The Guardian Companion to
the General Election 2001

The Guardian Companion to the General Election

2001

guardian.co.uk/politics

Edited by Julian Glover
Associate editor: Thomas Happold

ATLANTIC BOOKS

LONDON

First published in 2001 by Atlantic Books,
an imprint of Grove Atlantic Ltd

Sub Editor: Charlotte Thompson
Researcher: Joseph Piercy

1 2 3 4 5 6 7 8 9

A CIP catalogue record for this book is
available from the British Library.

ISBN 1 903809 03 7

Printed in Great Britain by Omnia Books Ltd
Design by LewisHallam

Atlantic Books
An imprint of Grove Atlantic Ltd
29 Adam & Eve Mews
London W8 6UG

Contents

Campaigns

Election Day

Constituencies

Introduction

Alan Rusbridger

After a decade and two general elections in which the direction of British politics has been anything but certain, polling day this year marks a return to a strange sort of political normality. The result seems hardly in doubt and the consequences far from earth-shattering (barring a possible referendum on the euro). Record numbers of voters are likely to stay at home and many more will vote without enthusiasm.

This is odd, given that in the perturbing winter of 2000–01 the nation experienced national crises of the sort many thought had been left behind with flares, Austin cars and Jim Callaghan. The petrol crisis, flooding, foot and mouth, rail chaos and disaster... Why have none of these made the 2001 general election one of national urgency?

Is it, as George Monbiot argues on p. 13, because voters no longer see these events as ones politicians can control? Or perhaps Simon Hoggart is right to point out (p. 9) that a parliament of poodles hardly cries out for enthusiastic support?

Yet much has been achieved since 1997, as David Walker explains (p. 65) in his introduction to policy. Hugo Young writes (p. 11) about the rise of a federal Britain. Larry Elliott (p. 68) describes the apparent triumph that Gordon Brown has had with his handling of the economy. And John Carvel (p. 78) looks at an education system that may be about to blossom after years of failure.

Nor, as Michael White makes clear (p. 3), was the last parliament a quiet one for the political parties themselves. Four major parties – the Conservatives, the Lib Dems, the SNP and Plaid Cymru – go into the campaign with new leaders. And both the Conservatives and, to a lesser extent Labour, are unsure about their place in the ideological spectrum. Ken Livingstone, after all, is a monument to remind us that not everything in the past four years has worked out as Tony Blair would have liked.

So it would be a mistake to write off this election as an irrelevance. Great things are at stake – not just this country's future relationship with the European Union, but the course of its political development. Will a re-energised Labour government return to complete its modernisation of the constitution, perhaps even accepting the Guardian's case for a republic? Or will a chastened Tony Blair creep back into Downing Street with a slashed majority and an empty policy slate? Might William Hague even surprise us all (as Jonathan Freedland imagines in his piece on p. 98) and win? These things matter. In the pages that follow, I hope they are explained, as well.

Alan Rusbridger is the Guardian's editor.

Party abbreviations used in this book

Alliance – Alliance party of Northern Ireland

BNP – British National party

Con – Conservative party

DUP – Democratic Unionist party

IUP – Independent Unionist party

Lab – Labour party

LD – Liberal Democrat party

PUP – Progressive Unionist party

PC – Plaid Cymru

Ref – Referendum party

SDLP – Social Democratic and Labour party

SF – Sinn Fein

UKip – UK Independence party

UDP – Ulster Democratic party

UUP – Ulster Unionist party

NoC – No overall control

List of Tables

Old Parliament, New Politics

It ain't over till it's over

Michael White

"Whatever you do, don't believe the opinion polls," snapped a weary Labour MP at the end of a long Sunday spent canvassing the marginal seat in southern England that he had captured in the Great Landslide of 1997. "We're finding there are a lot of people out there who haven't made up their minds."

It was an odd remark to make in late February. Surely this was supposed to be an election where people had made up their minds long ago? Despite that rictus smile and his gratingly-inclusive rhetoric, Tony Blair was going to win a historic second term for Labour: no Labour government in the 20th century had managed to win a proper working majority in two successive elections.

It is impossible to underestimate the extent to which that fact has haunted the first Blair administration. After 18 grim, frustrating years in opposition a generation of Labour politicians had emerged, hungry for power, not just for its own sake (though there was that too) but in order to *do* things.

It was an ambitious agenda. They wanted to tackle hard-core unemployment and social exclusion in the name of the "opportunity society", boost investment in people and new technologies as well as long-neglected public services, to reform an over-centralised constitution and take the paranoia and neurosis out of relations with Europe. They even talked grandly of restoring a confident "civic society" eroded by a century of decline and retreat.

Blair knew from the start that it would take at least two terms to achieve this vision. It is the central issue of the coming campaign. Will voters accept Labour's assurances that the new school roofs and hospitals that are at last in view are the down payment on a more fundamental re-structuring of society? Or will William Hague's taunts that Labour is "all spin and no substance" strike a cynical chord with voters? Hague's tactics are deliberate, ministers say. He is the first opposition leader in history who would prefer people not to vote at all.

Early efforts to rebrand Britain as a young country, even a cool one were, admittedly, clumsy. "Modernise" was a better word and Blair gradually came to prefer it. Gordon Brown set the pace on the fifth day of the new order when he granted independence to the monetary policy committee of the Bank of England to set interest rates. The City was impressed, as it was when the new chancellor doggedly stuck to the Conservative spending plans he had inherited for the first two years in office.

Whenever the author of those plans, Ken Clarke, protested that he himself would never have stuck to them, it was the cue for Brown and Blair to remind voters of the roller-coaster boom and bust years of Tory economic management that had left them a mountain of debt to pay off.

The freeze on spending was the crucial strategic decision of the government and it carried a price tag. Labour has only won three proper working majorities, by 143 seats in 1945, and by 97 in 1966 after a narrow win in 1964. The Attlee government of 1945 created the post-war order that lasted until the Thatcher years, including the national health service, a socialist institution so popular that it survived even her flying handbag. Though the 1966 government had solid social reforms to its credit it proved an economic failure.

The biggest landslide of all was 1997. With 179 seats more than all the other parties combined, it served to rekindle the fires of expectation that Labour's campaign had been designed to douse. Why couldn't this government do anything it wanted, from banning fox-hunting to restoring the link between pensions and earnings? Key ministers preferred to placate mythical Middle England, offsetting a radical gesture here with some reactionary rhetoric there, and never admitting in the Daily Mail's hearing that it was putting taxes up. Determined, above all, to establish their credentials as sound economic managers they did not start pumping money into the NHS and the school system on the scale that modernisation required until the third year in office. By that stage even the hapless Tories had managed to make stealth taxes an issue.

Labour activists were disappointed. Heartland voters wondered if this public school lawyer with fashionable metropolitan habits was really "one of us"? There might have been real trouble if so many experienced Tory hands hadn't quit the field after their routing at the polls. But the Tories picked the 36-year-old ex-Welsh secretary, William Hague, instead of the bruiser, Ken Clarke, to succeed John Major, whose premiership had been crippled by in-fighting, most bloodily over Europe.

Hague took time to find his feet (and lose his baseball cap) and had to focus his efforts on re-consolidating the core Tory vote, the millions who had voted for the Referendum and UK Independence parties in 1997 or the 2m of them who stayed at home. Even with Michael Portillo back on board after his Kensington and Chelsea by-election win in 1999, the shadow cabinet's ineptitude gave the Blairites useful room for manoeuvre. Its tendency to reverse not just Major's policies but its own, discouraged the Murdoch and Rothermere press, which Blair had wooed so tenderly, from slipping back to its natural anti-Labour habits.

In any case, the new prime minister, four days short of his 44th birthday, could sleep soundly in the flat above the shop knowing that, if his own leftwing gave him trouble (it rarely did), he could turn to Paddy Ashdown and the 46 Liberal Democrat MPs. They had been swept into Westminster on Labour's tide, partly through luck and tactical voting, but also as a tribute to Ashdown's decision to end equidistance and cosy up to Blair.

Ashdown's unconsummated passion for the project was one of the disappointments of the 1997 parliament for constitutional reformers of the centrist persuasion. They proved hard to please. Mr Blair had presided over more constitutional reform than any prime minister since 1832, another anti-Tory landslide year. It included devolution, the Human Rights Act, Freedom of Information, reform at the Bank of England, a smattering of PR elections, even 100 years after Keir Hardie mooted it – the expulsion of all but 92 hereditary legislators. Blair and Robin Cook, his foreign secretary, went so far as to set up a Lib–Lab consultative committee to the annoyance of their colleagues.

Ashdown, whose diaries later revealed how close he had got to achieving coalition politics in 1997, remained disappointed. When he duly stood down as Liberal Democrat leader in 1999 and became Sir Paddy (but not United Nations supremo in Kosovo as he had once hoped), Charles Kennedy beat Simon Hughes to the vacancy, as most people expected.

Kennedy was a Highland Scot but few people realised he was also secular Britain's first Catholic political leader for 300 years. He had a more realistic view of progress: he even ducked confrontation over Blair's waning enthusiasm for PR elections at Westminster, though he did echo Ashdown's complaint that failure to hold the promised referendum on membership of the eurozone in 1997 or 1998 was a lost opportunity. If they are right, predict some, that fateful delay might one day trigger a No vote that could destroy the Blair premiership.

"Where's the beef, Charlie?" asked some more ardent Lib Dems. Mr Kennedy neither jogged, policy-wonked, nor arm-wrestled on BBC radio's Today programme. True, he had won a famous victory in the Romsey by-election of May 2000 by taking anti-asylum sentiment head-on. In his amiable way Kennedy claimed to be appealing to fair play and the growing anti-political mood. But will his laid-back style give Hague a chance to win back southern seats lost to tactical anti-Tory votes in 1997? And will the post-election mathematics at Westminster give him any more leverage over Blair than the very little leverage that 46 MPs has given him?

Such imponderables kept the pundits employed and guaranteed that, however dull the campaign might (or might not) prove to be, the results would be interesting. Hartlepool, for example, may be the Enfield Southgate of the season with the twice-dropped Peter Mandelson as the whipping boy for voter disappointment as Portillo was the last time round. And foot and mouth disease may serve to eradicate Labour from rural Britain.

All the same, smart, metropolitan dinner party chat in the winter before the election focussed on the size of Labour's overall majority. Would it be bigger than last time? Some people looked at Hague's poll ratings and thought it might be. Labour HQ in Millbank mischievously targeted a dozen Tory seats for capture, just to pile on the pressure. "I sometimes sit there wishing I could set up a consultancy and give them lessons in opposition," murmured one cabinet minister.

Not even Mandelson's second resignation from cabinet over the Hinduja passport affair on January 24 seemed to unsettle the opinion polls, however much it left the prime minister bereft of his closest cabinet chum, a buffer against rampant Brownism in the campaign planning and beyond. Blair would be much more assured than the untested opposition leader he had been in 1997, MPs predicted, and the Labour campaign team might be less split by factions. But Mandelson's energy and his sensitivity to the aspirations of floating voters – Worcester Woman and Mondeo Man had been rebranded as Pebbledash People by some pollsters – would be missed.

Tory efforts to portray Labour as sleazier than the Tories under Major, with scandals over Ecclestone, Robinson, Mandelson (twice), Vaz, even Lord Irvine's "cash for wigs" fundraising letter, were noted by voters, the polls confirmed. But that made little apparent difference. During the fuel protests in the autumn of 2000 the Conservatives had taken a poll lead for the first time since the sterling crisis of 1992. It did not last. Labour's lead bounced back to 26% according to Gallup, 15% according to ICM's poll for the Guardian, the one the Tories most fear because they use ICM too. Mr Hague – Billy Bandwagon to the Millbank scriptwriters – duly changed his tax-and-spend policy tack again.

The harsh political fact as the campaign gets into gear is that, to an extent unimaginable in Thatcher's heyday, the central economic battle is being fought on Labour's terms: how much can the government sensibly tax and wisely spend rebuilding public services? Hague, Portillo and David Willetts promise to match most of the spending and cut taxes by "saving on waste", a formula that deserves (and gets) derision. But the sum in dispute is a mere £8bn, 0.8% of a £1,000bn economy. It seems more of a managerial disagreement than an ideological chasm.

Sensible Labour types, the ones who thought Blair would win by 50 seats in 1997 (deep down Blair thought that himself), asked each other if the majority would be above or below 100. That was more important to Hague. In the face of brutal poll results and depressingly buoyant economic data ("Things Can't Get Better for Blair", said a headline in the Daily Telegraph) his unswerving self-belief was even more remarkable than Blair's recurrent jitters.

The Tory leader behaved as if he couldn't lose, while on bad days the Labour leader behaved as if he might. Pop psychologists wondered if Hague's confidence was rooted in his idyllic south Yorkshire childhood, the baby brother in a close, horribly-normal middle class family? And was Blair's edginess the product of an upbringing marred by parental illness and early death? Or, as Tory pundits insisted, by his lack of core beliefs, a man who rarely knew what to think until Mandelson or Alastair Campbell told him?

Either way Hague's buoyant spirits did not impress voters who regularly derided his personal qualities and conceded, often through gritted teeth, that Blair was doing a good job. So much so that even Thatcherite Tories like Alastair McAlpine could be heard openly wondering whether they would have been wiser to pick the arch-European Ken Clarke, as Major's successor. He was perceived as having Hague's resilience *plus* the gravitas and experience the younger man so clearly lacked.

Hague knows he must run a good campaign and win a credible result to stay in his job. It would be wonderful, his supporters tell each other, if they could win or even deny Labour a majority in England so that its power at Westminster depends on devolved Welsh and Scottish votes. But morale is fragile and few believe it. Senior Tories who solemnly declare their belief in victory (that would mean an extra 170 seats) calmly admit in the next sentence that an extra 40 or so Tory seats (taking them up to 200 or 220) will probably be enough to save William's shaven head. Loyalists politely refrain from adding that this is partly because many Conservative MPs fear that under the Hague-devised leadership rules rank-and-file activists might pick Ann Widdecombe instead of Portillo, let alone the indestructible Clarke, to succeed him.

Long-term political strategists are already looking far beyond the coming election, as Blair himself demonstrated when he unexpectedly rose to Hague's challenge across the Commons dispatch box in February. "Of course an early assessment of Gordon Brown's famous five tests of Britain's compatibility with the euro means within two years", the prime minister said. A statement of the obvious, but newspapers went wild.

Some Labour insiders privately predict that, assurances to Rupert Murdoch notwithstanding, that translates into a rapidly-escalated timetable for an early referendum provided ministers and their pollsters believe they can turn around the large No majority against the single currency, a sentiment that is believed to be wide but shallow.

As always it will depend on what happens in the world beyond the chancellor's control, in the uncertainties of the United States economy under George Bush and in the global markets where the euro has fared badly. As Brown put the finishing touches to his prudent-but-crafty March 7 budget all such speculation was still too far ahead of the game, though the brooding chancellor himself knows so well that his own chances of becoming prime minister in 2005–6 depend on fine-tuning the euro-judgement.

It helped that he, far more than Blair (whose enthusiasm is as much political as economic) is agnostic. No such charge could be levelled against Hague in the run-up to the election. He and his closest advisers persist in believing that their Save the Pound battle-cry will touch a deep nerve in the voters' psyches. Did they not win a famous victory (8% ahead of Labour, admittedly on a 23% turnout) in the June 1999 European elections by hardening their line during the campaign?

Polls suggest otherwise. Voters do seem fond of the strong pound that buys more holiday pesetas than it used to, albeit at the cost of selling less Welsh steel to Spanish industry. But they are more concerned about the need to invest in reform of public services, especially education and the NHS, but also the criminal justice system and the public transport network, groaning at the seams as much on remote Pennine stretches of the M62 motorway as in the London Underground.

Which takes us back to the bull point. Unlike every previous Labour government since 1923 that has spent first and retrenched later, this one has placed itself brilliantly to meet such expectations by stuffing money down the public sector's throat as election day looms. It is money that it miraculously had at its disposal after four years in power because the economy has held up remarkably well. Yet Iron Gordon had refused to distribute it earlier in the electoral cycle.

As was widely observed at the time, the chancellor may have married Sarah Macaulay in August 2000, but he still kept Prudence's picture on his desk at the Treasury, to the quiet annoyance of Labour traditionalists and the vocal protests of Lib Dems and Nationalists. Brown and Blair have many disagreements, but they will campaign this spring united in a Presbyterian conviction that sound public finance is the bedrock of economic stability and growth.

Voters will be told again and again that these are the necessary prerequisites to better schools and hospitals in a customer-based Knowledge Economy. Lawyer Blair talks a lot about e-commerce and the internet. But there is little evidence that he turns to last.minute.free-holiday.com to book his annual trips to Italy and France, the heart of Europe he so often invokes in speeches. Significantly perhaps, Brown usually holidays at his own expense on Cape Cod, closer to Harvard's policy wonks and its bulging libraries.

Aware of charges that the government has become complacent or arrogant (charges that helped to cripple Harold Wilson in 1970), Blair and his team have taken to thanking voters for allowing them to modernise Britain. They will campaign apologetically for not having done enough fast enough, promising to deliver assorted 10 years plans in the new parliament, and hoping against hope to offload the embarrassing dome in Greenwich before Hague makes it the campaign symbol of Labour extravagance and vacuity.

Hague has other targets, such as the rise in violent crime (though not all crime), the seemingly insoluble problem of asylum-seekers heading for Dover from southern Europe and Asia. Labour's Queen's Speech produced a raft of measures designed to shrink the target area. Jack Straw's 10 year crime plan in late February was part of that strategy.

But Blair's real hope, confirmed by private polling, lies in Hague's Billy Bandwagon tendency to jump aboard passing issues highlighted by Sun editorials, and the well-remembered legacy of boom and bust economics under Thatcher and Major. It has become the Tory equivalent of Labour's own albatross, the 1978–9 Winter of Discontent.

"Recessions, negative equity, unemployment, expensive mortgages, people even blame the Tories for the break-up of their marriages," one senior Downing Street strategist enthusiastically confided. No wonder the promised Tory tax cuts for pensioners and families seem to make little impact. It is still too soon to be forgiven or forgotten.

Try as they may the Hague team sounds to many Tories (and Tory tabloids) like New Labour wannabes on days when they aren't sounding a bit too much like Austria's Jorg Heider on the EU or asylum-seekers, important issues to their core voters. "We do not have an ideology," Hague told the BBC. Indeed not, and it shows.

None the less Hague, who needs an improbable 8% overall swing to win outright, persists in saying he will surprise everyone and win, as Ted Heath did in 1970. The fixed odds were as loaded in Wilson's favour then as they were in early 2001, noted Stuart Wheeler, the highly-numerate spread bet millionaire, when he gave Hague £5 million to level the playing field.

Out in the field hardline Eurosceptics and countryside campaigners have rallied, as much against Blair as for Hague. From the disaffected left Greens and Socialist Alliance candidates hope to damage Blair's prospects as Ralph Nader did Al Gore's in the US elections in November. Consumer choice applies to politics too.

It is hardly surprising then that Millbank strategists fret over stay-at-home voters, against apathy and Hague-induced cynicism, even as they quietly focus their efforts and their hi-tech, customised email-shots on saving key marginals. It is not over yet. Hence the cold Sunday evening report from that class of 97 Labour MP who will only lose on a 6% swing. "There are a lot of people out there who have not made up their minds."

Michael White is the Guardian's political editor.

Poodle parliament
Simon Hoggart

There was no real reason to suppose that the sensational 1997 election result would create a sensational parliament. Yes, almost one third of the people who voted Tory five years earlier failed to do so this time. Yes, the number of Tory MPs was halved. Yes, if Labour had won just 20 seats more, they would have held an incredible two-thirds of all parliamentary seats. But it would have been foolish to imagine that from the astonishing avalanche of new members, an excitingly free, independent and thoughtful parliament would emerge.

On the contrary, if some parliaments win sobriquets – the long parliament, the rump parliament, etc – then this one could be called the poodle parliament. To be fair, the growth of lickspittle questioning had begun long before Labour surged into power, and had been heartily encouraged by John Major. Beset by rebellious and rebarbative backbenchers, he had often been willing to give government posts to those who offered the most fulsome support and hence the most welcome respite in the House of Commons. But any hopes that Labour would run things differently were quickly dashed.

At the beginning of each day's session, for instance, MPs who had questions tabled – plus any others who were anxious to make life easier for their superiors – were issued with long and detailed "fact" sheets. These listed all the questions in order, provided ripostes to likely Conservative claims, and suggested "helpful" supplementaries by which backbenchers with an eye to their own future could offer supportive remarks to ministers in the guise of probing questions. Question time was less than ever a chance for MPs to grill the executive on behalf of their constituents. Instead it became a parade of formalised, party-political combat.

Sometimes even this ritual process went dreadfully wrong. During one prime minister's question time in November 2000, the whips issued the same grovelling supplementary to two Labour MPs. When one of them, Caroline Flint, rose to speak she stuttered that she couldn't put a question because someone had already asked it. This was one of the low spots of the entire parliament.

Andrew Mackinlay, however, the tough, outspoken MP for Thurrock, won plaudits from all sides when he protested about obsequious questions and declared how disappointed he had been to see the practice continue. Another Labour rebel, the wealthy QC Robert Marshall-Andrews, lost any hopes he had of a ministerial job when, speaking at a dinner for the Society of Labour Lawyers, he made a joke at the expense of Derry Irvine, soon to become lord chancellor. He later instituted the Golden Pager Award, to be given annually to the MP who asked the greasiest question of the year. It seemed a fitting memorial to the whole parliament.

The problem was not eased by the Tories, perhaps the most ineffective opposition anyone can recall. In part this was due to their small numbers; the average government generally has 90-plus members, including whips and members of the Lords. Nearly all of these must be shadowed by the opposition, and with only 165 MPs to draw from, the new Tory leader William Hague was obliged to give front-bench positions to around half of his members. You can't do this without a loss of quality, a loss exacerbated by his decision to clear out as many former ministers as he could. Not only had six cabinet members been defeated in the election, but many who had survived – including disappointed leadership candidates such as Michael Heseltine and Ken Clarke – decided that the time had come to retreat to the backbenches and their various directorships. On top of this, Hague fired heavy-hitters such as Michael Howard, Peter Lilley and John Redwood. The widely liked and respected Sir George Young left the shadow cabinet to stand unsuccessfully for Speaker. The return of Michael Portillo, swiftly offered the key post of shadow chancellor, gave Mr Hague some relief, but the fact remained that for much of the parliament, apart from himself, only one other member of the shadow cabinet had been in a real cabinet.

The consequence was that a largely successful minister such as David Blunkett was shadowed by the inexperienced Theresa May, and feebler operators such as Stephen Byers, Chris Smith and John Prescott were matched against lightweights such as Angela Browning, Peter Ainsworth and Archie Norman. None of these managed to land many punches on those in power. Often the House had to wait for contributions from the likes of Heseltine, Clarke, Major, Redwood and John Selwyn Gummer – all backbenchers now – if members wanted to hear a coherent, informed and well-argued attack on the government.

There are many causes for the apparent decline. The Labour government has barely hidden its contempt for parliament, which it regards largely as a rubber-stamping mechanism. This is especially apparent when it comes to highly controversial measures such as the reduction in trial by jury and the part-privatisation of air traffic control, all privately opposed by a majority of Labour MPs. The national debate has tended to shift further and further into the media and away from the Commons, where rules of procedure can mean that important events may not be debated for weeks. With the growth of round-the-clock news coverage, MPs frequently prefer to be interviewed live on air than wait in the hopes of being called to give their opinions to a largely empty chamber.

The new Speaker, Michael Martin, replaced the exceedingly popular Betty Boothroyd in October 2000. While some feel he has been unjustly criticised for his lacklustre control of the House, few believe that he matches his predecessor either in public esteem or parliamentary skills.

There were some highlights, however. The best debate of the year was probably the first on fox hunting, held at the tail-end of 1997. That featured what some regard as the finest speech of the parliament: a passionate, ferocious, enraged diatribe against hunting from Ann Widdecombe, the acknowledged star of the Tory front bench.

It also included what might be the best joke of the parliament. Michael Heseltine was speaking, rather pompously it must be said, about methods of killing foxes. "Why do we flush something out?" he asked rhetorically.

"Ask Mrs Thatcher!" shouted Denis MacShane, Labour MP for Rotherham. The gale of laughter that followed provided one of those rare parliamentary moments when a single interjection can destroy an entire speech.

Simon Hoggart is the Guardian's parliamentary sketchwriter.

A federal Britain

Hugo Young

The first general election after devolution exposes an issue and widens a wound in the body politic. What exactly, one has to ask, is this election for? How much power is draining away from the parliament that will receive a freshly mandated 659 MPs? How much of the process is now symbol, and how much reality?

Parliament is our sovereign law-making body, with the power to do anything for which a majority of the 659 heroes of democracy can be persuaded to vote. It is indeed the formal epicentre of the system. The executive power of Tony Blair's first government may have obscured that, thanks to the sheer size of the majority Labour won in 1997. Indeed, the role of MPs was diminished, paradoxically, by that heavy load of them on one side of the benches. If a semi-landslide brought back something like parity between the main parties, the Commons would soon assert itself as the cockpit where the government could lose as often as it wins.

There is something irreducible about the drama of the democratic moment that will shortly decide how the Commons is filled. The majority really does count. The difference between government and not-government is absolute. The place where this has become most dramatically clear is Washington where, even with a disputed mandate, the administration of George W Bush has glided with effortless assurance into the seats of power.

A parliamentary election, besides being capable of just such closeness, has the added magnetism of combining in itself a decision about the powers held separately in the United States by the Congress and the presidency. The coming event should be an awesome political climax.

Yet why do I, for the first time in my life, experience tremors of heretical disbelief when I pass that great parliamentary building in Westminster? Gazing up at Big Ben these past few years, I've begun to see it as the icon of a theme park rather than a cauldron of democracy. It is a magnificent sight: none more resonant, especially at night, in the entire democratic world. But what goes on inside? In the real world, is it truly sovereign? Is that where power actually resides? Once the parliament of an empire, does this place continue to be the parliament of even a single nation?

Perhaps 80% of the government decisions that affect Scotland are no longer decided under those ancient rafters. The setting-up of the Scottish parliament means that 72 of the MPs at Westminster are no longer responsible for much of public life as it touches their constituents. Welsh devolution, although less drastic, is also a harbinger of power disappearing from Westminster.

Those are two tranches of MPs that the coming election will return, in a way, as impostors, only partially connected to the mandate of legitimacy that they need to do the work they do. Similar enfeeblement comes from other directions. The global power of corporations, and the sheer speed at which trillions of dollars move about, somewhat confine the agenda that any tribunes of the people can seriously expect to influence. So does the encroaching writ of the European Union. A decade ago,

Jacques Delors famously declared that before long 80% of the social and economic laws affecting Europe would be decided in Brussels. It never came to that, and now the tendency is to try and move the other way. But Europe is a mighty force for the rearrangement of sovereignty. The best that MPs can do is invigilate the decisions of the EU collective after the event, which they don't work hard enough to do. Perhaps they know an irresistible force when they see one. Whatever the reason, the European verities add to the impression that the sound and fury we are about to witness is, in part, a charade.

Parliament remains, of course, sovereign. It can overturn devolution, cancel the Treaty of Rome, even pass statutes that purport to defy the laws of global economics. The Commons could re-declare itself as the potent centre of what it means to be British. And the democracy of the nation-state does matter. Even without trying to undo the surrenders it has been forced to make to geo-political realities, parliament makes vital decisions at the margin and even, occasionally, on matters of "moral" consequence where MPs are graciously allowed to vote with their conscience. The 659 do make a difference.

Their very existence, like the election that will produce them, is what distinguishes countries such as Britain from great tracts of Africa and Asia on which the Mother of Parliaments somehow failed to graft a permanent culture of functioning democracy. As a citizen, therefore, one wants an election that is open and uncorrupt, and engages the maximum number of people to turn out and vote. All the same, MPs perform a diminished function. If there is another Labour landslide, it is hard to imagine that they will be listened to any more by the second Blair government than the first. There is an element of the parade about what they do.

Their presence is vital, as a massive, immovable guarantee against dictatorship. But MPs have seen their importance inexorably reduced, and have consciously passed laws to that effect. They watch the world from sidelines more distant than their Victorian forebears could have imagined. The theatre to which we're about to return them is unattended, to a degree unthinkable even 30 years ago – but for reasons that perhaps show more public realism than MPs themselves are ready to acknowledge.

Vote early. And vote often, if the day coincides with local elections. But be aware how the sentiment around the sacred act has dimmed. As you picture that great neo-Gothic palace by the Thames, understand where the seats of power, and therefore the real challenges to democracy, have moved.

Hugo Young is a Guardian columnist.

Politics not parliament

George Monbiot

When Tony Benn announced his intention to retire as an MP he said he was "leaving parliament to go into politics". He didn't need to explain what he meant. To the thousands of activists championing the issues governments have neglected, parliament has been peripheral to the life of the nation for years.

It's not hard to see why. The first and most obvious reason is that MPs are no longer permitted to represent their constituents. The lavish use of the parliamentary whip, the increased efficiency of the party machines, the fudged reform of the House of Lords, the marginalisation of even the cabinet as the government is run by unelected advisers, have all helped to sever the links between the people and their representatives.

As the government is gradually removed from effective, democratic supervision, unprecedented opportunities emerge for undemocratic lobbying. While petitions signed by one million electors are binned, Rupert Murdoch is admitted to Downing Street every time he knocks. All governments, aware that the best way to acquire power is to appease those who possess it, are enlisted by the powerful to marginalise dissent. But this government has been so comprehensively captured by its lobbyists that it has marginalised itself.

There is, both Tony Blair and Gordon Brown have assured us, "no alternative" to neoliberal globalisation. This leads to, although they would never express it this way, the gradual privatisation of everything, brokered by means of the Private Finance Initiative and the forthcoming General Agreement on Trade in Services. It means the deregulation of business activities, resulting in even lower environmental, workplace and consumer standards. It means fiscal policies whose purpose is to provide "a more competitive environment" for business, which translates as a long-term shift from corporate to personal taxation.

None of these issues are subject to debate, as all three major parties are courting the same corporate constituency. National sovereignty, for example, is an issue only when the European Union suggests raising the standards to which business must conform. Its deregulatory measures, by contrast, are never construed as a danger to democracy. The gravest of all recent challenges to sovereignty was the Multilateral Agreement on Investment. Had this global measure been approved, it would have permitted corporations to sue governments for the removal of any laws restricting their ability to make money. But when it was debated in parliament, the Conservative benches were empty. When, on the day of its negotiation, the home secretary, Jack Straw, was asked about the agreement, he admitted that he had never heard of it.

So the electorate is left to wonder why, in a state that has never been richer, public services are falling apart, the state pension is dwindling and schools are being privatised. Why, though no one wants them, are we being forced to accept genetically modified crops? Why has the government that promised traffic reduction, rail renationalisation and integrated transport instead relaunched the road building programme?

Why does Tony Blair refuse to rule out British participation in the deadly farcical Nuclear Missile Defence programme?

While the government insists that there is no alternative, those seeking to promote one are treated as dangerous outcasts. Non-violent campaigners have been reclassified as terrorists by the new Terrorism Act, while the Investigatory Powers Act and the new Criminal Justice Act allow the security services to intercept emails and raid computers without a warrant. Yet, in the absence of an independent, investigative press, peaceful protest is now among the few means of raising the issues that will determine the future course of most people's lives. We are, as a result, entering a new age of activism.

Until recently, protest in Britain has been fragmentary and confused. But suddenly the dissenters appear to be coalescing, and a coherent, radical opposition movement is beginning to emerge. Socialists, anarchists and greens seem to be laying aside their differences in order to campaign against global neoliberalism. Even the farmers who joined the fuel protests are beginning to talk to environmentalists, as both sides come to see that corporate power threatens small businesses and the ecosystem in equal measure and foot and mouth rampages through the countryside. While the turnout for the general election promises to be one of the lowest on record, the protests scheduled for the G8 summit in Genoa in July are likely to number among the biggest held.

These are, as a result, exciting times. While extra-parliamentary activism will make little difference to the outcome of this election, the concerns it expresses will become harder to ignore. With or without the help of a marginalised parliament, Britain's politics at future elections will bear little resemblance to those of 2001.

George Monbiot is a Guardian columnist.

Events 1997–2001

May 1 1997	Labour wins general election with a majority of 179.
May 6 1997	The Bank of England is granted independence. A monetary policy committee is established to set interest rates.
June 19 1997	William Hague is elected leader of the Conservative party.
June 30 1997	British rule ends in Hong Kong, the colony returns to China.
July 2 1997	Gordon Brown promises an extra £3bn for health and education in his first Budget.
July 19 1997	The IRA announces a restoration of its ceasefire.
July 22 1997	Tony Blair invites Paddy Ashdown to join a cabinet committee on constitutional reform.
August 31 1997	Princess Diana dies in a car crash in Paris.
September 11 1997	Scotland votes in favour of establishing a Scottish parliament with tax raising powers.
September 18 1997	Wales narrowly votes in favour of establishing a Welsh assembly.
September 19 1997	Seven die in the Southall rail crash.
October 27 1997	Gordon Brown rules out British membership of the euro for the lifetime of the parliament.
November 10 1997	Labour promises to return a £1m donation to Bernie Ecclestone after controversy over its support for an exemption for Formula One from a Europe-wide ban on tobacco advertising.
March 1 1998	More than 200,000 march through London in support of the countryside and fox hunting.
April 10 1998	The UK and Irish governments and Northern Ireland parties sign the Good Friday agreement.
May 6 1998	London votes in favour of establishing a Greater London Authority led by a mayor.
May 22 1998	Northern Ireland and the Irish Republic vote in favour of the Good Friday agreement.
June 25 1998	Pro-Good Friday agreement parties take the majority of seats in the Northern Ireland Assembly elections.
July 5 1998	Labour apparatchiks turned lobbyists are accused of using their contacts within the government to gain privileged access for their clients in the so-called "cash for access" scandal.

August 15 1998	Real IRA bomb attack in Omagh kills 28.
October 17 1998	General Pinochet, the former dictator of Chile, is arrested in London.
October 27 1998	Welsh secretary Ron Davies resigns after a "moment of madness" on Clapham Common.
October 29 1998	Roy Jenkins's electoral reform commission recommends that "first-past-the-post" should be replaced by "alternative vote plus" for general elections.
December 2 1998	William Hague sacks Viscount Cranborne, the Conservative leader in the Lords for agreeing a secret deal with Tony Blair to let the government's proposals pass through the upper house if 92 hereditary peers are allowed to stay.
December 16 1998	The US and UK launch air strikes on Iraq.
December 23 1998	Peter Mandelson and Geoffrey Robinson resign after it is revealed that the millionaire treasury minister secretly loaned the trade and industry secretary £373,000 to buy a house.
January 1 1999	The euro replaces 11 national currencies.
February 20 1999	Welsh secretary Alun Michael narrowly beats Rhodri Morgan in a controversial contest for the leadership of the Welsh Labour party.
February 24 1999	The Metropolitan police is accused of institutional racism by the Macpherson report on the murder of Stephen Lawrence.
March 16 1999	The European commission resigns en masse after auditors find fraud and corruption in the commission.
March 24 1999	Nato launches air strikes against Yugoslavia. Romano Prodi is nominated president of the European commission.
May 6 1999	Labour wins the most seats, but no majority, in the Scottish parliament and Welsh assembly elections.
May 12 1999	Alun Michael is elected first secretary of Wales and forms a minority administration.
May 13 1999	Donald Dewar is elected first minister of Scotland and forms a coalition administration with the Liberal Democrats.
June 10 1999	Nato ends its air strikes after Slobodan Milosevic agrees to withdraw Yugoslav forces from Kosovo. Conservatives win the most seats in the European parliamentary elections.
August 1 1999	The EU lifts its export ban on British beef.
August 6 1999	Charles Kennedy is elected leader of the Liberal Democrats.

September 9 1999	Chris Patten's report on policing in Northern Ireland recommends a name-change for the Royal Ulster Constabulary and the recruitment of more Catholics.
October 5 1999	Thirty die in the Paddington rail crash.
October 11 1999	Peter Mandelson returns to the cabinet as Northern Ireland secretary.
November 20 1999	Jeffrey Archer stands down as Conservative candidate for London mayor after revelations that he asked a friend to commit perjury.
November 29 1999	David Trimble becomes first minister of Northern Ireland, leading an executive that includes Sinn Fein's Martin McGuinness.
November 31 1999	Michael Portillo wins the Kensington and Chelsea by-election.
December 31 1999	Millennium Dome holds opening ceremony.
January 16 2000	Tony Blair promises to raise health spending to the European average by 2006.
January 20 2000	John Wakeham's commission on reform of the House of Lords recommends that the majority of its members should continue to be appointed.
February 9 2000	Alun Michael resigns as first secretary of Wales.
February 15 2000	Rhodri Morgan is elected first secretary of Wales.
February 20 2000	Frank Dobson narrowly beats Ken Livingstone in a controversial contest to become the Labour candidate for London mayor.
March 2 2000	General Pinochet, the former dictator of Chile, flies home.
May 16 2000	BMW announces plans to sell off or close Rover.
May 4 2000	Ken Livingstone is elected mayor of London as an independent.
May 9 2000	The Phoenix consortium buys Rover for £10.
June 19 2000	Fifty-eight illegal immigrants are found dead in the back of a lorry in Dover.
July 12 2000	Betty Boothroyd announces that she is to stand down as Speaker of the House of Commons.
July 18 2000	In the Comprehensive Spending Review, Gordon Brown announces that public expenditure is to rise by £43bn over the next three years.
July 25 2000	Concorde crashes in Paris.
September 7 2000	Farmers and hauliers blockade Stanlow oil refinery in Ellesmere Port.
September 11 2000	The Privy Council grants the government emergency powers to distribute petrol to the emergency services.

September 13 2000	The NHS is put on an emergency footing because of the fuel crisis.
September 14 2000	Pickets calls off fuel blockades.
October 11 2000	Donald Dewar dies after suffering a brain haemorrhage in Edinburgh.
October 17 2000	Four die in Hatfield rail crash. Rail chaos follows.
October 23 2000	Michael Martin is elected speaker of the Commons.
October 26 2000	Henry McLeish is elected first minister of Scotland.
November 7 2000	The US presidential election fails to produce an immediate winner because of a dispute over the Florida ballot.
December 31 2000	The Dome closes.
January 20 2001	George W Bush is sworn in as US president.
January 24 2001	Peter Mandelson resigns over the Hinduja passport affair.
February 16 2001	The US and UK launch air strikes on Baghdad, Iraq.
February 19 2001	A herd of pigs are discovered to be carrying foot and mouth disease at the Cheale Meats abattoir in Essex.
February 28 2001	Selby rail crash.
March 7 2001	Gordon Brown gives pre-election budget, concentrating on helping children and the low paid.
March 9 2001	The Hammond report clears Peter Mandelson of lying.
March 15 2001	The agriculture secretary, Nick Brown, announces a programme to slaughter all farm animals suspected of carrying foot and mouth disease.

Politicians

The leaders

Anthony Charles Lynton Blair

PERSONAL DETAILS

Born: May 6 1953
Family: His father Leo was a barrister and former secretary of the Scottish Young
Communist League turned Conservative activist.
Marital status: Married to barrister Cherie Booth, the daughter of actor Tony
Booth. Four children.

Education
Schools: Durham Cathedral School and Fettes College, Edinburgh.
Universities: St John's College, Oxford.
Qualifications: Honours in law.

Employment history
Job: Barrister in the chambers of Derry Irvine, specialised in industrial and trade
union law.

Political career
Constituency: Sedgefield
Background: Apart from standing as the Conservative candidate in a school election
aged 11, showed little interest in politics until he left university, where he was
involved in a Christian discussion group. Joined the Labour party at 22.
Big break: After coming a poor third in the Beaconsfield by-election in 1982, was
selected for the safe Labour seat of Sedgefield in time for the 1983 general election.
Turning point: Reinvented Labour as New Labour and rewrote clause IV.
Positions: Became prime minister with a landslide in 1997. Elected party leader in
1994 after making his name as shadow home secretary.

Hinterland
Plays the electric guitar (was in a rock group, Ugly Rumours, at Oxford).
Committed Christian.

Quotes
"He could uphold his side of the debate about the rights and wrongs of everything better
than any boy in the school." *Dr Eric Anderson, former housemaster, headmaster of Eton*

"Tough on crime, tough on the causes of crime." *Tony Blair*

"The unbearable self-assurance of one who knows he is a member of a class
born to rule." *Andrew Rawnsley*

"I don't carry any baggage of an ideological kind." *Tony Blair*

William Jefferson Hague

PERSONAL DETAILS

Born: March 26 1961

Family: His father Nigel was director of a family-owned soft drinks firm in
      Yorkshire, which used to produce Hague Pop lemonade.

Marital status: Married to Ffion, his former assistant private secretary at the Welsh
      Office.

Education

Schools: Greasbrough primary and Wath-on-Dearne comprehensive, near
      Rotherham.

Universities: Magdalen College Oxford and INSEAD business school, France.

Qualifications: First class Honours in politics, philosophy and economics and an
      MBA with distinction.

Employment history

Jobs: Management consultant, McKinsey and company. Speechwriter for Geoffrey
      Howe.

Political career

Constituency: Richmond, Yorkshire

Background: Became interested in politics around the time of the 1974 general
      election and joined the Young Conservatives at 15.

Big break 1: Spoke at Conservative party conference aged 16.

Big break 2: After contesting his hometown seat of Wentworth in 1987, won the
      Richmond by-election in 1989, the last Tory to achieve such a feat for a
      decade.

Positions: Elected leader in 1997, easily beating the Europhile Ken Clarke in the
      third round by 92 votes to 70. Joined the government as parliamentary private
      secretary to chancellor Norman Lamont in 1990, after playing an active part in
      John Major's leadership campaign. Became Welsh secretary and the youngest
      cabinet minister in 50 years in 1995.

Hinterland

Spends an hour a day practising judo with his private secretary Sebastian Coe.

Quotes

"Roll back the frontiers of the state." *William Hague, 1977*

"Possibly another young Pitt." *Margaret Thatcher, 1977*

"A tragedy for the party." *Edward Heath*

"Impervious to the apprehension that he might just possibly be destined for total
failure." *Hugo Young, the Guardian*

Charles Peter Kennedy

PERSONAL DETAILS

Born: November 25 1959.
Family: The grandson of a crofter, his father Ian was an engineering draughtsman
    and well-known fiddle player.
Marital status: Single, but has a long-time girlfriend.

Education
Schools: Lochaber High School, Fort William.
Universities: Glasgow University and Indiana University (Fulbright Scholar).
Qualifications: Honours in politics, philosophy and English.

Employment history
First job: Reporter, BBC Radio Highlands.

Political career
Constituency: Ross, Skye and Inverness West
Background: Joined the Labour party aged 15, but switched to the Social Democrats
    at university.
Big break: Elected to parliament in 1983, scoring a surprise SDP victory in a
    Highland constituency where the Liberals had only gained 9% of the vote in
    1979.
Turning point: One of only two SDP MPs to defy David Owen and back merger
    with the Liberals in 1988.
Positions: Elected leader in 1999, narrowly defeating Simon Hughes by 56.6% to
    43.4% in the fourth round of voting. President of the Liberal Democrats,
    1990–94.

Hinterland
Appearing on game shows.

Quotes
"I believe in being serious about politics, though not in taking myself too seriously."
Charles Kennedy

"He likes a wee dram or three." *The Observer*

Top dog and underdogs
Patrick Wintour

Party political leaders in today's increasingly presidential election campaigns survive in a bubble of exhaustion, self-doubt, fear and extraordinary feats of logistics. Rumours abound and egos grate. Highs, as voters respond warmly to the candidate on the stump, or a poll that signals a turning of the tide, can be followed by moments of grim realism or explosive anger at some crass mistake within the campaign team. jIt all requires an extraordinary self-discipline, stagecraft and resilience.

For two candidates this time, the pressures will be a novel experience. In 1997 William Hague spent his time in the obscurity of Wales watching Tory held seats fall to Labour. Charles Kennedy can claim the experience of chairing the party's 1994 European election campaign, but spent much of 1997 in Skye. Only Blair has undergone the rigours of an election campaign.

No leader will be under greater personal pressure than the 40-year-old Hague, and no leader on the surface seems better equipped to handle it. He appears to have superhuman strengths of resilience and seems unaffected by criticism. Some put it down to judo, some to transcendental calm and others to his private belief that he doesn't expect to win this election.

The mystery is what kind of image he will present on the stump. He has flirted with so many different persona, it is difficult to predict. He has been the multicultural carnival jiver, the Sun-reading man in the white van, the political train spotter, the drunken Yorkshireman, the husband of glamour and the management consultant in the double-breasted suit. Yet his personal ratings remain doggedly miserable. He is widely seen as a drag on the party's poll standing. Despite the best efforts of Amanda Platell, the word wally is beginning to hang round his neck, along with Alastair Campbell's other sobriquet, Billy Bandwagon.

As a result many observers expect the story of the election to revolve round the slow disintegration of his campaign and the increasingly open scramble for his succession. For if the media collectively decides the election is over, and become bored by the Hague–Blair contest, they will train their sights on Hague's battle to retain the leadership. It will then be difficult for him to keep his agenda running.

He may also feel politically and physically isolated, for he has elected to forego London press conferences, in favour of a regional campaign in which he may receive more sympathetic press coverage. He will also try to reproduce some of the underdog spirit. But with two of his closest advisers, George Osborne and Danny Finkelstein, themselves fighting seats, he will be dependent on Michael Portillo and Franics Maude to keep him informed of the national picture and the mood within Central Office. To make matters worse, both men are out of sympathy with Hague's core vote campaign.

It is essential that Hague campaigns well on the stump and comes out of the election looking like a potential winner. Neil Kinnock in 1987 should be his model. If Hague retreats ever further back into the laager of Europe, asylum seekers and tax cuts, he is likely to be doomed.

By tradition, Tory MPs are not tolerant of failure. Few Conservative leaders have survived losing an election badly. Calculations abound but the message is straight-forward: Hague must gain seats.

Charles Kennedy also faces a difficult first outing on the stump. He has about 12% of the big parties' cash, and will rely on the broadcasting rules for TV impact. He does not have the enthusiasm for campaigns of his predecessor Paddy Ashdown. Indeed, some Liberal Democrat MPs believe Kennedy is so uneasy as party leader that he will resign after the election. Despite the bonhomie he displays in chat shows, he is prone to self-doubt. By nature he is a shy man who does not respond well to the inherent absurdities of the campaign trail. Kennedy relished the idea of TV debates between himself and the other leaders partly because it would give him the excuse to stay in London and prepare. He has even had to go on trial helicopter rides to cure himself of a fear of flying.

He does have the advantage of being a refreshing and unknown quantity for many voters. Two years after taking on the party leadership, voters still have surprisingly little feel for him. Some 46% of voters cannot express a view when asked. However, those that have formed an opinion do like him. A poll conducted by the party in February in 40 of its key seats show that Kennedy is trusted much more than the other two leaders.

His difficulty is that his key seats are spread across the country. In effect he will be running 50 different by-elections simultaneously whilst pretending he is running a national campaign. There are worrying signs that the Lib Dem vote has fallen back most in the south west, once a fortress for the party. The departure of Paddy Ashdown, a Yeovil MP, has depressed support in the Liberal Democrat stronghold. The party's strong pro-European views also do not help in a region so dependent on farming and fisheries.

Meanwhile Tony Blair enjoys thinking through the strategy behind campaigns, but is tired from four years at the helm in Downing Street. Instinctively, he knows when he is connecting with a campaign, and when it is missing the spot. He will have familiar and trusted faces around him, apart from Peter Mandelson, a loss to the Millbank esprit de corps. The usual team of Gordon Brown, Alastair Campbell, Philip Gould, Margaret McDonagh, Lord Irvine, and his pollster Greg Cook, will reassure him. Their aim will be to show Blair as a friendly figure in relatively small, warm and intimate surroundings – the opposite of the Sheffield rally of the 1992 election. He will be looking for what he describes as a vocabulary of achievement – a way of setting out the government's record without sounding arrogant.

Blair also needs a rhetoric to galvanise the Labour core vote, which has been turned off by politics and not turned on by him personally. It will mean many unconventional appearances on apolitical soft programmes – more Richard and Judy than Paxman and Wark.

His aides say the big trick is to prevent a sense of inevitable victory and keep the Hague threat alive to play up the need to get out and vote. High turnout, after all is essential for Blair to secure his coveted second term and a big majority.

Patrick Wintour is the Guardian's chief political correspondent.

Out with the old
Retiring MPs

Labour

Joe Ashton
Tony Benn
Dale Campbell-Savours
Malcolm Chisholm[1]
Judith Church
Eric Clarke
Lawrence Cunliffe
Ron Davies[2]
Maria Fyfe
Sam Galbraith[1]
Dr Norman Godman
Llin Golding
John Gunnell
John Home Robertson[1]
Jenny Jones
Dr Lynne Jones
Tess Kingham
John McAllion[1]
Henry McLeish[1]
John Marek[2]
John Maxton
Bill Michie
Rhodri Morgan[2]
John Morris
Mo Mowlam
Tom Pendry
Giles Radice
Allan Rogers
Jeff Rooker
Ted Rowlands
Robert Sheldon
Peter Snape
Peter Temple-Morris

Conservative

Sir Richard Body
Peter Brooke
Dr Michael Clark
Sir Peter Emery
David Faber
Sir Norman Fowler
Christopher Gill
Teresa Gorman
Archie Hamilton
Sir Edward Heath
Michael Heseltine
Sir Geoffrey Johnson Smith
Tom King
Sir Peter Lloyd
Sir Nicholas Lyell
John MacGregor
Sir David Madel
John Major
Andrew Rowe
John Townend
Charles Wardle
Bowen Wells
Sir Ray Whitney

Liberal Democrat

Paddy Ashdown
Ronnie Fearn
Donald Gorrie[1]
Richard Livsey
Robert Maclennan
Ray Michie
Jim Wallace[1]

Plaid Cymru

Dafydd Wigley[2]

Scottish National Party

Roseanna Cunningham[1]
Margaret Ewing[1]
Alasdair Morgan[1]
John Swinney[1]
Andrew Welsh[1]

Ulster Unionist Party

Ken Maginnis
John Taylor[3]

Independents

Ken Livingstone[4]
Thomas Graham

1. Member of the Scottish parliament
2. Member of the Welsh assembly
3. Member of the Northern Ireland assembly
4. Mayor of London

List complete as at 1 March 2001

In with the new
Andrew Roth

In this strange election we know half the winners before the counting begins: the 70 or so replacements for MPs retiring from safe seats. Labour's 30-odd replacements are mainly local worthies, selected by the one-member one-vote system (OMOV). One obvious exception is Chris Bryant, the openly-gay former Anglican priest and BBC head of European affairs, selected for the very safe seat of Rhondda, having fought Wycombe in the 1997 election. Born in Wales, he left at eight, and was initially a Tory in Oxford, alongside William Hague.

The new Tories inheriting safe seats reflect the continuing shift toward Europhobia. This is best illustrated by the capture of Henley, formerly the seat of Europhile Michael Heseltine, by Spectator editor Boris Johnson, and the takeover of Wycombe from retiring ultra-Europhile Sir Ray Whitney by Paul Goodman, the key link between the Telegraph newspapers and Conservative Central Office. These two show that the Eurosceptics' first team is moving onto the green benches.

They may make life uncomfortable for some former Tory MPs coming back for safer seats. It should be easy for Derek Conway, replacing Sir Edward Heath in Old Bexley, because he was a Eurosceptic when he was the MP for Shrewsbury. Alistair Burt, coming back as the replacement for Sir Nicholas Lyell in Bedfordshire North East, was initially a churchy Heathite in the wet Tory Reform Group and later a parliamentary private secretary to Kenneth Baker before losing Bury North. The mild Eurosceptic and talented former minister Andrew Mitchell, who lost marginal Gedling in 1997, is returning to the much safer seat of Sutton Coldfield after Sir Norman Fowler retires.

There is a more mixed message about Sir Paddy Ashdown's successor in Yeovil. David Laws, who took a double first in economics from King's College, Cambridge, made a fortune as vice president of J P Morgan and managing director of Barclays Bank before becoming the Lib Dems' director of policy and research. He fought hard for selection at Yeovil, to the extent that his opponents alleged he over-canvassed. An appeals panel upheld Mr Laws.

These safe successors seem likely to outnumber other new MPs because political opinions, with a blip last September, have long been frozen at roughly the same level as the last election: half supporting Labour, a third supporting the Tories, a fifth backing the Liberal Democrats. The puzzle for pundits is working out what percentage of this will be translated into votes in the ballot box. It's a big problem for New Labour because it has not warmed the cockles of working-class hearts in Labour's traditional areas. There, Labour can expect reduced majorities, without losing seats. The turnout in marginal seats is likely to be higher.

Marginals have long been crucial in deciding the result of elections. The outcome used to depend on changes in a fifth of the constituencies: 130 out of 659. This time changes may be limited to a mere 60 seats. The Tories, with increased funds, are going to concentrate on retaking at least 40 of the seats they lost in 1997. A gain of 50 seats would be seen as an endorsement for William Hague. The Tories hope to regain those seats considered so safe last time that cabinet ministers, such as Michael Portillo in Southgate and Roger Freeman in Kettering, spent their time defending other, more vulnerable seats. Portillo and Freeman have already found asylum in Kensington and Chelsea and in the Lords, but retaking their former seats is a matter of prestige for the party.

To regain target seats Tories are relying heavily on a score of former MPs thirsting for vengeance. In most cases this is useful, as in Dartford where Bob Dunn is well known as the former MP and candidate for almost 20 years, until he was defeated by Dr Howard Stoate in 1997. The return of another rightwinger, Viv Bendall, in Ilford North, is also arguable, but it makes less sense to rerun Lady Olga Maitland against Paul Burstow, the Lib Dem incumbent in Sutton and Cheam. Her reputation as a loose cannon on such issues as nuclear weapons and Serbia, seems to have been reinforced by her recent hostility to wheelybins.

There is an even larger question mark over fielding David Shaw, the former Tory MP for Dover, to retake Kingston and Surbiton from Lib Dem Edward Davey, who won in 1997 by a mere 56 votes. There are 12,811 Labour voters there, many of whom could be won over by the Lib Dems.

The tactical decision of the local selectors in Wellingborough is also suspect. The seat was won by Labour's Paul Stinchcombe with a majority of only 187 votes. But to dislodge him, the Tories have chosen travel agent Peter Bone, who famously boasted to a Tory conference that he hired staff for one pound an hour. That should infuriate the town's many warehouse workers on minimum wages.

The Lib Dems are worried about Romsey, where their great by-election victory has been overshadowed by the Tories' decision to select a local candidate. But they are more aggressive than expected elsewhere. In 1997 they doubled their seats in the House of Commons although their percentage of the national vote fell slightly. This was because their campaign chief, Chris (now Lord) Rennard, concentrated on picking winners for winnable seats. He is now confident that almost all the incumbent Lib Dem MPs, even those with slim majorities, can retain their seats because they have dug themselves in with the local people and press. He is determined to oust Labour from Falmouth and win at least three southwestern seats from the Tories: Teignbridge, Totnes and Tiverton.

Labour is "only" defending its 179 majority. But can it resist trying to pick off Tory Ian Bruce in Dorset South, who is holding on with only 77 votes? Or helping the Lib Dems oust David Prior from Norfolk North?

Andrew Roth is publisher of Parliamentary Profiles.

The next generation
Thomas Happold

Hilary Benn
Labour MP for Leeds Central

Though Hilary Benn inherited Tony Benn's charm, he didn't inherit his father's hard-left politics – he describes himself as a Benn but not a Bennite. Despite their political differences, father and son are close. The Benns are now one of Britain's most notable political dynasties – Hilary is the fourth successive Benn to sit as an MP. A former head of research at the manufacturing union, MSF and deputy leader of Ealing council, he was an advisor to David Blunkett at the department of education until he was selected to fight the Leeds Central by-election. Despite failing to inspire many of his future constituents to vote, he succeeded in holding the safe Labour seat. At Westminster he has made more of an impression. Displaying the Benn talent for ingenuity he came up with the bright idea of persuading the credit card companies to encourage people to register their wish to have their organs used for transplants after their death.

Charles Clarke
Labour MP for Norwich South

Once Neil Kinnock's chief of staff and now the minister responsible for reducing crime, Charles Clarke is used to tough jobs. He helped write Kinnock's celebrated conference attack on Derek Hatton and the leadership of Liverpool city council and took on Militant and all those he saw as standing in the way of Labour's long march back to electability. An instinctive loyalist, Clarke eschewed sycophancy as a means to achieve office. Despite voting for the government's cut to lone parent benefits, he opposed it in private – writing to the then social security secretary Harriet Harman to protest that it's "fundamentally wrong to discriminate financially against those who make the choice to be a parent and so do not seek work." His crumpled and bearded appearance suggests a trade union background; in fact he's the son of a former Whitehall mandarin and the product of a public school and Cambridge university.

Patricia Hewitt
Labour MP for Leicester West

Patricia Hewitt and Charles Clarke were the first of the 1997 intake of MPs to join the government, and it is not unlikely that they'll be the first to join the Cabinet too. Clever, but perhaps lacking in charm, Hewitt is the government's e-minister, responsible for encouraging the new economy. She came to prominence as the young leader of the National Council for Civil Liberties, famously attacking the record of Jim Callaghan's government at Labour's 1979 conference. Charges of opportunism followed her subsequent switch from the hard left to Kinnockite new realism. She served the Labour leader as his press secretary and policy co-ordinator for six years before becoming deputy director of the Labour-leaning think-tank, the IPPR. Hewitt has long campaigned for shorter hours and greater flexibility in the work place. Don't be surprised to see her appointed Britain's first woman Chancellor.

James Purnell
Labour candidate for Stalybridge and Hyde

James Purnell, the recently selected Labour candidate for the safe seat of Stalybridge and Hyde, was previously a member of the Guildford troika in Number 10 – one of three special advisors from the town. As the media specialist in its policy unit he worked with his childhood friends Liz Lloyd, also a policy adviser, and Tim Allen, Alastair Campbell's former deputy. It was Purnell who got them their jobs: he first worked for Tony Blair in the 1992 general election. Since then his rise has been swift. After working for Blair in opposition, he joined the IPPR and then the BBC as a senior policy consultant. But it hasn't been all smooth. As an Islington councillor Purnell had to issue a public apology to Liz Davies, after Labour's NEC refused to endorse her as a parliamentary candidate after, among other things, he accused her of 'inciting' a crowd at a fraught public meeting. Trusted by the prime minister, it's unlikely he'll spend long on the backbenches.

John Bercow
Conservative MP for Buckingham

Unlike most of the Tory front bench John Bercow seems to understand what opposition is all about. Schooled in the art of political street fighting in the left-dominated world of student politics, Bercow rose to become chairman of the notoriously right-wing Federation of Conservative Students. Elected to parliament in 1997, he made his mark in pursuit of Lord Simon, the BP boss-turned minister accused of impropriety for failing to register his portfolio of shares. Always aggressive, always on the attack, the terrier-like Tory sometimes bites off more than he can chew – he was derided recently for describing Cherie Blair as being "a cross between first lady and Lady Macbeth". Despite his spell as secretary of the Monday Club's immigration and repatriation committee, Bercow seems to share Michael Portillo's analysis that the Tory party needs to become more inclusive. He voted for the equalisation of the age of consent but is at pains to describe himself as "rampantly heterosexual".

David Cameron
Conservative candidate for Whitney

David Cameron has a lot in common with Shaun Woodward, the last Conservative candidate to stand for the safe Tory seat of Whitney. Both are married to heiresses – Samantha Sheffield, daughter of the Lincolnshire landowner Sir Reginald Sheffield in Cameron's case and Camilla Sainsbury, a member of the supermarket dynasty in Woodward's. Both have worked at Conservative Central Office. And both have had glittering futures predicted for them. Cameron differs from Woodward in having stuck with the Tory party, despite being present at one of its darkest hours. As a Treasury adviser, he watched the pound fall through the floor with his boss Norman Lamont. Apart from that blip, his career has been upward. Educated at Eton, he left Whitehall to head Carlton Communication's corporate affairs department. It is unlikely his rise will stop on the backbenches.

David Davis
Conservative MP for Haltemprice and Howden

David Davis is an outside bet to become the next Tory leader. And though much of this speculation has been prompted by his famous weekend phone calls, it does reflect the standing he has achieved as chairman of the Common's public accounts committee. After the last election, Davis shrewdly shunned a seat on the opposition front bench, preferring to attack the government from the committee corridor. There he has been remarkably successful, landing blows with reports on subjects ranging from social security fraud to hospital acquired infections. Ironically, the Eurosceptic Davis made his name as a whip, forcing the Maastricht treaty through the Commons – has was known as DD of the SS. Before parliament he was a successful businessman, sitting on the board of Tate and Lyle. What are his leadership chances? He has the advantage of appearing neither odd nor mad, but could be held back by his lack of oratorical skills.

Eleanor Laing
Conservative MP for Epping Forest

As a Conservative spokesman on Scotland, a land without Tory MPs, Eleanor Laing has a tough time of it. But as a witty and strong parliamentary performer she defies admiring male colleagues' attempts to find a less stilted word than feisty for her spirited Commons style. The daughter of a Conservative councillor, she started distributing Conservative leaflets aged 12. After Edinburgh University, where she was the first woman to be elected president of the union, Laing qualified as a solicitor. A short spell in a city law firm was followed by a five-year stretch as a special advisor. Economically dry, she tried to convince her boss, transport secretary John McGregor, to privatise the railways. Socially liberal, she spoke for an equal age of consent for gay sex in the Commons. As one of the few female Tory MPs, promotion seems inevitable.

David Heath
Liberal Democrat MP for Somerton and Frome

If he keeps his marginal seat, David Heath could become a rare thing after the general election – a well-known Liberal Democrat MP. Born into a liberal and nonconformist family, Heath joined the Liberal Party aged 16 and was elected the youngest-ever county council leader at 31. He also inherited his father's profession, qualifying as an optician after studying at St John's College, Oxford with Tony Blair. In parliament he showed his liberal credentials by voting against the government's total ban on handguns. But, despite his local government background and beard, Heath displays a healthy disrespect for the tenet of liberal "pavement politics". As an MP of a largely rural constituency and former breeder of Tamworth pigs, he was one of the first politicians to recognise the danger and call for action against BSE. Heath is one of the Liberal Democrats' most effective parliamentary performers.

Thomas Happold is a freelance political journalist.

Parties

Labour
Kevin Maguire

"This party is a moral crusade or it is nothing." Harold Wilson's call to arms easily transfers to Tony Blair's lips in one of his more messianic moments but the current Labour leader's promised land would be unrecognisable to his predecessor.

The vast majority of members now, as four decades ago, are more interested in social democracy than socials and Blair has risked alienating the party's bedrock supporters with talk of the big tent and the third way. Elected with a thumping majority in 1997, Blair has often found himself in the unusual position of being more popular in the country as a whole than in the Labour party he heads.

After the 2001 election Blair must impose himself fully on Labour or the party may reassert itself on Blair. Certainly, the uneasy alliance of recent years is unlikely to hold as traditionalists tussle with modernisers. Key to the Blair vision of a radical century, rather than a Labour era, is coalition with the Liberal Democrats through proportional representation, to unite the centre ground and outflank both left and right. The second volume of former Liberal Democrat leader Paddy Ashdown's diaries details how dearly Blair wanted such an alliance, only to be thwarted by Labour's thumping majority.

Few Labour members share that enthusiasm and Blair's ability (or inability) to pull it off, together with a decision on the euro referendum, may ultimately define his spell in No 10.

The smart money among cabinet members is that Blair will achieve neither goal before stepping down mid-term to pave the way for Gordon Brown to become only Labour's sixth prime minister in more than 100 years. If re-elected, speculation of the "will-he-won't-he" variety can be expected to dog Blair from the day he returns to Downing Street. The inevitable uncertainty will also revive the simmering rivalry between the Blair-Brown camps in which every word or action is forensically examined for signs of a leadership bid from the chancellor.

But it is at the grassroots that Labour has a growing problem. Membership, according to the party's own figures, has slipped from 405,000 at the last election to under 380,000. The official total is considered grossly inflated and some in Millbank suggest it may be nearer 300,000 as veterans resign from a party that no longer resembles the one they joined and new recruits melt away from lack of commitment.

Enthusiasm is also waning among activists, as witnessed by the turnout in the contest for constituency seats on the national executive committee. Fewer than one in four bothered to cast their votes. Low morale is pinned partly on a series of "control freak" rows that left activists disenchanted.

In 1999, Blair backed Frank Dobson to be London mayor but the electorate supported Ken Livingstone. The prime minister similarly miscalculated in Wales a year before by imposing Alun Michael in Cardiff before accepting the inevitability of Rhodri Morgan. In Scotland old Labour warhorse Dennis Canavan was deemed insufficiently "new" for the Edinburgh parliament. He quit the party and subsequently won his seat as an independent. And Millbank's imposition of handpicked European candidates proved an umitigated disaster as party workers stayed at home and the Tories topped the poll.

Millbank has recently shown signs of realising that heavy-handed interventions can be counterproductive and, if the party's organisation is to thrive during the next four years, Blair will need to pay more heed to its members. The prime minister has had little time for internal opponents, complaining of "negativism" and "self-mutilation" on the left. Whether he likes it or not, as fair-weather stars and big business desert Labour, he will be forced to rely on traditional supporters such the unions to sustain the party.

Blair may dislike comparisons with Wilson (bright, initially inspirational, ultimately disappointing?) but could do worse than reflect on why people join the Labour party.

Kevin Maguire is the Guardian's chief reporter.

Conservatives
Nicholas Watt

William Hague will fight his first general election as Conservative leader supported by a party machinery that outstrips the creaking operation in place when John Major presided over the worst Tory defeat since 1906.

Conservative Central Office has been transformed since the 1997 election – thanks to the generosity of the party's billionaire treasurer Lord Ashcroft – allowing the Tories to establish a highly efficient "war room" with a staff of 60. By the time Mr Hague steps aboard his battle bus, Central Office will have been hard at work for months targeting more than 100 seats the Tories must regain to achieve a decent result, though not an overall victory.

Tory strategists believe that the reforms at Central Office, which helped them win the 1999 European elections, will place them in a strong position. Few people are seriously talking of a victory, but there are hopes that the Tories can achieve a significant dent in Labour's historic majority.

Behind the public confidence, however, many strategists admit in private that their campaign will be severely weakened across a range of fronts. The first problem is one of motivation. Outside Mr Hague's small inner circle, hardly a soul in the party believes the Tories can win. Without the whiff of power, Central Office faces a monumental challenge in motivating the foot soldiers who will form the backbone of the Tory campaign.

Even if the leadership does motivate its grassroots activists, their numbers have been so depleted over the past decade that constituencies will struggle to drum up enough "door knockers". Tory councillors, the most important force on the ground, have become a rare breed. In 1979, when Margaret Thatcher won her first election, the Tories boasted more than 12,000 councillors. This has nearly halved to just over 6,700, which is 2,000 fewer than Labour.

Tory strategists admit privately that they are also struggling to boost party membership which has slipped to just over 300,000 – the lowest level since the first world war. This has delighted the Tories' opponents who have noticed that a once mighty machine is a shadow of its former self. During last year's disastrous Romsey by-election, when Mr Hague lost one of his safest seats, most of the Tory activists had to be drafted in from outside.

Despite this gloomy backdrop, Mr Hague insists that he is on course to repeat Edward Heath's 1970 victory when he came from behind to unseat Harold Wilson. As a sign of Tory resolve, a bank of 60 computers has been set up in a special call centre in Smith Square to target 2.5 m floating voters in the 180 target seats the Tories must regain to win the election. By polling day the call centre will have contacted 1.25 m swing voters by telephone. This is half the number of voters needed for a Tory victory, showing that Central Office strategists have abandoned any hope of making it to Downing Street. All the swing voters will be sent a mailshot from Mr Hague.

The call centre serves, however, to demonstrate the gulf between the finely tuned operation in Central Office and the shaky machinery on the ground. Thanks to Lord Ashcroft's millions, the Tories have spent a fortune identifying the sort of voters who are most likely to switch back from Labour. But this information has not been gleaned from the doorsteps. Instead, the Tories have used sophisticated computer "demographic profiling" techniques to draw up a database of their target voters.

The 180 seats on the target list have been carefully graded. Seats near the top, such as Enfield Southgate, the 26th target seat where the Tories need a swing of 1.5%, will be left largely alone.

Shadow cabinet ministers will instead fan out to seats further down the list. Residents of seats such as The Wrekin (51st) can expect plenty of visits from the likes of Ann Widdecombe and Michael Portillo. The final seats on the Tories' 180-strong target list – around 60 – will receive less resources because Central Office is privately writing them off.

Central office is ensuring that resources on the ground are carefully targeted by operating a "twinned seat" strategy, which is run by the party's 12 new area regional campaign directors. So called "majority seats" have been twinned with "target seats" to ensure that activists devote their energy to seats where the Tories face a real battle. Strategists hope that the scheme will motivate activists who think their candidate is going to win to offer support to activists who fear that their candidate is heading for certain defeat.

Mr Hague enters the campaign, his aides insist, convinced that he can make it to Downing Street. Tory pessimists simply hope that he makes it over the "Foot benchmark" – winning more than the 209 seats Labour picked up in its dismal 1983 election, which would be a gain of 44 Tory seats on 1997.

Nicholas Watt is a Guardian political correspondent.

Liberal Democrats
Lucy Ward

Charles Kennedy will fight his first general election as Liberal Democrat leader without the benefit of the proportional voting system that his party had hoped to secure from co-operation with Labour.

Since Kennedy took over from the energetic Paddy Ashdown, enthusiasm for the Lib-Lab cooperation "project" has cooled almost to freezing point, with the prospect of the Lib Dems' longed-for referendum on PR receding over the horizon. That leaves the Lib Dems, as ever, attempting to wring maximum success from the traditional first-past-the-post system, primarily by treating the general election campaign as a series of fiercely contested by-elections.

With an election war chest of £3m compared with the £15m or so filling the Labour and Tory coffers, party strategists know it makes financial and electoral sense to focus resources on a limited number of constituencies. While the mantra "every seat is a target seat" will be repeated in public, effort will be concentrated on defending the Lib Dems' existing 47 Westminster seats and targeting another 20, with another 30 within the party's sights if the Conservative vote collapses badly.

In all but a handful of their key seats, the Lib Dems are battling with Tories. Strategists point to the surprise Romsey by-election victory, where the party overturned an 8,500 Tory majority, as evidence that many traditional Conservatives are unhappy with William Hague's swing to the right, and that Labour supporters are still prepared to vote tactically to keep out Tory candidates.

The party's performance may surprise thanks to its traditional ability to pick up protest votes from disaffected supporters of both main parties. Although its policy portfolio is little changed from 1997, it now stands to the left of Labour on issues such as social justice and public sector funding. One-nation Tories disenchanted with the Hague stance on asylum seekers or Europe may be tempted to give the Lib Dems a try – secure in the knowledge that they will never have to pay the tax increases the party advocates. Labour supporters frustrated at the slow pace of change may do the same.

Kennedy, not recognised by many voters but trusted by those who know him, will pull no punches in attacking Hague, though his assault on Tony Blair will depend on whether the Labour manifesto renews a so-far broken promise to hold a referendum on electoral reform.

Without the personal chemistry of Blair or Ashdown, Lib–Lab cooperation – with fair votes as the bait – has broken down, with the historic joint cabinet committee on hold since last summer and a breakdown in talks over the future of the second chamber. But in the cold light of the election campaign such Westminster machinations will have little impact: clear orange water separating the party from Labour may even help. After the election, however, another significant Labour majority would force Kennedy to find a clearer line on Lib-Lab relations.

Lucy Ward is a Guardian political correspondent.

Other parties
Julian Glover

More than 100 political parties – a record – ran candidates at the last general election and a similar number are likely to try again in 2001. One thing unites them: a shared hatred of the "other" word.

The term, used by pollsters to describe the political small fry, hides a multitude of enthusiasms and ideas that deserve kinder attention. Some may be mad – the New Millennium Bean party – some sad – the No Candidate Deserves My Vote! party – and some bad – the National Front – but most are just unfairly neglected.

Only at election time, when the broadcasters are obliged to mention every parliamentary candidate in their reports and evening political slots are given to some minor parties, does their existence even intrude into the public consciousness. But this is changing, slowly. The political fringe is moving away from the margins and into serious contention for power. The share of the vote achieved by "others" makes this clear. In 1951 99.5% of the national vote went to the big three parties. Years later, in 1997, "others" gained 7%.

Since then proportional representation has seen Green candidates elected to the European and Scottish parliaments and the London assembly and three members of the Eurosceptic, dispute-ridden, UK Independence party have gone to Brussels.

Parties such as these mean business. Ukip and the Greens will have a presence on ballot papers all over the land on polling day. So will some smaller but still serious political forces such as the Cornish nationalist Mebyon Kernow ("our philosophy is based on four cornerstones: it is Cornish, Green, left-of-centre and decentralist") and the Liberal party, run by a former MP whose message is that he is *not* a Liberal Democrat. The Liberals have unexpected pockets of strength, such as Exeter and Liverpool.

In 1997 one "other" party almost broke out of the fringe. Jimmy Goldsmith's Referendum party put out a sceptical message that won plenty of attention although few votes – 2.6% – on polling day. After the election the party was accused by some Conservatives of helping let Labour in by the back door, just as in the United States Ralph Nader found himself unpopular with Democrats after Al Gore's defeat. This charge, in the British case, was unfair. Research shows that plenty of Referendum votes came from Labour and especially the Lib Dems. In fact some Conservatives may have been saved from defeat by the Referendum party's role in diluting their opponents.

This time round there is no Referendum party. Ukip will try to fill the gap, but without the Goldsmith millions it will fail. Their polar opposite, the breakaway Pro-European Conservative party, seems to have been stillborn.

In fact 2001 may prove rather a dull year for "others". The bouncy men and women from the Natural Law party are not going to stand again. Neither will Screaming Lord Sutch – he killed himself in October 1999, although he lives on as spiritual president of a party that plans to put up candidates all over the place.

And before anyone claims that the Monster Raving Loony party proves that the fringe groups are all mad, consider these past Loony policies, now law: votes for 18-year-olds, opening the airwaves to commercial radio, the abolition of the 11+ test, all-day pub opening and a passports for pets plan. A rather better track record of implementation than say, the Labour manifesto of 1983. Yet that genuinely loony document was enough to launch a certain Tony Blair all the way to No 10.

Julian Glover is launch editor of Guardian Unlimited politics.

Scotland
Gerald Seenan

In the early 1980s, London newspapers decided to take on the indigenous press north
of the border with a panoply of Scottish editions. But they soon learned that they
had to give news emanating from England a Scottish resonance. It became known as
putting a kilt on a story.

Something similar will be happening in politics at this election. Many of the core
issues that the Conservatives, Labour and the Liberal Democrats will be slugging out
– education, the health service, police – are all matters now devolved to the Scottish
parliament. So the election north of the border will either have to be fought on different issues entirely – leaving Labour, in particular, at a disadvantage – or politicians
will have to resort to the newspaper tactic of putting a kilt on their policies.

For Labour things will be tough. Education and health may be Tony Blair's priorities, but no Westminster MP has a say on these matters in Scotland. There is also a
major divergence between Labour in Edinburgh and London on these issues – from
the abolition of tuition fees to the commitment to free long-term care for the elderly
– which will not be lost on Labour's only credible opposition in Scotland: the Scottish
National party.

Sleight of hand, on both sides, will be required. Labour will shout about smaller
class sizes and homework classes; the SNP will fire back with the exam crisis that saw
thousands of Scottish school pupils receive incorrect Higher results. In theory, none
of these issues has anything to do with a general election: Labour's pledges apply to
England, the exam crisis is a matter for Holyrood. But that's just the theory.

Fighting the election north of the border on Westminster matters – pensions, tax,
social security – would make for a dull and slim contest. Labour strategists in
Scotland are already worried that a wave of apathy caused by remoteness from
Westminster will cost them seats, so a dull contest is the last thing they want.

The new Scottish secretary, Helen Liddell – the self-styled Hammer of the Nats –
will also be looking forward to taking on the SNP. The death of Donald Dewar has
left Labour feeling the void of a seasoned campaigner, but Liddell will be a match for
Alex Salmond, who will lead the SNP in the Commons. Liddell, though, has her work
cut out. Labour has held fairly steady in the polls since 1997, but the scale of its win in
Scotland in 1999 means that even a slight swing could lose the party seats.

This is also a key election for the SNP. The creation of the Scottish parliament has
generated a fundamental question: what does the party stand for at Westminster?
Independence is the obvious answer, but the party has recently played down its
commitment to separation. Salmond – who never really shone in Holyrood as he did
in the Commons – will lead a group of unknowns now that the party's main talent is
based in Edinburgh. Salmond and his band of hopefuls will carry, whether they like
it or not, the perception that this election is a litmus test on the state of support for
independence, which has dwindled from its high point a year before the Scottish
elections.

But for the Conservatives, at least, there are benefits to be found in this new brand of take-your-pick, Holyrood-Westminster politics. They cannot but improve on their 1997 Westminster performance – when every Scottish Conservative MP lost their seat – yet they also have an advantage: at least two of their main policies are equally powerful on both sides of the border.

Keeping the pound and ruling out the euro for the lifetime of the next parliament has as much resonance in Thurso as it does in Kent. And a commitment to abolish tax on savings is unaffected by geography. It is on these issues that Malcolm Rifkind's Conservative campaign stands its best chance of clawing back a handful of seats. But it will not be an easy ride: the party still languishes a poor third in the polls, is lack-lustre at Holyrood and there is only a slim chance that even Rifkind will win back his Edinburgh seat.

That leaves only the Liberal Democrats, currently enjoying power in the first coalition government in mainland Britain since the second world war. But power hasn't brought them electoral reward: they have come fourth in Scottish by-elections – often only narrowly ahead of the Scottish Socialists – and they are constrained by the same problem as Labour: their key policies are irrelevant in Scotland.

Gerald Seenan is a Guardian Scotland correspondent.

Wales
David Torrance

Wales has had its share of political upheaval since the Labour landslide of 1997, but the new National Assembly for Wales has, in one way or another, made its mark on the United Kingdom – no longer does the Principality's entry in the Encyclopedia Britannica read: For Wales, see England.

But the resignations and bitter leadership contests of the past two years are not likely to be factors at the next general election. In a departure from Wales' politically radical past, the voters are not about to give any of the four parties cause for celebration, or alarm.

Unlike in Scotland, where most traditional election issues are now devolved matters, the campaign in Wales is likely to resemble any other general election fight, with Labour-dominated South Wales slugging it out with pockets of support in the north for Plaid Cymru – Labour's main challenger.

The creation of the assembly nearly two years ago will have a minimal impact on the battle for the green benches. While the assembly has flexed its narrow remit slightly – with recent freezes on prescription charges and free school milk as testament – they are hardly the sort of issues that arouse passions in the valleys.

But the fact that Labour and the Liberal Democrats now share a cabinet table in Crickhowell House, following a surprise coalition forged late last year, will inevitably cause problems in the respective parties' campaigns. Should Labour's first minister Rhodri Morgan criticise his Liberal Democrat deputy Mike German as a political opponent, or praise him as a coalition ally?

Although one quarter of Welsh seats are expected to change hands at the election, the majority of these shifts will be the result of long-serving Labour members retiring to the red benches in the upper chamber, together with three Plaid MPs standing down to concentrate their energies in Cardiff Bay.

Morgan will undoubtedly be Labour's major asset during the campaign, and with a 60% approval rating, the member for Cardiff West should at least keep the party faithful on side, even if some floating voters drift elsewhere.

The amiable Welsh secretary Paul Murphy will also figure prominently in the election battle. Having made it clear he wishes to remain as Wales' voice in the Westminster cabinet, he has everything to prove in maintaining Labour's 45% opinion poll share – down 10% since 1997.

If Plaid's present 15% poll rating holds up, it should be able to claim at least the four seats snatched from Labour during the first assembly elections in 1999 – Conwy, the Rhondda, Islwyn and Llanelli – for Westminster too, as well as its number one target seat of Carmarthen East and Dinefwr.

The Conservatives, meanwhile, have no Welsh representatives in the Commons but enjoy a 25% poll rating, raising their hopes of regaining Monmouth (won in the Welsh election) and possibly one or two more seats in the north, although far from the 10 seats predicted by assembly leader Nick Bourne.

And the Liberal Democrats expect to hold their two seats, under their new leader, the Montgomeryshire MP Lembit Öpik who, despite an unhealthy obsession with meteorites, has quickly established himself as a competent and witty media performer.

But in the familiarity stakes, Plaid has everything to lose from the recent resignation of its main asset in 1997, former leader Dafydd Wigley. His successor, the rather bland and high-pitched Ieuan Wyn Jones, suffers the same problem as his newly incumbent Scottish counterpart, John Swinney – inexperience and a damagingly low public profile.

Plaid will also have a lot of thinking to do about policy. Their call is no longer full independence for Wales – despite popular perception – but parity with Scotland in terms of legislative muscle. Its biggest problem will come in communicating this to a largely disinterested electorate.

While Plaid's rallying cry will be tax raising powers and primary legislative powers, Labour will shy away from controversy and promote the status quo, as will the Conservatives. The Lib Dems, too, want to see more powers transferred to Cardiff Bay, but as part of a much wider set-up in their mythical federal United Kingdom.

Constitutional issues rarely capture the electorate's imagination, especially in the principality, where it can never be far from any politician's mind that the original devolution referendum scraped home by a frighteningly small margin less than four years ago.

David Torrance is a freelance writer.

Northern Ireland

Rosie Cowan

As the rest of the country makes its mind up over tax, health and education policies, many voters in Northern Ireland will use the general election to pass judgement on the state of the political process, still faltering three years after the Good Friday agreement was signed.

For the first time the fiercest battle will be waged between pro and anti-agreement unionists. The Province's largest party, the Ulster Unionists, hold nine of the 18 Westminster constituencies. They are, however, bitterly split with six of the current MPs against the peace deal, something the anti-accord Democratic Unionists, who have three seats, are keen to exploit.

Meanwhile Sinn Fein, with two sitting MPs, expect the most promising results since the 1950s. They will duel for the nationalist vote with the SDLP, which has strong majorities in its three constituencies.

The election is already an unwelcome guest at the negotiating table where the parties are trying to keep the fledgling Stormont government alive. Even if only a few seats change hands the two largest and more moderate parties, the Ulster Unionists and SDLP, who captured 32.7% and 24.1% of the 1997 vote, could lose considerable ground to the DUP and Sinn Fein, who got 13.6% and 16.1% respectively.

This ballot will be a defining moment for Ulster Unionism and especially its leader, David Trimble, who is already under pressure for sharing power with Sinn Fein without an IRA arms handover. It will be difficult to accept any further compromise on weapons before the voters have their say.

A total of 71.1% of the people in Northern Ireland backed the agreement in the 1998 referendum. But exit polls showed that while 96% of Catholics supported it, only 55% of Protestants did. Any fall in the vote for pro-accord Ulster Unionist candidates will make it harder for Mr Trimble to claim he represents majority unionist opinion.

Ian Paisley's DUP will be aiming to replicate their success in last autumn's South Antrim by-election. Willie McCrea, who lost his Mid-Ulster seat by fewer than 2,000 votes to Sinn Fein's Martin McGuinness in 1997, capitalised on the ambiguous position of Ulster Unionist David Burnside, a former supporter of the agreement who turned sceptic. The Ulster Unionists blamed apathy for the poor turnout but the DUP, which had not previously opposed them for the seat, managed to overturn a 16,000-vote majority to win by just 800 votes.

The UUP leader could also be hit by the loss of one of his staunchest supporters, Ken Maginnis, who is standing down from his Fermanagh and South Tyrone seat after 18 years. Pro-agreement James Cooper is the new candidate but the DUP's Maurice Morrow could split the unionist vote, which would boost Sinn Fein and the SDLP.

Mr Trimble's maverick deputy, John Taylor, is also retiring from his Strangford constituency, and Iris Robinson, of the DUP, who topped the Strangford poll in the

1998 Stormont assembly elections, will fight a high profile campaign to try and scale the 5,000-vote Ulster Unionist majority.

Two other constituencies could see very close races. In West Tyrone anti-agreement Ulster Unionist Willie Thompson won in 1997 by 1,161 votes, with the SDLP and Sinn Fein neck and neck behind him. In North Down UK Unionist Bob McCartney, who opposes the peace deal, beat the Ulster Unionists by 1,449 votes.

Rosie Cowan is the Guardian's Ireland correspondent.

The men who paid for the election
David Hencke

Conservative

NAME: **Stuart Wheeler**
DONATION: £5m
DESCRIPTION: 65 year old Old Etonian and Douglas Hurd lookalike. Millionaire owner of spread betting company, IG Index, which was floated for £90m and is predicting a Labour victory. No previous history of large political donations. Says he wants to redress the Labour business balance and give William Hague a chance.

NAME: **Michael Ashcroft**
DONATION: £1.5m
DESCRIPTION: Controversial Conservative party treasurer, former tax exile, who has come back to Britain from Belize, where he has established roots. Highly successful businessman, he came to the Tories aid in the darkest hour after the 1997 defeat.

NAME: **Paul Sykes**
DONATION: £2m
DESCRIPTION: Eurosceptic property developer and IT millionaire who came back into the Tory fold last year. Has promised to spend anything up to £20m to keep the pound – more likely to offer a tenth of that.

Labour

NAME: **Lord Hamlyn**
DONATION: £2m
DESCRIPTION: Publisher and philanthropist who decided to give Labour a big donation – a self made man – will not want anything in return.

NAME: **Lord Sainsbury**
DONATION: £2m
DESCRIPTION: Minister of Science and Innovation – with responsibility for Britain's tiny space programme. Made a fortune turning his family firm into a giant supermarket chain. Generous donor to the arts, including the Sainsbury wing at the National Gallery.

NAME: **Christopher Ondaatje**
DONATION: £2m
DESCRIPTION: Anglo-Canadian financier who has endowed a wing of the National Portrait Gallery and is a key supporter of the re-development of London's South Bank arts complex. A Former Tory donor who became disillusioned with the party's Eurosceptic stance and switched his support to Labour.

Labour and the unions
Seumas Milne

In the run-up to the 1997 election, relations between Labour and the trade unions that founded the party reached a nadir. As Tony Blair made ritually contemptuous noises about organised labour in an effort to reposition the party as business's champion, his up-and-coming lieutenant Stephen Byers famously floated the prospect of a complete rupture of links with the unions, at a Blackpool fish supper. Disgruntled trade union officials muttered bitterly about walking before they were pushed, even as they signed the cheques that still paid the lion's share of Labour's election expenses.

Four years on, the scene is markedly different. Union leaders have regular access to ministers at all levels and the TUC has overseen a steady colonisation of Whitehall. Unions have challenged and changed policy on the floor of Labour's conference and they are signing hundreds of new agreements on the back of the hard-fought right to union recognition legislation. Meanwhile the government has defied the CBI's public warnings and increased the minimum wage by 11% – and all talk of breaking Labour's links with the unions has been scrubbed from the agenda, at least for now. New Labour discovered – notably during the fuel tax protests of September 2000 – that it needed the unions after all.

For all the attention paid to the £2m donations from the party's rich friends, it will once again be the unions who stump up the bulk of its election expenses, along with countrywide organisational support in the constituencies. But unlike in 1997, the Labour hierarchy is making little attempt to conceal the extent of the unions' involvement in the campaign, such as their drive to sign up hundreds of thousands of postal voters in advance of polling day. A visible relationship with the 7m-strong trade union movement is now a reassuring signal to core Labour voters disappointed with the government's delivery. It also has the advantage of highlighting a more accountable and transparent form of party funding at a time when Labour is on the back foot over tradeoffs with its private business donors.

But the return of trade union influence should not be exaggerated. Not only is the power of the unions much less than it was under the last Labour government, it is much less than that wielded by business and the corporate sector, whether party donors or not. As a rule, the lower-profile and more marginal the issue, the greater the progress the trade unions can expect to make. But when it comes to set-piece policy conflicts, new Labour's "pro-business" instincts almost invariably prevail. This is the case over pensions, air traffic control privatisation, the private finance initiative and the draft European directive giving workers rights to be informed and consulted about their employers' plans.

How the significant, but subaltern, role that the trade unions have carved out for themselves with the Blair administration might evolve during a second term depends crucially on the performance of the economy and the political direction of the government. The expected first-term public sector pay explosion never materialised and ministers will hope that planned spending increases and union loyalty will continue to defuse the danger of industrial pressure from below. But there are concerns on the union side that the government is already running out of steam and failing to develop the more radical agenda that could cement the loyalty and see the relationship through more difficult economic times ahead.

Seumas Milne is the Guardian's labour editor.

Labour MPs who rebelled against the government, 1997–2000

Parliamentary rebellions were both less frequent and less threatening to the government than in the 1992 parliament. However significant outbreaks of dissent did occur, although none succeeded in defeating the government. The major ones are listed below.

Lone parent benefits
December 10 1997
47 Labour MPs voted against the government's proposed cut to the lone parent supplement to child benefit, 14 government backbenchers abstained and a junior Scottish Office minister, Malcolm Chisholm resigned. Conservative support gave the government a 350 majority.

University tuition fees
June 8 1998
33 Labour MPs defied the government whips and opposed plans to abolish student maintenance grants, another 15 abstained. The government's majority was 137.

Newspaper pricing
July 8 1998
25 Labour MPs backed a rebel amendment to the government's competition bill challenging the tactics of Rupert Murdoch's News Corporation. It called for a lower threshold in the definition of market domination in the national newspaper industry to make it easier for the authorities to investigate predatory pricing and fine offenders. The amendment was defeated by 301 to 68.

Disability benefits
May 20 1999
66 Labour MPs opposed the government's proposals to remove entitlement to incapacity benefit for those who have made no national insurance contributions in the previous two years, while 14 abstained. The government's majority was 40.

Legal aid reform
June 22 1999
21 Labour MPs supported a rebel amendment to the government's access to justice bill, calling for legal aid to be retained for the disabled and less well off in personal injury cases. The amendment was defeated by 291 to 173.

Pensions
April 3 2000
41 Labour MPs backed a rebel amendment calling for the restoration of the link pensions and earnings. The revolt followed an inflation-linked rise in the state

pension of 75p a week. The amendment to the child support, pensions and social security bill was defeated by 240 to 75.

Freedom of information
April 5 2000
35 Labour MPs supported a strengthening of the government's freedom on information bill and backed a rebel amendment to force ministers to allow disclosure of the factual basis behind their policy decisions. The amendment was defeated by 311 votes to 202.

Part-privatisation of air traffic control
May 9 2000
46 Labour MPs opposed the government's plans to part-privatise Britain's air traffic control system. The government's majority was 60.

Table 1 Issues on which Labour MPs rebelled against the government, 1997–2000

Labour MP	Lone parent benefits	University tuition fees	Newspaper pricing	Incapacity benefits	Legal aid reform	Pensions	Freedom of information	Privatisation of air traffic control
Diane Abbot	•	•	•	•		•		
John Austin	•		•					
Harry Barnes	•			•		•		•
Tony Benn	•	•	•	•	•	•	•	•
Andrew Bennett		Teller		•				•
Roger Berry	•			•				
Harold Best	•		•	•				
Ronnie Campbell	•	•		•		•	Teller	
Dennis Canavan[1]	•	•		•				
Jamie Cann				•				
Martin Caton	•			•		•		
David Chaytor	•			•				•
Malcolm Chisholm	•							
Michael Clapham				•		•		
David Clark							•	
Tom Clarke				•				
Tony Clarke				•		•		
Ann Clwyd	•		•	•		•	•	•
Harry Cohen		•			•			
Michael Connarty						•		•
Frank Cook	•				•	•	•	
Robin Corbett							•	
Jeremy Corbyn	•	•	•	•	•	•	•	•
Jim Cousins			Teller			•	•	
David Crausby				•				
Ann Cryer	•	•		•				•
John Cryer	•	•		•	•	•		•
John Cummings				•				
Lawrence Cunliffe		•						
Tam Dalyell		•		•	•		•	•
Ian Davidson				•		•		•

	Lone parent benefits	University tuition fees	Newspaper pricing	Incapacity benefits	Legal aid reform	Pensions	Freedom of information	Privatisation of air traffic control
Denzil Davies		•		•	•			
Hilton Dawson	•							
Janet Dean								•
Andrew Dismore								•
Jim Dobbin	•					•		•
Brian Donohoe								•
Gwyneth Dunwoody	•		•	•			•	
William Etherington	•	•		•				
Frank Field				•				•
Mark Fisher				•	•	•	•	
Jim Fitzpatrick		•						
Paul Flynn			•					•
Derek Foster							•	
Maria Fyfe	•	Teller		•				•
Neil Gerrard			Teller	•		•	•	
Ian Gibson	•			•				
Norman Godman	•		•	•		•		•
Llin Golding							•	
Eileen Gordon								•
Bernie Grant	•	•						
David Hinchliffe	•			•			•	
Kelvin Hopkins	•	•	•		Teller	Teller	•	
Alan Hurst					•	•		
Brian Iddon	•			•		•		
Eric Illsley				•				
Jenny Jones				•				
Jon Owen Jones							•	
Lynne Jones	•	•	•	•	•	•	•	•
Alan Keen								•
Tess Kingham				•				
David Lepper								•
Terry Lewis	•	•	•	•		•		•
Ken Livingstone[2]	•	•	•		•			
Andrew Love							•	
John McAllion	•	•	•	•				
Christine McCafferty				•				
John McDonnell	•	Teller	•	•	•	•		•
Kevin McNamara	•							
Andrew Mackinlay				•			•	
Alice Mahon	•	•		•	•	•	•	•
John Marek	•	•						•
David Marshall				•				
Jim Marshall		•		•	•		•	
Bob Marshall-Andrews			•	•	•	•	•	
Bill Michie	•		Teller		•	•	•	Teller
Austin Mitchell		•						
Julie Morgan				•		•	•	
Chris Mullin			•					
Denis Murphy				•				
Kerry Pollard		•		•		•		
Ray Powell		•						
Gordon Prentice	•			•		•	•	•
Gwyn Prosser								•
Allan Rogers		•						
Ted Rowlands		•		•				
Martin Salter								•

	Lone parent benefits	University tuition fees	Newspaper pricing	Incapacity benefits	Legal aid reform	Pensions	Freedom of information	Privatisation of air traffic control
Phillip Sawford						•		
Brian Sedgemore	•			•		•		
Jonathan Shaw	•							
Alan Simpson	•	•		•	Teller	•	•	•
Marsha Singh						•		
Dennis Skinner	•	•		•	•	•	•	•
Llewellyn Smith	•	•		•	•	•	•	•
George Stevenson				•		•		•
Ian Stewart	•	•				•		
Roger Stott				•				
Gavin Strang								•
David Taylor								•
Desmond Turner				•				•
Joan Walley						•		
Bob Wareing	•			•				•
Betty Williams				•			•	•
David Winnick	•		•	•				•
Audrey Wise	•	•	•	•	•			
Mike Wood	•		•	•		•	•	Teller
Tony Wright							•	
Derek Wyatt		•					•	

1 Dennis Canavan was expelled from the Labour party, March 25 1999
2 Ken Livingstone was expelled from the Labour party, April 3 2000

Free votes in Parliament 1997–2001

Free votes proved extremely troublesome for the government. Equalising the age of consent and banning fox hunting might have easily got through the Commons, but the Lords was another matter. The major free votes are listed below.

Handgun ban
June 11 1997
MPs voted by 384 to 173 to extend the ban on handguns to include .22 weapons. The ban was backed by the SNP and all but six Labour MPs and opposed by the Conservatives and Liberal Democrats.

Age of consent
February 10 2000
Michael Portillo abandoned his previous opposition and joined Labour and Liberal Democrat MPs in backing the lowering of the age of consent for gay sex to 16. 263 MPs approved the change against 102.

Embryo research
December 19 2000
MPs voted to relax the rules governing the "stem cell" branch of research into human embryos. The new regulations were endorsed by 366 votes to 174.

Fox hunting
January 17 2001
MPs voted by 387 to 174 to support a ban on fox hunting in England and Wales. The alternative options were both rejected. Retaining the status quo by 399 to 155 and licensing hunting under a code of conduct by 382 to 182, suggesting only 27 MPs regard the so-called middle way as their preferred option.

Cabinet

Prime Minister
Tony Blair MP

Deputy Prime Minister and Secretary of State for the Environment, Transport and the Regions
John Prescott MP

Chancellor of the Exchequer
Gordon Brown MP

Foreign Secretary
Robin Cook MP

Lord Chancellor
Lord Irvine of Lairg

Home Secretary
Jack Straw MP

Education and Employment Secretary
David Blunkett MP

Leader of the House of Commons
Margaret Beckett MP
Ann Taylor MP (moved to Whips' Office, July 27 1998)

Chief Whip
Ann Taylor MP
Nick Brown MP (moved to Agriculture, July 27 1998)

Culture, Media and Sport Secretary
Chris Smith MP

Cabinet Office Minister
Dr Marjorie Mowlam MP
Dr Jack Cunningham MP (left the government, October 11 1999)
David Clark MP (sacked, July 27 1998)

International Development Secretary
Clare Short MP

Social Security Secretary
Alistair Darling MP
Harriet Harman MP (sacked, July 27 1998)

Agriculture Minister
Nick Brown MP
Dr Jack Cunningham MP (moved to Cabinet Office, July 27 1998)

Leader of the House of Lords
Baroness Jay of Paddington
Lord Richard (sacked, July 27 1998)

Trade and Industry Secretary
Stephen Byers MP
Peter Mandelson MP (resigned after home loan scandal, December 23 1998)
Margaret Beckett MP (moved to lead the House of Commons, July 27 1998)

Health Secretary
Alan Milburn MP
Frank Dobson MP (left the government to run for Mayor of London, October 11 1999)

Scottish Secretary
Helen Liddell MP
Dr John Reid MP (moved to Northern Ireland, January 24 2001)
Donald Dewar MP (left the government to become First Minister of Scotland, May 17 1999)

Welsh Secretary
Paul Murphy MP
Alun Michael MP (left the government to become First Secretary of Wales, July 28 1999)
Ron Davies MP (resigned after a "moment of madness" on Clapham Common, October 27 1998)

Northern Ireland Secretary
John Reid MP
Peter Mandelson MP (resigned over Hinduja
passport affair, January 24 2001)
Dr Marjorie Mowlam MP (moved to Cabinet Office,
October 11 1999)

Defence Secretary
Geoffrey Hoon MP
George Robertson MP (left the government to
become Secretary General of NATO,
October 11 1999)

Chief Secretary to the Treasury
Andrew Smith MP
Alan Milburn MP (moved to Health,
October 11 1999)
Stephen Byers MP (moved to Trade and Industry,
December 23 1998)

Transport Minister*
Lord Macdonald of Tradeston
Helen Liddell MP (moved to Trade and Industry,
July 28 1999)
Dr John Reid MP (moved to Scotland, May 17 1999)
Gavin Strang (sacked, July 27 1998)

* Non-Cabinet member invited to Cabinet since July 27 1998.

Shadow Cabinet 1997

**Conservative Party Leader and
Leader of the Opposition**
William Hague MP

Shadow Chancellor of the Exchequer
Michael Portillo MP
Francis Maude MP (moved to Foreign Affairs,
February 1 2000)
Peter Lilley MP (made Deputy Leader,
June 1 1998)

Shadow Foreign Secretary
Francis Maude MP
John Maples MP (sacked, February 1 2000)
Michael Howard MP (stood down from the front
bench, June 15 1999)

Shadow Home Secretary
Ann Widdecombe MP
Sir Norman Fowler MP (stood down from
the front bench, June 15 1999)
Sir Brian Mawhinney (stood down from
the front bench, June 1 1998)

Conservative Party Chairman
Michael Ancram MP
Lord Parkinson (stood down from the front bench,
October 6 1998)

Shadow Environment Secretary
Archie Norman MP
John Redwood MP (sacked, February 1 2000)
Gillian Shephard MP (stood down from
the front bench, June 15 1999)
Sir Norman Fowler MP (moved to Home Affairs,
June 1 1998)

**Shadow Education and Employment
Secretary**
Theresa May MP
David Willetts MP (moved to Social Security,
June 15 1999)
Stephen Dorrell MP (stood down from
the front bench, June 1 1998)

**Shadow Leader of the House of Commons
and Constitutional Affairs**
Angela Browning MP
Sir George Young MP (stood down from the
front bench to stand for Speaker, September 26
2000)
Gillian Shephard MP (moved to Environment,
June 1 1998)

Opposition Chief Whip
James Arbuthnot MP

Shadow Culture Secretary
Peter Ainsworth MP
Francis Maude MP (made Shadow Chancellor,
June 1 1998)

Shadow Cabinet Office Minister*
Andrew Lansley MP

Shadow International Development Secretary
Gary Streeter MP
Alastair Goodlad (left parliament, June 1 1998)

Shadow Social Security Secretary
David Willetts MP
Iain Duncan Smith MP (moved to Defence,
June 15 1999)

Shadow Agriculture Minister
Tim Yeo MP
Michael Jack MP (resigned to be able to increase
his earnings to pay for his children's education,
August 1 1998)
David Curry MP (resigned over the Shadow
Cabinet's decision to oppose membership of
the euro, November 1 1997)

Shadow Leader of the House of Lords
Lord Strathclyde
Viscount Cranborne (sacked after agreeing
a secret deal with Tony Blair over reform of the
House of Lords, December 2 1998)

Shadow Trade and Industry Secretary
David Heathcoat-Amory MP
Angela Browning MP (made Shadow Leader of
the House of Commons, September 26 2000)
John Redwood MP (moved to Environment,
June 15 1999)

Shadow Health Secretary
Liam Fox MP
Ann Widdecombe MP (moved to Home Affairs,
June 15 1999)
John Maples MP (moved to Defence,
June 1 1998)

Shadow Northern Ireland Secretary
Andrew Mackay MP

Shadow Defence Secretary
Iain Duncan Smith MP
John Maples MP (moved to Foreign Affairs,
June 15 1999)
Sir George Young (made Shadow Leader of
the House of Commons, June 1 1998)

Shadow Chief Secretary to the Treasury
Oliver Letwin MP
David Heathcoat-Amory MP (moved to Trade
and Industry, September 26 2000)

Shadow Transport Minister**
Bernard Jenkin MP

Conservative Party Deputy Leader***
Peter Lilley MP (sacked after making a speech
disowning Thatcherism, June 15 1999)

Constitutional Spokesman****
Liam Fox MP (move to Health, June 15 1999)
Michael Ancram MP (moved to Conservative
Central Office, June 1 1998)

* The position became a shadow cabinet one with the
appointment of Andrew Lansley, June 15 1999.
** The position became a shadow cabinet one with the
appointment of Bernard Jenkin, June 15 1999.
*** The position was abolished after Peter Lilley's departure,
June 15 1999.
**** The position was merged with that of shadow leader of
the House of Commons.

Liberal Democrat front bench

Leader
Charles Kennedy MP

Deputy Leader
Alan Beith MP

Economy
Matthew Taylor MP

Foreign Affairs
Menzies Campbell MP

Home Affairs
Simon Hughes MP

Education and Employment
Phil Willis MP

**Environment, Transport,
the Regions and Social Justice**
Don Foster MP

Transport
Michael Moore MP

Shadow Leader of the House of Commons
Paul Tyler MP

Constitution, Culture and Sport
Robert Maclennan MP

International Development
Jennifer Tonge MP

Social Security
Steven Webb MP

Agriculture, Rural Affairs and Fisheries
Colin Breed MP

Leader in the House of Lords
Lord Rodgers of Quarry Bank

Trade and Industry
Dr Vincent Cable MP

Health
Nick Harvey MP

Scotland
Ray Michie MP

Wales
Richard Livsey MP

Table 2 Guardian/ICM opinion polls, 1992–2001

	Con %	Lab %	Lib Dem %	Others %	Lab lead %
1992 general election	**43**	**35**	**18**	**4**	**-8**
May 92	45	34	17	4	11
Jun 92	45	36	16	4	9
Jul 92	45	36	15	5	9
Aug 92	41	36	17	5	5
Sep 92	39	35	19	6	4
Oct 92	38	38	19	5	0
Nov 92	36	40	19	5	4
Dec 92	36	41	18	5	5
1992 average (post election only)	**41**	**37**	**18**	**5**	**4**
Jan 93	39	37	18	6	2
Feb 93	37	39	18	5	2
Mar 93	36	41	18	5	5
Apr 93	34	39	21	5	5
May 93	32	38	24	6	6
Jun 93	31	38	26	6	7
Jul 93	32	37	25	6	5
Aug 93	30	36	27	6	6
Sep 93	29	40	26	5	11
Oct 93	36	39	20	4	3
Nov 93	34	38	24	4	4
Dec 93	31	42	23	4	11
1993 average	**33**	**39**	**23**	**5**	**6**
Jan 94	31	43	21	5	12
Feb 94	30	44	21	5	14
Mar 94	29	44	22	5	15
Apr 94	30	42	22	5	12
May 94	29	44	24	4	15
May 94	30	44	20	6	14
Jul 94	31	44	21	4	13
Aug 94	28	49	19	5	21
Sep 94	33	45	18	4	12
Oct 94	32	49	15	4	17
Nov 94	31	49	16	3	18
Dec 94	31	49	17	4	18
1994 average	**30**	**46**	**20**	**5**	**16**
Jan 95	30	48	18	4	18
Feb 95	31	49	17	4	18
Mar 95	27	52	17	4	25
Apr 95	26	51	18	5	25
May 95	29	48	19	4	19
Jun 95	24	53	19	4	29
Jul 95	32	47	17	3	15
Aug 95	31	48	17	5	17
Sep 95	31	48	17	4	17
Oct 95	29	49	17	5	20
Nov 95	30	47	19	4	17
Dec 95	31	48	16	4	17
1995 average	**29**	**49**	**18**	**4**	**20**
Jan 96	26	48	22	4	22
Feb 96	31	47	19	4	16
Mar 96	31	45	20	4	14
Apr 96	29	50	17	4	21
May 96	28	45	21	5	17
Jun 96	30	46	19	5	16
Jul 96	30	45	21	4	15
Aug 96	33	45	19	3	12

	Con %	Lab %	Lib Dem %	Others %	Lab lead %
Sep 96	32	47	16	5	15
Oct 96	31	49	16	3	18
Nov 96	34	47	15	4	13
Dec 96	31	50	15	4	19
1996 average	**31**	**47**	**18**	**4**	**16**
Jan 97	31	48	16	4	17
Feb 97	32	48	15	4	16
Mar 97	30	48	16	6	18
1997 general election	**31**	**44**	**17**	**7**	**13**
Jun 97	23	62	14	2	39
Jul 97	23	61	12	4	38
Aug 97	29	55	12	4	26
Sep 97	24	60	10	6	36
Oct 97	23	59	13	4	36
Nov 97	30	52	14	4	22
Dec 97	29	50	17	4	21
1997 average (post election only)	**26**	**57**	**13**	**4**	**31**
Jan 98	30	48	17	5	18
Feb 98	31	47	18	4	16
Mar 98	33	46	17	5	13
Apr 98	31	48	16	6	17
May 98	29	50	16	5	21
Jun 98	29	51	16	4	22
Jul 98	27	52	17	4	25
Aug 98	31	47	17	4	16
Sep 98	29	48	17	6	19
Oct 98	29	51	15	5	22
Nov 98	27	51	17	5	24
Dec 98	29	49	16	6	20
1998 average	**30**	**49**	**17**	**5**	**19**
Jan 99	30	50	15	5	20
Feb 99	28	49	16	6	21
Mar 99	29	52	16	4	23
Apr 99	28	50	17	5	22
May 99	28	51	16	6	23
Jun 99	29	46	19	7	17
Jul 99	31	48	16	5	17
Aug 99	30	48	16	6	18
Sep 99	32	45	16	8	13
Oct 99	32	45	17	6	13
Nov 99	34	44	15	7	10
Dec 99	29	48	17	6	19
1999 average	**30**	**48**	**16**	**6**	**18**
Jan 00	30	47	17	6	17
Feb 00	29	44	18	9	15
Mar 00	32	44	16	8	12
Apr 00	32	45	15	8	13
May 00	34	41	18	7	7
Jun 00	32	43	17	8	11
Jul 00	35	42	17	6	7
Aug 00	34	44	17	5	10
Sep 00	38	34	22	7	4
Oct 00	35	40	19	6	5
Nov 00	34	40	20	7	6
Dec 00	34	44	16	6	10
2000 average	**33**	**42**	**18**	**7**	**9**
Jan 01	34	44	16	6	10
Feb 01	32	47	15	7	15

Policy

Did Things Get Better?

David Walker

A Guardian/ICM poll taken in February 2001 showed that Labour in power had one remarkable achievement under its belt. It had educated the public to think it was as fiscally continent as the Tories. In February 1997 49% of those polled believed that once Labour came to power it would spend more than the Tories. Four years later that figure was 24%. Indeed, more people believed the Tories would spend more if they achieved office.

This turnaround stemmed from Labour's key promise in the run-up to the 1997 election: to stick to Tory spending plans for the first two years. Perhaps it was "existentially" necessary to sunder Labour from its past. But from it grew an enervating sense of disappointment in Labour ranks and among the public at large. Where, people asked, where the better schools and surgeries they thought Labour would build – though Labour's formal promises in 1997 promised nothing of the kind.

Besides, only a third of the public actually cast their ballots for Tony Blair in 1997, which might imply that most people had willed either the status quo or minimal change. Nonetheless the buzz had been that Labour would be better for public services and though that has eventually been proved to be true, the differences after four years are not as dramatic as expected. They couldn't be when, in aggregate, the UK state as a proportion of GDP declined. In John Major's last year the ratio of government spending to GDP was 41.2%. It will still be less than that 40.6% when Gordon Brown's extensive spending plans are realised by March 2004. The economy, of course, is growing so the physical resources available for public services will expand. Still, Labour's Third Way has not been a bonanza for public services. Blairism offered no fundamental recalibration of the importance of government in our society or economy.

Yet the first Blair government has been busy. Its large majority tramped through the lobbies passing a raft of laws. A book could be written enumerating the policy initiatives and plans, made and accomplished. (We wrote it)

An audit of the Blair term might note, first, that there are no signs of improvement on what Labour ministers themselves identified as the battleground of modern governance: productivity. On it depends the capacity of the economy to break through the limits that have kept annual growth below 3%. Labour no longer believes the state should own significant economic assets nor plan in any traditional sense. Its main job is making markets more competitive, pulling down barriers to trade and improving the quality of the factors of production.

But government can aid science and research – so improving capital – and above all it can educate and train. Labour would say that it has. The Blair cabinet can notch up improved educational attainments in the primary sector and continuing improvements at exams for 16- and 18-year-olds. The expansion of higher education has continued, unimpeded by Labour's introduction of university tuition charges and the abolition of student maintenance grants. A start has been made on reshaping vocational education. But British productivity rates remain below those in both the United States and the allegedly bloated welfare states of France and Germany.

Fearful of saying anything remotely critical about business or the British system of free enterprise, Labour ministers were never heard to speculate about one possible reason – deformations in the business culture and corporate sector. Instead the chancellor, Gordon Brown, led a chorus extolling enterprise, blaming culture for being insufficiently attuned to economic opportunity, but never addressing the structure of economic power as a possible cause of under-achievement.

But if Labour did not affect such fundamentals as productivity, it did manage to accomplish some traditional goals of socialism, including making Britain a fairer place. Changes were small in scale but noteworthy. The combined impact of Labour's changes in tax and social security increased the income of the bottom 10th of households by some 8%, over £8 a week, and it cut the income of the richest 10th by 0.5%, or £4.74 a week. Economic growth (2.6% on average since 1997) may have pulled the income distribution at large into an even more unequal shape. Labour's measures hindered rather than helped that outcome.

A ledger of achievements is hard to compile because Labour policies often contradicted each other. For example, in fulfilment of a 1997 manifesto promise, Gordon Brown cut VAT on domestic fuel to 5%: in other words, he encouraged the consumption of fossil fuels. His levy on climate change, due to be introduced in April 2001, is meant to do the opposite. It was bitterly resisted by industrialists, though it will be critical in cutting emissions of greenhouse gases in line with promises made at the Kyoto summit.

Devolution of power to the new parliament in Edinburgh and, to a lesser extent, the Cardiff assembly was not accompanied by reform at Westminster. The creation of a London mayor and assembly was not matched by a coherent reappraisal of Whitehall's relationship with elective local government in England. A "liberal" approach to matters of sexual orientation led Labour to equalise the age of consent and seek the abolition of Clause 28 (accomplished by the Scottish parliament but not at Westminster, after the conservative majority in the House of Lords mobilised).

A "progressive" approach to justice for young people was accompanied by a punitive policy for adult offenders leading to a 6,000 increase in the prison population from 1997 onwards, even though no greater number of criminals was being caught. A muscular determination to uphold human rights in the Balkans did not prevent Labour pursuing commercial opportunities in China, despite the regime's record. The reconfiguration of the UK's defence after a widely-praised review still left room for procurement decisions that had more to do with trade and constituency interest than military posture.

The social account is especially full, in principle as much as in practice. The various new deals promised that nobody was going to be left out of the labour market. The Sure Start programme was introduced for poor young children; the incomes of poor families with children were greatly augmented; and money was found for pensioners, not across the board but concentrated on the poorest.

Schools, especially primaries, have been given new focus and teachers are returning to the public's esteem and, after rises in April 2001, the pecking order of salaries.

At work Labour established the minimum wage and for the first time gave workers a formal right to belong to a trade union.

Of course all judgements must be interim. The great spending increase announced in July 2000 only comes on stream in April 2001. Tony Blair likes to point out how little Margaret Thatcher accomplished in her first term – she had barely thought of privatisation. But if Thatcherism was invented on the run, Labour has shown a dismaying unwillingness to rethink the dogmas it acquired in opposition: what else explains Gordon Brown's insistence on privatisation schemes for air traffic control and the London Underground?

The watchword of a second Labour terms seems to be "delivery". But Blairite ministers did not show much interest in the nuts and bolts of public administration, especially the role of elected local authorities in providing "national" services. Expectations have been built up, despite the comparatively modest increment in public spending to meet them.

This raises a wider question about government. The Blair government did little or nothing to counter the trend towards a lack of confidence in public officials. Early scandals increased the public's cynicism. The shady dealings of Ecclestone, Robinson, Mandelson et al, soured the atmosphere further. It quickly felt like business as usual. Indifference and suspicion spread through bus queues, wine bars and pubs and were picked up with growing alarm by Labour in its own focus groups.

John Dunn, the Cambridge political theorist, speculated that Western politics in this post-socialist, post cold war age was going to be "irritable, reactive and myopic". Is there a better way of describing public feeling during the September 2000 fuel protests? The proportion of people expressing attachment to a political party continued to fall. Voters may feel that representative institutions themselves are weakening and little that the Blair government has done, devolution included, seems likely to arrest the trend.

Perhaps the government's economic success is a contributory factor. We are losing confidence in political leaders because we no longer think we need them, in the economic realm above all. The view may rest on a mistaken short-term idea that macro economic problems have been "solved". Formerly the left wanted the state to intervene and steer the economic ship. The right resented government, but neither side denied its capacity or importance. Now in the age of the Third Way, that has been replaced by indifference.

David Walker is editor of the Guardian's analysis page and joint author of Did Things Get Better? – An Audit of Labour's Successes and Failures (Penguin £6.99).

Economy
Larry Elliott

From the stroke of midnight that marked the end of 1999 and the start of 2000, life went sour for Tony Blair. The Millennium Dome, the flu epidemic that swept through the national health service, the botched attempt to stop Ken Livingstone becoming mayor of London, the fuel crisis. Everything seemed to be going wrong for Labour. Everything, that is, except the economy.

For the first time since it first formed an administration in the 1920s, Labour was in the happy position of approaching an election with the economy set fair. Clement Attlee, Harold Wilson and Jim Callaghan had all been beset by a host of economic troubles – sterling crises, devaluation's, spending cuts, failed incomes policies – on the eve of elections. But Tony Blair had the luxury of picking a polling date safe in the knowledge that unemployment was falling, inflation was below its target and the treasury coffers were brimming with cash.

It is an article of faith for psephologists that strong economies win elections and for once Labour has managed to align the economic and political cycles. So, as the good economic news rolled in during the first few months of 2001 Labour extended its lead over the Conservatives even during the political furore that surrounded the resignation for the second time of Peter Mandelson.

In actual fact, Labour simply continued what the Conservatives had started after Britain's departure from the exchange rate mechanism in September 1992. The difference was that John Major and Kenneth Clarke got no credit for strong growth, falling unemployment and quiescent inflation: Tony Blair and Gordon Brown did.

Brown's one big macroeconomic change was to give the Bank of England control over the setting of interest rates, a bombshell dropped by the chancellor just days after the 1997 election. The overt reason for the move was Brown's desire to take the politics out of interest-rate decisions, the covert reason was to take the financial markets out of politics. Labour had been undone so many times by what Harold Wilson used to call the Gnomes of Zurich that this time the party was taking no chances. The strategy worked. Blair was the first Labour prime minister who was not faced with the problem of a plunging pound; on the contrary, sterling was rather too strong for the comfort of manufacturing.

Brown also kept fiscal policy tight, particularly in Labour's first two years, when the government actually spent less than Kenneth Clarke had envisaged in his last budget. This helped Labour's reputation for managerial competence, but by the time the spending shackles were removed the impact of the squeeze was being felt across the public sector. The chancellor had argued that the scale of his spending commitments – real increases of 6.1% for health and 5.4% for education – showed that his policy was "prudence for a purpose". His critics said that by the end of Labour's first four years in office, discretionary spending would have increased at a slightly lower rate than under Major. They added that a less rigid chancellor would have spotted earlier the political pitfall of the 75p a week increase in pensions in 2000.

However, by the end of the parliament it was clear that Labour was setting the terms of the economic debate, obliging the Conservatives to pledge that they would match Brown's increases for health and education. Michael Portillo and William Hague adopted independence for the Bank of England, the minimum wage and Brown's plans for a tax break for families with children.

The latter, the replacement for the married couples' allowance, was indicative of Brown's approach. He was an inveterate tinkerer with the tax and benefits system, bringing in a host of tax credits designed to target help on the most needy. On the upside, this "redistribution by stealth" resulted in hefty increases for those on the lowest incomes. The downside was that "targeting" benefits entailed a massive extension of means testing.

Leaving to one side the question of whether Britain should join the euro, Labour's challenges for a second term are threefold. Firstly, it has to show that its stewardship of a well-functioning economy was no flash in the pan and that it can continue to spend the vast sums needed to rebuild the public sector. Secondly, it has to extend the benefits of growth to those regions and districts where unemployment and poverty remain stubbornly high. Finally, Brown's attempts to encourage enterprise, innovation and the creation of a more-skilled workforce has so far only scratched the surface of Britain's historic failing of low investment and poor productivity.

Larry Elliott is the Guardian's economics editor.

Legislation

Finance (No 2) Act 1997
– windfall tax on utilities, pension fund changes

Bank of England Act 1998
– transfer of operational responsibilities for monetary policy to bank

Competition Act 1998
– competition commission, tightening of rules on mergers

Electronic Communications Act 2000
– allowed e-signature and other commercial uses of the internet

Financial Services and Markets Act 2000
– set up the Financial Services Authority and compensation scheme

Government Resources and Accounts Act 2000
– introduced resource budgeting, expanded remit of National Audit Office

Source: *Did Things Get Better?* (Penguin £6.99)

Quotes

"No return to short termism, no return to Tory boom and bust."
Gordon Brown, 2000

"You [Gordon Brown] have done what all Labour chancellors have done: to increase taxes and the only difference is that you're much stealthier about it."
William Hague, 2000

Table 3 Public attitude to parties' economic competence, 1992–2000
Best party on managing the economy

	Con %	Lab %	Lib Dem %	None/Don't know %
Jan 17–21 1992	41	25	8	25
Sept 16–20 1993	23	25	13	38
May 19–23 1994	25	33	12	29
July 21–24 1995	22	33	4	40
Mar 22–25 1996	24	33	6	35
Feb 21–24 1997	34	30	5	30
May 21–24 1998	19	40	4	36
Jan 20–25 2000	22	40	4	33

Source: Mori

Table 4 Economic data, 1979–2001

	GDP £m	Annual inflation %	Income tax basic rate %	Corporation tax main rate %	Taxation as % GDP	Unemployment
1979	196,211	13.4	30	52	34.3	1,063,700
1980	227,747	18	30	52	36	1,351,000
1981	251,290	11.9	30	52	38.2	2,152,400
1982	274,290	8.6	30	52	38.7	2,521,900
1983	301,809	4.6	30	50	38.3	2,761,900
1984	324,636	5	30	45	38.3	2,887,800
1985	352,870	6.1	30	40	38.1	2,997,300
1986	381,567	3.4	29	35	37.9	3,066,600
1987	417,073	4.2	27	35	37.1	2,779,600
1988	465,903	4.9	25	35	37	2,253,100
1989	509,047	7.8	25	35	36.9	1,768,000
1990	550,521	9.5	25	34	36.6	1,648,100
1991	579,071	5.9	25	33	36.3	2,267,800
1992	606,027	3.7	25	33	35.1	2,741,600
1993	635,531	1.6	25	33	34.1	2,876,600
1994	682,300	2.4	25	33	34.5	2,598,600
1995	715,028	3.5	25	33	35.6	2,289,700
1996	760,281	2.4	24	33	35.4	2,087,500
1997	813,974	3.1	23	31	35.8	1,584,500
1998	862,462	3.4	23	31	37.3	1,347,800
1999	896,988	1.5	23	30	37.5	1,248,000
2000	n/a	3	22	30	n/a	1,088,800
2001	n/a	2.7*	22	30	n/a	1,005,000*

*data applies to Jan 2001 only
Source: HM Treasury, Office of National Statistics

Table 5 Public sector net debt, 1993–2000

	£bn	% GDP
1993–94	249.4	37.4
1994–95	289.3	41
1995–96	321.3	43.1
1996–97	348.5	44
1997–98	352.9	41.9
1998–99	348.7	39.7
1999–00	340.1	36.8

Source: Office of National Statistics

Table 6 Unemployment*, 1992–99

Ranking	Country	1999 %	1998 %	1997 %	1996 %	1995 %	1994 %	1993 %	1992 %
1	Luxembourg	2.3	2.7	2.7	3	2.9	3.2	2.6	2.1
2	Switzerland	3	3.5	4.2	3.9	3.5	3.8	4	3.1
3	Norway	3.2	3.3	4.1	4.9	5	5.5	6.1	6
4	Netherlands	3.3	4.1	5.2	6.3	6.9	7.1	6.6	5.6
5	Austria	3.8	4.5	4.4	4.3	3.9	3.8	4	
6	United States	4.2	4.5	4.9	5.4	5.6	6.1	6.9	7.5
7	Portugal	4.5	5.2	6.8	7.3	7.3	7	5.7	4.3
8	Japan	4.7	4.1	3.4	3.4	3.1	2.9	2.5	2.2
9	Denmark	5.2	5.2	5.6	6.8	7.2	8.2	10.2	9.2
10	Ireland	5.7	7.6	9.9	11.7	12.3	14.4	15.6	15.4
11	**United Kingdom**	**6.1**	**6.3**	**7**	**8.2**	**8.7**	**9.6**	**10.5**	**10**
12	New Zealand	6.8	7.5	6.6	6	6.3	8.2	9.5	10.3
13	Hungary	7.1	8	8.9	10.1	10.4	11	12.1	9.9
14	Australia	7.2	8	8.5	8.5	8.5	9.7	10.9	10.8
15	Sweden	7.2	8.3	9.9	9.6	8.8	9.4	9.1	5.6
16	Canada	7.6	8.3	9.1	9.6	9.4	10.4	11.4	11.2
17	Czech Republic	8.8	6.5	4.8	3.9	4.1	4.4	4.4	
18	Germany	8.8	9.4	9.9	8.9	8.2	8.5	7.9	4.5
19	Belgium	9.1	9.5	9.4	9.7	9.9	10	8.8	7.2
20	Finland	10.2	11.4	12.6	14.5	15.2	16.7	16.4	11.6
21	France	11.2	11.8	12.3	12.4	11.7	12.3	11.7	10.4
22	Italy	11.4	11.8	11.7	11.7	11.6	11.2	10.2	8.9
23	Spain	15.9	18.8	20.8	22.2	22.9	24.1	22.7	18.4

* People of working age who are without work, available for work and taking specific steps to find it.
Source: OECD

Table 7 GDP per capita (US$ adjusted for current purchasing power parity) 1992–1999

Ranking	Country	1999	1998	1997	1996	1995	1994	1993	1992
1	Luxembourg	41,356	37,331	35,743	33,927	33,556	31,811	29,862	28,184
2	United States	33,836	32,262	30,798	29,194	27,895	26,834	25,505	24,517
3	Switzerland	28,672	27,338	26,373	25,205	25,661	24,369	23,652	23,024
4	Norway	28,133	26,147	26,705	25,460	23,306	21,944	21,389	20,393
5	Denmark	26,770	25,584	24,647	24,237	22,974	21,327	19,760	18,793
6	Canada	26,424	25,203	24,300	23,323	22,901	20,808	19,678	18,899
7	Iceland	26,338	25,279	24,168	23,446	22,250	19,632	18,836	18,447
8	Netherlands	25,923	24,678	23,158	21,875	21,249	19,583	18,552	18,181
9	Australia	25,590	24,226	23,139	22,429	21,845	19,885	18,828	17,822
10	Ireland	25,404	22,700	21,347	18,713	18,117	16,003	14,552	13,903
11	Belgium	24,845	23,804	22,878	22,270	21,838	20,666	19,749	19,160
12	Austria	24,646	23,582	22,900	22,387	21,454	20,373	19,490	18,888
13	Japan	24,628	24,102	24,474	24,001	22,644	21,238	20,689	20,136
14	Germany	23,819	22,904	22,256	21,601	21,404	20,152	18,952	18,952
15	Italy	23,065	22,160	20,988	20,937	20,119	18,856	17,865	18,298
16	Sweden	23,017	21,845	21,063	20,527	19,952	18,372	17,468	17,579
17	**United Kingdom**	**22,876**	**22,050**	**20,977**	**19,965**	**18,630**	**17,981**	**17,239**	**17,026**
18	Finland	22,723	21,780	20,464	19,422	18,856	16,703	15,977	15,200
19	France	22,067	21,209	20,410	20,294	20,197	19,133	18,636	18,903
20	New Zealand	18,629	17,785	17,701	17,296	17,051	16,005	15,043	14,038
21	Spain	18,215	17,027	16,451	15,904	15,218	14,250	13,918	13,782
22	Portugal	16,576	15,592	15,294	14,313	13,765	12,857	11,971	11,497
23	Korea	16,059	14,384	15,367	14,602	13,603	11,719	10,616	9,591
24	Greece	15,140	14,327	13,568	13,359	12,828	11,877	11,188	10,826
25	Czech Republic	13,366	12,939	13,053	13,039	12,365	11,014	10,439	9,780
26	Hungary	11,275	10,445	9,826	9,322	9,064	8,391	8,050	7,759
27	Poland	8,671	8,183	7,310	7,359	7,022	5,838	5,344	4,961
28	Mexico	8,447	7,879	7,535	7,209	6,833	6,983	6,743	6,472
29	Turkey	6,335	6,544	6,371	5,999	5,638	5,280	5,562	5,105

Source: OECD

Table 8 Government spending in real terms, 1992–2000

	1992–93	1993–94	1994–95	1995–96	1996–97	1997–98	1998–99	1999–00 estimated
	£bn	£bn	£bn	£bn	£bn	£bn	£bn	£bn
Education	36.9	37.9	39.1	39	38.3	38.4	38.4	40.1
Health	40.3	40.7	42.3	43	43.1	43.8	44.6	47.8
Transport	14.8	13.4	13.6	12.6	10.7	9.4	8.6	8.5
Housing	7.4	6.1	6	5.6	4.9	3.8	3.7	3.5
Law and order	16.6	16.9	17.3	17.3	17.2	17.4	17.4	18.7
Defence	26.6	25.8	25.3	23.7	22.6	21.6	22.6	22.4
International development	3.5	3.5	3.6	3.6	3.1	3	3.2	3.3
Culture, media and sport	3.6	3.5	3.7	3.8	3.9	4.3	4.9	5.2
Social Security	93	98.9	100.1	101.7	102.5	100.6	99.5	101
Total government expenditure	**318.3**	**324.1**	**334.5**	**333.4**	**335.5**	**333.3**	**331**	**336.8**

Source: HM Treasury

Table 9 Government spending plans, 2000–2004

	2000–01 £bn	2001–02 £bn	2002–03 £bn	2003–04 £bn
Education (including local government spending)	46	49.7	53.7	58.1
NHS	44.7	48.7	52.8	57.1
Defence	23.6	23.8	24.2	24.9
International development	2.9	3.1	3.3	3.6
Culture, media and sport	1	1.1	1.2	1.3
Social security benefits	99.1	104.9	108.6	113.5
Total government expenditure	**368.3**	**393.7**	**417.8**	**442.6**

Source: HM Treasury, Budget 2001

Health
Anthony Browne

Tony Blair warned just before the last election: "We have only 24 hours to save the national health service." So has it been saved? The only thing that can be said for certain is that it hasn't been lost: the NHS is still there, in much the shape as it was before, lurching from crisis to crisis, but with far less public confidence in either it or the medical profession.

The one concrete Labour commitment – one of the famous five pledges – was to cut waiting lists by 100,000 and this has been achieved. The pledge was then promptly abandoned, largely because it was meaningless to patients (although not NHS bureaucrats) and because it distorted clinical priorities (hospitals ploughed through the quick operations and let the complex ones languish). What matters to patients is how long they wait, not how many others are waiting, and waiting times rather than numbers are now the thrust of the government's targets. So far, Labour has had little impact on waiting times for operations, although it has made some progress in fast tracking the referral for urgent suspected cancer cases to two weeks.

Perhaps the main advance was the launch of the NHS Direct telephone service, which has proved popular with patients, and the meningitis vaccination scheme, which has sharply cut deaths from the disease.

But for most patients the experience of the NHS will be little different now than when Labour was elected. The NHS deteriorated in the first couple of years under Labour because the government stuck to Conservative spending plans, almost freezing spending on the NHS despite growing demand. That led to the winter crisis of 1999/2000, in which high levels of flu brought the NHS to an almost complete collapse. Scandals such as Alder Hey, Bristol Royal Infirmary, Harold Shipman and Rodney Ledward simultaneously helped damage confidence not just in the health service but in doctors as well.

With bitter attacks from newspapers – and endless stories about the UK's appalling cancer and heart disease survival rates – public confidence in the NHS waned rapidly, provoking the government to pledge vast sums of money, and a radical national plan to modernise it. The extra money was widely welcomed, and allowed the government to go on a recruitment spree for doctors and nurses in developing countries, but will fail to deliver the prime minister's pledge to bring spending on health up to European levels. The national plan – announced by Tony Blair himself – has been widely derided for being too timid to make much difference. Instead there have been lots of headline grabbing measures such as appointing TV foodie Lloyd Grossman to improve NHS meals.

The government sees itself in a battle to save the principle of a tax-funded free-for-everyone NHS: if it doesn't get it right, public demands for abandoning it would be irresistible. Most critics – including those on the Labour backbenches – believe that the government became serious about improving the NHS too late, and it will certainly have difficulty using its track record with the NHS as a reason to be re-elected.

If things carry on as they have for the last four years, Blair may not have saved the NHS, but merely stayed its execution.

Anthony Browne is the Observer's health editor.

Legislation

National Health Service (Private Finance) Act 1997
– empowered health trusts to enter into PFI deals

Foods Standards Act 1999
– set up Food Standards Agency with the aim of protecting public health

Health Act 1999
– abolished GP fund-holding, established primary care trusts and Commission for Health Improvement

Source: *Did Things Get Better?* (Penguin £6.99)

Quotes

"The truth is that our services are much the worst in Europe."
Lord Winston, 2000

"We set out to transform the NHS. We always said it would take time. And it will. That does not mean we have failed."
Tony Blair, 2001

Table 10 Public attitudes to the NHS, January 2001

Thinking about the NHS and from what you know or have heard, since Labour was elected in May 1997 do you think the following things have got better or worse or have they stayed the same?

Standards of treatment for patients in the NHS (%)

Better	24
Worse	20
Stayed the same	49
Don't know	7

Standards of hygiene in NHS hospitals (%)

Better	11
Worse	44
Stayed the same	30
Don't know	15

The length of time patients have to wait before receiving treatment (%)

Better	19
Worse	37
Stayed the same	35
Don't know	9

The service provided by GPs or family doctors (%)

Better	29
Worse	18
Stayed the same	49
Don't know	4

Source: Mori

Table 11 Outcomes of calls to NHS Direct, April to June 1999

England	%
April to June 1999	
Nurse advice given:	
Self-care advice	35
Advised urgent GP visit (within 24 hours)	24
Advised a routine GP visit	15
Advised a visit to accident and emergency	12
Advised patient to contract other professionals	8
Arranged for an emergency ambulance	3
Other/call aborted	2
All calls receiving nurse advice (=100%) (thousands)	165
Other calls (thousands)	37
All calls (thousands)	202

Source: Department of Health

Table 12 NHS hospital waiting lists by region,1999[1]

	Less than 6 months %	6 months but less than 12 %	12 months or longer %	Average time spent waiting (months)
North and Yorkshire	77	22	–	3.9
North West	76	20	4	4.1
Trent	74	21	5	4.3
West Midlands	79	18	3	3.8
Anglia and Oxford	74	22	5	4.3
North Thames	69	24	7	4.8
South Thames	69	25	6	4.8
South and West	76	20	4	4.1
England	74	22	4	4.3
Wales	–	11	–	–
Scotland[2]	86	12	1	2.4
Northern Ireland	63	19	18	–

1 At 31 March. People waiting for admission as either in-patient or day case.
2 Figures are at 31 March 1998.

Source: Department of Health; National Assembly for Wales; National Health Service in Scotland; Department of Health and Social Services, Northern Ireland

Education
John Carvel

Tony Blair promised before the 1997 election: "Education will be our number one priority, and we will increase the share of national income spent on education as we decrease it on the bills of economic and social failure."

His pledge was only partly delivered. Over the last two years there has been record real terms growth in spending on state schools and that upward trend is projected to continue. But this followed two years of sticking close to the static spending projections of the previous Conservative administration. The result was that the education budget over the lifetime of Mr Blair's first term of office barely matched that spent by John Major.

The resources were sufficient, however, to deliver on Labour's key pre-election pledges. Universal nursery education for all four-year-olds was provided for all parents wanting it, and some progress was made in providing extra provision for three-year-olds. Infant class sizes were cut on a faster schedule than was envisaged in 1997. Almost 500,000 children aged 5–7 were in overcrowded classes of more than 30 when Labour took office. The promise was to reduce that to zero within a five-year parliamentary term. By September 2000, the number had been reduced to 30,000 and the pledge was set to be delivered completely at the start of the new school year in September 2001.

Targets to improve standards of literacy and numeracy in primary schools were also close to delivery. The promise was to increase the proportion of 11-year-olds reaching the expected "level 4" standard in English from 57% in 1996 to 80% by 2002. Last summer 75% reached the standard and the target is now being raised to 85%. For maths the target was to raise the pass rate from 54% to 75%. Last summer 72% reached the standard and the maths target is also being raised to 85%. These improvements in performance were coupled with a trebling of investment in school buildings, rising from £683m in 1996–97 to £2.1bn in 2000–01.

Those signs of progress did not give teachers the morale boost that might have been expected, given the unpopularity of the previous Conservative administration in most parts of the profession. This was partly due to Labour ministers' determination to distance themselves from teachers' unions and show the rigour of their approach to raising classroom standards.

Leaders of the profession were appalled by an early decision to name and shame persistently failing schools. They were perplexed by Mr Blair's attachment to Chris Woodhead, chief inspector of schools in England, who continued, until early retirement last year, to batter teachers' morale by castigating their failings. He then turned to castigating the education secretary David Blunkett in the press.

Labour party traditionalists were also dissatisfied by the failure to scrap selective grammar schools. Mr Blunkett, had made it clear in opposition that he would not be "distracted" from the drive towards improved standards by wasting energy on reforming the structure of secondary education. As promised, the future of the grammar schools was left to ballots of local parents. But the rules for triggering those ballots were complex and the voting arrangements looked stacked against pro-comprehensive parents. There was only one local ballot and all the grammar schools remained intact.

The government's proposals for partial selection in specialist secondary schools and remarks by the prime minister's press secretary about "bog standard" comprehensives left doubts about the extent of Labour's opposition to selection at 11.

Selection remains a dividing issue between the parties. The Conservatives were going into the election proclaiming William Hague's plan to liberate schools from Whitehall and local authority control. His "free schools" plan would channel £4bn directly to schools, equivalent to £540 per pupil. Schools would take on extra responsibility for services such as transport and be allowed to decide their spending priorities, salary levels and admissions policies. According to Mr Hague, this would lead to the creation of new grammar schools.

The emphasis of education policy during the last parliament was on improving standards in primary schools. Whatever the result of this election, attention will shift to performance in secondary schools and universities. The challenges for the next few parliaments include action to remedy the dip in performance of pupils in the first three years of secondary school, when motivation falls and disaffection too often takes hold.

Politicians have to avoid encouraging further polarisation of schools, as parents seek out the best and shun the poor performers. Another danger is the loss of creativity in education at schools struggling to meet exam targets. The most immediate danger is the recruitment crisis. Initiatives to raise standards will flounder in classes without teachers and schools without heads.

John Carvel is the Guardian's social affairs editor.

Legislation

Education (Schools) Act 1997
– abolished assisted places

Schools Standards and Framework Act 1998
– established action zones, allowing more central intervention

Teaching and Higher Education Act 1998
– established General Teaching Council, reorganising teacher training, student fees

Learning and Skills Act 2000
– set up new Learning and Skills Council and new youth service, Connexions

Source: *Did Things Get Better?* (Penguin £6.99)

Quotes

"Read my lips. No selection by examination or interview."
David Blunkett, 1995

"Ask me my three main priorities for government, and I tell you: education, education and education."
Tony Blair, 1996

"I say it is now time that these old universities open their doors to women and to people from all backgrounds. And we are determined that in the next 10 years the majority of young people will be able to get higher education."
Gordon Brown, 2000

"David Blunkett has presided over a set of initiatives that have wasted taxpayers' money, distracted teachers from their real responsibilities and encapsulated the worst of the discredited ideology that has done so much damage since the 1960s."
Chris Woodhead, former chief inspector of schools, 2001

Table 13 Public attitudes to comprehensive education, February 2001

Do you approve or disapprove of the idea of comprehensive secondary education?

	%
Approve	72
Disapprove	18
Don't know	10

The government has said that it plans to turn half of all state secondary schools into partly selective schools specialising in areas such as technology, the arts, media or sport. Do you approve or disapprove of this plan?

	%
Approve	58
Disapprove	31
Don't know	11

Source: ICM

Table 14 Spending on education by country as % GDP, 2000

Ranking	Country	%
1	Sweden	6.8
2	Norway	6.6
3	Denmark	6.5
4	Finland	6.3
5	New Zealand	6.1
6	Austria	6
7	France	5.8
8	Poland	5.8
9	Portugal	5.8
10	Canada	5.4
11	Switzerland	5.4
12	United States	5.2
13	Iceland	5.1
14	Belgium	4.8
15	Spain	4.7
16	Italy	4.6
17	**United Kingdom**	**4.6**
18	Czech Republic	4.5
19	Germany	4.5
20	Hungary	4.5
21	Ireland	4.5
22	Mexico	4.5
23	Korea	4.4
24	Australia	4.3
25	Netherlands	4.3
26	Luxembourg	4.2
27	Japan	3.6
28	Greece	3.5

Source: OECD

Social Justice
Malcolm Dean

Tony Blair was unequivocal in opposition: "If the next Labour government has not raised the living standards of the poorest by the end of its time in office, it will have failed."

After the worst of beginnings – cuts to lone parent benefit and later a squeeze on incapacity benefit – the government has comfortably fulfilled this test. By April 2002, about 1.2m children and 800,000 adults will have been lifted out of poverty. This is the biggest improvement for poor children since the welfare state was launched in 1948. All families will have gained (by almost £850 a year) but poor families will have gained the most (about £1,500). Yet this still means twice as many children are living in poverty (which is set at below half the average income) at the end of this parliament as there were at the end of the last Labour government in 1979.

Ministers have ambitious plans. They set themselves the goal in 1999 of lifting all children out of poverty by 2019. With child poverty increasing threefold in the three decades up to 1997 – from 1.4m in 1968 to 4.4m in 1997 – the challenge is daunting. Britain has the third worst rate of child poverty in the developed world. A new 10-year goal aims to halve child poverty by 2009. A new child tax credit of up to £520 a year for households earning under £40,000, plus an integrated child credit are designed to help achieve this goal. Other support for poor families is being funnelled through the Sure Start, an imaginative scheme that extends support to parents living in deprived areas through a variety of different projects involving mentors, advisers and advice centres.

The most disadvantaged group in the first term have been people without work or children. These people – disabled, unemployed, chronically sick – have watched others being helped while their benefits have stayed linked to prices. The second poorest group are elderly people who have only a basic pension, which was reduced in value by £30 a week for single people and £48 for married couples by Margaret Thatcher's decision to end its link with earnings. Labour's minimum income guarantee grants all pensioners £90 a week by April, 2001, but it still requires pensioners to claim it. Ministers should have done more to ensure that everyone actually receives this benefit.

Labour has also failed to reform the social fund. This was set up to help poor people buy exceptional items, such as cookers, which have to be replaced. In 1988 the Tories replaced a grant-giving scheme with a service that mainly provided loans. This trend towards loans continues with 1.8m loans being given compared to 225,000 grants in 1998/99. Labour's national commission on social justice rightly described the system in 1994 as "perhaps the most soul-destroying aspect of income support" but there is still no commitment to reform.

Meanwhile the Tories have signalled their intention to make savings on social security by reducing Labour's welfare programme. Working family tax credits, which supplement workers on low income, will be abolished. Sure Start is expected to be curtailed. The Tory emphasis will be on targeted tax reductions, but these have kept changing during the past six months. An earlier promise to restore the married couples tax allowance has been altered to allow married couples with children under 11 to add a non-working parent's tax allowance to the working partner. The concession would be worth about £1,000 a year but would only help 20% of parents.

Malcolm Dean is an assistant editor of the Guardian.

Legislation

National Minimum Wage Act 1998
– established minimum payments in employment

Disability Rights Act 1999
– set up Disability Rights Commission with powers to help disabled people

Employment Relations Act 1999
– gave unions statuary right to be recognised and various new rights at work

Protection of Children Act 1999
– childcare organisations to refer names of individuals considered unsuitable to work with children to a central list

Tax Credits Act 1999
– brought in Working Families' Tax Credit

Welfare Reform and Pensions Act 1999
– stakeholder pensions, changed pension rights on divorce

Care Standards Act 2000
– created commission regulating homes and council to oversee training of social workers

Carers and Disabled Children Act 2000
– councils to support those caring for people with long-term illnesses or disability

Children (Leaving Care) Act 2000
– councils to continue support for children previously in their care

Race Relations Amendment Act 2000
– made police and other public authorities subject to race equality laws

Source: *Did Things Get Better?* (Penguin £6.99)

Quotes

"There is something rather punitive and cruel about these [lone parent benefit] cuts."
Alice Mahon, 1997

"It's [welfare reform] the big idea."
Tony Blair, 1997

"A minimum wage would push up inflation and cost over a million jobs."
Michael Portillo, 1994

"I want to tell this house that the next Conservative government will not repeal the national minimum wage."
Michael Portillo, 2000

Table 15 Public attitudes to equality, October 2000

Britain is becoming a fairer and more equal society.

	%
Agree	51
Disagree	42
Don't know	7

Source: ICM

Table 16 Adults and children in poverty, 1979–99

	ADULTS			CHILDREN		
	Total population m	Number in poverty m	Total population %	Total population m	Number in poverty m	Total population %
1979	54	5	9	13.8	1.4	10
1994–5	55.8	13.3	24	12.7	4	31
1998–9	56.6	14.3	25	12.8	4.5	35

Source: Child Poverty Action Group

Transport

Keith Harper

Labour's transport policy has failed because of its inability to recognise that the public expected it to act. The voters gave the party a huge majority to improve Britain's deficient transport infrastructure only to find that Tony Blair's main concern was to keep Middle England on side. Mondeo man is crucial to Labour winning a second term and the party does not want to fail him.

John Prescott's reign at the Department of Transport has been disappointing. As the only serious heavyweight in the cabinet with an empathy for the issue, Mr Prescott had been expected to stake his claim as being the most forward-thinking transport minister for years. But he became a victim of Gordon Brown's tight control on the public purse and Mr Blair's belief, unfounded as it turned out, that transport was not a priority.

So Mr Prescott's transport white paper was delayed until 1998 and when it did arrive, contained a mishmash of proposals largely inherited from the Tories. With a declared intention to do nothing about the roads, the government staked a considerable part of its reputation on giving the railways a much-needed boost. Ministers have rightly attacked the structure and strategy of the privatised network but after four years in government their only achievement has been to set up son of British Rail, the Strategic Rail Authority, a body which has so far been unable to produce a strategy for the industry.

During Labour's time in government, rail passenger use has grown by 30%, the largest increase since after the second world war, and a sign that road congestion is forcing people to find other methods of transportation. But this has been against the background of a legacy of neglect and poor investment, culminating in last year's Hatfield rail crash and the mayhem that followed.

Labour's much heralded plans to invest £180bn in transport over the next 10 years might be seen as a timely contribution towards improving the transport infrastructure, but the figures are misleading. Two thirds will come from the private sector, and taking railways alone, only £15bn will be squeezed out of the chancellor's pocket over the next five years. As we approach the election, the industry is already saying that it is not enough.

Labour's other great arm of reform, congestion charging, has hardly got off the ground. Local authorities have been given the powers to impose charges on their citizens so long as the money raised is spent on improving local transport, such as park and ride schemes, better buses and train services. Only London's mayor, Ken Livingstone, has shown enthusiasm for the idea, and he is facing opposition from several inner London boroughs and powerful interest groups who are seeking exemption.

Yet banning cars from city centres at peak hours is a popular plan. If Mr Livingstone proceeds with it, he will almost certainly succeed. It will be the prelude for other big cities to copy, but it will take the indefatigable mayor at least another two years before he sees positive results.

The Tories have remained quiet on transport, mainly because their hasty privatisation of rail has largely contributed to the crisis the industry faces today. When they speak they seek to attract the motorists' vote and call for speed levels to be raised on motorways, a proposal which has little support even among motoring organisations. The Liberal Democrats want Railtrack to be taken into public ownership, as do many MPs. But the government believes that the industry cannot go backwards, and has to make do with what it has got. Yet the voters are so disillusioned that a promise to re-nationalise rail could actually increase Labour's popularity at the polls.

Whichever party is returned, the days of Mr Prescott's super ministry are numbered. It has proved to be an unworkable colossus. Environment and transport need to be linked, but regional policy and housing should be separated. Rail will need a new direction. The government will have to exercise more central control since it is spending the bulk of the taxpayers' money that has been appearing in dividends paid out to Railtrack shareholders. Terminal 5 at Heathrow airport will be approved and a start will be needed on airport expansion generally, especially in the crowded southeast. Turning public transport round will take several decades. None of the political parties have yet come to terms with it.

Keith Harper is the Guardian's transport editor.

Legislation

Transport Act 2000
– set up Strategic Rail Authority, privatisation of air traffic control, congestion charges

Source: *Did Things Get Better?* (Penguin £6.99)

Quotes

"We want to improve public transport and make it more attractive so that people will use their cars less."
John Prescott, 1997

"The re-railing programme following the Hatfield crash will take a number of months and passenger delays are inevitable."
Gerald Corbett, Railtrack, 2000

Table 17 Public attitudes to transport disruption, December 2000

As you may know, there has been considerable disruption to rail services and travel by road over the last few months. Which of these, if any, do you think is most to blame for recent disruptions to transport in Britain?

	%
The Labour government	24
The previous Conservative government	33
Railtrack	45
The train companies	36
The fuel protestors	8
Global warming	6
Other	5
None of these	1
Don't know	3

And to what extent, if at all, have you personally been affected by recent disruption to transport in Britain?

	%
A great deal	7
A fair amount	16
Not very much	33
Not at all	44
Don't know	1

Source: Mori

Table 18 Petrol and diesel duties, 1992–2000

	Petrol, pence per litre	Unleaded petrol, pence per litre	Diesel, pence per litre
Mar 92	27.79	23.42	22.85
Mar 93	30.58	25.76	25.14
Nov 93	33.14	28.32	27.7
Nov 94	36.14	31.32	31.32
Dec 94	36.14	31.32	31.32
Nov 95	39.12	34.3	34.3
Nov 96	41.68	36.86	36.86
Jun 97	45.1	40.3	40.3
Mar 98	49	44	45
Mar 99	52.88	47.21	50.21
Mar 00	50.89	48.82	48.82

Source: Institute of Fiscal Studies

Environment and agriculture
Ros Taylor

"This sandbag," John Prescott told the UN climate conference at the Hague in November 2000, "means a lot to my country." He indicated an object lying next to the podium. "Two weeks ago, much of my country was under water." When people experienced storms and droughts, the transport and environment secretary added, they knew something was wrong and that climate change affected them.

It was scarcely Prescott's fault that the Hague conference ended without a deal, and amid recriminations from France's environment minister. (Dominique Voynet described him as an "inveterate macho" after he claimed that it was her intransigence that had blocked progress. For her part, she believed that Prescott's proposals gave too much leeway to the US.)

But the failure of the talks, which left him "gutted", shook faith in Prescott's ability to broker a deal on the international stage. The fact that they coincided with Britain's worst floods in 50 years was an irony that was not lost on him – even if his declaration that the floods were a "wake-up call" was widely interpreted as a demand for better flood defences rather than a cut in greenhouse gas emissions. The sandbag, it turned out, began to look more and more like a symbol of the same patch-and-fix approach to environmental catastrophe which had contributed to the floods.

Prescott's stint at the DETR began on a high note at the Kyoto climate conference in 1997, where Britain's proactive stance was widely praised. The Kyoto delegates agreed to try to cut carbon emissions by 5.2% by 2012; Britain has since pledged to cut them by 20%. The Climate Change Levy on polluting industries is in place. The Countryside and Right to Roam Act is backed up by a promise to ensure 95% of nationally important wildlife sites are in a "favourable condition" by 2010. You can even type your postcode into the Environment Agency's website and find details of which businesses are allowed to pollute the area.

Nonetheless, Labour's environmental policies have relied on the carrot rather than the stick to persuade polluters to mend their ways. The chancellor has cut duty on ultra-low sulphur fuel and bio-diesel, and the government makes much of its subsidies for household insulation and biotechnology. Businesses, too, will shortly receive 100% tax breaks if they invest in environmental technologies.

Disappointingly, it proved easier for Labour to throw a bone to one flank of the green lobby in the form of a fox-hunting ban than to tackle public transport and invest in renewable energy. That ban has been the cause of uproar in rural Britain, uproar that has dogged Nick Brown's two-and-a-half years as minister for agriculture. Brown lifted his predecessor's ban on the sale of beef on the bone, and worked to put British beef back on sale in Europe's shops. But he failed to lift the mood of smouldering anger that led country dwellers to feel that they had been forgotten by an urban, and suburban, government.

No event made this clearer that the foot and mouth outbreak of February 2001. Though it closed down much of rural Britain it left towns comparatively unaffected.

The opposition could find little wrong in the government's rapid reaction, but did its best to exploit rural Britain's sense of dismay. One immediate political impact was the postponement of the planned Countryside March, which aimed to bring the country-side to London on 18 March.

To an extent, Labour's problems with rural Britain were more about tone than policy. Farmers did not feel that the government represented them. They sensed a country changing without them. Even as foot and mouth worsened, the government reassured the nation that the disease was "under control" and that the countryside was not (as had first been suggested) "closed for business". Though many areas worst hit by the outbreak contained small, upland sheep farms, urban Britain associated the outbreak with mass agri-business. Mr Brown's extension of culling to include many healthy animals – an announcement the minister mishandled in the Commons – only served to widen the divide. While some farmers protested that they would not let the slaughterman through their gates, public concern seemed to drift towards the hard-hit (and much larger) tourist sector. Some in New Labour even wondered privately whether the loss of the politically unsympathetic farming industry was much of a problem.

It was a sorry end to Tony Blair's first term: one that ministers will have to rectify once the general election is out of the way.

Ros Taylor is editor of Guardian Unlimited education.

Legislation

Fossil Fuel Levy Act
– 'climate change' tax on energy used by companies

Countryside and Rights of Way Act 2000
– walkers' rights of way over open country

Fur Farming (Prohibition) Act 2000
– banned the keeping of animals for their fur

Source: *Did Things Get Better?* (Penguin £6.99)

Quotes

"He [Tony Blair] and his inner circle still think that the environmental agenda is against people, against science, against business and against the poor."
Charles Secret, Friends of the Earth, 2000

"It is time to reawaken the environmental challenge as part of the core of British and international politics."
Tony Blair, 2000

Table 19 Public attitudes to the environment, October 2000

The government should give a higher priority to environmental policy even if it means penalising car drivers?

	%
Agree	54
Disagree	39
Don't know	6

Source: ICM

Table 20 Emissions of carbon dioxide, 1990 and 1997

	1990	1997	% change
Luxembourg	11	9	-20
Germany	943	831	-12
United Kingdom	**568**	**530**	**-7**
France	354	359	1
Sweden	51	52	2
Italy	391	402	3
Austria	55	60	8
Belgium	105	116	10
Netherlands	153	169	11
Finland	52	59	14
Greece	71	83	17
Spain	204	243	19
Denmark	53	64	21
Ireland	30	36	22
Portugal	39	48	23

Source: Eurostat

Culture and sport

Fiachra Gibbons

If you were to judge New Labour's cultural achievements on the Millennium Dome –
and William Hague will be hoping the public does – the Blairs should be looking for
removal men.

Which would be a pity. For although the folly of allowing the world's biggest
diaphragm to be built at Greenwich was pretty well the prime minister's own, Blair
can justly plead that it wasn't all his idea. Indeed, it was that wily undercover
Welshman Michael Heseltine who dreamed up Britain's first £1bn political booby
trap – what's £1,000m between friends? – to hobble the incoming government. And
Simon Jenkins, the Tory columnist and grandee, can claim credit for persuading Blair
not to spend the money on something useful.

It has to be said, Culture Secretary Chris Smith was entirely blameless. He was one
of those who argued in private against the dome, and made strenuous, though not
entirely successful, efforts to keep it off his patch, finally managing to nudge it into
John Prescott's Ministry for Disasters.

Despite the low farce over the new Wembley, Smith has been one of the sleeper
successes of cabinet room. In the March Budget he finally persuaded the chancellor
to deliver on the promise of free admission to museums and galleries. His handling of
the protracted negotiations over the future of the BBC, the thorny issue of sport on
terrestrial TV and the Covent Garden soap opera, showed that rare mix of canniness
and far-sightedness. Those qualities are now, albeit a little late in the day, being turned
to the dire situation of the performing arts. All of which makes rumours that culture
may be swallowed up by a swollen education department all the more odd. The
lessons of Prescott's superministry clearly have not been learned.

Smith did have the good fortune to be around as all those grand lottery projects
greenlighted by the Conservatives opened their doors. History will no doubt remember John Major as the greatest patron of arts' buildings since the Borgias. The big
problem, of course, is no one could afford to do anything in them.

New Labour's major failing – much of which can be laid at the chancellor's door –
is that for more than two years Smith was not able to do much more than issue press
releases and make encouraging noises, all of which formented frustration in the arts
world.

The Tories? Well, the Tories have Peter Ainsworth. Even on the sitting duck issue
of the dome he was beaten to the punch by the mercurial Liberal Democrat MP for
Lewes, Norman Baker, who was not even his party's official spokesman. Ainsworth's
ideas for the arts are, to put it charitably, vague. Less bureaucracy and trust funds are
his big ideas, though even he doesn't seem terribly convinced.

Fiachra Gibbons is the Guardian's arts correspondent.

Legislation

National Lottery Act 1998
– created National Lottery Commission

Source: *Did Things Get Better?* (Penguin £6.99)

Quotes

"This [the Dome] is going to be a huge asset for the country as a symbol of British confidence, a monument to our creativity and a fantastic day out."
Tony Blair, 1998

"The dome. Hindsight is a wonderful thing, and if I had my time again, I would have listened to those who said governments shouldn't try to run big visitor attractions."
Tony Blair, 2000

Table 21 Public attitudes to the Millennium Dome, September 2000

What do you think the Millennium Dome has done for the reputation of Britain?

	%
Greatly enhanced it	0
Slightly enhanced It	6
Made no difference	41
Slightly damaged it	28
Greatly damaged it	23
Don't know	3

What do you think the Millennium Dome has done for the reputation of Tony Blair's government?

	%
Greatly enhanced it	0
Slightly enhanced it	2
Made no difference	24
Slightly damaged it	38
Greatly damaged it	33
Don't know	4

Source: ICM

Table 22 Chris Smith and Peter Ainsworth's cultural highlights

Chris Smith's cultural highlights since 1997

1. Ian Holm as King Lear at the Cottesloe, National Theatre
2. Peter Brook's Hamlet at Bouffe du Nord Theatre, Paris
3. The Silver Tassie at the English National Opera, Mark Anthony Turnage
4. Ian Bostridge singing Schubert songs at the Queen's Hall, Edinburgh Festival
5. NDT2 (contemporary dance) at Sadler's Wells
6. The new Walsall Art Gallery, excellence and access brilliantly combined
7. Warrior, the BBC at its very best
8. Terence Davies' film House of Mirth
9. England v Australia rugby international, Twickenham, November 2000 (with a thrilling finish)
10. Arsenal v Everton, 1998, the match that clinched the league championship for Arsenal – shortly followed by the double of the FA Cup

Peter Ainsworth's cultural highlights since 1998

1. Opening of Tate Modern, 2000
2. Treasures of Rome, Royal Academy 2001
3. Cirque du Soleil's Quidam 2001
4. Men Do Not Go To War Over Women, BAC 2000
5. England v West Indies at Lords
6. Numerous BBC Proms 1998–2000
7. Ballet Rambert, Sadlers' Wells 1998
8. Macbeth, Shakespeare 4 Kidz
9. Merchant of Venice, Young Vic 2000
10. Rape of Lucretia, British Youth Opera, Royal Festival Hall 2000

Chris Smith has been culture secretary since 1997.
Peter Ainsworth has been shadow culture secretary since 1998.

Home affairs
Alan Travis

"Tough on crime, tough on the causes of crime" was one of Labour's most successful slogans in the run-up to its landslide victory in 1997.

The slogan combined an appeal to the law and order instincts of the Daily Mail reader with the belief of the Guardian-reading classes that tackling crime means tackling problems deeply rooted in society.

But while some imaginative policies have been introduced to curb crime in the medium-to-long term, they have proved less visible than the political auction in which each party seeks to outdo the others to prove their "lock 'em up" credentials.

Police numbers rose from 110,000 to 125,000 between 1979 and 1997 and budgets almost doubled in real terms. Yet recorded crime soared over the same period.

A similar pattern has occurred under New Labour: the government's 10-year strategy for cutting crime, announced in late February 2001, included a commitment to introduce 2,660 more prison places.

It is time to realise that the most effective policies – such as cutting long-term unemployment, truancy, drug abuse, homelessness and poor parenting – are not necessarily those that produce immediate results.

In the face of rising crime figures Labour must resist the temptation to follow populist ideas and avoid imposing blanket "zero tolerance" arrest policies. It should avoid, too, increasingly punitive mandatory sentences on the alleged "criminal classes", which pay little regard to the seriousness of the crime. Labour should also quietly drop its authoritarian experiments, such as child curfews.

The next Labour government should show its determination to tackle both crime and the causes of crime by building on its current target to cut car-related offences by 30% – and announce an even more ambitious long-term objective: halving the rate of acquisitive crime from the peak it reached in 1992. This would involve a huge extension of the government's crime reduction programme, based on policies that pass one simple test: do they work?

Prison governors cannot cope with offending behaviour in overcrowded conditions. A legal limit needs to be set on the numbers in each prison with the "jail full" sign going up when it is reached. Literacy programmes need to undergo rapid expansion.

The next Labour government should give a further injection of resources into our asylum system so that the current backlog of 60,000 cases can be brought down further. The rapid processing of asylum claims is the most effective deterrent to the abusive asylum seeker. While they wait for their claims to be resolved, asylum seekers should be allowed to work. Those who are unable to work should be paid benefits and the voucher system should be scrapped.

Britain must resist European moves to redefine the Geneva Convention on asylum so that it covers only the victims of direct state persecution. It should endorse the decisions of the British courts, which say the right to asylum covers those, such as rape victims, whom the state fails to protect.

The commission for racial equality should be merged with the equal opportunities commission into a more powerful human rights commission. The incorporation of the European convention of human rights needs to acknowledge changes in the past 50 years in the rights of women, gays, and ethnic groups.

Alan Travis is the Guardian's home affairs editor.

Legislation

Firearms (Amendment) Act 1997
– banned private ownership of firearms

Crime and Disorder Act 1998
- created anti-social behaviour and new parenting orders and curfews

Criminal Justice (Terrorism and Conspiracy) Act 1998
– powers to arrest and detain people suspected of terrorism overseas

Access to Justice Act 1999
– changed legal aid, allowed 'no fee' litigation

Youth Justice and Criminal Evidence Act 1999
– allowed courts to refer young offenders for non-custodial programmes

Criminal Justice and Court Services Act 2000
– new laws on sex offenders and reform of probation service

Regulation of Investigatory Powers Act 2000
– reworked powers of security services to intercept messages sent via internet

Terrorism Act 2000
– extended terrorism measures outside Northern Ireland context, removed need for annual review of counter terrorism legislation

Source: *Did Things Get Better?* (Penguin £6.99)

Quotes

"Tough on crime, tough on the causes of crime."
Tony Blair, 1993

"It is time for zero tolerance of the yob culture."
Tony Blair, 2000

"The Tony Martin case lit a touch paper that has led to an explosion of anger among the mass of law-abiding British people who no longer feel the state is on their side. I understand that outcry and I share it."
William Hague, 2000

"The Macpherson report has been used to brand every officer and every branch of the force as racist, has contributed directly to a collapse of police morale and recruitment and has led to a crisis on our streets."
William Hague, 2000

Table 23 Public attitudes to police and race, February 2000

From what you have seen or heard, do you think most police officers are. . .?

	%
Very racist	3
Tend to be racist	18
Tend not to be racist	27
Are not racist	30
Don't know	20

Do you think police officers tend to be more or less racist than people generally, or is there no real difference?

More racist	11
Less racist	6
No real difference	73
Don't know	11

Do you agree or disagree that whatever their intentions, the way the police operate, leads to unfair discrimination against black or Asian people?

Agree	30
Disagree	49
Don't know	21

Do you agree or disagree that the police are learning from the mistakes they made during the investigation into the murder of black teenager, Stephen Lawrence?

Agree	75
Disagree	12
Don't know	13

Source: ICM

Table 24 European asylum applications per 1,000 of population, 2000

Ranking	Country	Applications	Applications per 1,000 of population
1	Belgium	48,650	4.7
2	Ireland	10,920	2.9
3	Netherlands	43,895	2.8
4	Switzerland	17,660	2.5
5	Norway	10,840	2.4
6	Austria	18,285	2.3
7	Denmark	10,075	1.9
8	Sweden	16,285	1.8
9	**United Kingdom**	**97,485**	**1.6**
10	Luxembourg	585	1.3
11	Germany	78,565	1.0
12	France	43,990	0.7
13	Finland	2,835	0.5
14	Greece	3,005	0.3
15	Spain	7,235	0.2
16	Portugal	200	0.0

Source: Home Office

Table 25 Recorded crime in England and Wales, 1979–2000

	Number of offences (000s)	Violent offences	Number of offences per 100,000 population
1979	2,536.70	129,285	5,159
1980	2,688.20	133,359	5,459
1981	2,963.80	139,912	5,971
1982	3,262.40	151,261	6,577
1983	3,247.00	153,873	6,546
1984	3,499.10	159,252	7,047
1985	3,611.90	170,604	7,258
1986	3,847.40	178,203	7,707
1987	3,892.20	198,829	7,773
1988	3,715.80	216,214	7,396
1989	3,870.70	239,858	7,681
1990	4,543.60	249,904	8,986
1991	5,276.20	265,085	10,403
1992	5,591.70	284,199	10,943
1993	5,526.30	294,231	10,777
1994	5,253.00	310,332	10,212
1995	5,100.20	310,936	9,880
1996	5,036.60	344,766	9,719
1997	4,598.30	347,064	8,841
1998–9[1]	4,481.80	331,843	8,584
1998–9[2]	5,109.10	605,801	9,785
1999–00[2]	5,301.20	703,101	10,111

1 Estimates had pre-April 1998 counting rules been in place.
2 New counting rules.

Source: Home Office

Constitution
Jonathan Freedland

When historians come to judge Labour's first term in office, they may regard constitutional reform as its most radical achievement. A government condemned for control freakery in its handling of internal party management has in fact given away more power than any administration since Clement Attlee presided over the dismantling of the British empire.

Whether by creating a parliament in Scotland, assemblies in Wales and Northern Ireland or a mayoralty in London, Labour has remade the landscape of the British constitution. This is no abstract achievement, for the way a nation governs itself affects how it is governed. By changing our constitution, we hope not only to get a neater looking system but also better railways, schools or hospitals.

A clear case of unfinished business is the House of Lords. Labour's partial reform of the second chamber, by removing all but 92 of the hereditary peers, was a welcome first step, but it has created a new set of problems. The Lords continues to hold up the government's legislative programme, except that Labour can no longer dismiss it as an entirely fraudulent body, selected by aristocratic bloodline.

It has acquired a spurious legitimacy, even though it is hardly more democratic than the blue-blooded house it replaced. The government should move swiftly in its second term to put aside the timidly conservative proposals of the Wakeham commission and opt for a fully elected second chamber.

Chosen separately from the House of Commons, these committees would be wholly independent, out of reach of government whips and unswayed by patronage from Downing Street. At last, we would have a legislature distinct from the executive, a feature of almost every advanced democracy but our own.

Labour should extend the separation of powers in another, much less discussed direction: by peeling the judiciary away from the executive. At present, judges are appointed by an unelected member of the cabinet, the lord chancellor. Instead, Labour should honour its earlier commitment to create an independent judicial appointments commission: that body could nominate judges, who would then have to be ratified by the justice committee of a reformed second chamber.

Nor can the Commons leave itself out of this process of change. So long as the executive is drawn from the majority party in the Commons, it is naive to expect the lower house to behave independently: the government, by definition, will always get its way in the end. More realistic is to seek reforms to the way the house works.

In 1997 Labour promised a referendum on a new voting system for the Commons: it should honour that promise in the next term. It should also make good on its rhetoric of modernisation by dragging Westminster's working procedures out of the Victorian age. Labour should say yes to normal daytime office hours, yes to electronic voting – and yes even to breastfeeding in the chamber.

Jonathan Freedland is the Guardian's policy editor.

Legislation

Referendum (Scotland and Wales) Act (1997)
– legal basis for referendums on establishing a Scottish Parliament with tax-varying powers and a Welsh Assembly

Government of Wales Act (1998)
– established Welsh Assembly

Greater London Authority (Referendum) Act (1998)
– provided for vote on new London arrangements

Human Rights Act (1998)
– incorporated the European Convention on Human Rights

Scotland Act (1998)
– gave Scotland an elected parliament with tax-varying powers

European Parliament Elections Act (1999)
– allowed 1999 and subsequent European parliamentary elections to be conducted on 'regional lists'

Greater London Authority Act (1999)
– established the GLA through elections for mayor and assembly

House of Lords Act (1999)
– ended automatic right of hereditary peers to sit and vote in Lords

Freedom of Information Act (2000)
– new rights of access to official documents

Local Government Act (2000)
– executive mayors and other changes in council business

Political Parties, Elections and Referendums Act (2000)
– established new elections commission to oversee contests

Representation of the People Act (2000)
– allowed voting experiments

Source: *Did Things Get Better?* (Penguin £6.99)

Quotes

"We are committed to a referendum on the voting system for the House of Commons."
Labour manifesto, 1997

"A process [devolution] that could destroy the United Kingdom itself."
William Hague, 1997

"Devolution is a process, not an event."
Ron Davies, 1999

"The biggest ever decentralisation of government, giving power back to people, in British history."
Tony Blair, 2001

Table 26 Public attitudes towards mayors and devolution, April 2000

Do you think that other large cities in Britain should have directly elected mayor, similar to the new mayor of London or should they leave local government in its present form?

	%
Have elected mayor	22
Leave elected government in present form	61
Don't know	18

From what you have seen or heard do you think the Scottish parliament and Welsh assembly have been on the whole a good idea or a bad idea?

	%
Good idea	48
Bad idea	26
Don't know	26

Source: ICM

Regional policy

Peter Hetherington

Tony Blair came to power with a token commitment to answer the English question: should eight regions have a degree of devolution to match a transfer of power to Scotland, Wales and Greater London? In reality, he hoped the question would go away. Regionalism was a policy that dare not speak its name. Bruised by policy skirmishes, selection battles and the emergence of differing priorities in Edinburgh and Cardiff, the prime minister frequently dismissed talk of a north-south divide as a dangerous over-simplification. Now it has come back to haunt him.

He will go into the election with a regional dimension of sorts. Eight regional development agencies (RDAs) have been established to bring poorly performing areas up to the national average. Their budgets will increase by £500m to £1.7bn by 2003–4. But they have yet to deliver.

Consequently Tony Blair has to answer how, in the first three years of New Labour, the north-south divide widened. According to the latest figures, the wealth of his adopted north east compared with the national average (as measured by GDP per head) has fallen from 78.4% to 77.3% in other words, 23% below the norm. London, by contrast, tops a national prosperity table at 30% above. Not for nothing did the trade and industry secretary Stephen Byers, a constituency neighbour of Tony Blair, declare late in February in a series of damage-limitation briefings that there were still "unacceptably wide gaps" between regions.

Byers knows that, whatever national opinion polls may show, traditional Labour voters in the north east and elsewhere are restless as employment growth slows down and jobs in traditional industries disappear. This might explain why a string of senior ministers, notably the chancellor Gordon Brown and most recently Tony Blair himself, have supported the case for English devolution with varying degrees of enthusiasm.

Several other issues have clearly concentrated political minds. There is a growing unease, particularly in the north east, over the Scottish parliament's diverging policies – especially in education, health, welfare and industry – and a view throughout the wider north that the growing wealth of the south east has failed to trickle down to the less favoured parts of England. Too many old Labour stalwarts are disillusioned for comfort.

In March, the prime minister told business leaders in Cardiff that Labour was prepared to devolve power to the English regions where there is the "consent of the people". A month earlier, Gordon Brown linked the debate to broader constitutional questions: "Our reforms show that we are entering an era in which national government, instead of directing, enables powerful regional and local initiatives to work. Where Britain becomes. . . a Britain of nations and regions where there are many and not just one centre of initiative and energy for our country."

The Campaign for the English Regions, an increasingly influential pressure group, saw this as a significant policy shift. Ever the minister with the keenest political antennae,

Brown knows that passions south of the border are running high, particularly in the north east – the political home of Tony Blair, Stephen Byers, Alan Milburn, and a clutch of other ministers. Its MPs are looking enviously north of the border at a rapidly diverging political culture.

In truth, Brown's message is more about creating a US-style enterprise climate through the RDAs, underpinned with tax incentives and government grants, than an old-Labour culture propping up subsidised industries. He speaks warmly of John Prescott, the one senior minister who has been pushing the case for English devolution, using the RDAs as the first building block. He has certainly come close to the deputy prime minister's call for full-blooded elected regional government as the next great constitutional challenge. But he has still hedged his bets.

Even regional sceptics in the government are coming to realise that a constitutional head of steam is building up. Intriguingly, some senior Tories have parted company with William Hague by acknowledging (in the words of David Shakespeare, the Conservative chairman of the south east regional assembly) that the "regional genie is out of the bottle".

Statutory assemblies represent the other regional building block. Comprising councillors, businessmen, trade unionists and voluntary groups, they have been created in the south and the seven other regions with full-time secretariats to monitor the work of the RDAs (some concordats have been signed) and assume some strategic planning and transport functions. At present, they have few other powers. But after the election, they could bare their teeth.

Tony Blair has all but accepted the case for a green paper setting out the options for regional government after the election. John Prescott is also pressing for legislation early in the next term to trigger off a series of referendums to test public opinion on regional government. Of course, creating full-blown assemblies after that represents a big constitutional step. But, as Gordon Brown has shown, it is no longer a pipe dream.

Peter Hetherington is the Guardian's regional affairs editor.

Legislation

Regional Development Agencies Act (1998)
– established business-led agencies in English regions

Local Government Act (1999)
– councils to operate 'best value' regimes and compulsory competitive tendering abolished

Source: *Did Things Get Better?* (Penguin £6.99)

Quotes

"Regional chambers are a start to decentralisation in the English regions. Our next step must be to deepen regional accountability."
John Prescott, 2001

Northern Ireland

Rosie Cowan

Tony Blair will go down in history as the prime minister who sealed the Good Friday agreement and handed power back to local politicians in Northern Ireland, after 30 years of murder and mayhem.

But no government can afford to grow complacent about the troubled province. The wrangling between unionists, nationalists and republicans, over police reform, the decommissioning of paramilitary weapons and the scaling down of British security is far from over. Equally, the threat from dissident terrorism both in Ulster and in mainland Britain continues.

John Major's administration laid the groundwork for the progress that followed, with the 1993 Downing Street declaration and 1995 Joint Framework document. But it was Mr Blair, with help from his ally, the United States president Bill Clinton, who finally persuaded most of the main players to sign on the dotted line in April 1998.

It was to be more than two years after the peace deal was signed, and a false start that ended in suspension, before Mr Blair was able to devolve power to the four-party coalition at Stormont in May 2000. Even now, the foundations are fragile, with first minister David Trimble's Ulster Unionist party bitterly split over whether it can remain in government with Sinn Fein while the IRA refuses to hand over its guns. Nationalists and republicans were furious at Peter Mandelson's handling of the police reform bill, which they believe watered down Chris Patten's original proposals, and negotiations are still ongoing to try and resolve the matter.

Northern Ireland may not be a vote-catcher on the UK mainland, but many people are aware of and appreciate the unprecedented time and effort Mr Blair has devoted to it. He often flies to Belfast at a moment's notice to talk through the night with all sides, and welcomes the party leaders, including Sinn Fein's Gerry Adams, to Downing Street, at regular intervals.

The political process, which several times has appeared on the brink of collapse, has been pulled back from the edge by deals forged by Mr Blair, although the price was the dwindling confidence of Ulster's majority unionist community. The IRA took the highly symbolic step of opening up several of its secret arms dumps to international inspectors but critics have dismissed this as an empty gesture, pointing out no guns have actually been handed over or destroyed.

Both Labour and Conservatives were glad to see the agreement in place but putting it into action has brought splits in the bipartisan approach of recent years. William Hague has condemned the government for forging ahead with the early release of paramilitary prisoners, even though no weapons have been permanently decommissioned, while punishment attacks and, in some cases, murder continues.

The Tories were also critical of elements of police reform, including the dropping of the Royal Ulster Constabulary's name, which deeply angered unionists, and the drastic reduction in police numbers, even though a strong dissident paramilitary threat remains. Mr Blair however sees the agreement in its entirety as the only way forward for the province and is determined to press ahead to try and make the political institutions, police and criminal justice reforms work.

Northern Ireland may not be a make-or-break issue for UK voters and its future is far from certain, but many recognise the complexity of its problems and applaud any politician willing to roll their sleeves up and get sincerely involved.

Rosie Cowan is the Guardian's Ireland correspondent.

Legislation

Northern Ireland Act (1998)
– established devolved assembly and north–south council

Police (Northern Ireland) Act (2000)
– changed name of the Royal Ulster Constabulary

Source: *Did Things Get Better?* (Penguin £6.99)

Quotes

"When I arrived, I said I felt the hand of history on our shoulders. Today [Good Friday] I hope that the burden of history can at long last be lifted from them."
Tony Blair, 1998

Europe
Andrew Osborn

At the last election Labour promised that the party would make Britain "a leader in Europe" and drag it kicking and screaming off the EU's sidelines where its voice had become feeble and fractious. Better to be in and engaged rather than a sulky member of the club who carped and complained but never came up with any positive alternative proposals was the thinking at Millbank towers.

There was only one problem – Britain was not and is not signed up to the single currency – the EU's most ambitious project since the single market. The challenge which faced the government was therefore considerable: to make Britain's voice heard and heeded around the negotiating table in Brussels while staying firmly out of the single most important EU project of the moment.

The task was not made easier by the fact that Britain's relations with its European partners have long been bedevilled by the media's often rabid Euroscepticism and the public's knee-jerk hostility to all things emanating from Brussels.

How, the argument goes, could Tony Blair claim to be "a good European" if his country continued to stick two fingers up to the EU's most visionary and community-minded project to date – economic and monetary union. But by and large – and despite this huge handicap – Labour have confounded their critics and delivered, for the most part, on pre-election promises they made in 1997.

To say that Britain after some four years of a Labour government is "a leader in Europe" would be to overstate the case. France and Germany, despite their emerging differences and a marked decline in influence, still run the show. Britain has, however, made serious headway and been adept and sometimes highly skilled at defending its national interest and shaping the EU agenda on key issues.

When it comes to the EU's nascent new defence capability for example – the Rapid Reaction Force – Britain has been in the vanguard of its development despite fierce criticism back at home.

The landmark Treaty of Nice, negotiated in December 2000, was another victory for Labour's constructive approach to Europe. The government skilfully fought its corner and managed to retain the national veto in key policy areas such as tax and social security. All of the so-called redlines – the policy areas where the UK could not afford to give ground – were staunchly defended while an equitable and satisfactory re-weighting of votes in Britain's favour was negotiated.

Tony Blair has also been successful at playing the European statesman. In a thoughtful speech in October 2000 in Warsaw he spelt out his vision of how the EU should develop and became the first European leader to say he wanted the 12 mostly eastern European countries to join the EU by 2004. Nobody else had dared suggest a date up to then and his speech went down well in European capitals.

On the euro Labour's policy is clear: the prime minister has personally promised a referendum within two years of the next parliament. Nor has Labour ever wavered from its belief that its five self-imposed economic tests must be met before it will recommend that the UK sign up to the single currency. High-minded promises to reform the EU's lamentable common agricultural policy have, however, failed to materialise and Labour has been singularly poor at presenting the public with the potential benefits of joining the euro as well as the pitfalls.

Keith Vaz, the minister for Europe, is the fourth person to hold the post in as many years and like his predecessors he has failed to inspire. But on the whole, Labour has performed on Europe and delivered most of what it promised.

In contrast, the Tories have become increasingly hostile to Britain's membership of the EU itself, let alone the single currency. They oppose a referendum on the euro in the next parliament and want to renegotiate Britain's relationship with Europe to prevent what they see as an inexorable slide "by stealth" towards a fabled European superstate.

William Hague is blunt: he effectively wants an opt-out on anything from Brussels that he doesn't like in a kind of pick n' mix EU.

The implications of such a move are grave and Tory aides freely admit that it would signal the beginning of Britain's slow withdrawal from the EU altogether. The choice at the election is therefore clear: engagement or disengagement.

Andrew Osborn is a Guardian correspondent based in Brussels.

Legislation

European Communities (Amendment) Act (1998)
– incorporated Amsterdam treaty

Source: *Did Things Get Better?* (Penguin £6.99)

Quotes

"We believe in being in Europe not run by Europe."
William Hague, 2000

"Joining the Euro is in my view a sensible thing for this country to do in practice."
Tony Blair, 2001

Table 27 Public attitudes to the euro, 1992–2000

Autumn	For	Against	Don't know
	%	%	%
1992	30	58	11
1993	27	63	10
1994	31	58	11
1995	36	54	9
1996	29	60	10
1997	29	59	12
1998	36	48	16
1999	25	59	16
2000	21	63	16

Source: Eurobarometer

Foreign affairs
Simon Tisdall

Labour's idealistic attempt to give an ethical dimension to the conduct of its foreign policy quickly ran into problems after the party took office and Robin Cook became foreign secretary.

Supporters could see scant moral justification for the continuing economic sanctions and bombing of Iraq, for example, and were disappointed by Labour's failure to crack down on Britain's arms export trade with repressive regimes.

Opponents accused Labour of hypocrisy when it refused to take a tougher line over Russian human rights abuses in Chechnya and after it invited China's president, Jiang Zemin, to make a state visit despite his government's repression of dissent.

In a key restatement of policy aims, Cook dropped the ethical tag in a definitive policy speech at Chatham House in January, 2000. In order to meet the demands of the new "internationalist century", he said, Britain would follow four guiding principles.

These were a recognition that globalisation required the building of diplomatic and trade bridges, rather than barriers; that the global interest was increasingly the national interest; that a global community should adhere to "universal values" (including human rights); and that a Britain influential in Europe would consequently wield greater influence worldwide.

Cook's bridge-building approach meant in practice a reinforcement of existing links, including the most important – that with the US. Disappointing hopes on the left that Labour in office would adopted a more distanced approach to some aspects of United States policy, Blair lost no time in cementing a close personal relationship with Bill Clinton. When George Bush took office, he and Cook tried to pull the same trick with early visits to Washington.

But Cook's policy of "critical engagement' also led to the restoration or strengthening of relations with former foes such as Libya's Colonel Gadafy, the mullahs of Iran, Argentina, and with Fidel Castro's Cuba. London, at times, appeared to be trying to pull its US ally along in its wake.

Critical engagement was also applied to relations with Russia and China, although in practice it was more engaged than critical. Blair went out of his way to cultivate Boris Yeltsin's little known successor, Vladimir Putin, despite his authoritarian tendencies and concerted efforts to challenge US global leadership (especially over the controversial proposed US National Missile Defence system that Blair had endorsed in principle).

Once the delicate 1997 handover of Hong Kong had been completed, Labour tended to emphasise the importance of trade and economic relations with China over concerns about lack of democracy.

But following the dictum that Britain would do what it could, where it could, when it could, within the limits of its diminished power, Cook and Blair did not hesitate to step into the Sierra Leone and East Timor conflicts when they thought a British presence could make a difference and would bolster the UN. Other crises – in Zimbabwe and Pakistan – seemed to be beyond their ability to resolve. And when it came to the Arab–Israeli conflict, Britain could only stand and watch as US-led mediation efforts collapsed and violence ensued.

The biggest foreign policy test for Labour came not in Africa or Asia or the Middle East, however, but in the Balkans. Although the Kosovo intervention of 1999 was deeply controversial and militarily flawed, it was at bottom ethically motivated. And in the end, it did succeed both in stopping ethnic cleansing and fatally undermining Slobodan Milosevic.

Simon Tisdall is a Guardian comment writer.

Quotes

"Our foreign policy must have an ethical dimension."
Robin Cook, 1997

"We have made a very plain promise to the Kosovar people. To walk away now would not merely destroy NATO's creditability. More importantly, it would be a breach of faith to thousands of innocent civilians whose only desire is to live in peace and took us at our word: to protect them from military suppression."
Tony Blair, 1999

"Our strength with the United States is not just an asset [for the UK], it is potentially a European one. Britain can be the bridge between the EU and the US."
Tony Blair, 2000

Table 28 Public attitudes to Kosovo war, March–May 1999

Is Britain right or wrong to have joined in the NATO bombing of Yugoslavia?

	Mar 99 %	Apr 99 %	May 99 %
Right	55	76	70
Wrong	27	16	21
Don't know	18	8	8

Source: Mori

Campaigns

Politics ×3

Jonathan Freedland

In the spring of 2001, just as pre-election fever was building, the big hit in London's West End was Life ×3, a play that imagined the same night turning out three very different ways. Jonathan Freedland imagines how election night and the years after might follow the same pattern.

Scenario 1

Election night 2001 turned out to be a very strange affair. To those who were there, the sense of deja vu was inescapable: it was a re-run of 1997. Old Tory bastions, snatched by Labour four years earlier, fell to Labour for a second time. When Stephen Twigg held onto Enfield Southgate – scene of his famous 1997 victory over Michael Portillo – the Labour faithful knew that, once again, it was their night.

The majority was not as large, but it was still a comfortable three figures. There were fewer women – no photos of "Blair's Babes" in the papers – but no one blamed the voters for that: Labour had simply failed to select as many female candidates.

Still, the party's mood had never been better. Tony Blair had broken Labour's curse: the party had won a full second term for the first time in its history. He was hailed as a hero, waving and smiling as he entered Downing Street once again for a stroll in the spring sunshine. And this time the crowds did not wave union flags, but Labour party flags.

Later that would seem like an omen. For, buoyed by a fresh mandate, the Labour government was transformed. It shook off the nervousness that had dogged it during the first term and suddenly found its voice. It swatted away its critics, merrily moving ahead with partial privatisation of air traffic control and the London Underground. The voters had vindicated them: why should they listen to their critics?

Within a year Blair – rather than his chancellor, Gordon Brown – was telling the House of Commons that the notorious "five economic tests" for British entry into the single currency had been met. He promptly called a referendum for May 2002.

What followed was the most spirited, hoarse-throated political campaign anyone in Britain could remember. Journalists from around the world came to report on "the battle for the soul of an island nation", as nightly TV debates jostled with radio phone-ins to air the arguments. In the end the support of both government and business, some slick TV broadcasts and a sense of inevitability combined to produce one of the greatest upsets in political history: the Yes side won.

The knock-on effects were huge. Tony Blair's position became so strong that Gordon Brown began to despair of ever inheriting the top job himself. Early in 2003 he stunned the country by resigning from the cabinet – to become head of the new European central bank.

All the talk of succession now switched to Jack Straw, who had replaced Robin Cook as foreign secretary the weekend after the election. Commentators were struck by Straw's new liberal tone on international issues – speaking of his "regret" at letting

Augusto Pinochet off the hook a few years earlier – and guessed he was trying to endear himself with the Labour activists who would one day choose a new leader. Meanwhile his successor as home secretary, David Blunkett, also showed a caring, sharing side to his character – a sharp change from his first days in the job when he had vowed to be "tougher than Michael Howard". As for Blair, he seemed keen to go on and on.

In the Tory party, all was disarray. Having replaced William Hague as leader after the election debacle in 2001, Michael Portillo was seen as fatally damaged for having lost the euro referendum. His party felt confused: vaguely left on social issues, right on Europe – with neither approach seeming to work. Portillo survived a second leadership contest with Ann Widdecombe and gambled that, with Europe out of the way, he could refashion his party in the "compassionate conservative" image of President Bush. Privately he believed that only that approach could win an election – not the next one, but the one after that.

Scenario 2

Election night 2001 turned out to be a very strange affair. What the polls had said would be a coronation felt like an anti-climax. As the returns came in, it was clear Labour would win – but it hardly felt like a ringing endorsement. William Hague had managed to gain enough seats to push Labour's majority below the psychologically crucial 100-mark.

The impact was immediate. Muttered talk of a challenge for the Tory leadership faded; Hague was granted a reprieve and, for the second time in his career, Michael Portillo had to pull out the multiple telephone lines he'd installed in his Westminster office. Soon afterwards, Portillo announced he was quitting politics for good. He pursued a media career instead, sitting in for Sue Lawley as an occasional presenter of BBC radio's Desert Island Discs.

But the impact was greatest on Labour. The party had lost seats in 2001 because its own supporters had stayed at home while Tory voters had been much more motivated, which meant the wide gap of the pre-election polls had narrowed on voting day.

Labour drew two conclusions. First, they would never win a referendum on the euro – not if the Tories were that energised and Labour supporters that apathetic. So, in the autumn of 2002, as the government's own two-year deadline came closer, Gordon Brown told the House of Commons his famous "five economic tests" had not been met and there would be no referendum.

Second, the party realised it had to win back its core supporters. In the autumn conference of 2001, the words "new Labour" did not appear on the stage set for the first time in years: from now on it was just Labour. Quietly Brown shelved the partial privatisation plans that had so antagonised users of the London Underground but air passengers continued to worry about the sell-off of air traffic control. With John Prescott safely on the backbenches, Brown even made moves to renationalise part of the railways.

Indeed, with the shine coming off Blairism, Brown embarked on a not-so-subtle charm offensive from the left. He appeared once more on Tribune platforms, he made his 15-minute individual chats with every Labour MP a twice-yearly affair. When the

Scottish National party, running an old style Labour programme, made huge gains in the Scottish parliament elections of 2003, Brown took that as a warning – and increased the leftward pace.

The chancellor's stealth campaign paid off. In November 2004 a haggard-looking Tony Blair – who had never quite found his rhythm in the second term – gave an interview with Richard and Judy that sounded like a resignation speech. He was gone by the afternoon – replaced by a humble Gordon Brown.

Scenario 3

Election night 2001 turned out to be a very strange affair. For the first time in TV history, viewing figures grew larger as the night went on – as audiences tuned in to see the greatest dramatic twist since Bruce Willis in The Sixth Sense.

First came Enfield and Edgbaston, then Clywd West and Ayr, then Worcester and Brighton and Hove, until finally David Dimbleby could contain himself no more: the Conservatives had pulled off a turnaround like no other. William Hague would be prime minister.

There instantly followed a rush of resignations. Peter Snow was first to go, followed by the heads of the major polling organisations, who had all got it spectacularly wrong. Next came Tony Blair, who fell on his sword for failing to lead Labour to his cherished second term. There was a rumour that the newspaper pundits and TV talking heads, who had confidently predicted a Labour landslide, would resign. But, oddly enough, not one of them did.

Hague's first move was to ask Ann Widdecombe to build a series of detention camps for asylum seekers – not near Dover or the south coast, but in Scotland (which had stayed stubbornly loyal to Labour). Next he asked Lord Dacre (formerly Paul Dacre, editor of the Daily Mail) to pilot a bill updating and expanding the reach of Section 28, banning the promotion of homosexuality in schools.

Hague, with less fanfare, continued Labour's policy of increased spending on education and health. The Daily Telegraph hailed Hague's policies as neo-Powellism: a little to the left on public services and to the right on the culture wars.

As for Labour, war of a distinctly retro kind broke out. The London mayor Ken Livingstone mounted a challenge for the party leadership, running against the entire New Labour project. He seemed set for victory until someone remembered that he was no longer a party member. Instead, junior minister Peter Hain emerged as Tony Blair's successor after he published diaries revealing that he had never believed in Blairism. As for the former prime minister, he joined up with old chum Peter Mandelson and the two went into business together – as media consultants.

Jonathan Freedland is the Guardian's policy editor.

In the blue corner
Steve Hilton

Innovation was the hallmark of the Tory election campaign in 1997, on which I worked as the party's advertising account manager. Gone were the days of back to back meetings, each quaintly assigned to a specific task: "media management", "daily planning", "week ahead". In the groundbreaking Conservative campaign of spring 1997, all this tradition was swept away in favour of the rolling 24-hour crisis meeting, to which everyone was invited and at which anything could be discussed.

On one occasion this threw up the delicious spectacle of the head of the prime minister's policy unit applying his considerable (or, "not inconsiderable", as his boss no doubt would have said) intellectual skills to the weighty question of: Conservative policy on Britain's negotiating position at the Amsterdam summit? The most appropriate organisational model for school? Welfare reform? No, the issue at stake was how best to 'unveil' a 200ft version of the Tory election poster.

Debate raged. Hyde Park? No, they'd never give us permission. The façade of Conservative Central Office in Smith Square? It was bound to go wrong. Arsenal football ground (I'm not kidding)? We'd lose the vote of every Spurs fan.

Even with the brainpower of the party's top policy wonks, we couldn't crack it. Eventually, we plumped for a truly innovative solution – Maurice Saatchi's back garden. It should be pointed out at this stage that Maurice Saatchi's back garden is about half of West Sussex, just in case you were worried about logistics. But then we encountered a further problem: how could the Prime Minister actually unveil it? It was a little trickier than popping outside Central Office for a 5 minute photo opportunity after a press conference.

Again, the answer lay in innovation. Rather than actually standing in front of the poster physically, in the old fashioned way, John Major would "unveil" the message ('Britain Is Booming, Don't Let Labour Blow It' since you ask), by flying over it in a helicopter and pointing at it, with a film crew in tow. Genius! It worked perfectly. So one day, sandwiched between dealing with the seemingly endless old saga of Neil Hamilton and the latest new saga of sleaze, the PM found himself flying over Sussex looking out of the helicopter window.

"Look", he suddenly exclaimed. "Who left that poster there? Isn't it one of ours? Call those idiots at the advertising agency and tell them to get it up on a proper billboard."

There was innovation in other areas too. No more boring old 'message of the day': let's have 10, or 20, if John Major is making an evening speech. No more laboriously crafted calculations of the specific ways in which a Labour government would affect people's lives: let's just call Labour a "bunch of wankers" and be done with it.

Amazingly enough, though, the greatest innovation of all, was to conduct the campaign in a friendly atmosphere. I was the Tory party's campaign co-ordinator in the 1992 election and I remember that extended campaign as representing three months of almost unbearable tension and hard work. In 1997, on the other hand, it was laugh-a-minute nearly all the way. This was chiefly due to three people whose irrepressible good cheer kept us all going in the face of circumstances that would have sent even Claire Rayner into a tailspin of depression.

These heroic characters were Charles Lewington, the party's communications director, Michael Trend MP, the deputy chairman of the party, and Howell James, John Major's political secretary, whose line in gallows humour would have qualified him as the French Revolution's Perrier Award winner.

Probably because there wasn't a single person in Central Office who ever believed that we could actually win the election, the mood throughout was strangely unreal.

Sure, we all went through the motions and did the odd all-nighter surrounded by pizza boxes, but we didn't work *that* hard. (Except the party chairman, Brian Mawhinney, who absorbed almost inconceivable pressure better than anyone I've ever seen). This half-jokey atmosphere was occasionally disconcerting.

On a night before a major campaign launch, instead of fine-tuning the details till two in the morning, I found myself in the pub round the corner at 9pm, discussing the itinerary of a man dressed in a chicken suit with Charles Lewington and Alex Aitken, a press officer dubbed 'chicken controller'.

Oh how we laughed in those heady days! It wasn't until the early hours of May 2 that the smiles were wiped off our faces. But I'm looking forward to the Tory party's campaign this time round. I have a feeling it is going to be even more innovative than the last one.

Steve Hilton was the Conservative party account manager at M&C Saatchi during the 1997 general election.

In the red corner

Benjamin Wegg-Prosser

About two weeks into the 1997 general election campaign, working at the heart of New Labour, it finally dawned on me: I was bored. Even though I had spent a fortnight watching the Conservatives fall to pieces as Labour's campaign swept all before it I was fed up. I decided to complain to my boss, Peter Mandelson, that there wasn't enough to do.

Perhaps I was being a selfish brat, or I wasn't doing my job properly. We all had our tasks, and by the size of the result clearly did them well. It was just that there were few moments of panic, chaos or excitement. I had been expecting dramatic last-minute decisions and a constant flow of adrenaline. There wasn't much and I was disappointed.

Successful election campaigns are won long before polling day. John Major lost the 1997 election on Black Wednesday in September 1992. After then all Labour had to do was show the voters it was credible. It did that successfully and the result was never in doubt. By the time the election was called there was not much to do other than implement plans that had been worked out months in advance.

It is a tribute to the organisation and professionalism of Labour's campaign that many bright and able people had little to do for long periods of time. If called upon we could have been busier and there were a few crucial figures who were rushed off their feet. But those on the periphery, like me, often had little to do. We used to devise games to keep ourselves occupied. Our favourite happened during Sky News coverage of the morning press conferences. Anyone who hadn't sneaked into the theatre (there was a ban on staff sitting in the auditorium) would stare at the scenes on the monitors. We'd predict which political hack would be picked by Gordon Brown to ask the next question. An outsider listening would have been amazed at the fun we had as we chirped along to the broadcast: "He'll go for Michael Brunson now" or "you're wrong, he's got to do PA," and the occasional "Oh no, he's forgotten Robin Oakley."

The other source of excitement was mealtimes. Having worked in Millbank for nearly 18 months before the campaign I'd become used to the lack of creature comforts. However, after Major fired the starting gun a canteen opened that served excellent fried breakfasts and other delicacies. More importantly a tea trolley would appear at 4pm and an undignified rush would follow to secure one of the scones or Danish pastries. Peter Mandelson would refuse the trolley then, typically, he'd try what everyone else had bought. As ever he both charmed and infuriated in equal measure.

The early evening news bulletins provided the final piece of entertainment for the day. The staff would crowd round the TVs to watch the news and see the fruits of their labour on air. As if we were in the coliseum in Rome, we would boo when a Tory appeared and cheer when a Labour spokesperson took to the airwaves. You could judge Labour's performance on any given day by the number of positive murmurings from the audience at the end of a campaign report.

In between shouting at the television and stuffing our faces there would be reports from the front. Before the election those of us in Millbank had been rather proud of our privileged positions inside the war room. As the boredom set in the shine soon wore off and we realised that the real action was taking place in the 70 key seats that Labour were targeting across Britain. Our smugness turned to jealousy when friends and colleagues would ring up from outside London asking for the line to take on various national issues. They'd often be too busy to gossip after business had been done, but when they weren't we'd be regaled with tales of Tory chaos over its European policy, Labour's massive popularity in the country and days spent briefing future cabinet ministers on matters of national importance.

By the final week of the campaign most members of staff in party HQ had fled to these target constituencies to support their colleagues who were making a real difference to the election result. I joined Peter Mandelson in Hartlepool the day before the election – everyone's work had been done in London and we wanted a bit of fun on the ground before it was all over.

Benjamin Wegg-Prosser is the publisher of the Guardian's politics and environment website.

Trouble in the nursery

David Ruffley MP

New Labour is socialism by other means. That is why a second Labour term means more of a nanny state, more interference and more of a culture of dependency. Tony Blair may attack the unions and woo middle England but this is just posturing from a political ham. It is Gordon Brown who will do the real damage in a second term.

Lucky Gordon's performance so far flatters to deceive. His Tory economic inheritance and the fact that he has never been tested in real economic adversity conceals Labour's continuing flaws.

The tax system will grow hideously more complex. The Working Family Tax Credit and the Children's Tax Credit will be now superseded by the Integrated Child Credit. As if that isn't enough, there's the ETC (Employment Tax Credit) and the PTC (Pensioner Tax Credit) to come after the election. No wonder that Tolley's, the tax bible, has nearly doubled in size.

Byzantine Brownian tax and benefits have also extended means testing. Whilst 38% of OAPs were hit by a means test in 1997, 58% will be next year. Worse, Brown has brought middle-income earners into the dependency culture and will lure them even further into means testing in a second term. He calculates that the middle classes will hardly be able to complain about distribution lower down the scale if they themselves are getting some of the action.

Saving, so central to personal responsibility, has crashed to chronically low levels. Higher taxation of personal and occupational pensions this term will be compounded in the next by the ratcheting up of the minimum income guarantee to levels that make it nonsensical for those on lower incomes to save through the new stakeholder pension. The result? More state dependency.

Productivity – the main driver of economic growth – is poor and will not improve as Brown finds more ways of taxing business, which will in turn stifle enterprise. Businesses already pay £5bn extra tax per year and it will go on rising. The hydra-headed growth of regulation, which has seen 3,000 extra regulations passed – a post-war record – will mean more death by red tape strangulation.

Ignore the prime minister's patriotic epiphanies. Labour signed integrationist treaties at Amsterdam and Nice and they will sign the Mother of all inter-governmental treaties, scheduled for the first half of the next parliament. That will mean more autonomy for the Euro-army; and qualified majority voting will be extended by stealth to some new tax areas, industry and transport policy. Most worryingly, expect Blair to go for a referendum on the euro with a Millbank-rigged, weasel-worded question designed to bamboozle the electorate.

If Labour win the election there will be a price to pay in poorer economic performance, deteriorating public services, and European appeasement. As for five more years of Lucky Gordon? Gawd help us all. The ordure will hit the fan sooner than everyone thinks.

David Ruffley is Conservative MP for Bury St Edmunds.

The weakest link

Peter Kilfoyle MP

One can never underestimate the Tories' political resilience. The party has a chameleon-like ability to reinvent itself. In those areas in which they are choosing to fight, Labour needs to challenge their arguments line by line, word by word.

For example, Tories would love an election about the euro. The Tories are increasingly hostile to all matters European. Wild allegations about giving up the pound are symptoms of a deeper malaise. They have both racist and xenophobic elements to their insular attitude to the European Union. Many within their ranks want to withdraw from Europe, regardless of its effect on national interests. Indeed, the Labour party must show that Tory recidivism in this critical area explodes their claim to be the patriotic party of the United Kingdom.

However, their xenophobic and racist elements do not stop at the European Union. Those baser political instincts resonate in the fears whipped up about asylum seekers and immigration. Once again, British traditions of tolerance and fair play are being undermined by the Tory shift to the far right. Their regressive approach is intolerable in a multi-racial society

There also remains a dogged belief that the Tories have a natural political aptitude for national defence. It merges imperceptibly into their anti-Europe obsessions. Thus, their opposition to a European Rapid Reaction Force – now accepted by President Bush – is absolute, despite the support of the recently retired armed forces chief, Sir Charles Guthrie. William Hague's presumptuous support for "Sons of Star Wars" was based on prejudice, rather than consideration of its wider impact.

Similarly, the Tories consider law and order to be their particular manor. The home secretary Jack Straw can match them in terms of harsher sentences; but the key to that famous slogan – tough on crime: tough on the causes of crime – is in the second phrase. Social policy has to ameliorate the conditions in which crime prospers. Economic policy must give every citizen a share in national prosperity. The Tories have nothing to offer in these areas.

That leaves the countryside as their last redoubt. To believe that hunting will outweigh much-needed public services in the countryside electoral balance is risible. Nor will opportunistic attacks on the handling of foot and mouth sit well with the party that gave the countryside 11 years of equivocation over BSE. Perhaps a reminder of Tory failure in the countryside – such as 18 years lost in the reform of the Common Agricultural Policy – is overdue.

In their desperation, the Tories and their media allies will throw mud at Labour. To its credit, Labour is expected to be purer than Caesar's wife. Some gullible voters will forget the Tory record, and harbour doubts. Labour must disabuse them of their concerns, and concentrate on their record of responsibility and responsiveness.

Peter Kilfoyle is Labour MP for Liverpool Walton.

The non-voting party

David McKie

Here is a conventional view of the 1997 election result. Labour, with 43% of the vote, smashed the Tories, who took barely 30%. The swing from Conservative to Labour was a mighty 10%, much the biggest since 1945. The result was a Labour landslide, giving Tony Blair a majority topping even that of Attlee. It promised to put him in power for a decade. After 18 years of Tory rule, the country had voted decisively in favour of change.

And here is a less conventional analysis. The election showed no popular urgency or excitement. Despite its titanic majority, Labour attracted the support of fewer than one in three of those entitled to vote. Its share of the total electorate, as opposed to its share of the total vote, was a mere 30.9% – less than the 32.4% John Major had taken when he won by only 21 seats five years earlier; less even than Labour's share of the electorate in 1970, when Harold Wilson lost to Edward Heath.

The conventional analysis overlooks three main points: the bias towards Labour in the electoral system, which the boundary commissioners failed to rectify before the 1997 election; the effectiveness of tactical voting against the Conservatives; and the fact that turnout fell.

In 1992, when the result was in doubt, 77.7% of those entitled to vote took their chance to do so. In 1997, when the Conservatives appeared to be finished, the figure was 71.5% – the lowest for 60 years.

Here's a still less conventional version. Pretend that the stay-at-homes constituted their own political party. It is an unreal calculation, of course, since many could never have voted. Indeed thousands of people named on the electoral register were dead. But it may at least help to offset conventional calculations based only on shares of the vote, which treat those who stay away as if they did not exist.

On this basis, then, what we might call the Non Voting party (NVP) had almost as triumphant an election as Labour. Labour increased its support among those eligible to vote by 4.3 percentage points to 30.9%. But the NVP's share of the electorate jumped by over 6 points to 28.6%. That put them an easy second to Labour – far ahead of the Tories (21.9%) and Liberal Democrats (12%). In Inner London, they even topped Labour, with 37.5% of the electorate behind them, compared to Labour's 35%.

And that cannot be simply explained by a swing from the Tories to the apathy ticket. As John Curtice and Michael Steed show in their statistical appendix to the Nuffield study of the election turnouts fell most heavily in Labour seats. "Labour's heartland's," they say "were distinctly apathetic about their party's surge to victory." All the evidence suggests that this trend has continued. Turnout in by-elections where the likely outcome is not in doubt always tend to be low – but never as consistently low as they were in the life of the 1997 Labour government. In the Leeds Central by-election, turnout reached a nadir: 19.6%.

Some of this can be put down to the first-past-the-post electoral system. There is

Table 29 The decline of the two-party system

	share of vote won by Labour & the Conservatives	share of electorate won by Labour & the Conservatives
1945	87.6	66.0
1950	89.6	77.5
1951	96.8	79.9
1955	96.1	73.7
1959	93.2	73.3
1964	87.5	67.4
1966	89.9	68.2
1970	89.5	64.4
1974 Feb	75.1	59.2
1974 Oct	75.0	54.7
1979	80.8	61.4
1983	70.0	50.8
1987	73.1	55.0
1992	76.3	59.0
1997	73.9	52.2

less incentive to get out and vote in somewhere like Barnsley, where Labour success is certain, than in somewhere like Battersea, where every vote is needed to turn the Conservatives out. But that is not the whole story. As the Labour leadership increasingly came to note, it could also reflect a politics which, with the rise of New Labour, had become more and more geared to the needs and aspirations of middle class Britain, offering less and less to those who had least. Political exclusion, to go with the much debated social exclusion.

As the table shows, the NVP has had good days before: both in 1970 and the second election of 1974, when although the result was in doubt, almost 3 in 10 eligible voters decided not to cast a ballot. But what was happening in 1997 appeared to reflect a more general change in the political culture. It might be called the rise of the shop-around vote.

Back in the 1940s and 1950s, political allegiances were stable and hard to shift. Many voted out of family tradition or an almost tribal loyalty to their party of choice, despite the persistence of rationing, a fuel crisis in February 1947 (which kept the country shivering through a cruel winter) and the devaluation of September 1949.

Labour survived, just about, in 1950. But the party won an even bigger share of the electorate in 1951, when they lost. A swing of 5% or more in a by-election in those days was an event. No government lost a seat in a by-election between 1945 and February 1957, when the Conservatives lost Lewisham North to Labour. The turbulence that began with the Liberal triumphs at Torrington (1958) and Orpington (1962) signalled the beginning of much more turbulent politics. But even so the swings at general elections were modest: discontent did not normally preface defection.

From 1945 through to 1970, elections remained largely a two-party affair, with around 90% of the vote, sometimes more, going to the Conservatives or to Labour (see table above). Then came the resurgence of the Liberals, and the rise of the nationalist parties in Scotland and Wales.

At the 1997 election, with parties opposed to Britain's involvement in Europe muscling in on the action, nearly 7% of electors voted for parties that had once been dismissed as "others". And where once to switch party loyalty had been something of a traumatic experience, now younger, more pragmatic generations contemplated it as a matter of course. Likewise the old traditions that saw voting as part of the civic responsibility to which one was educated, were collapsing. Electoral shopping-around included the option of not going shopping at all.

As the 2001 election approaches, it looks as though the Non Voting party might be set for its best result ever.

David McKie is an assistant editor of the Guardian.

Elect for change
David Hencke

The rules of politics are about to change, for the next general election will be the first to be supervised by the Electoral Commission. This matters: from now on the public will know more about what Britain's politicians spend and where they get their cash from. The new body came into existence on 16 February 2001, as a result of a tough report from the anti-sleaze watchdog, Lord Neill's Committee on Standards in Public Life. The committee had been asked by Tony Blair to recommend ways in which to implement Labour's manifesto commitment on electoral reform: banning foreign donors, declaring large donations and introducing limits on campaign spending.

From February 2001 foreign donations to parties – but not to candidates – were outlawed. All other donations above £5,000 to national parties and £1,000 to constituency parties, will have to be declared to the commission. MPs will also have to publish any donation worth £1,000 or more. British companies will also have to get shareholders' permission if they want to donate £5,000 or more to a political party. The maximum spending allowance of any political party contesting every parliamentary seat is fixed at £15m for the forthcoming campaign. In future the commission wants the figure to fall.

The first publication of political donations is scheduled for April 30 2001, when all 107 registered parties have to make returns to the commission. Just days before a possible polling day, this could have a big impact.

Different and more stringent rules apply during the election campaign itself. Once Tony Blair has announced the date, any donation received after that has to be made public within seven days. During the campaign there will also be limits on what are known as "third party" organisations, such as business groups and trade unions, which will be limited to spending £1m, around 5% of the total election allowance, on any project to back the big parties. Returns from the election will normally have to be sent to the commission within three months of polling day.

This election campaign will be a testing period for the new commission. A spring election will mean that not all of the Political Parties, Elections and Referendums Act will be in force. The ban on foreign donations applies to parties, but candidates can still receive donations from anywhere in the world until July 1. And no candidate has to declare donations above £50 until then either.

The commission will be thus enforcing a partial act and some difficult judgements will have to be made. The ban on foreign donors, for example, is not as simple as it seems. In Northern Ireland foreign donations are to be allowed for the next four years, but tough rules ensure that they cannot be transferred to the mainland.

Citizens from the European Union, the Commonwealth (including its newest member, Mozambique) and British-registered but foreign-owned trading companies can all give money to political parties. Thus Mohamed Al Fayed, an Egyptian passport holder and former large donor to the Tories, cannot give a personal donation but he can contribute through Harrods, because most of its business is in Britain. To make matters more complicated, a wealthy foreigner resident in the UK could buy a Commonwealth passport over the internet from St Kitts, Belize or Nevis for some £33,000 and then donate as much as he or she liked.

Neither will there be an immediate clampdown on British voters resident overseas. The proposal to reduce the residential qualification overseas from 20 to 15 years does not apply until the election after next.

The biggest headache for party organisers will be complying with the law to ensure that all their expenditure is declared and above board. A complex explanation of the rules is available on the Electoral Commission's website (electoral-commission.gov.uk). If the election is on May 3, for example, the main parties will also have to absorb the £75,000 spending limit for the council elections within the parliamentary campaign budget. There are also strict rules on what constitutes campaign expenditure. Free mailing and party political broadcasts are not counted against the bill, but the design costs of advertisements or food and drinks provided at a press conference are very much part of the costs.

If parties get it wrong the commission can call in the police and organisations could face prosecution under the new act. The head of the Electoral Commission, Sam Younger, currently director general of the British Red Cross, has admitted that he has a tough task ahead of him to sort out the "grey areas".

"The idea that we will have something cut and dried and perfect in place before an election is cloud cuckoo land," he has said. "There are a lot of difficult and controversial things to resolve."

He is worried about the increasingly political role of Alastair Campbell, the prime minister's press secretary, and Jonathan Powell, his chief of staff. They are paid by the taxpayer until the election is called but the commission is going to consider whether they should move to the Labour party payroll at an earlier stage.

"It's important in an era where the public is above all looking for transparency to be able to put your hand on your heart and say I'm making a reasonable effort at the distinction between what is party business and what is government business," he says. "We ought to be moving further and further towards making very clear distinctions."

He is also worried about the dominance of multi-millionaire donors such as Stuart Wheeler and Lord Hamlyn, who gave £5m and £2m respectively to the Tory and Labour parties.

Whatever the result of the election, the most interesting event in the following weeks is likely to be a candid report from Mr Younger and his fellow commissioners on what must happen next.

David Hencke is the Guardian's Westminster correspondent.

Poll vault

Nick Sparrow

The 1992 general election was universally regarded as a disaster for the polls. 1997 by contrast was hailed as a success. But closer inspection suggests that the polling companies were saved from embarrassment in 1997 only because Labour's victory was so huge that no one noticed that once again most pollsters got the result wrong.

Indeed the average error in the final polls' estimate of each party's share was, at 2%, the third worst since 1945. Most polls significantly overestimated Labour's lead.

Yet none of the companies that conduct regular polls have made any significant change to their methodologies since 1997.

Recent results make this clear. On average, over the past year Gallup has had Labour ahead by 15 points, Mori has had the party ahead by 16 points and ICM in the Guardian has recorded an average nine point Labour lead. The differences between the polling companies are more or less identical to those recorded during the 1997 election campaign.

As in 1997, polls by Gallup and Mori produce very similar results, despite the fact that Gallup and ICM conduct polls by telephone and Mori persist with face-to-face quota samples. (The differences between ICM and the others result from different question wording and the weighting procedures applied to the poll data.)

What are voters to make of all this variation? In an attempt to resolve the problem that different polls say different things it is tempting to add them all up and rely on an average result. In fact the average is rarely the true figure – election day tends to show that the true figure is closer to one extreme or the other of the polling companies' findings.

In other words Labour are likely to have been ahead of the Tories by 16% or more over the past year - the upper end of recent poll findings – or 9% or less – the bottom end.

This is a big gap. It may not be critical if Labour maintains a lead of 10% or more - the polls will be seen to have 'got it right' even if, as in 1997, they substantially over-estimate Labour's lead.

But if the lead drops into single figures each percentage point could potentially have a big impact on the seats each party can expect to win.

All this uncertainty over conventional polls means that the 2001 election will see a range of other techniques come into play. In particular, online polling over the web has attracted plenty of attention, even if results so far have been mixed.

ICM Research has already set up the BBC News Online 1000, an online panel of 1,000 people, and will use the panel to track voter attitudes to the parties and campaign issues. It will not, however, be used to estimate party support.

Such research is easily criticised simply because fewer than 50% of the population is available on-line and the demographic profile of the online population is quite different to the whole population. Yet these polls, when weighted appropriately, produce credible results.

Interactive TV polls, automated telephone polls and even WAP polls may also be attempted. The rationale for sponsors of such surveys will be to show that plausible and robust data can be collected using the new technology they hope to sell in a variety of commercial environments.

Some – including political parties – are not so interested in the horse race aspects of the campaign that tends to dominate the media. Parties in particular are keen to find messages that will turn a few thousand swing voters in the key marginal seats.

Such voters, recruited to focus groups, talk freely about the issues that matter to them and the remedies they would like to see to problems. They pore over suggested initiatives, campaign ideas, party political broadcasts and posters. The moderator of such discussions is an intermediary, allowing senior politicians to hear what ordinary voters think of them and their ideas.

This type of research allows politicians to develop a small number of key messages about themselves and against the opposition. Quantitative polls may then monitor how effectively the messages are getting across.

And as in the United States last year, expect the media to run their own focus groups in the hope of unearthing what the parties are up to.

The results may be fun. But even in the US, where daily tracking polls became a routine part of campaign life, voters had to wait until Florida had declared to find out the name of their next president. This side of the Atlantic, the race isn't looking quite so close. Even so, polls are bound to be only part of the story.

Nick Sparrow is managing director of ICM Research.

Media battle

Emily Bell

Political parties spent some £20m during the 1997 general election to shape their media message. Most of this money was wasted. Politicians and spin doctors agree about this privately but rarely acknowledge it in public. Though newspapers, billboards and political TV slots do affect the public mood over years, they rarely change things in the space of a four-week campaign.

This won't stop the parties dedicating huge resources to promoting their messages in 2001. Modern elections are effectively a month-long continuous press conference. Senior spin doctors approach the campaign from the perspective of a news editor rather than a politician. Most private campaign meetings are more about interviews, pictures and deadlines than policies. You would expect nothing else with former Fleet Street executives Alastair Campbell, Blair's press secretary and Amanda Platell, Hague's communications guru calling the shots. They are supported respectively by Lance Price and Nick Wood, both seasoned political hacks.

As a former BBC journalist, Lance Price, Labour's communication director, knows that of the different media outlets, it is TV and radio that count. Yet putting a message across on TV at election time is a fine art. Broadcasters are constrained by rules governing the amount of air time given to each party and unlike newspapers there are no influential proprietors or outspoken columnists to weight the scales. Andrew Marr, the BBC's new political editor, is a man with impeccable reformist, almost Blairite roots. This has caused him trouble with the right-wing press who have accused him of being No 10's mouthpiece. The attacks will only make him keener to emerge from the election with a reputation for even-handedness.

Elections in newspapers are much more rough and tumble. What matters surprisingly little is the overt name calling. True, an inspired political poster – such as Saatchi & Saatchi's 'Labour Isn't Working' during the 1979 election – attracts attention. And a sharp front page – the Sun's 1992 Kinnock light bulb splash 'Will the Last Person in Britain Please Turn Off the Lights' is a prime example – might make people laugh. But both worked because they captured a mood, rather than shaped it.

Did the Sun really win the election for the Tories in 1992, as it claimed? "You have to stress the significance of the press during an election," says one former tabloid editor, "but at the end of the day you are only really telling your readers what they already know – such as the suggestion that Kinnock was not really national leader material."

In fact papers follow voters. The Sun will back Labour in 2001 because the paper's owner and editor are sure that Labour will win. A Sun that came out for William Hague would look foolish when its readers stayed away from the Tories in droves.

So what will count in 2001? With the result of this election seen as a foregone conclusion, political reporters on all the national papers will be under pressure to come up with insights into Labour's plans for a second term and likelihood of a Tory leadership challenge after polling day.

The major parties will use the media to push their key messages. These will have been clarified in detailed research in the 18 months prior to the election and then brought to life by visits and announcements.

Labour's focus will constantly remind the press about the state of the economy. This is no surprise given that Gordon Brown is in overall control of Labour's campaign. He will chair the morning press conferences and bore the hacks about the strength of the economy.

It is harder to pinpoint the areas which the Tories will focus on, a reflection on the lack of clarity that has dogged their communications since the 1997 election. Only William Hague's Eurosceptic stance has won him support in the press and right-wing newspapers would be following this agenda, regardless of whether he was leader. Admittedly his strong performances in the Commons have gained him favourable column inches but in this media age few voters pay much attention to how our politicians perform in parliament.

Both parties will rely on the fact that broadcast journalists rely almost exclusively on papers when setting their agenda. Today's Guardian front page splash often becomes tomorrow's TV row.

But more than that, the parties will use Britain's regional media to their advantage. The regional front in the media battle is a hidden, but vital. Regional broadcasts are seen by the spin doctors as a malleable medium and respected by the viewers. Regional papers can be flattered by offers of interviews with political leaders and do not always ask the challenging questions put by hardened national writers in the Westminster lobby.

This shift to the regions helped Labour perform better in terms of the numbers of seats it won in the 1992 election than its share of the vote suggested it should. The strategy was developed in 1997 and secured a massive majority in Westminster – out of all proportion to the level of support in the country.

In 2001 everyone will try to play the regional game. Politicians will accuse the national media of missing the point as they pander to the regional writer who are trusted by their audiences. So, when you hear Tony Blair have a go at journalists in London, just remember how good that sounds to voters north of Watford.

Emily Bell is editor-in-chief of Guardian Unlimited.

Snapshot of an election
Martin Argles

The next general election will be the sixth I have covered as a photographer. It will mean another four weeks watching politicians roam the country posing for the right shot against schools, new tech industries and unfortunate members of the public. In this, the ultimate battle of spin, years of contrived imagery will be condensed into a month of fast-fire picture taking and photo opportunities piling up in an uncritical and meaningless mass. As a snapper on one of the leader's battle buses, I must try to sort out the real from the hype.

The people behind the party machines, smiling behind clenched teeth, need photographers at election time, but they don't need to love us. Divorce is on the cards right from the start and is confirmed the minute the ballot boxes are sealed. In this relationship the politician and the photographer are always on different sides.

It's not that they ignore what we say. "We took your advice," a spin doctor told me at last year's Labour party conference. I had mentioned that Tony Blair had avoided his trademark praying-hand gesture in his conference speech. The year before I had taken a photographic version of one of Francis Bacon's screaming pope paintings: hands together, mouth agape. It had struck a political image-maker's anxiety button as being too heavy on Christian symbolism.

Somewhere in the prime minister's psyche is an unreconstructed evangelist trying to get out, but his team want to keep it safely hidden. That means there should be no pictures of the man with his arms outstretched, embracing the flock or even worse, images that hint at the crucifixion. And no pictures either of nose picking or ear scratching. And none with young children who might puke, poke an eye or scream in terror at his approach.

Of course that sets a challenge for photographers on the election trail. We want to take the picture that politicians would rather not see. The craft of the spinner imposes daily anxieties on its practitioners. Their relationship with photographers is a complicated one where desire for the favourable image and fear of the embarrassing one are often fractions of a second away.

Their reaction, of course, is to reduce exposure to mundane levels. "Have you got what you want?" they ask during some dull walk about. Well, no, actually, I'd prefer the minister to be dancing naked in the rain, or at least using a facial expression that betrays what he is really thinking. Yet it rarely happens. Spinners need us to promote the message, not to show the anxieties and conflicts that might expose politicians as men of human failings and political uncertainty.

Never was this more clear than during John Major's premiership. His habit of pushing his glasses up his nose with one finger made him look donnish, which was considered the wrong image. Swinging a cricket bat with teenagers was better, holding up large dead fish was not quite as good. Disaster struck when he was pictured during a formal dinner, head clasped in hands as though in despair. Apparently he was trying to recall a limerick to spice up his speech, but the image was taken not long before the election, while those "bastards", the euro-rebels, were at their worst. Bad timing, bad picture.

Since the fall of Margaret Thatcher, the Tories' sense of the importance of image has trailed that of New Labour, the party with which the image makers have achieved their greatest triumph. In 1997 the post-election orchestration began the morning Tony Blair entered office. The exhausted media pack was entertained by the sight of crowds of party workers and their families outside No 10, waving union flags and cheering wildly as though they were members of the grateful electorate. Then Blair and his family walked purposefully up Downing Street, waving at the cameras and groups of civil servants in the Foreign Office across the road, to achieve the correct sense of drama in front of the famous door.

Next day a bleary-eyed, tousled Cherie answered the door of the Blair home in Islington in a nightdress and bare feet, looking like any housewife in the land who had just packed the kids off to school. Mathew Polak snapped an award-winning picture. You might think that this unspun image would have upset the spinners, but no, they were delighted. Poor Cherie paraded deshabille for the sake of a political fiction. The era of post-spin had arrived.

It went on from there. But as reality sank in and the image of the prime minister as leader of the nation and an international statesman became the preferred visual iconography, the opportunity to present anything else became ever more restricted, only occasionally enlivened by a sweaty shirt or the odd rotten tomato.

Meanwhile the other lot have a hair problem – or rather lack of hair problem. The answer, apparently, is to crop it to a stubble, which just might appeal to the youth vote and conceal William Hague's premature baldness. Hague's wife, the beautiful Ffion, wore a different dress (one memorably and inaccurately trailed to us snappers as being see-through) at each party conference and so provided some good images, but Hague himself remains stubbornly short both in stature and in the public recognition of his shadow cabinet. Ann Widdecombe and Michael Portillo are a photographer's godsend but I defy anyone to get a memorable image of Peter Ainsworth (the shadow minister for culture, media and sport).

So that is a snapshot of the world of the political photographer. A bizarre place where the worst pictures tell a thousand lies and the best might just betray a political truth. A world where image formers, with their eyes on TV news bulletins, conceal and obstruct while appearing to help and where politicians are persuaded to hide their true selves for the sake of an unconvincing political image. Personally I think they can all afford to relax.

Martin Argles is a Guardian photographer.

Online, off message

Julian Glover

In the coming general election politics on the web faces a simple test: will anything that happens on the internet alter the way people vote?

If the answer is yes, the election will be remembered as a defining moment: the shattering of television's 50-year spell on national political life. If the answer is no, internet activists will have to scale back all their talk about the web being a liberating force and admit that it is a young and still minor challenger to the massed ranks of the senior media.

Intangible, fast-changing and heavily-promoted, politics seems a juicy product for the new economy. Britain's living rooms are filling up with computers and the web has inquisitive websites to serve them – the Guardian's political site among them (guardian.co.uk/politics). MPs and candidates have all invested in a growing and intermittently impressive online presence. For all that, though, Britain doesn't yet seem ready for its first e-election. Dot.com gloom seems to have pervaded even the political world.

The parties certainly think so. As a senior Labour election strategist confided recently, he expects the internet to have no impact on the next general election – and would be happy if that were the case.

That's partly because politicians see the internet as something they can't control – and in most cases, can't even use. Every party has its site, but it's a safe bet the leader has never logged on. There are no established tactics for spinning over the net: users have too much power and politicians see it as something that runs the risk of corrupting their message.

This is all positive, of course. If politicians are scared of the net, there is a chance it can be used to shape how they behave. But there is a more dispiriting reason for their scepticism. All Britain's political parties have learnt the lessons of last year's presidential election in the United States. It was supposed to be the first internet election, with the candidates being put under pressure by ordinary web-using voters. Yet even the net failed to stop the Republicans taking Florida and in the months since the counting stopped several large US political websites have gone to the wall.

Although both candidates ran massive web operations, most people who viewed the sites already knew who they were going to vote for. Al Gore and George Bush learned the trick of using the net as a massive, free, advertising space.

But the internet is much more than that. The question is how its strengths can be best applied to politics and whether they will be in time for polling day. There are several tricks that will sort this out. The first is one that the parties keep quiet about: the internet is an excellent tool for internal communication within organisations, especially disparate ones such as political parties. The Lib Dems have long used electronic communication to send campaign messages around the country. Now all the parties do it. So even if voters don't realise it, the election is already shaped by online activity – in fact the net already matters as much as Labour's famed pagers.

A second way the net might come to bear in this election is through a basic technology: email. Perhaps half the people who vote on polling day will have email addresses. If Britain follows the pattern of the US last year, many of them will have seen jokes about politicians, or been asked to help on a campaign, or contribute money, or lobby a cause. No doubt pressure groups will mail out lists of candidates sympathetic to their case, whether cat lovers or anti-abortionists.

So wise activists in the weeks before polling day will pay attention to their email strategies, and perhaps even the way they use mobile text messages, a technology unavailable in the US. But emails are dull. For the internet to count in the way that print journalism and television already does, sensations will have to happen on the web, in full interactive Technicolor.

The likelihood is that this election will be safe, predictable and massively ignored by voters. But there is a chance that some person, event or issue might set things on a different course and the web is perfect for catching and controlling political sparks – whether about the price of petrol or the dominance of global capitalism.

It's too early to say what the issue might be. But if this election is to catch alight it will be the internet that provides the match. And after that no politician will risk overlooking it again.

Lessons from America
Martin Kettle

Does Al Gore's defeat and George W Bush's election in November 2000 hold lessons for Britain's politicians as they enter the 2001 general election? The answer is – maybe.

The British political class is obsessed with US politics, and the US presidential election is the only event that takes place beyond Britain's shores that is of any real interest to British politicians. Whether British politicians really understand the US, though, is another question. It is a large, diverse and faraway country of which the British know much less than they think they do. Part of the reason for this is that our political cycles have recently seemed to move loosely in parallel. Democrat Jimmy Carter and Labour's Jim Callaghan were overwhelmed by the politics of inflation in the 1970s. Republican Ronald Reagan and Tory Margaret Thatcher presided over the conservative revolution of the 1980s. At the start of the 1990s, George Bush Sr and John Major struggled to maintain the momentum of their iconic predecessors. In the late 1990s, Bill Clinton and Tony Blair walked the third way hand in hand.

On the face of it, therefore, the election of George W Bush in November 2000 ought to be good news for William Hague and bad news for Blair. That was certainly Hague's hope when he went to the Republican convention in Philadelphia in August 2000, just as it was Blair's fear as he and his lieutenants sat in Downing Street on the night of November 7 and saw Al Gore appear to fall just short.

Yet the 36-day battle for Florida and the circumstances of Bush's election have made comparisons and lessons more than usually hazardous. What meaningful conclusions can a British politician draw from a contest in which the winner got half a million votes less than the man he defeated? Or in which the fate of the US rested on whether a few hundred elderly Jewish women in Palm Beach had the eyesight and the strength to cast their votes in the way they intended? Or in which a chief justice who was once described as "way to the right of Pat Buchanan" had the casting vote in deciding which contender he would swear in on the steps of the Capitol building five weeks later? The answers to these questions do not say much about how to fight the election in Basildon or Bradford or Bournemouth.

Yet there is little sign that British politicians – and in particular political campaigners – take such warnings seriously. Labour, whose links with the Clinton/Gore Democrats are unusually close (though not as close as they like to pretend), has taken Gore's defeat (which in most other electoral systems would have been a victory) very much to heart. The Conservatives, whose Republican links are much looser, feel that the tide is moving rightwards again. The truth, though, is that British politicians who take a special interest in the US – a designation that unites Gordon Brown and the once influential Peter Mandelson – have drawn the lessons from the 2000 election that confirm their own prejudices and self-interests.

There are three important lessons to draw from the US election. The first is that when a party of the centre-left switches to govern in a centre-right way, it risks alienating its left-wing support while at the same time failing to hold on to its new right-wing support. Gore lost the White House because he lost the left, sufficient of whom voted for Green candidate Ralph Nader to prevent Gore from capturing states like Florida and New Hampshire. The message for Labour is that unless it is more successful than the Democrats at energising its support on the left, it will lose elections, as it did in the European elections of 1999 and the London mayoral contest 12 months later, through a combination of defections and indifference.

The second lesson is that in an imperial power in which right-wing views are unusually strong, and in which men vote to the right of women, it is hard to stop a skilful candidate who promises a big tax cut, especially when times are good and when the last president has an undeniably tacky side. That, in essence, is why Bush beat Gore. The US is much further to the right than Britain, Clinton was an embarrassment, times were good and Bush ran a better (though not necessarily more honest) campaign than Gore. The big lesson from the US is that there is no big lesson from the US.

Except perhaps for one. In 1996, voter turnout for a presidential election slumped to its lowest figure. A year later in Britain, general election turnout fell too, though to a level that the US can only dream about.

After these two experiences, the conventional wisdom – turning New Labour's campaign song on its head – was that things could only get worse. Indifference was pronounced to be the modern condition. Politics was said to be irrelevant. And yet, in November 2000, the turnout in a presidential election that was widely (and wrongly) dismissed as both boring and about nothing rose again.

Who knows, it could even happen here too.

Martin Kettle is the Guardian's Washington correspondent.

Election Day

Watch me, watch my brother
Jonathan Dimbleby

This will my second outing as ITV's anchorman for the big night. The first was exhilarating beyond belief. The 1997 election was, of course, the most dramatic in a generation, and it was by far the biggest challenge of its kind I had faced.

Determined to show that ITN could deliver an even better public service than the BBC, ITV's guiding spirits had decided to make a heavier investment in the network's election coverage than ever before. We were to have a spectacular studio constructed in the atrium at ITN's headquarters. There were to be scores of outside broadcast cameras in constituencies across the UK, a journalist at every count, a dedicated team with behind-camera expertise - all led by ITV News' editor-in-chief, Nigel Dacre. There had been months of detailed discussion, preparation, and rehearsal. And we were to be on air, without any commercial breaks for 18 hours.

Our Mori exit poll, finalised before we went on air at 10pm, was in line with other polls conducted before the campaign. Even so - despite Bob Worcester's calm and prescient reassurance - we could scarcely believe the scale of the projected landslide. Minutes before the start of the programme, I fiddled yet again with my opening script, inserting the term "seismic" and adding an obligatory health warning to the effect that opinion polls can be wrong.

Like others, I am used to mainlining on adrenalin before a big programme but, once the titles start to roll, I am usually fatalistic. If it all goes hideously wrong, we know we have done our best. If it is my fault, I'll be out of a job. On the other hand, I comfort myself, I would get more time for the family and the farm. Even so, as the second hand approached the witching hour, I was not exactly heedless of the challenge with which I had been entrusted. I felt my pulse: mercifully it was even and slow.

And then we were away. It was a roller coaster night. First the speculation with the genial and expert Mike Brunson alongside me, then came the first result, the early marginals, the emerging certainty that our exit poll was going to be almost bang on target. Our performance was unscripted ad-libbery, trying to find words other than "seismic" to convey the fact that Labour was cutting a swathe through the Tory jungle and felling all manner of big beasts. We noted the rictus smiles of cabinet ministers destined for the wilderness and the heroic attempts by Labour bigwigs to display the modesty and decorum expected of wannabee statesmen. Scores of results came at an accelerating pace, scores of interviews, debate, analysis, speculation, gossip, jokes, and then the carefully-orchestrated spontaneity of the dawn jamboree on the South Bank.

At 6.30am, I took to a camp bed in my dressing room, eyes shut but wide awake. Ninety minutes later, I changed my contact lenses, had a shave and then we were off again. We covered the scenes outside Tony Blair's house, his motorcade from Islington to Buckingham Palace and all the rest, until we finally came off air at 4.30pm on Friday afternoon.

It had been a marathon but I was far too elated to notice. I went off to present my Any Questions programme for BBC Radio 4 and finally, at around midnight, I met my brother for a celebration. Not of the result itself you understand – we remain impartial in such matters – but of "our" election. We also drank a health to my mother. She had hired an extra television set and was thus able to claim to each of us that she had watched the entire drama from gavel to gavel with equal loyalty to both channels. I have no doubt she will be just as loyal this time round.

As for the rest of the nation? Well, it has to be ITV, doesn't it?

Jonathan Dimbleby will present ITV's election night coverage.

A duty to party
Paul Macinnes

Politics and parties don't go together. Staggering around accidentally breaking things while on the hunt for a bag of crisps is alien to the political classes, more interested as they are in policy, public service and acts of auto-eroticism. Even the term "political party" is an oxymoron that buffs its cufflinks in the face of debauchery. But for some strange reason, this rule of thumb does not apply on election night. No, on election night – for one night only – it all hangs out.

Unfortunately the only real hanging out to be seen after the 1987 and 1992 elections, were assorted hoorays dangling from the windows of Conservative central office. With Neil Kinnock getting his celebrations in beforehand, the arrival of another five years of Tory rule was commemorated solely by standing around in the cold waving plastic union flags (made in Taiwan), eating beef sandwiches provided by an officious woman from down the road, or contentedly patting one's wallet.

Indeed, the opportunity to have a half-decent election night party may have contributed towards the Tories' defeat in 1997. The country broke out into a sweat of festivity on the night of May 1. There was a party going on everywhere. Even those people who never stayed up beyond Newsnight were carousing until dawn. Citizens, it seemed, were making a choice not just between the past and the future, but between a nice glass of sherry and a six pack of continental lager. In my case, being a forward-thinking liberal, the lager won.

It must be said that without booze, the night would not have been what it was. The cries that accompanied the demise of Michael Portillo, cheers that seemed to echo from household to household, would not have been as loud. The protracted attempts by the family Follett to open a bottle of champagne would not have seemed so surreal. And without booze would anybody have made it through the night long enough to witness Mandelson and Kinnock trying to cut a rug to "Things Can Only Get Better?"

So, if you want to have a proper party, the drink comes first. But television does come a close second. Information is vital on election night, and to make sure you catch the result from Bristol West as soon as it happens, the television cannot be turned up loud enough. Having two sets on at the same time is also advisable. Not only does it increase the sense of being at the epicentre of events but, by comparing the coverage on BBC and ITV, you can remember what you pay your licence fee for. You can log onto the internet as well – www.guardian.co.uk/politics, of course.

The final ingredient is stupid games and preferably games stupid enough to last through the night. A sweepstake on the final result is one, although quite disheartening for the person who draws a Tory majority; a game of soundbite bingo another ("He said '????'! Full house!"). Another trick is to build a sparse wig from cotton wool and attach it to an unsuspecting reveller. From then on that person is Peter Snow, and must be prepared to offer spurious predictions whenever summoned – just a bit of fun…

You could even build your own swing-o-meter – the games need never end. So on election night, please remember to have the loudest party you can. It's your democratic duty.

Paul Macinnes is editor of the Guardian's football website.

A vote for the wise

Alan Travis

The scale of Tony Blair's landslide victory in 1997, when a record 409 Labour MPs were elected, owed as much to the rise of tactical voting as to the increase in the party's national share of the vote. But will tactical voting have as big an impact on polling day in 2001? Conventional wisdom says that there will be less of it this time – but nobody can yet estimate how much less.

In 1997 tactical voting certainly mattered. More people than ever before – about 10% of voters compared with 9% in the previous election – were so alarmed at the prospect of a Conservative government that they were prepared to put aside their own political preferences and support whichever opposition party was best able to defeat the local Tory.

Research[1] into the outcome of the election found that if each party's share of the vote since 1992 had been uniform across the country, Labour would have ended up with a majority of 131 MPs rather than the 179 that Mr Blair has enjoyed for the past four years.

It was this small 1% rise in tactical voting that was to prove decisive. The number of voters involved was out of all proportion to its impact on key marginal seats. Academics have estimated that the Tories lost at least 25 seats as a result of tactical voting and the Liberal Democrats more than doubled the number of their MPs, to 46.

But what about 2001? The first factor is, of course, that there is no longer a deeply unpopular Conservative government to be removed. Labour and Liberal Democrat supporters may still be prepared to vote for a second-choice party to prevent the return of the Conservatives but tactical voting is unlikely to be as potent a factor as it was in 1997.

One interesting finding from a recent Guardian/ICM poll about voting intentions showed that although turnout is likely to be at a record low in Labour's heartland seats, where there are large majorities, it seems as though it might hold up in the key marginal seats the party needs to win. This is known as "differential turnout". The poll may indicate that in the top 150 marginal battleground seats voters are acutely aware that in the first-past-the-post system their votes can have a much greater impact than those cast for a party loyalist who lives in a safe seat.

Some people claim that constituency opinion polls can have a profound effect. In 1997 an Observer/ICM survey was credited with contributing to the shock exit of Michael Portillo in Enfield Southgate because it revealed that the Labour candidate was the clear challenger for second place and this increased the level of tactical voting. But there were actually few such polls in 1997.

It was argued at the time that if a similar poll had been held in Michael Howard's Folkestone and Hythe constituency the former home secretary would also have lost his seat. In fact there are about half a dozen other Tories who hold their seats on only 35% to 39% share of the vote, with the Labour and Liberal Democrat vote split on 25% each.

Some Labour optimists hope that tactical voters in these constituencies will have long memories and with "one more heave" will throw out some more famous Tory names. A lack of a clear second place challenger in most of these seats will prevent that happening.

This time though, watch out for a revival of a strange beast not seen in any great number since the 1970s: the anti-Labour tactical voter. Few predict its return on any great scale – the vast bulk of Conservative voters have little history of voting for other parties and there are few Labour/Liberal Democrat marginal seats where it would make a difference. The most marginal is Conwy, which Labour currently holds with a majority of 1,596 or 3.84%.

But it is possible that anti-Labour tactical voting could see some Labour MPs being ousted by second-place Conservatives as disillusioned Liberal Democrat voters switch.

One major factor might limit this backlash against the Labour government. Essentially New Labour and the Liberal Democrats are occupying the same ground now as they did in 1997. Lib Dems may not give their votes as enthusiastically as they did last time but they are even less likely to vote Conservative and risk the return of a Tory government.

1 CREST paper 64: New Labour, New Tactical Voting? Geoffrey Evans, John Curtice and Pippa Norris.

Alan Travis is the Guardian's home affairs editor.

Who counts the votes?

Thomas Happold

Therese LePore lived a life of blameless obscurity until last year's presidential vote, when as elections supervisor of Palm Beach county in Florida she found herself at the centre of the biggest elections scandal for over a century. Palm Beach's dimpled chads put her on the world's front pages, George W Bush in the White House and the mechanics of elections under the microscope.

None of Britain's returning officers have yet achieved such notoriety. After a brief moment in the limelight they return to the shadows. Do you remember who announced Stephen Twigg's victory over Michael Portillo's in Enfield Southgate? It was Gordon Smith, if, like most of Britain, you've forgotten.

Britain's manual counts offer fewer opportunities for disaster than America's scanning machines but cock-ups do happen. Former Tory health minister Gerry Malone successfully challenged the result in Winchester in 1997, after losing by two votes. The high court ruled that the election had to be rerun, because 55 unstamped ballot papers hadn't been counted. Despite his court triumph, Malone lost again.

On election night, though the returning officer is nominally in-charge, most of the work is done by an even more obscure local government official, the electoral services officer. This figure books the polling stations, employs staff and deals with the candidates' electoral agents.

A typical polling station is staffed by a presiding officer and two poll clerks. They tick people off the electoral register, stamp their ballot papers and, after the polls have closed, record the number of ballot papers issued and take the ballot box to the count.

A typical count has over 60 tellers. Each ballot box must be verified – its contents counted and the total checked against the presiding officer's record of issued ballot papers. Then the ballot papers are separated into piles of votes for each candidate. These are then divided into bundles of 20, which are placed in the candidate's tray at the centre of the hall. Each candidate has their own tray, which is divided into a number of compartments and runs alongside those of the other candidates. Each compartment is filled with five bundles of 20, allowing each candidate to see how many votes they've received.

Candidates can witness the count, as can their counting agents. These political figures are strictly prohibited from touching the ballot papers, although they can ask for any bundle to be recounted. All spoiled or doubtful ballot papers must be shown to the candidates.

When all the ballot papers have been counted, the returning officer informs the candidates of the result. A candidate can request a recount, but the decision is up to the returning officer – he can refuse a request if he believes it to be unreasonable.

Then it is time for the announcement – the returning officer's brief moment in the limelight, when the victor strives to appear humbled, the defeated magnanimous. Back in the count the ballot papers are bagged up and sent, with the election return, to the clerk of the Crown at the lord chancellor's department. They are then kept for a year and then destroyed.

Table 30 This table offers a rough guide to likely declaration times in 2001, based on the 1997 election. (Note that several results were delayed by recounts.)

1	Sunderland South	22:46	59	Keighley	01:01
2	Hamilton South	23:07	60	Vale of Clwyd	01:01
3	Wrexham	23:38	61	Midlothian	01:02
4	Sunderland North	23:45	62	Darlington	01:03
5	Houghton & Washington East	00:05	63	Leeds East	01:03
6	Barnsley Central	00:15	64	Solihull	01:03
7	Bootle	00:19	65	Wallasey	01:03
8	Manchester Blackley	00:19	66	Rhondda	01:04
9	Birmingham Edgbaston	00:20	67	Bassetlaw	01:05
10	Warley	00:23	68	Bradford South	01:06
11	Ashton under Lyne	00:26	69	Sheffield Attercliffe	01:06
12	Portsmouth North	00:26	70	Pontefract & Castleford	01:07
13	Birmingham Ladywood	00:30	71	Alyn & Deeside	01:08
14	Crosby	00:31	72	Newcastle-upon-Tyne East & Wallsend	01:08
15	Salford	00:31	73	Kirkcaldy	01:09
16	Worsley	00:32	74	Moray	01:09
17	Eccles	00:34	75	Coventry North East	01:11
18	Barnsley West & Penistone	00:35	76	Cynon Valley	01:11
19	Tyne Bridge	00:35	77	Gateshead East & Washington West	01:11
20	Oldham West & Royton	00:39	78	Greenock & Inverclyde	01:11
21	Birmingham Yardley	00:41	79	Guildford	01:11
22	Clwyd South	00:41	80	Liverpool West Derby	01:11
23	Leigh	00:41	81	Newcastle-upon-Tyne North	01:11
24	Barnsley East & Mexborough	00:44	82	East Lothian	01:12
25	Southport	00:44	83	Sheffield Hallam	01:12
26	Birmingham Hall Green	00:45	84	Birkenhead	01:13
27	Leeds Central	00:45	85	Bolton North East	01:13
28	Sheffield I leeley	00:45	86	Bradford North	01:14
29	West Bromwich West	00:46	87	Halifax	01:14
30	Basildon	00:47	88	Liverpool Riverside	01:14
31	Stalybridge & Hyde	00:47	89	Makerfield	01:14
32	Wolverhampton South East	00:47	90	North West Durham	01:15
33	Dunfermline East	00:49	91	Pendle	01:15
34	Norwich North	00:49	92	Putney	01:15
35	Cunninghame South	00:51	93	Angus	01:16
36	West Bromwich East	00:51	94	Birmingham Sparkbrook & Small Heath	01:17
37	Hemsworth	00:52	95	Normanton	01:17
38	South Shields	00:52	96	Easington	01:18
39	Wolverhampton South West	00:52	97	Leeds West	01:18
40	Newcastle-upon-Tyne Central	00:53	98	Stirling	01:19
41	Oldham East & Saddleworth	00:53	99	Stockport	01:20
42	Dudley South	00:54	100	Montgomeryshire	01:21
43	Hartlepool	00:54	101	Stourbridge	01:21
44	Sheffield Central	00:54	102	Upminster	01:21
45	Manchester Gorton	00:55	103	Weston-super-Mare	01:21
46	Northavon	00:55	104	Blaydon	01:22
47	Wolverhampton North East	00:55	105	Perth	01:22
48	Denton & Reddish	00:56	106	Sheffield Brightside	01:22
49	Motherwell & Wishaw	00:56	107	Delyn	01:23
50	Battersea	00:57	108	Rochdale	01:23
51	Bolton South East	00:57	109	Islwyn	01:24
52	Livingston	00:57	110	Liverpool Garston	01:24
53	Great Grimsby	00:58	111	Liverpool Wavertree	01:24
54	Portsmouth South	00:58	112	Clydesdale	01:25
55	Hazel Grove	00:59	113	Middlesbrough	01:25
56	Wirral South	00:59	114	Clydebank & Milngavie	01:26
57	Wirral West	00:59	115	Linlithgow	01:26
58	Sedgefield	01:00	116	North Tyneside	01:26

117 Southampton Test	01:26	
118 Aldridge-Brownhills	01:27	
119 Knowsley North & Sefton East	01:28	
120 Bournemouth East	01:29	
121 Central Fife	01:29	
122 Wigan	01:29	
123 Cheadle	01:30	
124 Shipley	01:30	
125 Cumbernauld & Kilsyth	01:31	
126 Dundee East	01:31	
127 Heywood & Middleton	01:31	
128 Sheffield Hillsborough	01:31	
129 St. Helens South	01:31	
130 Stockton South	01:31	
131 Halesowen & Rowley Regis	01:32	
132 Poole	01:32	
133 Chingford & Woodford Green	01:33	
134 Hull East	01:34	
135 Rotherham	01:34	
136 Stretford & Urmston	01:34	
137 Ynys Môn	01:34	
138 Blaenau Gwent	01:35	
139 Birmingham Perry Barr	01:36	
140 Cunninghame North	01:36	
141 Cleethorpes	01:37	
142 Knowsley South	01:37	
143 Sittingbourne & Sheppey	01:37	
144 Bolton West	01:38	
145 Leeds North West	01:38	
146 Newport East	01:38	
147 Harwich	01:39	
148 Liverpool Walton	01:39	
149 Tooting	01:39	
150 Glasgow Baillieston	01:40	
151 Hamilton North & Bellshill	01:40	
152 Manchester Central	01:40	
153 Vale of Glamorgan	01:40	
154 Aberavon	01:41	
155 Ayr	01:41	
156 Hove	01:41	
157 Southampton Itchen	01:41	
158 Wakefield	01:41	
159 Bournemouth West	01:42	
160 Caernarfon	01:43	
161 Jarrow	01:43	
162 Glasgow Kelvin	01:44	
163 Hornchurch	01:44	
164 Kingswood	01:44	
165 Coventry South	01:45	
166 Glasgow Anniesland	01:45	
167 Yeovil	01:45	
168 Bedford	01:46	
169 Caerphilly	01:46	
170 Hull West & Hessle	01:46	
171 Leicester South	01:46	
172 Dundee West	01:47	
173 East Kilbride	01:47	
174 Leyton & Wanstead	01:47	
175 Wentworth	01:47	
176 Coventry North West	01:48	
177 Ogmore	01:48	
178 Stockton North	01:48	
179 Walsall South	01:48	
180 Glasgow Rutherglen	01:49	
181 Mansfield	01:49	
182 Bishop Auckland	01:50	
183 Hull North	01:51	
184 Dunfermline West	01:52	
185 Eastwood	01:52	
186 Glasgow Govan	01:52	
187 Gower	01:52	
188 Leicester West	01:52	
189 Pudsey	01:52	
190 Neath	01:53	
191 Redcar	01:53	
192 Scunthorpe	01:53	
193 Holborn & St. Pancras	01:54	
194 Hyndburn	01:54	
195 Bath	01:55	
196 Leicester East	01:55	
197 Meirionnydd Nant Conwy	01:55	
198 Romford	01:55	
199 Woodspring	01:55	
200 Croydon North	01:56	
201 Hertsmere	01:56	
202 Barking	01:57	
203 Dumfries	01:57	
204 Edinburgh South	01:57	
205 Bradford West	01:58	
206 Coatbridge & Chryston	01:58	
207 Manchester Withington	01:58	
208 St. Helens North	01:58	
209 Walsall North	01:58	
210 Walthamstow	01:58	
211 Morley & Rothwell	01:59	
212 Bridgend	02:00	
213 Cardiff Central	02:01	
214 Huddersfield	02:01	
215 Kilmarnock & Loudoun	02:01	
216 Durham North	02:02	
217 Gloucester	02:02	
218 Newcastle-under-Lyme	02:02	
219 Brentwood & Ongar	02:03	
220 Carrick, Cumnock & Doon Valley	02:03	
221 Glasgow Shettleston	02:03	
222 Swansea East	02:03	
223 Wythenshawe & Sale East	02:03	
224 Bury North	02:04	
225 Dudley North	02:04	
226 Reigate	02:04	
227 South Suffolk	02:04	
228 Newport West	02:05	
229 Nuneaton	02:05	
230 Swansea West	02:05	
231 Altrincham & Sale West	02:06	
232 Erith & Thamesmead	02:06	
233 Middlesbrough South & East Cleveland	02:06	
234 Torfaen	02:06	
235 Aberdeen South	02:07	
236 Carlisle	02:07	
237 Epping Forest	02:07	
238 Streatham	02:07	
239 Carshalton & Wallington	02:08	
240 Kensington & Chelsea	02:08	

243	Torbay	02:09	305	Glasgow Maryhill	02:32
244	Glasgow Springburn	02:10	306	High Peak	02:32
245	Hampstead & Highgate	02:10	307	Islington North	02:33
246	Harrogate & Knaresborough	02:10	308	Macclesfield	02:33
247	Rother Valley	02:10	309	Paisley North	02:33
248	Croydon Central	02:11	310	Rushcliffe	02:33
249	North Tayside	02:11	311	Wycombe	02:34
250	Airdrie & Shotts	02:12	312	Edinburgh West	02:35
251	Beverley & Holderness	02:12	313	Lincoln	02:35
252	Cardiff West	02:12	314	Yorkshire East	02:36
253	Edinburgh East & Musselburgh	02:12	315	Hendon	02:37
254	Broxbourne	02:14	316	Pontypridd	02:37
255	Ceredigion	02:14	317	Ross, Skye & Inverness West	02:37
256	Dagenham	02:14	318	West Suffolk	02:37
257	Glasgow Cathcart	02:15	319	Ashfield	02:38
258	Merthyr Tydfil & Rhymney	02:15	320	Falkirk West	02:38
259	Strathkelvin & Bearsden	02:15	321	Greenwich & Woolwich	02:38
260	Western Isles	02:15	322	Northampton North	02:38
261	Aberdeen Central	02:16	323	Tynemouth	02:38
262	Cheltenham	02:16	324	Aberdeen North	02:39
263	Stoke-on-Trent North	02:17	325	Ilford North	02:39
264	Amber Valley	02:18	326	Ilford South	02:40
265	Galloway & Upper Nithsdale	02:18	327	Brighton Pavilion	02:41
266	Dumbarton	02:19	328	Edmonton	02:41
267	Cardiff North	02:20	329	Llanelli	02:41
268	Ochil	02:20	330	Mitcham & Morden	02:41
269	Stoke-on-Trent Central	02:20	331	Twickenham	02:41
270	Waveney	02:20	332	Birmingham Selly Oak	02:42
271	Falkirk East	02:22	333	Dewsbury	02:42
272	Stoke-on-Trent South	02:22	334	Rossendale & Darwen	02:42
273	Sutton & Cheam	02:22	335	Bury South	02:43
274	Bromley & Chislehurst	02:23	336	City of York	02:43
275	Mid Dorset & Poole North	02:23	337	Tatton	02:43
276	Wimbledon	02:23	338	West Renfrewshire	02:44
277	Edinburgh North & Leith	02:24	339	Fylde	02:45
278	Havant	02:24	340	Isle of Wight	02:45
279	Shrewsbury & Atcham	02:24	341	North East Fife	02:45
280	Ealing North	02:25	342	Wansdyke	02:45
281	Meriden	02:25	343	Canterbury	02:46
282	Monmouth	02:25	344	Wyre Forest	02:46
283	North East Hertfordshire	02:25	345	Doncaster North	02:47
284	Burnley	02:26	346	Islington South & Finsbury	02:47
285	Camberwell & Peckham	02:26	347	Gillingham	02:48
286	Birmingham Hodge Hill	02:27	348	Preston	02:48
287	Broxtowe	02:27	349	Edinburgh Pentlands	02:49
288	Eastleigh	02:27	350	Birmingham Northfield	02:50
289	Leeds North East	02:27	351	Bromsgrove	02:50
290	Vauxhall	02:27	352	Bristol North West	02:51
291	Batley & Spen	02:28	353	Hayes & Harlington	02:51
292	City of Durham	02:29	354	St. Albans	02:51
293	Glasgow Pollok	02:29	355	Wansbeck	02:52
294	Lewisham Deptford	02:29	356	Warrington South	02:52
295	Oxford East	02:29	357	Carmarthen East & Dinefwr	02:53
296	Colne Valley	02:30	358	East Worthing & Shoreham	02:53
297	Elmet	02:30	359	Enfield North	02:53
298	Crewe & Nantwich	02:31	360	Finchley & Golders Green	02:53
299	Croydon South	02:31	361	Hammersmith & Fulham	02:53
300	Gordon	02:31	362	Hornsey & Wood Green	02:53
301	Warrington North	02:31	363	New Forest East	02:53
302	Birmingham Erdington	02:32	364	North Southwark & Bermondsey	02:53
303	Brent North	02:32	365	Calder Valley	02:54
304	Cardiff South & Penarth	02:32	366	Orpington	02:54

367	Banff & Buchan	02:55	429	Rutland & Melton	03:18
368	Derby South	02:56	430	South West Surrey	03:18
369	Taunton	02:57	431	Thurrock	03:18
370	Uxbridge	02:57	432	Windsor	03:18
371	Bexhill & Battle	02:58	433	Great Yarmouth	03:19
372	Surrey Heath	02:58	434	Horsham	03:19
373	Beckenham	02:59	435	North Swindon	03:19
374	Gedling	02:59	436	Scarborough & Whitby	03:19
375	Luton South	02:59	437	Erewash	03:20
376	New Forest West	02:59	438	Plymouth Sutton	03:20
377	Paisley South	02:59	439	Stafford	03:20
378	Tonbridge & Malling	02:59	440	Burton	03:21
379	Bexleyheath & Crayford	03:00	441	Dover	03:21
380	Brighton Kemptown	03:00	442	Newbury	03:21
381	Luton North	03:00	443	Basingstoke	03:22
382	South Swindon	03:00	444	Esher & Walton	03:22
383	Sutton Coldfield	03:00	445	Feltham & Heston	03:22
384	Ealing Acton & Shepherds Bush	03:01	446	Hackney North & Stoke Newington	03:22
385	North West Norfolk	03:01	447	Salisbury	03:22
386	Worcester	03:01	448	South Cambridgeshire	03:22
387	Enfield Southgate	03:02	449	Workington	03:22
388	Haltemprice & Howden	03:02	450	Bristol East	03:23
389	Harlow	03:02	451	Exeter	03:23
390	Lewisham West	03:03	452	North Devon	03:23
391	Ruislip-Northwood	03:03	453	Congleton	03:24
392	Bognor Regis & Littlehampton	03:04	454	Crawley	03:24
393	Gravesham	03:04	455	Doncaster Central	03:24
394	North Wiltshire	03:05	456	Gosport	03:24
395	Westmorland & Lonsdale	03:05	457	Brentford & Isleworth	03:25
396	Brigg & Goole	03:06	458	City of Chester	03:26
397	Derby North	03:06	459	Somerton & Frome	03:26
398	Dartford	03:07	460	Tamworth	03:26
399	Mid Sussex	03:07	461	Brent South	03:27
400	Tottenham	03:07	462	Huntingdon	03:27
401	Edinburgh Central	03:08	463	Colchester	03:28
402	Northampton South	03:08	464	Folkestone & Hythe	03:28
403	Stroud	03:08	465	Bosworth	03:29
404	Bridgwater	03:09	466	Woking	03:29
405	Conwy	03:09	467	Eltham	03:30
406	Harrow West	03:09	468	Poplar & Canning Town	03:31
407	Hemel Hempstead	03:09	469	Runnymede & Weybridge	03:31
408	Preseli Pembrokeshire	03:09	470	Lewisham East	03:32
409	Tunbridge Wells	03:09	471	Wantage	03:32
410	North Thanet	03:10	472	Wells	03:33
411	Chorley	03:11	473	Devizes	03:34
412	South Thanet	03:12	474	Richmond Park	03:35
413	Stevenage	03:13	475	Witney	03:35
414	Wellingborough	03:13	476	Hitchin & Harpenden	03:36
415	Castle Point	03:14	477	North Essex	03:36
416	Bristol West	03:15	478	Ribble Valley	03:36
417	North West Leicestershire	03:15	479	Spelthorne	03:36
418	Staffordshire Moorlands	03:15	480	Milton Keynes South West	03:37
419	Brent East	03:16	481	Warwick & Leamington	03:37
420	West Ham	03:16	482	Worthing West	03:38
421	Wokingham	03:16	483	Maidenhead	03:39
422	Blackburn	03:17	484	Christchurch	03:40
423	Hastings & Rye	03:17	485	South Staffordshire	03:40
424	Chesterfield	03:18	486	Cannock Chase	03:41
425	Fareham	03:18	487	Ipswich	03:41
426	Halton	03:18	488	Tweeddale, Ettrick & Lauderdale	03:41
427	Harrow East	03:18	489	East Ham	03:42
428	Old Bexley & Sidcup	03:18	490	Eastbourne	03:42

491	Carmarthen West & South Pemrokeshire	03:43
492	Louth & Horncastle	03:43
493	Roxburgh & Berwickshire	03:43
494	Saffron Walden	03:43
495	Faversham & Mid Kent	03:44
496	North East Derbyshire	03:44
497	Dulwich & West Norwood	03:45
498	North East Cambridgeshire	03:46
499	Redditch	03:46
500	Ryedale	03:46
501	Don Valley	03:47
502	Sevenoaks	03:47
503	Suffolk Coastal	03:47
504	Westbury	03:49
505	Inverness East, Nairn & Lochaber	03:50
506	Caithness, Sutherland & Easter Ross	03:52
507	Medway	03:52
508	Bristol South	03:53
509	Hackney South & Shoreditch	03:54
510	Hertford & Stortford	03:54
511	Rayleigh	03:55
512	Ealing Southall	03:56
513	Maidstone & the Weald	03:56
514	Telford	03:57
515	Ellesmere Port & Neston	03:58
516	Maldon & East Chelmsford	04:00
517	Chesham & Amersham	04:01
518	North Norfolk	04:01
519	East Surrey	04:02
520	Kingston & Surbiton	04:03
521	North Shropshire	04:04
522	Harborough	04:05
523	Mid Worcestershire	04:05
524	Copeland	04:06
525	Rugby & Kenilworth	04:06
526	Watford	04:07
527	North East Hampshire	04:08
528	Bolsover	04:11
529	Newark	04:11
530	Totnes	04:11
531	Hereford	04:12
532	Chipping Barnet	04:13
533	Billericay	04:14
534	Bracknell	04:14
535	Penrith & the Border	04:14
536	Henley	04:15
537	Sherwood	04:15
538	Sleaford & North Hykeham	04:16
539	Torridge & West Devon	04:16
540	Weaver Vale	04:17
541	Nottingham North	04:18
542	The Wrekin	04:18
543	Loughborough	04:19
544	Mid Bedfordshire	04:22
545	Milton Keynes North East	04:22
546	Chatham & Aylesford	04:23
547	Norwich South	04:23
548	North Dorset	04:24
549	Selby	04:24
550	Banbury	04:25
551	Morecambe & Lunesdale	04:25
552	Stone	04:25
553	Bethnal Green & Bow	04:26
554	Cotswold	04:26
555	West Derbyshire	04:26
556	Aldershot	04:27
557	South Ribble	04:27
558	Welwyn Hatfield	04:27
559	Reading East	04:28
560	North West Cambridgeshire	04:29
561	Oxford West & Abingdon	04:29
562	Braintree	04:31
563	Eddisbury	04:31
564	Epsom & Ewell	04:31
565	Nottingham East	04:32
566	Grantham & Stamford	04:33
567	Mole Valley	04:33
568	South West Devon	04:33
569	Regents Park & Kensington North	04:35
570	Slough	04:35
571	East Hampshire	04:39
572	Blaby	04:40
573	Gainsborough	04:40
574	West Chelmsford	04:40
575	Ashford	04:41
576	Bury St. Edmunds	04:41
577	Devonport	04:41
578	North Cornwall	04:41
579	Romsey	04:41
580	Reading West	04:43
581	Chichester	04:44
582	Beaconsfield	04:47
583	North Warwickshire	04:48
584	South West Norfolk	04:50
585	South East Cornwall	04:51
586	South Norfolk	04:51
587	West Lancashire	04:51
588	North West Hampshire	04:52
589	Wealden	04:53
590	Corby	04:54
591	Cities of London & Westminster	04:55
592	South Derbyshire	04:55
593	Lewes	04:56
594	Peterborough	04:58
595	Mid Norfolk	04:59
596	Vale of York	04:59
597	West Worcestershire	04:59
598	North East Bedfordshire	05:00
599	Charnwood	05:02
600	Teignbridge	05:03
601	Arundel & South Downs	05:04
602	Tewkesbury	05:04
603	Blackpool South	05:05
604	Cambridge	05:10
605	Blackpool North & Fleetwood	05:14
606	Boston & Skegness	05:18
607	Southend West	05:20
608	South Holland & the Deepings	05:22
609	South West Bedfordshire	05:22
610	Orkney & Shetland	05:23
611	Nottingham South	05:25
612	Stratford-on-Avon	05:27
613	Central Suffolk & Ipswich North	05:28
614	East Devon	05:30

615	South West Hertfordshire	05:31
616	Barrow & Furness	05:33
617	West Dorset	05:35
618	South East Cambridgeshire	05:38
619	Falmouth & Camborne	05:39
620	Lichfield	05:40
621	Aylesbury	05:43
622	Lancaster & Wyre	05:43
623	Rochford & Southend East	05:46
624	Buckingham	05:47
625	Leominster	05:55
626	Hexham	06:05
627	Forest of Dean	06:07
628	Tiverton & Honiton	06:13
629	Truro & St. Austell	08:11
630	St. Ives	10:59
631	Berwick-upon-Tweed	11:16
632	Argyll & Bute	11:43
633	Blyth Valley	12:00
634	Brecon & Radnorshire	12:18
635	South Dorset	12:23
636	Skipton & Ripon	13:03
637	North Down	13:23
638	Kettering	13:27
639	Strangford	13:49
640	Lagan Valley	13:54
641	East Londonderry	14:02
642	Richmond	14:05
643	Belfast West	14:11
644	South Antrim	14:15
645	North Antrim	14:29
646	Belfast North	14:38
647	Foyle	14:41
648	Fermanagh & South Tyrone	14:50
649	South Down	14:50
650	Mid Ulster	14:58
651	Newry & Armagh	16:18
652	Belfast South	16:23
653	Belfast East	16:35
654	Daventry	16:35
655	East Antrim	16:35
656	Ludlow	16:35
657	Upper Bann	16:35
658	West Tyrone	17:58
659	Winchester	18:18

Source: election.demon.co.uk

Constituencies

Table 31 Conservative targets

'Targets' are defined as seats in which the challenging party came second in 1997 or won in Scottish or Welsh elections or where the sitting MP has changed party since 1997.

Ranking	Constituency	Currently held by	Majority %	Swing required %	Current majority
1	Leominster*	Lab			
2	Romsey**	Lib Dem			
3	Witney***	Lab			
4	Winchester****	Lib Dem	0.0	0.0	2
5	Torbay	Lib Dem	0.0	0.0	12
6	Kingston & Surbiton	Lib Dem	0.1	0.1	56
7	Somerton & Frome	Lib Dem	0.2	0.1	130
8	Wellingborough	Lab	0.3	0.2	187
9	Kettering	Lab	0.3	0.2	189
10	Milton Keynes North East	Lab	0.5	0.2	240
11	Rugby & Kenilworth	Lab	0.8	0.4	495
12	Northampton South	Lab	1.3	0.7	744
13	Eastleigh	Lib Dem	1.4	0.7	754
14	Romford	Lab	1.5	0.8	649
15	Lancaster & Wyre	Lab	2.2	1.1	1,295
16	Harwich	Lab	2.3	1.1	1,216
17	Castle Point	Lab	2.3	1.2	1,116
18	Norfolk North West	Lab	2.3	1.2	1,339
19	Harrow West	Lab	2.4	1.2	1,240
20	Bristol West	Lab	2.4	1.2	1,493
21	Weston-Super-Mare	Lib Dem	2.4	1.2	1,274
22	Braintree	Lab	2.6	1.3	1,451
23	Lewes	Lib Dem	2.7	1.3	1,300
24	Shrewsbury & Atcham	Lab	3.0	1.5	1,670
25	Colchester	Lib Dem	3.0	1.5	1,581
26	Enfield Southgate	Lab	3.1	1.5	1,433
27	Devon West & Torridge	Lib Dem	3.3	1.7	1,957
28	Northavon	Lib Dem	3.4	1.7	2,137
29	Gillingham	Lab	3.9	2.0	1,980
30	Taunton	Lib Dem	4.0	2.0	2,443
31	Sittingbourne & Sheppey	Lab	4.2	2.1	1,929
32	Sutton & Cheam	Lib Dem	4.5	2.2	2,097
33	Clwyd West	Lab	4.6	2.3	1,848
34	Stroud	Lab	4.6	2.3	2,910
35	Falmouth & Camborne	Lab	5.0	2.5	2,688
36	Richmond Park	Lib Dem	5.2	2.6	2,951
37	Hastings & Rye	Lab	5.2	2.6	2,560
38	Warwick & Leamington	Lab	5.7	2.8	3,398
39	Shipley	Lab	5.7	2.8	2,996
40	Chatham & Aylesford	Lab	5.7	2.8	2,790
41	Newark	Lab	5.8	2.9	3,016
42	Wirral West	Lab	5.8	2.9	2,738
43	Aberdeenshire West & Kincardine	Lib Dem	6.2	3.1	2,662
44	Wimbledon	Lab	6.2	3.1	2,980
45	Eastwood	Lab	6.2	3.1	3,236
46	Reading West	Lab	6.2	3.1	2,997
47	Finchley & Golders Green	Lab	6.3	3.2	3,189
48	Thanet South	Lab	6.4	3.2	2,878
49	Ilford North	Lab	6.6	3.3	3,224
50	Hemel Hempstead	Lab	6.6	3.3	3,636
51	The Wrekin	Lab	6.7	3.3	3,025
52	Upminster	Lab	6.7	3.4	2,770
53	Putney	Lab	6.8	3.4	2,976
54	Selby	Lab	6.8	3.4	3,836
55	Croydon Central	Lab	7.0	3.5	3,897

56	Perth	SNP	7.1	3.5	3,141
57	Bexleyheath & Crayford	Lab	7.1	3.5	3,415
58	Hammersmith & Fulham	Lab	7.1	3.6	3,842
59	Gedling	Lab	7.3	3.6	3,802
60	Twickenham	Lib Dem	7.4	3.7	4,281
61	Reading East	Lab	7.6	3.8	3,795
62	Brighton Kemptown	Lab	7.7	3.8	3,534
63	Leeds North West	Lab	7.8	3.9	3,844
64	Hove	Lab	8.2	4.1	3,959
65	Dartford	Lab	8.3	4.2	4,328
66	Stafford	Lab	8.3	4.2	4,314
67	Portsmouth South	Lib Dem	8.4	4.2	4,327
68	Bradford West	Lab	8.5	4.3	3,877
69	Monmouth	Lab	8.5	4.3	4,178
70	Colne Valley	Lab	8.6	4.3	4,840
71	Isle of Wight	Lib Dem	8.8	4.4	6,406
72	Wansdyke	Lab	8.8	4.4	4,799
73	St Albans	Lab	8.8	4.4	4,459
74	Tayside North	SNP	9.1	4.6	4,160
75	Ribble South	Lab	9.2	4.6	5,084
76	Scarborough & Whitby	Lab	9.4	4.7	5,124
77	Portsmouth North	Lab	9.6	4.8	4,323
78	Broxtowe	Lab	9.6	4.8	5,575
79	Birmingham Edgbaston	Lab	10.0	5.0	4,842
80	Oxford West & Abingdon	Lib Dem	10.3	5.1	6,285
81	Wolverhampton South West	Lab	10.5	5.2	5,118
82	Watford	Lab	10.5	5.2	5,792
83	Brent North	Lab	10.5	5.3	4,019
84	Welwyn Hatfield	Lab	10.6	5.3	5,595
85	Edinburgh Pentlands	Lab	10.6	5.3	4,862
86	Gravesham	Lab	10.9	5.4	5,779
87	Loughborough	Lab	10.9	5.5	5,712
88	Swindon South	Lab	11.0	5.5	5,645
89	Calder Valley	Lab	11.1	5.5	6,255
90	Devon North	Lib Dem	11.3	5.6	6,181
91	Cornwall South East	Lib Dem	11.3	5.6	6,480
92	Battersea	Lab	11.3	5.7	5,360
93	Stourbridge	Lab	11.4	5.7	5,645
94	Burton	Lab	11.6	5.8	6,330
95	Pudsey	Lab	11.8	5.9	6,207
96	Brecon & Radnorshire	Lib Dem	11.9	5.9	5,097
97	Medway	Lab	12.0	6.0	5,354
98	Morecambe & Lunesdale	Lab	12.1	6.1	5,965
99	Southport	Lib Dem	12.2	6.1	6,160
100	Hendon	Lab	12.3	6.2	6,155
101	Ealing North	Lab	12.4	6.2	7,170
102	Wyre Forest	Lab	12.6	6.3	6,946
103	Forest of Dean	Lab	12.6	6.3	6,343
104	Hereford	Lib Dem	12.7	6.3	6,648
105	Hornchurch	Lab	12.9	6.5	5,680
106	Batley & Spen	Lab	13.1	6.5	6,141
107	Harrogate & Knaresborough	Lib Dem	13.1	6.5	6,236
108	Cheltenham	Lib Dem	13.2	6.6	6,645
109	St Ives	Lib Dem	13.3	6.7	7,170
110	Galloway & Upper Nithsdale	SNP	13.4	6.7	5,624
111	Brigg & Goole	Lab	13.7	6.8	6,389
112	Redditch	Lab	13.7	6.8	6,125
113	Bristol North West	Lab	13.8	6.9	11,382
114	Keighley	Lab	13.9	6.9	7,132
115	Moray	SNP	14.0	7.0	5,566
116	Gloucester	Lab	14.3	7.1	8,259
117	Bury North	Lab	14.3	7.1	7,866

118	Enfield North	Lab	14.3	7.2	6,822
119	Worcester	Lab	14.4	7.2	7,425
	Labour loses majority				
120	Bolton West	Lab	14.4	7.2	7,072
121	Wirral South	Lab	14.6	7.3	7,004
122	Ayr	Lab	14.6	7.3	6,543
123	Stirling	Lab	14.9	7.5	6,411
124	Tamworth	Lab	15.0	7.5	7,496
125	Newbury	Lib Dem	15.1	7.5	8,517
126	Peterborough	Lab	15.1	7.6	7,323
127	Erewash	Lab	15.1	7.6	9,135
128	Edinburgh West	Lib Dem	15.2	7.6	7,253
129	Leeds North East	Lab	15.3	7.6	6,959
130	High Peak	Lab	15.4	7.7	8,791
131	Swindon North	Lab	15.9	8.0	7,688
132	Elmet	Lab	16.2	8.1	8,779
133	Crosby	Lab	16.3	8.1	7,182
134	Gordon	Lib Dem	16.6	8.3	6,997
135	Blackpool North & Fleetwood	Lab	16.6	8.3	8,946
136	Cardiff North	Lab	16.8	8.4	8,126
137	Bedford	Lab	17.0	8.5	8,300
138	Harrow East	Lab	17.1	8.5	9,738
139	Chorley	Lab	17.1	8.6	9,870
140	W Bromwich West	Lab	17.1	8.6	3,232
141	Norwich North	Lab	17.2	8.6	9,470
142	Bath	Lib Dem	17.3	8.6	9,319
143	Great Yarmouth	Lab	17.7	8.9	8,668
144	Cleethorpes	Lab	18.2	9.1	9,176
145	Sheffield Hallam	Lib Dem	18.2	9.1	8,271
146	City of Chester	Lab	18.8	9.4	10,553
147	Derby North	Lab	18.9	9.5	10,615
	Conservatives largest party with 307 seats				
148	Exeter	Lab	18.9	9.5	11,705
149	Dewsbury	Lab	19.3	9.7	8,323
150	Northampton North	Lab	19.3	9.7	10,000
151	Dumfries	Lab	19.5	9.7	9,643
152	Vale of Glamorgan	Lab	19.5	9.8	10,532
153	Warrington South	Lab	19.6	9.8	10,807
154	Staffordshire Moorlands	Lab	19.7	9.8	10,049
155	Montgomeryshire	Lib Dem	19.7	9.9	6,303
156	Dudley North	Lab	19.8	9.9	9,457
157	Middlesbrough South & EastCleveland	Lab	19.8	9.9	10,607
158	Plymouth Sutton	Lab	19.8	9.9	9,440
159	Birmingham Hall Green	Lab	20.1	10.1	8,420
160	Milton Keynes South West	Lab	20.3	10.1	10,292
161	Luton North	Lab	20.3	10.2	9,626
162	Preseli Pembrokeshire	Lab	20.6	10.3	8,736
163	Yeovil	Lib Dem	21.1	10.6	11,403
164	Halesowen & Rowley Regis	Lab	21.2	10.6	10,337
165	Amber Valley	Lab	21.2	10.6	11,613
166	Rossendale & Darwen	Lab	21.4	10.7	10,949
167	Ipswich	Lab	21.6	10.8	10,439
168	Dover	Lab	21.7	10.8	11,739
169	Coventry South	Lab	21.9	10.9	10,953
170	Corby	Lab	22.0	11.0	11,860
	Conservative majority of 1				
171	Harlow	Lab	22.0	11.0	10,514
172	Waveney	Lab	22.0	11.0	12,453
173	Truro & St Austell	Lib Dem	22.0	11.0	12,501
174	Tynemouth	Lab	22.0	11.0	11,273
175	Halifax	Lab	22.2	11.1	11,212

176	Stockton South	Lab	22.2	11.1	11,585
177	Carmarthen West & Pembrokeshire South	Lab	22.3	11.2	9,621
178	Stevenage	Lab	22.5	11.3	11,582
179	Roxburgh & Berwickshire	Lib Dem	22.6	11.3	7,906
180	Blackpool South	Lab	22.6	11.3	11,616
181	Tatton*****	Ind	22.7	11.4	11,077
182	Vale of Clwyd	Lab	22.9	11.4	8,955
183	Pendle	Lab	23.0	11.5	10,824
184	Crawley	Lab	23.2	11.6	11,707
185	Derbyshire South	Lab	23.3	11.6	13,967
186	Eltham	Lab	23.5	11.7	10,182
187	Luton South	Lab	23.5	11.7	11,319
188	Angus	SNP	23.7	11.8	10,189
189	Hyndburn	Lab	23.7	11.9	11,448
190	Cornwall North	Lib Dem	23.8	11.9	13,933
191	Kingswood	Lab	23.8	11.9	14,253
192	Lincoln	Lab	23.9	12.0	11,130
193	Hazel Grove	Lib Dem	24.0	12.0	11,814
194	Bury South	Lab	24.7	12.4	12,433
195	Fife North East	Lib Dem	24.8	12.4	10,356
196	Basildon	Lab	25.0	12.5	13,280
197	Bethnal Green & Bow	Lab	25.3	12.6	11,285
198	Nuneaton	Lab	25.3	12.7	13,540
199	Leicestershire North West	Lab	25.4	12.7	13,219
200	Edinburgh South	Lab	25.5	12.8	11,452
	Conservative majority of 31				

* Conservative MP Peter Temple-Morris resigned whip, November 21 1997.
** Gained by Liberal Democrats at by-election by 3,311 votes, May 4 2000.
*** Conservative MP Shaun Woodward defected to Labour, December 18 1999.
**** Retained by Liberal Democrats at by-election by 21,556, November 20 1997.
***** Won by independent Martin Bell in absence of Labour and Liberal Democrat candidates.

Table 32 Labour targets

Ranking	Constituency	Held by	Majority %	Swing required %	Majority
1	Brent East*	Independent			
2	Renfrewshire West**	Independent			
3	Dorset South	Con	0.2	0.1	77
4	Bedfordshire South West	Con	0.2	0.1	132
5	Hexham	Con	0.5	0.2	222
6	Lichfield	Con	0.5	0.2	238
7	Bury St Edmunds	Con	0.7	0.3	368
8	Meriden	Con	1.1	0.5	582
9	Boston & Skegness	Con	1.4	0.7	647
10	Uxbridge	Con	1.8	0.9	3,766
11	Bosworth	Con	2.0	1.0	1,027
12	Chipping Barnet	Con	2.1	1.0	1,035
13	Beverley & Holderness	Con	2.3	1.1	1,211
14	Norfolk Mid	Con	2.3	1.2	1,336
15	Eddisbury***	Con	2.4	1.2	1,185
16	Billericay	Con	2.5	1.2	1,356
17	Altrincham & Sale West	Con	2.9	1.5	1,505
18	Suffolk West	Con	3.8	1.9	1,867
19	Tweedale Ettrick & Lauderdale	Lib Dem	3.8	1.9	1,489
20	Basingstoke	Con	4.2	2.1	2,397
21	Norfolk South West	Con	4.2	2.1	2,464
22	Shropshire North	Con	4.3	2.1	2,195

* Labour MP Ken Livingstone was expelled, April 3 2000.
** Labour MP Tommy Graham was expelled, September 9 1998.
*** Held by Conservatives at by-election by 1,606 votes, July 22 1999.

Table 33 Liberal Democrat targets

Ranking	Constituency	Held by	Majority %	Swing required %	Majority
1	Teignbridge	Con	0.5	0.2	281
2	Wells	Con	0.9	0.5	528
3	Mid Dorset & Poole North	Con	1.3	0.7	681
4	Totnes	Con	1.6	0.8	877
5	Norfolk North	Con	2.2	1.1	1,293
6	Tiverton & Honiton	Con	2.8	1.4	1,653
7	Bridgwater	Con	3.3	1.6	1,796
8	Dorset West	Con	3.4	1.7	1,840
9	Eastbourne	Con	3.8	1.9	1,994
10	Conwy	Lab	3.8	1.9	1,596
11	Christchurch	Con	3.9	1.9	2,165
12	Surrey South West	Con	4.8	2.4	2,694
13	Orpington	Con	4.9	2.5	2,952
14	Dorset North	Con	5.2	2.6	2,746
15	Southend West	Con	5.6	2.8	2,615
16	Wiltshire North	Con	6.0	3.0	3,475
17	Cheadle	Con	6.1	3.0	3,189
18	Oldham East & Saddleworth	Lab	6.3	3.1	3,389
19	Aberdeen South	Lab	7.6	3.8	3,365
20	Worcestershire West	Con	7.8	3.9	3,846

Table 34 SNP targets

Ranking	Constituency	Held by	Majority %	Swing required %	Majority
1	Inverness East, Nairn & Lochaber	Lab	4.9	2.5	2,339
2	Glasgow Govan	Lab	9.0	4.5	2,914
3	Ochil	Lab	10.6	5.3	4,652
4	Kilmarnock & Loudoun	Lab	15.3	7.7	7,256
5	Argyll & Bute	Lib Dem	17.0	8.5	6,081
6	Renfrewshire West	Independent	20.1	10.0	7,979
7	Western Isles	Lab	22.2	11.1	3,576
8	Dundee East	Lab	24.6	12.3	9,961
9	Aberdeen North	Lab	26.1	13.0	10,010
10	Dumbarton	Lab	26.4	13.2	10,883

Table 35 Plaid Cymru targets

Ranking	Constituency	Held by	Majority %	Swing required %	Majority
1	Carmarthen East & Dinefwr*	Lab	8.3	4.1	3,450
2	Conwy*	Lab	28.2	14.1	11,717
3	Llanelli*	Lab	38.9	19.5	16,039
4	Cynon Valley	Lab	59.1	29.6	19,755
5	Rhondda*	Lab	61.1	30.5	24,931
6	Iswlyn*	Lab	74.2	37.1	26,995

*Won by PC in 1999 Welsh elections

Complete list of constituencies in the General Election

ABERAVON, S Wales. Rock solid Lab, really Port Talbot, threat to local steel industry

Candidates 97	97 votes	97%	92%	Candidates
John Morris (Lab)	25,650	71.3	67.1	Hywel Francis
Ron McConville (LD)	4,079	11.3	12.5	Chris Davies
Peter Harper (Con)	2,835	7.9	13.9	Ali Miraj
Phil Cockwell (PC)	2,088	5.8	4.8	Lisa Turnbull
Majority	21,571	60	53.2	

Electorate: 50,025 Turnout: 35,963 (71.9%)

ABERDEEN CENTRAL, NE Scotland. Safest Lab seat in a city where Lab is usually just ahead, oil industry

Candidates 97	97 votes	97%	92%	Candidates
Frank Doran (Lab)	17,745	49.8	43.1	Frank Doran
J Wisely (Con)	6,944	19.5	28.8	Stewart Whyte
Brian Topping (SNP)	5,767	16.2	17.6	Wayne Gault
John Brown (LD)	4,714	13.2	10.6	Eleanor Anderson
Majority	10,801	30.3	14.3	

Electorate: 54,257 Turnout: 35,616 (65.6%)

ABERDEEN NORTH, NE Scotland. Secure for Lab thanks to 3-way opposition, oil industry

Candidates 97	97 votes	97%	92%	Candidates
Malcolm Savidge (Lab)	18,389	47.9	35.1	Malcolm Savidge
Brian Adam (SNP)	8,379	21.8	22.5	Dr Alasdair Allan
James Gifford (Con)	5,763	15	18.6	Richard Cowling
Mike Rumble (LD)	5,421	14.1	23.8	Jim Donaldson
Majority	10,010	26.1	16.5	

Electorate: 54,302 Turnout: 38,415 (70.7%)

ABERDEEN SOUTH, NE Scotland. Mixed history, now Lab but SNP, LD outside bet, could even go Con

Candidates 97	97 votes	97%	92%	Candidates
Anne Begg (Lab)	15,541	35.3	23.9	Anne Begg
Nicol Stephen (LD)	12,176	27.6	26.7	Ian Yuill
Raymond Robertson (Con)	11,621	26.4	37.4	Moray Macdonald
Jim Towers (SNP)	4,299	9.8	12.1	Ian Angus
Majority	3,365	7.7	10.7	

Electorate: 60,490 Turnout: 44,062 (72.8%)

ABERDEENSHIRE WEST & KINCARDINE, NE Scotland. LD gain 97, close fight against Cons, Balmoral and rugged Cairngorm hills

Candidates 97	97 votes	97%	92%	Candidates
Robert Smith (LD)	17,742	41.1	34.7	Robert Smith
George Kynoch (Con)	15,080	34.9	45.1	Tom Kerr
Joy Mowatt (SNP)	5,639	13.1	12.5	John Green
Qaisra Khan (Lab)	3,923	9.1	6.8	Kevin Hutchens
Majority	2,662	6.2	10.4	

Electorate: 59,123 Turnout: 43,189 (73%)

AIRDRIE & SHOTTS, W Scotland. Secure base for Lab tough-nut Helen Liddell, SNP distant challengers

Candidates 97	97 votes	97%	92%	Candidates
Helen Liddell (Lab)	25,460	61.8	62.5	Helen Liddell
Keith Robertson (SNP)	10,048	24.4	18.1	Alison Lindsay
Nicholas Brook (Con)	3,660	8.9	14.9	Gordon McIntosh
Richard Wolseley (LD)	1,719	4.2	4.5	
Majority	15,412	37.4	44.3	

Electorate: 57,673 Turnout: 41,181 (71.4%)

ALDERSHOT, Hampshire. Always Con, military tradition, LDs fight on in hope

Candidates 97	97 votes	97%	92%	Candidates
Gerald Howarth (Con)	23,119	42.7	58.1	Gerald Howarth
Adrian Collett (LD)	16,498	30.5	26.4	Adrian Collett
Terence Bridgeman (Lab)	13,057	24.1	13.8	Luke Akehurst
Majority	6,621	12.2	31.7	
Electorate: 76,189 Turnout: 54,151 (71.1%)				

ALDRIDGE-BROWNHILLS, W Midlands. Lab might have won 97, instead Con radical Richard Shepherd

Candidates 97	97 votes	97%	92%	Candidates
Richard Shepherd (Con)	21,856	47.1	54.3	Richard Shepherd
Janos Toth (Lab)	19,330	41.7	33.3	Ian Geary
Celia Downie (LD)	5,184	11.2	12.4	Jim Whorwood
Majority	2,526	5.4	21	
Electorate: 62,441 Turnout: 46,370 (74.3%)				

ALTRINGHAM & SALE WEST, Greater Manchester. Cons shocked by near-defeat 97 – should be a stronghold
Cheshire commuters

Candidates 97	97 votes	97%	92%	Candidates
Graham Brady (Con)	22,348	43.2	54.5	Graham Brady
Jane Baugh (Lab)	20,843	40.3	26.4	Jane Baugh
Marc Ramsbottom (LD)	6,535	12.6	18.4	Christopher Gaskell
Majority	1,505	2.9	28.1	
Electorate: 70,625 Turnout: 51,782 (73.3%)				

ALYN & DEESIDE, NE Wales. Gladstone lived here, heavily Lab, ex-industrial, by Welsh border

Candidates 97	97 votes	97%	92%	Candidates
Barry Jones (Lab)	25,955	61.9	50.9	Barry Jones
Timothy Roberts (Con)	9,552	22.8	36.9	Mark Isherwood
Eleanor Burnham (LD)	4,076	9.7	9.7	
Majority	16,403	39.1	14	
Electorate: 58,091 Turnout: 41,948 (72.2%)				

AMBER VALLEY, Derbyshire. Con until 97 but doesn't look it, ex-coalmining, safe Lab now

Candidates 97	97 votes	97%	92%	Candidates
Judy Mallaber (Lab)	29,943	54.7	44.4	Judy Mallaber
Philip Oppenheim (Con)	18,330	33.5	46.5	Gillian Shaw
Roger Shelley (LD)	4,219	7.7	9.1	Kate Smith
Majority	11,613	21.2	2.1	
Electorate: 72,005 Turnout: 54,775 (76.1%)				

ANGUS, NE Scotland. Safe SNP like many rural Scots once Con seats, inc. Montrose and Arbroath

Candidates 97	97 votes	97%	92%	Candidates
Andrew Welsh (SNP)	20,792	48.3	39.2	Michael Weir
Sebastian Leslie (Con)	10,603	24.6	38.1	Marcus Booth
Catherine Taylor (Lab)	6,733	15.6	12.9	Ian McFatridge
Richard Speirs (LD)	4,065	9.4	8.8	Peter Nield
Majority	10,189	23.7	1.1	
Electorate: 59,708 Turnout: 43,076 (72.1%)				

ANTRIM EAST, Northern Ireland. Larne and Carrickfergus, urban, coastal, DUP longshot

Candidates 97	97 votes	97%	92%	Candidates
Roy Beggs (UUP)	13,318	38.7	43.6	Roy Beggs
Sean Neeson (Alliance)	6,929	20.3	25.1	John Mathews
Jack McDee (DUP)	6,682	19.5	22.7	Sammy Wilson
T Dick (Con)	2,334	6.8		
Majority	6,389	18.6	18.5	
Electorate: 58,963 Turnout: 34,353 (58.3%)				

ANTRIM NORTH, Northern Ireland. Paisley's stronghold, inc. Moyle, Ballymoney and Ballymena, scenic, 25% Catholic

Candidates 97	97 votes	97%	92%	Candidates
Rev Ian Paisley (DUP)	21,495	46.5	50.9	Rev Ian Paisley
James Leslie (UUP)	10,921	23.6	18.1	Lexie Scott
Sean Farren (SDLP)	7,333	15.9	14.3	Sean Farren
J McCarry (SF)	2,896	6.3	4.2	John Kelly
Majority	10,574	22.9	32.8	

Electorate: 72,411 Turnout: 46,186 (63.8%)

ANTRIM SOUTH, Northern Ireland. Safest UUP seat, agricultural, DUP by-election gain

Candidates 97	97 votes	97%	92%	Candidates
Clifford Forsythe (UUP)	23,108	57.5	71.4	David Burnside
Donovan McClelland (SDLP)	6,497	16.2	13.5	Sean McKie
David Ford (Alliance)	4,668	11.6	10.9	
H Smyth (PUP)	3,490	8.7		Dr William McCrea
Majority	16,611	41.3	57.8	

Electorate: 69,414 Turnout: 40,195 (57.9%)

ARGYLL AND BUTE, W Scotland. Huge, Gaelic speakers, LD since 87, new candidate gives SNP chance

Candidates 97	97 votes	97%	92%	Candidates
Ray Michie (LD)	14,359	40.2	23.8	Alan Reid
Neil MacCormick (SNP)	8,278	23.2	34.9	Agnes Samuel
Ralph Leishman (Con)	6,774	19	27.7	David Petrie
Ali Syed (Lab)	5,596	15.7	13.6	Hugh Raven
Majority	6,081	17	11.1	

Electorate: 49,451 Turnout: 35,720 (72.2%)

ARUNDEL & SOUTH DOWNS, W Sussex. Cons will never lose here, 53% vote even in 97, rich, rural

Candidates 97	97 votes	97%	92%	Candidates
Howard Flight (Con)	27,251	53.1	62.8	Howard Flight
John Goss (LD)	13,216	25.7	25.1	
Richard Black (Lab)	9,376	18.3	9.3	Charles Taylor
Majority	14,035	27.4	37.7	

Electorate: 67,641 Turnout: 51,337 (75.9%)

ASHFIELD, Nottinghamshire. Once-mining seat, rock solid Labour, base for defence minister Geoff Hoon

Candidates 97	97 votes	97%	92%	Candidates
Geoff Hoon (Lab)	32,979	65.2	54.9	Geoff Hoon
Mark Simmonds (Con)	10,251	20.3	32.6	Julian Leigh
Bill Smith (LD)	4,882	9.6	12.5	
Majority	22,728	44.9	22.3	

Electorate: 72,269 Turnout: 50,603 (70%)

ASHFORD, Kent. Fast-developing, Channel Tunnel town, Cons safe despite big Lab, LD votes

Candidates 97	97 votes	97%	92%	Candidates
Damian Green (Con)	22,899	41.4	54.6	Damian Green
John Ennals (Lab)	17,544	31.7	20	John Adams
John Williams (LD)	10,901	19.7	24.1	Keith Fitchett
Majority	5,355	9.7	30.5	

Electorate: 74,149 Turnout: 55,294 (74.6%)

ASHTON-UNDER-LYNE, Greater Manchester. Safe Lab, new candidate, threatened textile industry, Asian minority

Candidates 97	97 votes	97%	92%	Candidates
Robert Sheldon (Lab)	31,919	67.5	57	David Heyes
Richard Mayson (Con)	8,954	18.9	28.7	Tim Charlesworth
Tim Pickstone (LD)	4,603	9.7	11.9	Kate Fletcher
Majority	22,965	48.6	28.3	

Electorate: 72,206 Turnout: 47,280 (65.5%)

AYLESBURY, Buckinghamshire. Secure Con, active local LDs on council, London commuters

Candidates 97	97 votes	97%	92%	Candidates
David Lidington (Con)	25,426	44.2	57.3	David Lidington
Sharon Bowles (LD)	17,007	29.5	27.8	Peter Jones
Robert Langridge (Lab)	12,759	22.2	13.4	Keith White
Majority	8,419	14.7	29.5	

Electorate: 79,047 Turnout: 57,554 (72.8%)

AYR, W Scotland. Always close, likely Con gain. Lab won 97, Lab MSP (just) in 99 but Con in by-election

Candidates 97	97 votes	97%	92%	Candidates
Sandra Osborne (Lab)	21,679	48.4	42.6	Sandra Osborne
Phil Gallie (Con)	15,136	33.8	38.4	Phil Gallie
Ian Blackford (SNP)	5,625	12.6	11.2	Jim Mather
Clare Hamblen (LD)	2,116	4.7	7.5	
Majority	6,543	14.6	4.2	

Electorate: 55,829 Turnout: 44,756 (80.2%)

BANBURY, Oxfordshire. Always Con, rural, Lab near-success 97 may fade

Candidates 97	97 votes	97%	92%	Candidates
Tony Baldry (Con)	25,076	42.9	54.9	Tony Baldry
Hazel Peperell (Lab)	20,339	34.8	26.9	Leslie Sibley
Catherine Bearder(LD)	9,761	16.7	17.8	Tony Worgan
Majority	4,737	8.1	28	

Electorate: 77,456 Turnout: 58,446 (75.5%)

BANFF & BUCHAN, NE Scotland. Alex Salmond will win to lead party in Westminster, fishing jobs hit

Candidates 97	97 votes	97%	92%	Candidates
Alex Salmond (SNP)	22,409	55.8	50.8	Alex Salmond
William Frain-Bell (Con)	9,564	23.8	34.7	Alexander Wallace
Megan Harris (Lab)	4,747	11.8	8.6	Edward Harris
Neil Fletcher (LD)	2,398	6	5.9	
Majority	12,845	32	16.1	

Electorate: 58,493 Turnout: 40,178 (68.7%)

BARKING, E London. Strong Lab seat, industrial, skilled manual, base for ex-socialist Margaret Hodge

Candidates 97	97 votes	97%	92%	Candidates
Margaret Hodge (Lab)	21,698	65.8	52.2	Margaret Hodge
Keith Langford (Con)	5,802	17.6	33.9	Mark Page
Mark Marsh (LD)	3,128	9.5	13.9	
Majority	15,896	48.2	18.3	

Electorate: 53,682 Turnout: 32,964 (61.4%)

BARNSLEY CENTRAL, S Yorkshire. Utterly secure for Lab, but no coal mines these days

Candidates 97	97 votes	97%	92%	Candidates
Eric Illsley (Lab)	28,090	77	70.8	Eric Illsley
Simon Gutteridge (Con)	3,589	9.8	18.5	Ian McCord
Darren Finlay (LD)	3,481	9.5	18.5	
Majority	24,501	67.2	52.3	

Electorate: 61,133 Turnout: 36,485 (59.7%)

BARNSLEY EAST & MEXBOROUGH, S Yorkshire, 16th safest Labour, ex-mining seat

Candidates 97	97 votes	97%	92%	Candidates
Jeffrey Ennis (Lab)	31,699	73.1	72.9	Jeffrey Ennis
Jane Ellison (Con)	4,936	11.4	17.3	Matthew Offord
David Willis (LD)	4,489	10.4	9.7	Sharron Brook
Majority	26,763	61.7	55.6	

Electorate: 67,840 Turnout: 43,335 (63.9%)

BARNSLEY WEST & PENISTONE, S Yorkshire. Lab, home of Arthur Scargill, some LDs and Cons

Candidates 97	97 votes	97%	92%	Candidates
Michael Clapham (Lab)	25,017	59.3	58.3	Michael Clapham
Paul Watkins (Con)	7,750	8.4	28	William Rowe
Winifred Knight (LD)	7,613	18	11.7	Miles Crompton
Majority	17,267	40.9	30.3	

Electorate: 64,894 Turnout: 42,208 (65%)

BARROW & FURNESS, Cumbria. Remote, once Tory as Trident yard created jobs, now secure Lab

Candidates 97	97 votes	97%	92%	Candidates
John Hutton (Lab)	27,630	57.3	47.7	John Hutton
Richard Hunt (Con)	13,133	27.2	41.3	James Airey
Anne Metcalfe (LD)	4,264	8.8	10.9	Barry Rabone
Majority	14,497	30.1	6.4	

Electorate: 66,960 Turnout: 48,230 (72%)

BASILDON, Essex. Famous as 92 weathervane, massive Lab win 97, Cons might just overturn one day

Candidates 97	97 votes	97%	92%	Candidates
Angela Smith (Lab)	29,646	55.8	40.7	Angela Smith
John Baron (Con)	16,366	30.8	45.1	Dominic Schofield
Lindsay Granshaw (LD)	4,608	8.7	14.2	
Majority	13,280	25	4.4	

Electorate: 73,989 Turnout: 53,082 (71.7%)

BASINGSTOKE, Hampshire. Shock Lab near miss 97, usually very safe Con, new town, middle class

Candidates 97	97 votes	97%	92%	Candidates
Andrew Hunter (Con)	24,751	43.3	53.5	Andrew Hunter
Nigel Lickley (Lab)	22,354	39.1	25.1	Jon Hartley
Martin Rimmer (LD)	9,714	17	20.4	Steve Sollitt
Majority	2,397	4.2	28.4	

Electorate: 77,035 Turnout: 57,129 (74.2%)

BASSETLAW, Nottinghamshire. Really Worksop, very Lab but still 11,000 Con votes 97, new Lab candidate

Candidates 97	97 votes	97%	92%	Candidates
Joe Ashton (Lab)	29,298	61.1	53.4	John Mann
Martin Cleasby (Con)	11,838	24.7	35	Alison Holley
Mike Kerringan (LD)	4,950	10.3	11.6	Neil Taylor
Majority	17,460	36.4	18.4	

Electorate: 68,101 Turnout: 47,924 (70.4%)

BATH, Somerset. Elegant, rich long-term marginal, LD since 92, should hold, Cons dream of recapture

Candidates 97	97 votes	97%	92%	Candidates
Don Foster (LD)	26,169	48.5	46.9	Don Foster
Alison McNair (Con)	16,850	31.2	43.4	Ashley Fox
Tim Bush (Lab)	8,828	16.4	8.2	Marilyn Hawkings
Majority	9,319	17.3	3.5	

Electorate: 70,815 Turnout: 53,989 (76.2%)

BATLEY & SPEN, W Yorkshire. Con lost 97 but not badly, might even retake, mixed area, Asian minority

Candidates 97	97 votes	97%	92%	Candidates
Mike Wood (Lab)	23,213	49.4	43	Mike Wood
Elizabeth Peacock (Con)	17,072	36.4	44.7	Elizabeth Peacock
K Pinnock (LD)	4,133	8.8	11.3	K Pinnock
Majority	6,141	13	1.7	

Electorate: 64,209 Turnout: 46,965 (73.1%)

BATTERSEA, S London. Posh inner suburb, famous Con wins until 97, ex-Guardian reformist Lab MP

Candidates 97	97 votes	97%	92%	Candidates
Martin Linton (Lab)	24,047	50.7	41.3	Martin Linton
John Bowis (Con)	18,687	39.4	50.4	Lucy Shersby
P Keaveney (LD)	3,482	7.3	7.1	Siobhan Vitelli
Majority	5,360	11.3	9.1	

Electorate: 66,928 Turnout: 47,397 (70.8%)

BEACONSFIELD, Buckinghamshire. Blair stood once, hosted sleaze-hit Tim Smith, still 5th safest Con

Candidates 97	97 votes	97%	92%	Candidates
Dominic Grieve (Con)	24,709	49.2	63.7	Dominic Grieve
Peter Mapp (LD)	10,722	21.4	19.4	Stephen Lloyd
Alastair Hudson (Lab)	10,063	20	13.7	Stephen Lathrope
Majority	13,987 2	7.8	44.3	

Electorate: 68,959 Turnout: 50,201 (72.8%)

BECKENHAM, S London. Smart, locals say it's Kent, Con 97, MP quit, Lab near-win 97 by-election

Candidates 97	97 votes	97%	92%	Candidates
Piers Merchant (Con)	23,084	42.5	60.2	Jacqui Lait
Robert Hughes (Lab)	18,131	33.4	21.1	Richard Watts
R Vetterlein (LD)	9,858	18.1	16.7	Alex Feakes
Majority	4,953	9.1	39.1	

Electorate: 72,807 Turnout: 54,350 (74.7%)

BEDFORD, Bedfordshire. Lab unless a bad year, many Asian voters, mostly urban

Candidates 97	97 votes	97%	92%	Candidates
Patrick Hall (Lab)	24,774	50.6	36.4	Patrick Hall
Robert Blackman (Con)	16,474	33.7	45.4	Nicky Attenborough
Christopher Noyce (LD)	6,044	12.3	16.4	Michael Headley
Majority	8,300	16.9	9	

Electorate: 66,560 Turnout: 48,944 (73.5%)

BEDFORDSHIRE MID, Bedfordshire. Safe as houses – and home of London brickworks – Cons will always win here

Candidates 97	97 votes	97%	92%	Candidates
Jonathan Sayeed (Con)	24,176	46	62.4	Jonathan Sayeed
Neil Mallett (Lab)	17,086	32.5	19.8	James Valentine
Tim Hill (LD)	8,823	16.8	15.8	Graham Mabbutt
Majority	7,090	13.5	42.6	

Electorate: 66,979 Turnout: 52,516 (78.4%)

BEDFORDSHIRE NORTH EAST, Bedfordshire. Con, mainly rural, professional but Lab closer than expected 97

Candidates 97	97 votes	97%	92%	Candidates
Sir Nicholas Lyell (Con)	22,311	44.3	59.3	Alastair Burt
John Lehal (Lab)	16,428	32.6	20	Philip Ross
Philip Bristow (LD)	7,179	14.2	18.5	Dan Rogerson
Majority	5,883	11.7	39.3	

Electorate: 64,743 Turnout: 50,388 (77.8%)

BEDFORDSHIRE SOUTH WEST, Bedfordshire. Con close shave 97 with Lab 132 behind, won't happen again

Candidates 97	97 votes	97%	92%	Candidates
Sir David Madel (Con)	20,777	46.2	65.2	Andrew Selous
Andrew Date (Lab)	21,534	40.7	56.2	Andrew Date
Stephen Owen (LD)	7,559	14.3	16.6	Martin Pantling
Majority	132	0.2	30.5	

Electorate: 69,781 Turnout: 52,864 (75.8%)

BELFAST EAST, Northern Ireland. Very Protestant, shipbuilding (for the moment), DUP usually wins

Candidates 97	97 votes	97%	92%	Candidates
Peter Robinson (DUP)	16,640	42.6	54.5	Peter Robinson
Reg Empey (UUP)	9,886	25.3	-	Tim Lemon
Jim Hendron (Alliance)	9,288	23.8	27.3	David Alderdice
S Dines (Con)	928	2.4	-	Terry Dick
Majority	6,754	17.3	27.2	

Electorate: 61,744 Turnout: 39,029 (63.2%)

BELFAST NORTH, Northern Ireland. Includes Protestant Shankhill but now Catholics too, up for grabs

Candidates 97	97 votes	97%	92%	Candidates
Cecil Walker (UUP)	21,478	51.8	51.7	Cecil Walker
Alban Maginness (SDLP)	8,454	20.4	18.3	Alban Maginness
Jon Kelly (SF)	8,375	20.2	11.3	Gerry Kelly
Tom Campbell (Alliance)	2,221	5.4	7.7	Tom Campbell
Majority	13,024	31.4	33.5	

Electorate: 64,577 Turnout: 41,452 (64.2%)

BELFAST SOUTH, Northern Ireland. Middle class, academic voters, mixed support but UUP ought to hold

Candidates 97	97 votes	97%	92%	Candidates
Rev Martin Smyth (UUP)	14,201	36	52.7	Rev Martin Smyth
Dr Alasdair McDonnell (SDLP)	9,601	24.3	14.2	Dr Alasdair McDonnell
David Ervine (PUP)	5,687	14.4	-	
Steve Mcbride (Alliance)	5,112	12.9	15.7	Gerry Rice
Majority	4,600	11.7	37	

Electorate: 63,439 Turnout: 39,484 (62.2%)

BELFAST WEST, Northern Ireland. Very Nationalist, Gerry Adams will win here, voters key to peace process

Candidates 97	97 votes	97%	92%	Candidates
Gerry Adams (SF)	25,662	55.9	42	Gerry Adams
Dr Joe Hendron (SDLP)	17,753	38.7	44.2	Alex Attwood
Freddie Parkinson (UUP)	1,556	3.4	11.6	
J Lowry (WP)	721	1.6	-	
Majority	7,909	17.2	2.2	

Electorate: 61,785 Turnout: 45,885 (74.3%)

BERWICK-UPON-TWEED, Northumberland. Long time LD Alan Beith ought to be safe, Borders, rural

Candidates 97	97 votes	97%	92%	Candidates
Alan Beith (LD)	19,007	45.5	44.4	Alan Beith
Paul Brannen (Lab)	10,965	26.2	22.9	Martin Walker
Nick Herbert (Con)	10,056	24.1	32.8	Glen Sanderson
Majority	8,042	19.3	11.6	

Electorate: 56,428 Turnout: 41,803 (74.1%)

BETHNAL GREEN & BOW, E London. Poor, plus yuppies, Bangladeshi voters, star MP Oona King safe

Candidates 97	97 votes	97%	92%	Candidates
Oona King (Lab)	20,697	46.3	53.5	Oona King
Dr Kabir Choudhury (Con)	9,412	21.1	16.4	Shahagir Faruk
Syed Nurul Islam (LD)	5,361	12	25.8	Janet Ludlow
Majority	11,285	25.2	27.7	

Electorate: 73,008 Turnout: 44,682 (61.2%)

BEVERLEY & HOLDERNESS, E Yorkshire. Labour almost pulled off triumph 97, will revert to safe Con

Candidates 97	97 votes	97%	92%	Candidates
James Cran (Con)	21,629	41.2	54.5	James Cran
Norman O'Neill (Lab)	20,418	38.9	20.1	Philippa Langford
John Melling (LD)	9,689	18.4	25.3	
Majority	1,211	2.3	29.2	

Electorate: 71,916 Turnout: 52,942 (73.6%)

BEXHILL & BATTLE, E Sussex. Strong Con seat, seaside, managerial, many retired voters

Candidates 97	97 votes	97%	92%	Candidates
Charles Wardle (Con)	23,570	48.1	60.3	Greg Barker
Kathryn Field (LD)	12,470	25.5	28.9	Stephen Hardy
Robert Beckwith (Lab)	8,866	18.1	9.4	Anne Moore-Williams
Majority	11,100	22.6	31.4	

Electorate: 65,584 Turnout: 48,994 (74.7%)

BEXLEYHEATH & CRAYFORD, S London. No one expected Lab win here 97, amazing if it happens again

Candidates 97	97 votes	97%	92%	Candidates
Nigel Beard (Lab)	21,942	45.5	31.3	Nigel Beard
David Evenett (Con)	18,527	38.4	54.2	David Evennett
Francoise Montford (LD)	5,391	11.2	14.3	Nickolas O'Hare
Majority	3,415	7.1	22.9	

Electorate: 63,334 Turnout: 48,223 (76.1%)

BILLERICAY, Essex. Huge swing to Lab 97, famous MP Teresa Gorman standing down, commuters

Candidates 97	97 votes	97%	92%	Candidates
Teresa Gorman (Con)	22,033	39.8	57.6	John Baron
Paul Richards (Lab)	20,677	37.3	20	Amanda Campbell
Geoff Williams (LD)	8,763	15.8	22.3	Frank Bellard
Majority	1,356	2.5	35.3	

Electorate: 76,550 Turnout: 55,420 (72.4%)

BIRKENHEAD, Merseyside. Strong Lab seat, inner city, working class, high unemployment

Candidates 97	97 votes	97%	92%	Candidates
Frank Field (Lab)	27,825	70.8	63.6	Frank Field
John Crosby (Con)	5,982	15.2	25.1	Brian Stewart
Roy Wood (LD)	3,548	9	9.7	Roy Wood
Majority	21,843	55.6	38.5	

Electorate: 59,782 Turnout: 39,323 (65.8%)

BIRMINGHAM EDGBASTON, W Midlands. Leafy middle-class Birmingham, Lab gain 97, key test for Blair

Candidates 97	97 votes	97%	92%	Candidates
Gisela Stuart (Lab)	23,554	48.6	39.3	Gisela Stuart
Andrew Marshall (Con)	18,712	38.6	49.3	Nigel Hastilow
Jock Gallagher (LD)	4,691	9.7	10.1	Nicola Davies
Majority	4,842	10	10	

Electorate: 70,204 Turnout: 48,465 (69%)

BIRMINGHAM ERDINGTON, W Midlands. Strong Lab seat, inner city, white, includes Spaghetti junction

Candidates 97	97 votes	97%	92%	Candidates
Robin Corbett (Lab)	23,764	58.8	53.3	Robin Corbett
Anthony Tompkins (Con)	11,107	27.5	36.5	Oliver Lodge
Ian Garrett (LD)	4,112	10.2	10.2	Sandra Johnson
Majority	12,657	31.3	16.8	

Electorate: 66,380 Turnout: 40,407 (60.9%)

BIRMINGHAM HALL GREEN, W Midlands. Outer suburbs, middle class, Lab gain 97, should keep it

Candidates 97	97 votes	97%	92%	Candidates
Terry Davis (Lab)	22,398	65.6	38.3	Terry Davis
Ed Grant (Con)	8,198	24	46.1	Debbie Lewis
A Thomas (LD)	2,891	8.5	15.6	Tracey O'Brien
Majority	8,420	20.1	7.8	

Electorate: 58,767 Turnout: 41,819 (71.2%)

BIRMINGHAM HODGE HILL, W Midlands. Lab seat, inner city, skilled manual

Candidates 97	97 votes	97%	92%	Candidates
Stephen McCabe (Lab)	22,372	53.5	53.6	Stephen McCabe
Andrew Hargreaves (Con)	13,952	33.4	36.3	Chris White
Alastair Dow (LD)	4,034	9.6	9.2	
Majority	8,420	20.1	17.3	

Electorate: 56,066 Turnout: 34,147 (60.9%)

BIRMINGHAM LADYWOOD, W Midlands. Ultra safe – 74% vote – for Lab Clare Short, once Lib, Con

Candidates 97	97 votes	97%	92%	Candidates
Clare Short (Lab)	28,134	74.1	71.4	Clare Short
Shailesh Vara (Con)	5,052	13.3	20.4	Benjamin Prentice
Sardul Marwa (LD)	3,020	8	8.2	Mahmood Chaudhry
Majority	23,082	60.8	51	

Electorate: 70,013 Turnout: 37,977 (54.2%)

BIRMINGHAM NORTHFIELD, W Midlands. Once Con, now Lab, Hague needs to win but won't, Rover crisis

Candidates 97	97 votes	97%	92%	Candidates
Richard Burden (Lab)	22,316	57.4	45.9	Richard Burden
Alan Blumenthal (Con)	10,873	28	42.5	Nils Purser
Michael Ashell (LD)	4,078	10.5	11.6	Trevor Sword
Majority	11,443	29.4	3.4	

Electorate: 56,842 Turnout: 38,847 (68.3%)

BIRMINGHAM PERRY BARR, W Midlands. Secure Lab seat, urban, outer ring council estates

Candidates 97	97 votes	97%	92%	Candidates
Jeffrey Rooker (Lab)	28,921	63	51.9	
Andrew Dunnett (Con)	9,964	21.7	37.4	David Binns
Roy Hassall (LD)	4,523	9.9	10.8	Jon Hunt
Majority	11,443	29.4	14.5	

Electorate: 71,031 Turnout: 45,887 (64.6%)

BIRMINGHAM SELLY OAK, W Midlands. Once Con-Lab marginal, now Lab bastion, middle class

Candidates 97	97 votes	97%	92%	Candidates
Dr Lynne Jones (Lab)	28,121	55.6	46	Dr Lynne Jones
Graham Greene (Con)	14,033	27.8	42.3	Ken Hardeman
David Osborne (LD)	6,121	12.1	10.3	David Osborne
Majority	14,088	27.8	3.7	

Electorate: 72,049 Turnout: 50,550 (70.2%)

BIRMINGHAM SPARKBROOK & SMALL HEATH, W Midlands. Lab, inner city, locals want Asian MP

Candidates 97	97 votes	97%	92%	Candidates
Roger Godsiff (Lab)	26,841	64.3	63.1	Roger Godsiff
Kenneth Hardeman (Con)	7,315	17.5	25.6	Iftkhar Hussain
Roger Harmer (LD)	3,889	9.3	8	Qassim Afzal
Majority	19,526	46.8	37.5	

Electorate: 73,130 Turnout: 41,765 (57.1%)

BIRMINGHAM YARDLEY, W Midlands. Lab, hardworking LDs hope for shock gain, Con vote fading

Candidates 97	97 votes	97%	92%	Candidates
Estelle Morris (Lab)	17,778	47	34.9	Estelle Morris
John Hemming (LD)	12,463	33	34.5	John Hemming
Anne Jobson (Con)	6,736	17.8	30.2	Barrie Roberts
Majority	5,315	14	0.3	

Electorate: 53,058 Turnout: 37,787 (71.2%)

BISHOP AUCKLAND, Durham. Lab seat, ex-mining, working class, unexpectedly rural

Candidates 97	97 votes	97%	92%	Candidates
Derek Foster (Lab)	30,359	65.9	47.6	Derek Foster
Josephine Fergus (Con)	9,295	20.2	32.8	Fiona McNish
Les Ashworth (LD)	4,293	9.3	19.5	Chris Foote Wood
Majority	21,064	45.7	14.8	

Electorate: 66,754 Turnout: 45,981 (68.9%)

BLABY, Leicestershire. Strong Con seat, once Lawson's, suburban, middle class, outside Leicester

Candidates 97	97 votes	97%	92%	Candidates
Andrew Robathan (Con)	24,564	45.8	56.8	Andrew Robathan
Ross Willmott (Lab)	18,090	33.8	21.8	J David Morgan
Geoff Welsh (LD)	8,001	14.9	20.1	Geoff Welsh
Majority	6,474	12	35	

Electorate: 70,471 Turnout: 53,593 (76%)

BLACKBURN, Lancashire. Safe base for Jack Straw, industrial, large Asian community

Candidates 97	97 votes	97%	92%	Candidates
Jack Straw (Lab)	26,141	55	48.4	Jack Straw
S Sidhu (Con)	11,690	24.6	37.5	John Cotton
Stephen Fenn (LD)	4,990	10.5	11.5	Imtiaz Patel
Majority	14,451	30.4	10.9	

Electorate: 73,058 Turnout: 47,497 (65%)

BLACKPOOL NORTH & FLEETWOOD, Lancashire. Seaside, retirement, white collar, once Con marginal now Lab

Candidates 97	97 votes	97%	92%	Candidates
Joan Humble (Lab)	28,051	52.2	37.6	Joan Humble
Harold Elletson (Con)	19,105	35.5	49.8	Alan Vincent
Beverley Hill (LD)	4,600	8.6	12	Steven Bate
Majority	8,946	16.7	12.2	

Electorate: 74,989 Turnout: 53,748 (71.7%)

BLACKPOOL SOUTH, Lancashire. Ex-marginal, contains big local sights, Lab gain 97

Candidates 97	97 votes	97%	92%	Candidates
Gordon Marsden (Lab)	29,282	57	43.4	Gordon Marsden
Richard Booth (Con)	17,666	34.4	44.1	David Morris
Doreen Holt (LD)	4,392	8.6	12.1	Doreen Holt
Majority	11,616	22.6	0.7	

Electorate: 75,720 Turnout: 51,340 (67.8%)

BLAENAU GWENT, S Wales. Safe Lab seat, ex-mining, Michael Foot and Nye Bevan were MPs

Candidates 97	97 votes	97%	92%	Candidates
Llewellyn Smith (Lab)	31,493	79.5	79	Llewellyn Smith
Geraldine Layton (LD)	3,458	8.7	9.8	Edward Townsend
Margrit Williams (Con)	2,607	6.6	6.4	Huw Williams
Jim Criddle (PC)	2,072	5.2	4.8	Adam Ryaka
Majority	28,035	70.8	69.2	

Electorate: 54,800 Turnout: 39,630 (72.3%)

BLAYDON, Tyne & Wear. Strong Lab seat, ex-mining, partly rural, a few LD voters

Candidates 97	97 votes	97%	92%	Candidates
John McWilliam (Lab)	27,535	60	52.7	John McWilliam
Peter Maughan (LD)	10,930	23.8	26.7	Peter Maughan
Mark Watson (Con)	6,048	13.2	20.7	Mark Watson
Majority	16,605	36.2	26	

Electorate: 64,699 Turnout: 45,925 (71%)

BLYTH VALLEY, Northumberland. Lab seat, ex-mining, part new town

Candidates 97	97 votes	97%	92%	Candidates
Ronnie Campbell (Lab)	27,276	64.2	49.9	Ronnie Campbell
Andrew Lamb (LD)	9,540	22.5	33.5	Jeffrey Reid
Barbara Musgrave (Con)	5,666	13.3	15.6	Wayne Daley
Majority	17,736	41.7	16.4	

Electorate: 61,761 Turnout: 42,482 (68.8%)

BOGNOR REGIS & LITTLEHAMPTON, W Sussex. Always Con, seaside, pensioners

Candidates 97	97 votes	97%	92%	Candidates
Nick Gibb (Con)	20,537	44.2	56.9	Nick Gibb
Roger Nash (Lab)	13,216	28.5	13.5	George O'Neill
Dr J Walsh (LD)	11,153	24	26.7	Pamela Peskett
Majority	7,321	15.7	30.2	
Electorate: 66,480 Turnout: 46,443 (69.9%)				

BOLSOVER, Derbyshire. Strong Lab seat, famous for electing Dennis Skinner, skilled manual

Candidates 97	97 votes	97%	92%	Candidates
Dennis Skinner (Lab)	35,073	74	64.5	Dennis Skinner
R Harwood (Con)	7,924	16.7	25.3	Simon Massey
Ian Cox (LD)	4,417	9.3	10.2	Marie Bradley
Majority	27,149	57.3	39.2	
Electorate: 66,476 Turnout: 47,414 (71.3%)				

BOLTON NORTH EAST, Greater Manchester. Big Lab win 97, Cons may retake one day, industrial, urban

Candidates 97	97 votes	97%	92%	Candidates
David Crausby (Lab)	27,621	56.1	47.5	David Crausby
Robert Wilson (Con)	14,952	30.4	42.1	Michael Winstanley
Edmund Critchley (LD)	4,862	9.9	10.1	Tim Perkins
Majority	12,669	25.7	5.4	
Electorate: 67,930 Turnout: 49,207 (72.4%)				

BOLTON SOUTH EAST, Greater Manchester. Totally secure Lab seat, industrial, large Asian community

Candidates 97	97 votes	97%	92%	Candidates
Dr Brian Iddon (Lab)	29,856	68.9	54.3	Dr Brian Iddon
Paul Carter (Con)	8,545	19.7	28.7	Haroon Rashid
Frank Harasiwka (LD)	3,805	8.8	10.6	Frank Harasiwka
Majority	21,311	49.2	25.5	
Electorate: 66,459 Turnout: 43,349 (65.2%)				

BOLTON WEST, Greater Manchester. Lab marginal, key Con target seat, smart residential

Candidates 97	97 votes	97%	92%	Candidates
Ruth Kelly (Lab)	24,342	49.5	39.1	Ruth Kelly
Thomas Sackville (Con)	17,270	35.1	47.3	James Stevens
Barbara Ronson (LD)	5,309	10.8	13.2	Barbara Ronson
Majority	7,072	14.4	8.2	
Electorate: 63,535 Turnout: 49,160 (77.4%)				

BOOTLE, Merseyside. Safest Lab seat – 83% vote – inner city, high unemployment

Candidates 97	97 votes	97%	92%	Candidates
Joe Benton (Lab)	31,668	82.9	76.5	Joe Benton
Rupert Matthews (Con)	3,247	8.5	14.1	Judith Symes
Kiron Reid (LD)	2,191	5.7	6.5	Jim Murray
Majority	28,421	74.4	62.4	
Electorate: 57,284 Turnout: 38,223 (66.7%)				

BOSTON & SKEGNESS, Lincolnshire. Cons nearly lost in 97, won't be as close again, bracing seaside resort

Candidates 97	97 votes	97%	92%	Candidates
Sir Richard Body (Con)	19,750	42.4	50.8	Mark Simmonds
Philip McCauley (Lab)	19,103	41	28.2	Elaine Bird
Jim Dodsworth (LD)	7,721	16.6	21	Duncan Moffatt
Majority	647	1.4	22.6	
Electorate: 67,623 Turnout: 46,574 (68.9%)				

BOSWORTH, Leicestershire. Once Lab, Cons held on just 97, Leicester commuters

Candidates 97	97 votes	97%	92%	Candidates
David Tredinnick (Con)	21,189	40.6	51.6	David Tredinnick
Andrew Furlong (Lab)	20,162	38.7	26.4	Andrew Furlong
J Ellis (LD)	9,281	17.8	20.7	J Ellis
Majority	1,027	1.9	25.2	
Electorate: 68,113 Turnout: 52,153 (76.6%)				

BOURNEMOUTH EAST, Dorset. Traditional Con seat, some LD activity, seaside, retirement

Candidates 97	97 votes	97%	92%	Candidates
David Atkinson (Con)	17,997	41.4	55.5	David Atkinson
Douglas Eyre (LD)	13,651	31.4	31.1	Andrew Garratt
J Stevens (Lab)	9,181	21.1	12.8	
Majority	4,346	10	24.4	

Electorate: 61,862 Turnout: 43,428 (70.2%)

BOURNEMOUTH WEST, Dorset. LDs and Lab fight for second, Cons always first, many pensioners

Candidates 97	97 votes	97%	92%	Candidates
John Butterfill (Con)	17,115	41.7	52.5	John Butterfill
Janet Dover (LD)	11,405	27.8	27.4	Fiona Hornby
Dennis Gritt (Lab)	10,093	24.6	19,5	David Stokes
Majority	7,022	13.9	33	

Electorate: 62,028 Turnout: 41,072 (66.2%)

BRACKNELL, Berkshire. Very secure Con seat, partly new town, professional

Candidates 97	97 votes	97%	92%	Candidates
Andrew Mackay (Con)	27,983	47.4	60.4	Andrew Mackay
Anne Snelgrove (Lab)	17,596	29.8	20.2	Janet Keene
Alan Hilliar (LD)	9,122	15.4	19.4	Ray Earwicker
Majority	5,710	13.9	40.2	

Electorate: 79,292 Turnout: 59,091 (74.5%)

BRADFORD NORTH, W Yorkshire. Lab seat, declining textile industry, large Asian community

Candidates 97	97 votes	97%	92%	Candidates
Terence Rooney (Lab)	23,493	56.1	47.8	Terence Rooney
Rasjid Skinner (Con)	10,723	25.6	32.2	Zahid Iqbal
Terry Browne (LD)	6,083	14.5	18.7	David Ward
Majority	12,770	30.5	15.6	

Electorate: 66,228 Turnout: 41,895 (63.3%)

BRADFORD SOUTH, W Yorkshire. Comfortably safe for Lab these days, once Con target, inner city

Candidates 97	97 votes	97%	92%	Candidates
Gerry Sutcliffe (Lab)	25,558	56.7	47.6	Gerry Sutcliffe
Anne Hawkesworth (Con)	12,622	28	38.4	Graham Tennyson
Alex Wilson-Fletcher (LD)	5,093	11.3	13.7	
Majority	12,936	28.7	9.2	

Electorate: 68,391 Turnout: 45,058 (65.9%)

BRADFORD WEST, W Yorkshire. Inner city, Asian, rare Con surge 97 makes it odd Con target

Candidates 97	97 votes	97%	92%	Candidates
Marsha Singh (Lab)	18,932	41.5	53.2	Marsha Singh
Mohammed Riaz (Con)	15,055	33	33.8	Mohammed Riaz
Helen Wright (LD)	6,737	14.8	10.5	
Majority	3,877	8.5	19.4	

Electorate: 71,961 Turnout: 45,568 (63.3%)

BRAINTREE, Essex. Unexpected Lab gain 97, key Con target, mainly rural, white collar

Candidates 97	97 votes	97%	92%	Candidates
Alan Hurst (Lab)	23,729	42.7	27.4	Alan Hurst
Tony Newton (Con)	22,278	40.1	50.5	Brooks Newmark
Trevor Ellis (LD)	6,418	11.5	20.8	Peter Turner
Majority	1,451	2.6	32.1	

Electorate: 72,772 Turnout: 55,576 (76.4%)

BRECON & RADNORSHIRE, Mid Wales. Long time 3-way marginal, mainly rural, LD MP standing down

Candidates 97	97 votes	97%	92%	Candidates
Richard Livsey (LD)	17,516	40.8	35.8	Roger Williams
John Evans (Con)	12,419	29	36.1	Peter Gooderham
Chris Mann (Lab)	11,424	26.6	26.3	Huw Davies
Majority	5,097	11.8	0.3	

Electorate: 52,142 Turnout: 42,881 (82.2%)

BRENT EAST, N London. Urban home of ex-Lab mayor Ken Livingstone, Lab will regain

Candidates 97	97 votes	97%	92%	Candidates
Ken Livingstone (Ind)	23,748	67.3	52.8	Paul Daisley
Mark Francois (Con)	7,866	22.3	36.6	David Gauke
Ian Hunter (LD)	2,751	7.8	8.9	Nowsheen Bhatti
Majority	15,882	45	16.2	

Electorate: 53,548 Turnout: 35,272 (65.9%)

BRENT NORTH, N London. Big Lab gain 97, once thought safe Con, strongly Asian

Candidates 97	97 votes	97%	92%	Candidates
Barry Gardiner (Lab)	19,343	50.7	30.3	Barry Gardiner
Sir Rhodes Boyson (Con)	15,324	40.1	57.4	Philip Allott
Paul Lorber (LD)	3,104	8.1	10.6	Paul Lorber
Majority	4,019	10.6	27.1	

Electorate: 54,149 Turnout: 38,174 (70.5%)

BRENT SOUTH, N London. Majority non-white population, secure Lab but some Con activity

Candidates 97	97 votes	97%	92%	Candidates
Paul Boateng (Lab)	25,180	73	57.6	Paul Boateng
Stewart Jackson (Con)	5,489	15.9	31.1	Carupiah Selvarajah
Julian Brazil (LD)	2,670	7.7	9.5	Havard Hughes
Majority	19,691	57.1	26.5	

Electorate: 53,505 Turnout: 34,498 (64.5%)

BRENTFORD & ISLEWORTH, W London. Con lost badly 97, urban, large Asian community

Candidates 97	97 votes	97%	92%	Candidates
Ann Keen (Lab)	32,249	57.4	42.8	Ann Keen
Nirj Deva (Con)	17,825	31.8	45.6	Tim Mack
Gareth Hartwell (LD)	4,613	8.2	10.1	Gareth Hartwell
Majority	14,424	25.6	2.8	

Electorate: 79,058 Turnout: 56,135 (71%)

BRENTWOOD & ONGAR, Essex. Strong Con seat, commuting, managerial, many LDs on council

Candidates 97	97 votes	97%	92%	Candidates
Eric Pickles (Con)	23,031	45.4	57.6	Eric Pickles
Liz Bottomley (LD)	13,341	26.3	30.5	David Kendall
Marc Young (Lab)	11,231	22.1	10.9	Diana Johnson
Majority	9,690	19.1	27.1	

Electorate: 66,005 Turnout: 50,726 (76.8%)

BRIDGEND, S Wales. Lab seat, mainly urban, prosperous in parts

Candidates 97	97 votes	97%	92%	Candidates
Win Griffiths (Lab)	25,115	58.1	51.3	Win Griffiths
David Davies (Con)	9,867	22.8	35.7	Tania Brisby
Andrew McKinlay (LD)	4,968	11.5	10.3	
Majority	15,248	35.3	15.6	

Electorate: 59,721 Turnout: 43,261 (72.4%)

BRIDGWATER, Somerset. Con seat, LD missed 97, mainly rural, not rich

Candidates 97	97 votes	97%	92%	Candidates
Tom King (Con)	20,174	36.9	46.8	Ian Liddell-Grainger
Mike Hoban (LD)	18,378	33.6	29.7	Ian Thorn
Roger Lavers (Lab)	13,519	24.8	21.7	William Montieth
Majority	1,796	3.3	17.1	

Electorate: 73,038 Turnout: 54,622 (74.8%)

BRIGG & GOOLE, Humberside. Lab in 97 but must be Con target, skilled manual, docks

Candidates 97	97 votes	97%	92%	Candidates
Ian Cawsey (Lab)	23,493	50.2	35.7	Ian Cawsey
Donald Stewart (Con)	17,104	36.5	49.8	Donald Stewart
Mary-Rose Hardy (LD)	4,692	10	14.5	David Nolan
Majority	6,389	13.7	14.1	

Electorate: 63,648 Turnout: 46,802 (73.5%)

BRIGHTON KEMPTOWN, E Sussex. Lab marginal, seaside, white collar

Candidates 97	97 votes	97%	92%	Candidates
Dr Des Turner (Lab)	21,479	46.6	32.6	Dr Des Turner
Andrew Bowden (Con)	17,945	38.9	52.8	Geoffrey Theobald
Clive Gray (LD)	4,478	9.7	13.9	
Majority	3,534	7.7	20.2	

Electorate: 65,147 Turnout: 46,132 (70.8%)

BRIGHTON PAVILION, E Sussex. Huge Lab win 97, now looks safe, seaside, middle class

Candidates 97	97 votes	97%	92%	Candidates
David Lepper (Lab)	26,737	54.6	40.2	David Lepper
Sir Derek Spencer (Con)	13,556	27.7	45.3	David Gold
Kenneth Blanshard (LD)	4,644	9.5	12.3	Ruth Berry
Majority	13,181	26.9	5	

Electorate: 66,431 Turnout: 48,951 (73.7%)

BRISTOL EAST, Bristol. Typical of Tory collapse, lost by Con in 92, now utterly safe for Lab

Candidates 97	97 votes	97%	92%	Candidates
Jean Corston (Lab)	27,418	56.9	47.3	Jean Corston
Edward Vaizey (Con)	11,259	23.4	37.6	Jack Lo-Presti
Peter Tyzack (LD)	7,121	14.8	14.7	Brian Niblett
Majority	16,159	33.5	9.7	

Electorate: 68,990 Turnout: 48,201 (69.9%)

BRISTOL NORTH WEST, Bristol. Lab gain 97, secure if not safe, very urban

Candidates 97	97 votes	97%	92%	Candidates
Dr Doug Naysmith (Lab)	27,575	49.9	45.2	Dr Doug Naysmith
Michael Stern (Con)	16,193	29.3	38.8	Charles Hansard
Ian Parry (LD)	7,263	13.1	14.8	Peter Tyzack
Majority	11,382	20.6	6.4	

Electorate: 75,009 Turnout: 55,245 (73.7%)

BRISTOL SOUTH, Bristol. Least prosperous Bristol seat, very safe for Lab minister Dawn Primarolo

Candidates 97	97 votes	97%	92%	Candidates
Dawn Primarolo (Lab)	29,890	59.9	47.3	Dawn Primarolo
Michael Roe (Con)	10,562	21.2	33.2	Richard Eddy
S Williams (LD)	6,691	13.4	18	James Main
Majority	19,328	38.7	14.1	

Electorate: 72,393 Turnout: 49,859 (68.9%)

BRISTOL WEST, Bristol. Lab gained – just – from third 97, Con target, LD longshot, university

Candidates 97	97 votes	97%	92%	Candidates
Valerie Davey (Lab)	22,068	35.2	23.4	Valerie Davey
William Waldegrave (Con)	20,575	32.8	45.1	Pamela Chesters
Charles Boney (LD)	17,551	28	29.2	Stephen Williams
Majority	1,493	2.4	15.9	

Electorate: 84,870 Turnout: 62,641 (73.8%)

BROMLEY & CHISLEHURST, S London. Strong Con seat even in 97, outer suburbs, middle class

Candidates 97	97 votes	97%	92%	Candidates
Eric Forth (Con)	24,428	46.3	62	Eric Forth
Rob Yeldham (Lab)	13,310	25.2	17.2	
Dr P Booth (LD)	12,530	23.8	17.8	Geoff Payne
Majority	11,118	21.1	44.2	

Electorate: 71,104 Turnout: 52,738 (74.2%)

BROMSGROVE, Hereford and Worcester. Strong Con seat, commuting, managerial

Candidates 97	97 votes	97%	92%	Candidates
Julie Kirkbride (Con)	24,620	47.2	54.1	Julie Kirkbride
Peter McDonald (Lab)	19,725	37.8	30.7	Peter McDonald
Jennette Davy (LD)	6,200	11.9	13.8	Margaret Rowley
Majority	4,895	9.4	23.4	

Electorate: 67,744 Turnout: 52,207 (77.1%)

BROXBOURNE, Hertfordshire. Strong Con seat, stockbroker belt, white collar

Candidates 97	97 votes	97%	92%	Candidates
Marion Roe (Con)	22,952	48.9	62.3	Marion Roe
Ben Coleman (Lab)	16,299	34.7	21.4	David Prendergast
Julia Davies (LD)	5,310	11.3	16	Julia Davies
Majority	6,653	14.2	40.9	

Electorate: 66,720 Turnout: 46,976 (70.4%)

BROXTOWE, Nottinghamshire. Lab gain 97, Con target, suburban

Candidates 97	97 votes	97%	92%	Candidates
Dr Nicholas Palmer (Lab)	27,343	47	34	Dr Nicholas Palmer
James Lester (Con)	21,768	37.4	51	Pauline Latham
T Miller (LD)	6,934	11.9	13.8	David Watts
Majority	5,575	9.6	16.2	

Electorate: 74,144 Turnout: 58,137 (78.4%)

BUCKINGHAM, Buckinghamshire. Once elected Lab Robert Maxwell, now safe Con, mainly rural

Candidates 97	97 votes	97%	92%	Candidates
John Bercow (Con)	24,594	49.8	62.3	John Bercow
Robert Lehmann (Lab)	12,208	24.7	16.1	
Neil Stuart (LD)	12,175	24.6	20.9	Isobel Wilson
Majority	12,386	25.1	41.1	

Electorate: 62,945 Turnout: 49,398 (78.5%)

BURNLEY, Lancashire. Strong Lab seat, industrial, traditional

Candidates 97	97 votes	97%	92%	Candidates
Peter Pike (Lab)	26,210	57.9	53	Peter Pike
Bill Wiggin (Con)	9,148	20.2	30.6	Robert Frost
Gordon Birtwistle (LD)	7,877	17.4	16.4	
Majority	17,062	37.7	22.4	

Electorate: 67,582 Turnout: 45,245 (67%)

BURTON, Staffordshire. Lab gain 97, Cons must be hopeful of retaking, brewing industry

Candidates 97	97 votes	97%	92%	Candidates
Janet Dean (Lab)	27,810	51	41.2	Janet Dean
Ivan Lawrence (Con)	21,480	39.4	48.2	Maggie Punyer
David Fletcher (LD)	4,617	8.5	10.5	David Fletcher
Majority	6,330	11.6	7	

Electorate: 72,601 Turnout: 54,511 (75.1%)

BURY NORTH, Greater Manchester. Lab gained as expected 97, Cons need to win to form a government

Candidates 97	97 votes	97%	92%	Candidates
David Chaytor (Lab)	28,523	51.8	41.6	David Chaytor
Alastair Burt (Con)	20,657	37.5	49.7	John Walsh
Neville Kenyon (LD)	4,536	8.2	8.5	
Majority	7,866	14.3	8.1	

Electorate: 70,515 Turnout: 55,053 (78.1%)

BURY SOUTH, Greater Manchester. Once Con, now looks safe Lab, mixed seat

Candidates 97	97 votes	97%	92%	Candidates
Ivan Lewis (Lab)	28,658	56.9	44.6	Ivan Lewis
David Sumberg (Con)	16,277	32.3	46	Nicola Le Page
V D'Albert (LD)	4,227	8.4	9	Tim Pickstone
Majority	12,381	24.6	1.4	

Electorate: 66,568 Turnout: 50,326 (75.6%)

BURY ST EDMUNDS, Suffolk. Cons just avoided shock defeat 97, mainly rural, middle class

Candidates 97	97 votes	97%	92%	Candidates
David Ruffley (Con)	21,290	38.3	45.9	David Ruffley
Mark Ereira-Guyer (Lab)	20,922	37.7	26	Mark Ereira-Guyer
David Cooper (LD)	10,102	18.2	26.9	Richard Williams
Majority	368	0.6	19	

Electorate: 74,017 Turnout: 55,525 (75%)

CAERNARFON, NW Wales. Most Welsh-speaking seat, strong Plaid Cymru vote, castles and Snowdonia

Candidates 97	97 votes	97%	92%	Candidates
Dafydd Wigley (PC)	17,616	51	59	Hywel Williams
Difion Williams (Lab)	10,167	29.5	15.5	Martin Eaglestone
Elwyn Williams (Con)	4,230	12.3	19.2	Bronwen Naish
Mary McQueen (LD)	1,686	4.9	5.8	M Owain
Majority	7,449	21.5	39.8	

Electorate: 46,815 Turnout: 34,010 (72.7%)

CAERPHILLY, S Wales. Very strong Lab seat, ex-mining, valleys north of Cardiff

Candidates 97	97 votes	97%	92%	Candidates
Ron Davies (Lab)	30,697	67.8	63.7	Wayne David
Dr Ronald Harris (Con)	4,858	10.7	18.1	David Simmonds
Lindsay Whittle (PC)	4,383	9.7	9.6	Lindsay Whittle
Tony Ferguson (LD)	3,724	8.2	8.5	Rob Roffe
Majority	25,839	57.1	45.6	

Electorate: 64,621 Turnout: 45,269 (70%)

CAITHNESS, SUTHERLAND & EASTER ROSS, N Scotland. Hugely remote, retiring LD MP gives Lab, SNP chance

Candidates 97	97 votes	97%	92%	Candidates
Robert Maclennan (LD)	10,381	35.6	44.4	John Thurso
James Hendry (Lab)	8,122	27.8	15.6	Michael Meighan
Euan Harper (SNP)	6,710	23	18.3	John MacAdam
Tom Miers (Con)	3,148	10.8	21.6	Robert Rowantree
Majority	2,259	7.8	28.8	

Electorate: 41,566 Turnout: 29,172 (70.2%)

CALDER VALLEY, W Yorkshire. Con lost to Lab 97, must be target seat, mainly rural

Candidates 97	97 votes	97%	92%	Candidates
Christine McCafferty (Lab)	26,050	46.1	37.4	Chris McCafferty
Sir Donald Thompson (Con)	19,795	35.1	45.4	Sue Robson-Catling
Stephen Pearson (LD)	8,322	14.7	16.1	Michael Taylor
Majority	6,255	11	8	

Electorate: 74,901 Turnout: 56,466 (75.4%)

CAMBERWELL & PECKHAM, S London. Inner city, poor, high unemployment, safest Lab in London

Candidates 97	97 votes	97%	92%	Candidates
Harriet Harman (Lab)	19,734	69.3	60.4	Harriet Harman
Kim Humphreys (Con)	3,383	11.9	23.8	Johnathan Morgan
Nigel Williams (LD)	3,198	11.2	15.1	D McCarthy
Majority	16,351	57.4	36.6	

Electorate: 50,214 Turnout: 28,474 (56.7%)

CAMBRIDGE, Cambridgeshire. Lab made a stronghold since gain in 92, university, technology

Candidates 97	97 votes	97%	92%	Candidates
Anne Campbell (Lab)	27,436	53.4	39.7	Anne Campbell
David Platt (Con)	13,299	25.9	38.5	Graham Stuart
Geoffrey Heathcock (LD)	8,287	16.1	19.9	David Howarth
Majority	14,137	27.5	1.2	

Electorate: 71,669 Turnout: 51,339 (71.6%)

CAMBRIDGESHIRE NORTH EAST, Cambridgeshire. Strong Con seat, rural, flat fenland

Candidates 97	97 votes	97%	92%	Candidates
Malcolm Moss (Con)	23,855	43	53.5	Malcolm Moss
Virginia Bucknor (Lab)	18,754	33.8	13.6	Dil Owen
Andrew Nash (LD)	9,070	16.4	30.9	
Majority	5,101	9.2	22.6	

Electorate: 76,056 Turnout: 55,425 (72.9%)

CAMBRIDGESHIRE NORTH WEST, Cambridgeshire. Strong Con seat, rural, managerial, outside Peterborough

Candidates 97	97 votes	97%	92%	Candidates
Sir Brian Mawhinney (Con)	23,488	48.1	62.4	Sir Brian Mawhinney
Lee Steptoe (Lab)	15,734	32.2	25.9	Anthea Cox
Barbara McCoy (LD)	7,388	15.1	8.7	
Majority	7,754	15.9	36.5	

Electorate: 65,791 Turnout: 48,818 (74.2%)

CAMBRIDGESHIRE SOUTH, Cambridgeshire. Strong Con seat, rural, professional

Candidates 97	97 votes	97%	92%	Candidates
Andrew Lansley (Con)	22,572	42	58.5	Andrew Lansley
James Quinlan (LD)	13,860	25.8	24.9	Amanda Taylor
Tony Gray (Lab)	13,485	25.1	15.3	Joan Herbert
Majority	8,712	16.2	33.6	

Electorate: 69,850 Turnout: 53,683 (76.8%)

CAMBRIDGESHIRE SOUTH EAST, Cambridgeshire. Secure Con seat even in 97, semi-rural, professional

Candidates 97	97 votes	97%	92%	Candidates
James Paice (Con)	24,397	42.9	57.5	James Paice
Rex Collinson (Lab)	15,048	26.5	19.5	
S Brinton (LD)	14,246	25.1	21.2	Sal Brinton
Majority	9,349	16.4	36.3	

Electorate: 75,666 Turnout: 56,807 (75.1%)

CANNOCK CHASE, Staffordshire. Lab seat, power stations, small towns, intellectual MP Tony Wright

Candidates 97	97 votes	97%	92%	Candidates
Dr Tony Wright (Lab)	28,705	54.8	49	Dr Tony Wright
John Backhouse (Con)	14,227	27.2	38.2	Gavin Smithers
Richard Kirby (LD)	4,537	8.7	12.2	
Majority	14,478	27.6	10.8	

Electorate: 72,362 Turnout: 52,366 (72.4%)

CANTERBURY, Kent. Lab surge 97 but remained Con, mainly rural, university, middle class

Candidates 97	97 votes	97%	92%	Candidates
Julian Brazier (Con)	20,913	38.6	50.4	Julian Brazier
C Hall (Lab)	16,949	31.3	15.4	
Martin Vye (LD)	12,854	23.8	32.6	Peter Wales
Majority	3,964	7.3	17.8	

Electorate: 74,548 Turnout: 54,109 (72.6%)

CARDIFF CENTRAL, South Glamorgan. Lab marginal, LD target (winning in Welsh elections), residential

Candidates 97	97 votes	97%	92%	Candidates
Jon Owen Jones (Lab)	18,464	43.7	42	Jon Owen Jones
Jenny Randerson (LD)	10,541	24.9	21.4	Jenny Willott
David Melding (Con)	8,470	20	33.9	Gregory Walker
T Burns (SLP)	2,230	5.3	-	
Majority	7,923	18.8	8.1	

Electorate: 60,354 Turnout: 42,253 (70%)

CARDIFF NORTH, South Glamorgan. Prosperous city seat lost by Con 97, will stay Lab barring calamity

Candidates 97	97 votes	97%	92%	Candidates
Julie Morgan (Lab)	24,460	50.4	38.9	Julie Morgan
Gwilym Jones (Con)	16,334	33.7	45.1	Alastair Watson
Robyn Rowland (LD)	5,294	10.9	13.6	John Dixon
Dr C Palfrey (PC)	1,201	2.5	1.9	Sion Jobbins
Majority	8,126	16.7	6.2	

Electorate: 60,430 Turnout: 48,488 (80.2%)

CARDIFF SOUTH & PENARTH, South Glamorgan. Strong Lab seat, inner city, white collar

Candidates 97	97 votes	97%	92%	Candidates
Alun Michael (Lab)	22,647	53.4	55.5	Alun Michael
Caroline Roberts (Con)	8,786	20.7	33.6	Maureen Kelly-Owen
Dr Simon Wakefield (LD)	3,964	9.3	7.8	Rodney Berman
J Foreman (N Lab)	3,942	9.3	-	
Majority	13,861	32.7	21.9	

Electorate: 61,838 Turnout: 42,400 (68.6%)

CARDIFF WEST, South Glamorgan. Strong Lab seat, inner city, docks, MP leaving to lead Lab in Welsh Assembly

Candidates 97	97 votes	97%	92%	Candidates
Rhodri Morgan (Lab)	24,297	60.3	53.2	Kevin Brenan
Simon Hoare (Con)	8,669	21.5	32.9	Andrew Davies
Jacqui Gasson (LD)	4,366	10.8	10.9	Jacqui Gasson
G Carr (PC)	1,949	4.8	2.5	Delme Bowen
Majority	15,628	38.8	20.3	

Electorate: 58,198 Turnout: 40,277 (69.2%)

CARLISLE, Cumbria. Remote city with Lab tradition, Cons distant second

Candidates 97	97 votes	97%	92%	Candidates
Eric Martlew (Lab)	25,031	57.4	45.3	Eric Martlew
Richard Lawrence (Con)	12,641	29	41.2	Mike Mitchelson
Chris Mayho (LD)	4,576	10.5	13	
Majority	12,390	28.4	4.1	

Electorate: 59,917 Turnout: 43,607 (72.8%)

CARMARTHEN EAST & DINEFWR, W Wales. Only real PC target, likely to take from Lab, Welsh speaking, rural

Candidates 97	97 votes	97%	92%	Candidates
Dr Alan Wynne Williams (Lab)	17,907	42.9	41.5	Dr Alan Wynne Williams
Rhodri Glyn Thomas (PC)	14,457	34.6	29.1	Adam Price
Edmund Hayward (Con)	5,022	12	20.3	David N Thomas
Juliana Hughes (LD)	3,150	7.5	9.1	Dorian Evans
Majority	3,450	8.3	12.4	

Electorate: 53,079 Turnout: 41,732 (78.6%)

CARMARTHEN WEST & PEMBROKESHIRE, W Wales. Mixed, part urban Lab, part rural Pembrokeshire

Candidates 97	97 votes	97%	92%	Candidates
Nick Ainger (Lab)	20,956	49.1	38.5	Nick Ainger
Owen John Williams (Con)	11,335	26.6	35.5	Colin Schrader
Roy Llewellyn (PC)	5,402	12.7	15	Llyr Hughes Griffiths
Keith Evans (LD)	3,516	8.2	10.9	William Jeremy
Majority	9,621	22.5	3	

Electorate: 55,724 Turnout: 42,641 (76.5%)

CARRICK, CUMNOCK & DOON VALLEY, W Scotland. Strong Lab seat, ex-mining, coastal

Candidates 97	97 votes	97%	92%	Candidates
George Foulkes (Lab)	29,398	59.8	54.1	George Foulkes
Alistair Marshall (Con)	8,336	17	25.7	Gordon Miller
Christine Hutchison (SNP)	8,190	16.7	15	Tom Wilson
Derek Young (LD)	2,613	5.3	5.2	
Majority	21,062	42.8	28.4	

Electorate: 65,593 Turnout: 49,171 (75%)

CARSHALTON & WALLINGTON, S London. Suburban, LDs must fight to keep remarkable 97 gain

Candidates 97	97 votes	97%	92%	Candidates
Tom Brake (LD)	18,490	38.2	30.9	Tom Brake
Nigel Forman (Con)	16,223	33.5	49.7	Ken Andrew
Andrew Theobald (Lab)	11,565	23.9	17.7	
Majority	2,267	4.7	18.8	

Electorate: 66,038 Turnout: 48,423 (73.3%)

CASTLE POINT, Essex. Stunning Lab win 97, Con target, commuting, white collar

Candidates 97	97 votes	97%	92%	Candidates
Christine Butler (Lab)	20,605	42.4	24	Christine Butler
Dr Robert Spink (Con)	19,462	40.1	55.6	Dr Robert Spink
David Baker (LD)	4,477	9.2	19.2	Billy Boulton
Majority	1,143	2.3	31.6	

Electorate: 67,146 Turnout: 48,572 (72.3%)

CEREDIGION, W Wales. Once safe Liberal, recent PC success, rural, Welsh-speaking

Candidates 97	97 votes	97%	92%	Candidates
Cynog Dafis (PC)	16,728	41.6	30.9	Simon Thomas
Robert Harris (Lab)	9,767	24.3	18.6	David Grace
Dai Davies (LD)	6,616	16.5	26.5	Mark Williams
Felix Aubel (Con)	5,983	14.9	24	Paul Davies
Majority	6,961	17.3	4.5	

Electorate: 54,378 Turnout: 40,186 (73.9%)

CHARNWOOD, Leicestershire. Secure Con seat, commuting, managerial, between Leicester and Loughborough

Candidates 97	97 votes	97%	92%	Candidates
Stephen Dorrell (Con)	26,110	46.5	60.6	Stephen Dorrell
David Knaggs (Lab)	20,210	36	21.6	Sean Sheahan
Roger Wilson (LD)	7,224	12.9	17.8	
Majority	5,900	10.5	39	

Electorate: 72,692 Turnout: 56,173 (77.3%)

CHATHAM & AYLESFORD, Kent. Surprise Lab win 97, key Con target, mixed rural and urban

Candidates 97	97 votes	97%	92%	Candidates
Jonathan Shaw (Lab)	21,191	43.1	26.7	Jonathan Shaw
Richard Knox-Johnston (Con)	18,401	37.4	51.3	Sean Holden
Robin Murray (LD)	7,389	15	21.3	
Majority	2,790	5.7	24.6	

Electorate: 69,172 Turnout: 49,161 (71.1%)

CHEADLE, Greater Manchester. Prosperous, commuting, LD challenge but Cons expect to win

Candidates 97	97 votes	97%	92%	Candidates
Stephen Day (Con)	22,944	43.7	57.7	Stephen Day
Patsy Calton (LD)	19,755	37.7	29.6	Patsy Calton
Paul Diggett (Lab)	8,253	15.7	12.4	Howard Dawber
Majority	3,189	6	28.1	

Electorate: 67,627 Turnout: 52,463 (77.6%)

CHELMSFORD WEST, Essex. LD challenge to Con blocked by Lab surge 97, mainly rural, professional

Candidates 97	97 votes	97%	92%	Candidates
Simon Burns (Con)	23,781	40.6	54.8	Simon Burns
Martin Bracken (LD)	17,090	29.2	28.9	Stephen Robinson
Dr Roy Chad (Lab)	15,436	26.4	15.1	Adrian Longden
Majority	6,691	11.4	25.9	

Electorate: 76,086 Turnout: 58,577 (77%)

CHELTENHAM, Gloucestershire. Grand ex-Con town now looks secure for LD MP

Candidates 97	97 votes	97%	92%	Candidates
Nigel Jones (LD)	24,877	49.5	47.6	Nigel Jones
John Todman (Con)	18,232	36.2	44.2	Rob Garnham
Barry Leach (Lab)	5,100	10.1	6.7	
Majority	6,645	13.3	3.4	

Electorate: 67,950 Turnout: 50,303 (74%)

CHESHAM & AMERSHAM, Buckinghamshire. Strong Con seat, stockbroker belt, leafy hills

Candidates 97	97 votes	97%	92%	Candidates
Cheryl Gillan (Con)	26,298	50.4	63.4	Cheryl Gillan
M Brand (LD)	12,439	23.8	24.5	John Ford
P Farrelly (Lab)	10,240	19.6	10.4	Ken Hulme
Majority	13,859	26.6	38.9	

Electorate: 69,244 Turnout: 52,197 (75.4%)

CHESTER, CITY OF, Cheshire. Con lost 97, Lab now look secure, mixed urban voters

Candidates 97	97 votes	97%	92%	Candidates
Christine Russell (Lab)	29,806	53	40.6	Christine Russell
Gyles Brandreth (Con)	19,253	34.2	44.7	David Jones
David Simpson (LD)	5,353	9.5	13.6	Eleanor Burnham
Majority	10,553	18.8	4.1	

Electorate: 71,730 Turnout: 56,257 (78.4%)

CHESTERFIELD, Derbyshire. Ex-Tony Benn, LD target, new Lab, LD candidates

Candidates 97	97 votes	97%	92%	Candidates
Tony Benn (Lab)	26,105	50.8	47.3	Reg Race
Tony Rogers (LD)	20,330	39.6	35.8	Paul Holmes
Martin Potter (Con)	4,752	9.2	16.9	Simon Hitchcock
Majority	5775	11.2	11.5	

Electorate: 72,472 Turnout: 51,389 (70.9%)

CHICHESTER, W Sussex. Smart, safe Con seat, mainly rural, LDs distant second

Candidates 97	97 votes	97%	92%	Candidates
Andrew Tyrie (Con)	25,895	46.4	59.3	Andrew Tyrie
Dr Peter Gardiner (LD)	16,161	29	26.6	Lynne Ravenscroft
Charlie Smith (Lab)	9,605	17.2	11.4	Celia Barlow
Majority	9,734	17.4	32.7	

Electorate: 74,489 Turnout: 55,779 (74.9%)

CHINGFORD & WOODFORD GREEN, N London. Con, white collar, clever right-wing MP

Candidates 97	97 votes	97%	92%	Candidates
Iain Duncan Smith (Con)	21,109	47.5	61.4	Iain Duncan Smith
Tommy Hutchinson (Lab)	15,395	34.6	21	
Geoffrey Seeff (LD)	6,885	15.5	14.3	John Beanse
Majority	5,714	12.9	40.4	

Electorate: 62,904 Turnout: 44,448 (70.7%)

CHIPPING BARNET, N London. Con just held on 97, outer London, commuting, middle class

Candidates 97	97 votes	97%	92%	Candidates
Sydney Chapman (Con)	21,317	43	56.6	Sydney Chapman
Geoff Cooke (Lab)	20,282	40.9	26.2	
Sean Hooker (LD)	6,121	12.3	16.1	Sean Hooker
Majority	1,035	2.1	30.4	

Electorate: 69,049 Turnout: 49,565 (71.8%)

CHORLEY, Lancashire. Bellwether seat, now looks secure for Lab, semi-urban

Candidates 97	97 votes	97%	92%	Candidates
Lindsay Hoyle (Lab)	30,607	53	41.6	Lindsay Hoyle
Den Dover (Con)	20,737	35.9	45.8	Peter Booth
Simon Jones (LD)	4,900	8.5	12	Stephen Fenn
Majority	9,870	17.1	4.2	

Electorate: 74,387 Turnout: 57,706 (77.6%)

CHRISTCHURCH, Dorset. LD won in 93 by-election, Con retook 97, seaside, pensioners

Candidates 97	97 votes	97%	92%	Candidates
Christopher Chope (Con)	26,095	46.4	63.8	Christopher Chope
Diana Maddock (LD)	23,930	42.6	23.4	Dorothy Webb
Charles Mannan (Lab)	3,884	6.9	12.1	
Majority	2,165	3.8	40.4	

Electorate: 71,488 Turnout: 56,199 (78.6%)

CITIES OF LONDON & WESTMINSTER, Rare inner city safe Con seat, famous London sights

Candidates 97	97 votes	97%	92%	Candidates
Peter Brooke (Con)	18,981	47.3	59.3	Mark Field
Kate Green (Lab)	14,100	35.1	24.1	Mike Katz
Michael Dumigan (LD)	4,933	12.3	14.1	Martin Horwood
Majority	4,881	12.2	35.2	

Electorate: 69,047 Turnout: 40,155 (58.2%)

CLEETHORPES, Humberside. Once Con, now Lab likely hold, villages outside Grimsby, coast

Candidates 97	97 votes	97%	92%	Candidates
Shona McIsaac (Lab)	26,058	51.6	48	Shona McIsaac
Michael Brown (Con)	16,882	33.4	35.9	Stephen Howd
K Melton (LD)	5,746	11.4	14.7	Gordon Smith
Majority	9,176	18.2	12.1	

Electorate: 68,763 Turnout: 50,473 (73.4%)

CLYDEBANK & MILNGAVIE, W Scotland. Strong Lab seat, shipbuilding

Candidates 97	97 votes	97%	92%	Candidates
Tony Worthington (Lab)	21,583	55.2	50.3	Tony Worthington
Jim Yuill (SNP)	8,263	21.1	18.5	Jim Yuill
Nancy Morgan (Con)	4,885	12.5	21.5	Katherine Pickering
Keith Moody (LD)	4,086	10.5	9.5	Rod Ackland
Majority	13,320	34.1	28.8	

Electorate: 52,092 Turnout: 39,086 (75%)

CLYDESDALE, W Scotland. Strong Lab seat, ex-mining

Candidates 97	97 votes	97%	92%	Candidates
Jimmy Hood (Lab)	23,859	52.5	44.6	Jimmy Hood
Andrew Doig (SNP)	10,050	22.1	23.1	Jim Wright
Mark Izatt (Con)	7,396	16.3	23.4	Kevin Newton
S Grieve (LD)	3,796	8.4	8.2	
Majority	13,809	30.4	21.2	

Electorate: 63,428 Turnout: 45,412 (71.6%)

CLWYD SOUTH, NE Wales. Scenic, rugged, Welsh-speaking north Wales, safe Lab

Candidates 97	97 votes	97%	92%	Candidates
Martyn Jones (Lab)	22,901	58.1	49.8	Martyn Jones
Boris Johnson (Con)	9,091	23.1	30.2	Tom Biggins
Andrew Chadwick (LD)	3,684	9.4	11.1	
Gareth Williams (PC)	2,500	6.3	7.9	Dyfed Edwards
Majority	13,810	35	19.6	

Electorate: 53,495 Turnout: 39,383 (73.6%)

CLWYD WEST, NE Wales. 3-way marginal, Lab gain 97, could go back to Con or even PC

Candidates 97	97 votes	97%	92%	Candidates
Gareth Thomas (Lab)	14,918	37.1	30.9	Gareth Thomas
Rod Richards (Con)	13,070	32.5	48.5	Jimmie James
Eryl Williams (PC)	5,421	13.5	4.6	Elfred Williams
Gwyn Williams (LD)	5,151	12.8	15.7	Bobbie Feeley
Majority	1,848	4.6	17.6	

Electorate: 53,467 Turnout: 40,257 (75.3%)

COATBRIDGE & CHRYSTON, W Scotland. Strong Lab seat, industrial

Candidates 97	97 votes	97%	92%	Candidates
Tom Clarke (Lab)	25,694	68.3	61.8	Tom Clarke
Brian Nugent (SNP)	6,402	17	16.8	Peter Kearney
Andrew Wauchope (Con)	3,216	8.6	15.5	Patrick Ross-Taylor
Morag Daly (LD)	2,048	5.4	5.9	Alistair Tough
Majority	19,292	51.3	45	

Electorate: 52,024 Turnout: 37,612 (72.3%)

COLCHESTER, Essex. Urban, LD gain 97, could go Con or even Lab

Candidates 97	97 votes	97%	92%	Candidates
Bob Russell (LD)	17,886	34.4	32.7	Bob Russell
Stephan Shakespeare (Con)	16,305	31.4	42	Kevin Bentley
Roderick Green (Lab)	15,891	30.6	24.1	
Majority	1,581	3	9.3	

Electorate: 74,743 Turnout: 52,006 (69.6%)

COLNE VALLEY, W Yorkshire. Historic 3-way marginal, Lab gain 97, could just go Con, LDs finished

Candidates 97	97 votes	97%	92%	Candidates
Kali Mountford (Lab)	23,285	41.3	29.8	Kali Mountford
Graham Riddick (Con)	18,445	32.7	42	Philip Davies
Nigel Priestley (LD)	12,755	22.6	27	Gordon Beever
Majority	4,840	8.6	12.2	

Electorate: 73,338 Turnout: 56,411 (76.9%)

CONGLETON, Cheshire. Con seat, LD longshot, mainly rural, prosperous Cheshire middle class

Candidates 97	97 votes	97%	92%	Candidates
Ann Winterton (Con)	22,012	41.2	48.5	Ann Winterton
Joan Walmsley (LD)	15,882	29.7	31.7	David Lloyd-Griffiths
Helen Scholey (Lab)	14,713	27.5	19.2	John Flanagan
Majority	6,130	11.5	16.8	

Electorate: 68,873 Turnout: 53,419 (77.6%)

CONWY, NW Wales. Rare 4-way marginal, PC won Welsh elections 99, Lab took from Con 97, LDs just lose out

Candidates 97	97 votes	97%	92%	Candidates
Betty Williams (Lab)	14,561	35	25.8	Betty Williams
Rev Roger Roberts (LD)	12,965	31.2	31.4	Vicky Macdonald
D Jones (Con)	10,085	24.3	33.7	David Logan
Rhodri Davies (PC)	2,844	6.8	7.4	Ann Davies
Majority	1,596	3.8	2.3	

Electorate: 55,092 Turnout: 41,560 (75.4%)

COPELAND, Cumbria. Lakes fells plus remote urban coast and nuclear power, secure Lab

Candidates 97	97 votes	97%	92%	Candidates
Dr Jack Cunningham (Lab)	24,077	58.2	48.7	Dr Jack Cunningham
Andrew Cumpsty (Con)	12,081	29.2	43.4	Mike Graham
Roger Putnam (LD)	3,814	9.2	7.6	Mark Gayler
Majority	11,996	29	5.3	

Electorate: 54,263 Turnout: 41,345 (76.2%)

CORBY, Northamptonshire. Once steel town, then Con marginal, now looks secure for Lab

Candidates 97	97 votes	97%	92%	Candidates
Phil Hope (Lab)	29,888	55.4	43.9	Phil Hope
William Powell (Con)	18,028	33.4	44.5	Andrew Griffith
Ian Hankinson (LD)	4,045	7.5	10.2	Kevin Scudder
Majority	11,860	22	0.6	

Electorate: 69,252 Turnout: 53,957 (77.9%)

CORNWALL NORTH, Cornwall. Isolated, poor, Cornish coast, LD Paul Tyler made it LD bastion

Candidates 97	97 votes	97%	92%	Candidates
Paul Tyler (LD)	31,100	53.2	6.6	Paul Tyler
Nigel Linacre (Con)	17,253	29.5	44.3	John Weller
Annie Lindo (Lab)	5,523	9.4	47.4	
Majority	13,847	23.7	3.1	

Electorate: 80,076 Turnout: 58,581 (73.2%)

CORNWALL SOUTH EAST, Cornwall. LD took from Con 97, now Con longshot, rural, pretty sea ports

Candidates 97	97 votes	97%	92%	Candidates
Colin Breed (LD)	27,044	47.1	38.1	Colin Breed
Warwick Lightfoot (Con)	20,564	35.8	51	Ashley Gray
Dorothy Kirk (Lab)	7,358	12.8	9.2	Bill Stevens
Majority	6,480	11.3	12.9	

Electorate: 75,825 Turnout: 57,432 (75.7%)

COTSWOLD, Gloucestershire. Strong Con seat, rural, professional, contains Cirencester, Tewkesbury

Candidates 97	97 votes	97%	92%	Candidates
Geoffrey Clifton-Brown (Con)	23,698	46.4	54.4	Geoffrey Clifton-Brown
David Gayler (LD)	11,733	23	33.4	Angela Lawrence
David Elwell (Lab)	11,608	22.7	10.9	Richard Wilkins
Majority	11,965	23.4	21	

Electorate: 67,333 Turnout: 51,121 (75.9%)

COVENTRY NORTH EAST, W Midlands. Strong Lab seat, urban, large Asian community

Candidates 97	97 votes	97%	92%	Candidates
Bob Ainsworth (Lab)	31,856	66.2	49.6	Bob Ainsworth
Michael Barnett (Con)	9,287	19.3	28	Gordon Bell
Geoff Sewards (LD)	3,866	8	10.5	Dr Napier Penlington
Majority	22,569	46.9	21.6	

Electorate: 74,274 Turnout: 48,085 (64.7%)

COVENTRY NORTH WEST, W Midlands. Longtime Lab seat, urban, some Con voters

Candidates 97	97 votes	97%	92%	Candidates
Geoffrey Robinson (Lab)	30,901	56.9	51.2	Geoffrey Robinson
Paul Bartlett (Con)	14,300	26.3	37	Andrew Fairburn
Dr Napier Penlingotn (LD)	5,690	10.5	11.8	Geoffrey Sewards
Majority	16,601	30.6	14.2	

Electorate: 76,439 Turnout: 54,322 (71.1%)

COVENTRY SOUTH, W Midlands. Secure for Lab urban, professional, university

Candidates 97	97 votes	97%	92%	Candidates
James Cunningham (Lab)	25,511	50.9	34.7	James Cunningham
Paul Ivey (Con)	14,558	29	39.8	Heather Wheeler
Gordon MacDonald (LD)	4,617	9.2	9.2	
Majority	10,953	21.9	5.1	

Electorate: 71,826 Turnout: 50,124 (69.8%)

CRAWLEY, W Sussex. New town, white collar, Gatwick airport, should stay Lab

Candidates 97	97 votes	97%	92%	Candidates
Laura Moffatt (Lab)	27,750	55	40.3	Laura Moffatt
Josephine Crabb (Con)	16,043	31.8	44	Henry Smith
Harold De Souza (LD)	4,141	8.2	14.5	
Majority	11,707	23.2	3.7	

Electorate: 69,040 Turnout: 50,417 (73%)

CREWE & NANTWICH, Cheshire. Once Lab marginal, now very safe, twin towns

Candidates 97	97 votes	97%	92%	Candidates
Gwyneth Dunwoody (Lab)	29,460	58.2	47.6	Gwyneth Dunwoody
Michael Loveridge (Con)	13,662	27	38.9	Donald Potter
David Cannon (LD)	5,940	11.7	12.5	David Cannon
Majority	15,798	31.2	8.7	

Electorate: 68,694 Turnout: 50,605 (73.7%)

CROSBY, Merseyside. Massive Lab gain 97, Cons need 8% swing to retake, Liverpool commuters

Candidates 97	97 votes	97%	92%	Candidates
Claire Curtis-Thomas (Lab)	22,549	51.1	28.7	Claire Curtis-Thomas
Malcolm Thornton (Con)	15,367	34.8	48.7	Robert Collinson
Paul McVey (LD)	5,080	11.5	20	Tim Drake
Majority	7,182	16.3	20	

Electorate: 57,190 Turnout: 44,141 (77.2%)

CROYDON CENTRAL, S London. Lab gain 97, leading Con target, urban, white collar

Candidates 97	97 votes	97%	92%	Candidates
Geraint Davies (Lab)	25,432	45.6	31.5	Geraint Davies
David Congdon (Con)	21,535	38.6	55.5	David Congdon
George Schlich (LD)	6,061	10.9	13	Paul Booth
Majority	3,897	7	24	

Electorate: 80,152 Turnout: 55,799 (69.6%)

CROYDON NORTH, S London. Now safe Lab seat, Con revival looks distant prospect, suburban

Candidates 97	97 votes	97%	92%	Candidates
Malcolm Wicks (Lab)	32,672	62.2	44.4	Malcolm Wicks
Ian Martin (Con)	14,274	27.2	44.7	Simon Allison
Martin Morris (LD)	4,066	7.7	10.9	Sandra Lawman
Majority	18,398	35	0.3	

Electorate: 77,063 Turnout: 52,563 (68.2%)

CROYDON SOUTH, S London. Strong Con seat, even in 97, outer suburbs, managerial

Candidates 97	97 votes	97%	92%	Candidates
Richard Ottaway (Con)	25,649	47.3	61.7	Richard Ottaway
Charlie Burling (Lab)	13,719	25.3	16.3	Gerry Ryan
Steven Gauge (LD)	11,441	21.1	21.6	Anne Gallop
Majority	11,930	22	40.1	

Electorate: 73,787 Turnout: 54,199 (73.5%)

CUMBERNAULD & KILSYTH, W Scotland. Strong Lab seat, partly new town, SNP remote second

Candidates 97	97 votes	97%	92%	Candidates
Rosemary McKenna (Lab)	21,141	58.7	54	Rosemary McKenna
Colin Barrie (SNP)	10,013	27.8	28.9	David McGlashan
Ian Sewell (Con)	2,441	6.8	11.3	
J Biggam (LD)	1,368	3.8	5.8	
Majority	11,128	30.9	25.1	

Electorate: 48,032 Turnout: 36,024 (75%)

CUNNINGHAME NORTH, W Scotland. Lab, once Con target but no longer, ex-mining

Candidates 97	97 votes	97%	92%	Candidates
Brian Wilson	20,686	50.3	41	Brian Wilson
Margaret Mitchell (Con)	9,647	23.5	34.1	Dorothy Luckhurst
Kim Nicoll (SNP)	7,584	18.4	18.2	Campbell Martin
Karen Freel (LD)	2,271	5.5	6.7	
Majority	11,039	26.8	6.9	

Electorate: 55,526 Turnout: 41,129 (74.1%)

CUNNINGHAME SOUTH, W Scotland. Totally secure Lab seat, industrial

Candidates 97	97 votes	97%	92%	Candidates
Brian Donohoe (Lab)	22,233	62.7	52.9	Brian Donohoe
Margaret Burgess (SNP)	7,364	20.8	24.2	
Pamela Paterson (Con)	3,571	10.1	16.3	Eveline Archer
Erland Watson (LD)	1,604	4.5	6.2	
Majority	14,869	41.9	28.7	

Electorate: 49,543 Turnout: 35,444 (71.5%)

CYNON VALLEY, S Wales. Small valleys seat, traditionally Lab, ex-mining, working class

Candidates 97	97 votes	97%	92%	Candidates
Ann Clwyd (Lab)	23,307	69.7	69.1	Ann Clwyd
Alun Davies (PC)	3,552	10.6	11	Alun Davies
Huw Price (LD)	3,459	10.3	7	Ian Parry
Andrew Smith (Con)	2,262	6.8	12.9	Julian Waters
Majority	19,755	59.1	56.2	

Electorate: 48,286 Turnout: 33,424 (69.2%)

DAGENHAM, E London. Hit by part-closure of Ford plant but will stay Lab, Cons now nowhere

Candidates 97	97 votes	97%	92%	Candidates
Judith Church (Lab)	23,759	65.7	51.7	Jon Cruddas
James Fairre (Con)	6,705	18.5	36.9	Michael White
Tom Dobrashian (LD)	2,704	7.5	11.5	
Majority	17,054	47.2	14.8	

Electorate: 58,573 Turnout: 36,163 (61.7%)

DARLINGTON, Durham. Once marginal, now safe for Blairite minister Alan Milburn, urban, light industry

Candidates 97	97 votes	97%	92%	Candidates
Alan Milburn (Lab)	29,658	61.6	48.1	Alan Milburn
Peter Scrope (Con)	13,633	28.3	43	Tony Richmond
Les Boxell (LD)	3,483	7.2	8.3	Robert Adamson
Majority	16,025	33.3	5.1	

Electorate: 65,139 Turnout: 48,173 (74%)

DARTFORD, Kent. Lab gain 97, likely to be close, partly rural, white collar

Candidates 97	97 votes	97%	92%	Candidates
Dr Howard Stoate (Lab)	25,278	48.6	36.2	Dr Howard Stoate
Robert Dunn (Con)	20,950	40.3	50.9	Robert Dunn
Dorothy Webb (LD)	4,872	9.4	12.1	
Majority	4,328	8.3	14.7	

Electorate: 69,726 Turnout: 51,998 (74.6%)

DAVENTRY, Northamptonshire. Only Con win in Northants in 97, rural, middle class

Candidates 97	97 votes	97%	92%	Candidates
Timothy Boswell (Con)	28,615	46.3	57.8	Timothy Boswell
Ken Ritchie (Lab)	21,237	34.4	23.9	Kevin Quigley
John Gordon (LD)	9,233	15	17.6	Jamie Calder
Majority	7,378	11.9	33.9	

Electorate: 80,151 Turnout: 61,750 (77%)

DELYN, NE Wales. Con until 92, secure Lab since, industrial, coastal north Wales

Candidates 97	97 votes	97%	92%	Candidates
David Hanson (Lab)	23,300	57.2	46.9	David Hanson
Karen Lumley (Con)	10,607	26	39.6	Paul Brierley
Phil Lloyd (LD)	4,160	10.2	11	Tudor Jones
A Drake (PC)	1,558	3.8	2.5	Paul Rowlinson
Majority	12,693	31.2	7.3	

Electorate: 53,693 Turnout: 40,742 (75.9%)

DENTON & REDDISH, Greater Manchester. Lab seat, urban, skilled manual

Candidates 97	97 votes	97%	92%	Candidates
Andrew Bennett (Lab)	30,137	65.4	53	Andrew Bennett
Barbara Nutt (Con)	9,826	21.3	33.9	Paul Newman
Iain Donaldson (LD)	6,121	13.3	10	
Majority	20,311	44.1	19.1	

Electorate: 68,866 Turnout: 46,084 (66.9%)

DERBY NORTH, Derbyshire. Substantial Lab gain 97, mainly suburban, Cons distant prospect

Candidates 97	97 votes	97%	92%	Candidates
Bob Laxton (Lab)	29,844	53.2	40.9	Bob Laxton
Gregory Knight (Con)	19,229	34.3	48.4	Barry Holden
Robert Charlesworth (LD)	5,059	9	9.6	Robert Charlesworth
Majority	10,615	18.9	7.5	

Electorate: 76,115 Turnout: 56,143 (73.8%)

DERBY SOUTH, Derbyshire. Long term Lab seat, no longer marginal, urban, large Asian community

Candidates 97	97 votes	97%	92%	Candidates
Margaret Beckett (Lab)	29,154	56.3	48.3	Margaret Beckett
Javed Arain (Con)	13,048	25.2	40.9	Simon Spencer
Jeremy Beckett (LD)	7,438	14.4	10.8	Anders Hanson
Majority	16,106	31.1	7.4	
Electorate: 76,386 Turnout: 51,819 (67.8%)				

DERBYSHIRE NORTH EAST, Derbyshire. Always Lab seat, once mining, some Con voters

Candidates 97	97 votes	97%	92%	Candidates
Harry Barnes (Lab)	31,425	60.5	48.8	Harry Barnes
Simon Elliott (Con)	13,104	25.2	38.2	James Hollingsworth
Stephen Hardy (LD)	7,450	14.3	13	
Majority	18,321	35.3	10.6	
Electorate: 71,653 Turnout: 51,979 (72.5%)				

DERBYSHIRE SOUTH, Derbyshire. Former semi-rural base for Edwina Currie, now looks Lab certainty

Candidates 97	97 votes	97%	92%	Candidates
Mark Todd (Lab)	32,709	54.5	44.1	Mark Todd
Edwina Currie (Con)	18,742	31.3	47.2	James Hakewill
Rob Renold (LD)	5,408	9	8.3	
Majority	13,967	23.2	3.1	
Electorate: 76,672 Turnout: 59,967 (78.2%)				

DERBYSHIRE WEST, Derbyshire. White peak, rural, small towns, always Con, Lab surge 97, LDs faded

Candidates 97	97 votes	97%	92%	Candidates
Patrick McLoughlin (Con)	23,945	42.1	54.2	Patrick McLoughlin
Steve Clamp (Lab)	19,060	33.5	22.3	Steve Clamp
Christopher Seeley (LD)	9,940	17.5	23.5	Jeremy Beckett
Majority	4,885	8.6	30.7	
Electorate: 72,716 Turnout: 56,883 (78.2%)				

DEVIZES, Wiltshire. Strong Con seat, rural, onetime LD hope

Candidates 97	97 votes	97%	92%	Candidates
Michael Ancram (Con)	25,710	42.8	53	Michael Ancram
Tony Vickers (LD)	15,928	26.5	32.4	Helen Frances
Frank Jeffrey (Lab)	14,551	24.2	12	Aubrey Ross
Majority	9,782	16.3	20.6	
Electorate: 80,383 Turnout: 60,036 (74.7%)				

DEVON EAST, Devon. Strong Con seat, pensioners, rural, pensioners

Candidates 97	97 votes	97%	92%	Candidates
Peter Emery (Con)	22,797	43.4	12.2	Hugo Swire
Rachel Tretheway (LD)	15,308	29.1	52.5	Tim Dumper
Andrew Siantonas (Lab)	9,292	17.7	27.1	
Majority	7,489	14.3	25.4	
Electorate: 69,094 Turnout: 52,550 (76.1%)				

DEVON NORTH, Devon. Seaside and farms, ex-Jeremy Thorpe, now LD again, Con vote remains

Candidates 97	97 votes	97%	92%	Candidates
Nick Harvey (LD)	27,824	50.8	47.1	Nick Harvey
Richard Ashworth (Con)	21,643	39.5	45.7	Clive Allen
Annie Brenton (Lab)	5,347	9.8	5.9	
Majority	6,181	11.3	1.4	
Electorate: 70,350 Turnout: 54,834 (77.9%)				

DEVON SOUTH WEST, Devon. Very Con, even in 97, part Plymouth, part rural and coast

Candidates 97	97 votes	97%	92%	Candidates
Gary Streeter (Con)	22,659	42.9	57.6	Gary Streeter
Chris Mavin (Lab)	15,262	28.9	15.9	Chris Mavin
Keith Baldry (LD)	12,542	23.8	25.6	Phil Hutty
Majority	7,397	14	32	
Electorate: 69,293 Turnout: 52,817 (76.2%)				

DEWSBURY, W Yorkshire. Almost a marginal, though Lab since 87, urban, large Asian community

Candidates 97	97 votes	97%	92%	Candidates
Ann Taylor (Lab)	21,286	49.4	47.3	Ann Taylor
Paul McCormick (Con)	12,963	30.1	40	Robert Cole
Kingsley Hill (LD)	4,422	10.3	9.9	Ian Cuthbertson
Majority	8,323	19.3	7.3	

Electorate: 61,523 Turnout: 43,075 (70%)

DON VALLEY, S Yorkshire. Changing ex-mining seat outside Doncaster, secure Lab but some Con votes

Candidates 97	97 votes	97%	92%	Candidates
Caroline Flint (Lab)	25,376	58.3	50.6	Caroline Flint
Clare Gledhill (Con)	10,717	24.6	36.8	James Browne
Paul Johnston (LD)	4,238	9.7	11.1	Philip Smith
Majority	14,659	33.7	13.8	

Electorate: 65,642 Turnout: 43,557 (66.4%)

DONCASTER CENTRAL, S Yorkshire. Strong Lab seat, industrial, developing town

Candidates 97	97 votes	97%	92%	Candidates
Rosie Winterton (Lab)	26,961	62.1	54.3	Rosie Winterton
David Turtle (Con)	9,105	21	33.5	Gary Meggitt
Simon Tarry (LD)	4,091	9.4	11.8	
Majority	17,856	41.1	20.8	

Electorate: 67,965 Turnout: 43,443 (63.9%)

DONCASTER NORTH, S Yorkshire. Strong Lab seat, ex-mining, working class

Candidates 97	97 votes	97%	92%	Candidates
Kevin Hughes (Lab)	27,843	69.8	64.4	Kevin Hughes
Peter Kennerley (Con)	5,906	14.8	22.3	Anita Kapoor
Michael Cook (LD)	3,369	8.4	13.3	Colin Ross
Majority	21,937	55	42.1	

Electorate: 63,018 Turnout: 39,888 (63.3%)

DORSET MID & POOLE NORTH, Dorset. LD hope in 97, Con came out just ahead, suburban and rural

Candidates 97	97 votes	97%	92%	Candidates
Christopher Fraser (Con)	20,632	40.7	50.1	Christopher Fraser
Alan Leaman (LD)	19,951	39.3	38	Annette Brokke
David Collis (Lab)	8,014	15.8	11.9	
Majority	681	1.4	12.1	

Electorate: 67,049 Turnout: 50,733 (75.7%)

DORSET NORTH, Dorset. Con for 50 years but LD always second, worth watching, market towns, farms

Candidates 97	97 votes	97%	92%	Candidates
Robert Walter (Con)	23,294	44.3	56.5	Robert Walter
Paula Yates (LD)	20,548	39.1	37.4	Emily Gasson
John Fitzmaurice (Lab)	5,380	10.2	6	Mark Wareham
Majority	2,746	5.2	19.1	

Electorate: 68,922 Turnout: 52,587 (76.3%)

DORSET SOUTH, Dorset. Weymouth, Portland and rural surrounds, strong Lab vote 97 but Con just held

Candidates 97	97 votes	97%	92%	Candidates
Ian Bruce (Con)	17,755	36.1	50.9	Ian Bruce
Jim Knight (Lab)	17,678	35.9	20.8	Jim Knight
Michael Plummer (LD)	9,936	20.2	26.6	Andrew Canning
Majority	77	0.2	24.3	

Electorate: 66,317 Turnout: 49,182 (74.2%)

DORSET WEST, Dorset. Very rural seat, some seaside towns, LD target, Con held 97

Candidates 97	97 votes	97%	92%	Candidates
Oliver Letwin (Con)	22,036	41.1	50.9	Oliver Letwin
Robin Legg (LD)	20,196	37.7	36.2	Simon Green
Robert Bygraves (Lab)	9,491	17.7	13.0	Richard Hyde
Majority	1,840	3.4	14.7	

Electorate: 70,369 Turnout: 53,552 (76.1%)

DOVER, Kent. Port town, hit by Channel Tunnel, massive Lab gain from Con in 97

Candidates 97	97 votes	97%	92%	Candidates
Gwyn Prosser (Lab)	29,535	54.5	11.9	Gwyn Prosser
David Shaw (Con)	17,796	32.8	50.1	Paul Watkins
Mark Corney (LD)	4,302	7.9	38	Anthony Hook
Majority	11,739	21.7	12.1	

Electorate: 68,669 Turnout: 54,200 (78.9%)

DOWN NORTH, Northern Ireland. Curious independent tradition, now UKU, richest in province

Candidates 97	97 votes	97%	92%	Candidates
Robert McCartney (UKU)	12,817	35.1	40.7	Robert McCartney
Alan McFarland (UUP)	11,368	31.1	–	Peter Weir
Sir Oliver Napier (Alliance)	7,554	20.7	15.7	Stephen Farry
L Fee (Con)	1,810	4.9	–	
Majority	1,449	4	40.7	

Electorate: 63,010 Turnout: 36,566 (58%)

DOWN SOUTH, Northern Ireland. SDLP seat, mainly rural, some unionist votes too

Candidates 97	97 votes	97%	92%	Candidates
Edward McGrady (SDLP)	26,181	52.9	56.2	Edward McGrady
Dermot Nesbitt (UUP)	16,248	32.8	35.4	Dermot Nesbitt
Mick Murphy (SF)	5,127	10.4	3.6	Mick Murphy
J Crozier (Alliance)	1,711	3.5	2.5	
Majority	9,933	20.1	20.8	

Electorate: 69,855 Turnout: 49,486 (70.8%)

DUDLEY NORTH, W Midlands. Easy Lab win in 97 but could go Con in a good year, urban

Candidates 97	97 votes	97%	92%	Candidates
Ross Cranston (Lab)	24,471	51.2	45.5	Ross Cranston
Charles MacNamara (Con)	15,014	31.4	43.8	Andrew Griffiths
Gerry Lewis (LD)	3,939	8.2	9.7	Richard Burt
Majority	9,457	19.8	1.7	

Electorate: 68,835 Turnout: 47,808 (69.5%)

DUDLEY SOUTH, W Midlands. Once thought marginal, now seems safe Lab, urban Black Country

Candidates 97	97 votes	97%	92%	Candidates
Ian Pearson (Lab)	27,124	56.6	47	Ian Pearson
Mark Simpson (Con)	14,097	29.4	41.9	Jason Sugarman
Richard Burt (LD)	5,214	10.9	11.1	Lorely Burt
Majority	13,027	27.2	5.1	

Electorate: 66,731 Turnout: 47,902 (71.8%)

DULWICH & WEST NORWOOD, S London. Suburban, middle class but also secure Lab

Candidates 97	97 votes	97%	92%	Candidates
Tessa Jowell (Lab)	27,807	61	46.3	Tessa Jowell
Roger Gough (Con)	11,038	24.2	42.8	Nick Vineall
Susan Kramer (LD)	4,916	10.8	9.8	Caroline Pidgeon
Majority	16,769	36.8	3.5	

Electorate: 69,655 Turnout: 45,615 (65.5%)

DUMBARTON, W Scotland. Lab, ex-textile industry, SNP outside bet

Candidates 97	97 votes	97%	92%	Candidates
John McFall (Lab)	20,470	49.6	43.6	John McFall
Bill Mackechnie (SNP)	9,587	23.2	18.4	Iain Robertson
Peter Ramsay (Con)	7,283	17.6	29.7	Peter Ramsay
Alan Reid (LD)	3,144	7.6	7.8	
Majority	10,883	26.4	13.9	

Electorate: 56,229 Turnout: 41,264 (73.4%)

DUMFRIES, SW Scotland. Once Con (to 97) southern Scottish seat, inc. Gretna Green, hit by foot and mouth

Candidates 97	97 votes	97%	92%	Candidates
Russell Brown (Lab)	23,528	47.5	29.6	Russell Brown
Struan Stevenson (Con)	13,885	28	43.1	John Charteris
Robert Higgins (SNP)	5,977	12.1	14.8	Robert Fairbairn
Neil Wallace (LD)	5,487	11.1	11.7	John Ross Scott
Majority	9,643	19.5	13.5	

Electorate: 62,759 Turnout: 49,527 (78.9%)

DUNDEE EAST, NE Scotland. Lab seat, SNP longshot, urban

Candidates 97	97 votes	97%	92%	Candidates
John McAllion (Lab)	20,718	51.1	44.3	Iain Luke
Shona Robison (SNP)	10,757	26.5	32.1	Stewart Hosie
Bruce Mackie (Con)	6,397	15.8	18.4	Alan Donnelly
Dr G Saluja (LD)	1,677	4.1	4.3	Raymond Lawrie
Majority	9,961	24.6	12.2	

Electorate: 58,388 Turnout: 40,528 (69.4%)

DUNDEE WEST, NE Scotland. Strong Lab seat, urban

Candidates 97	97 votes	97%	92%	Candidates
Ernie Ross (Lab)	20,875	53.8	47.7	Ernie Ross
John Dorward (SNP)	9,016	23.2	24.6	Gordon Archer
Neil Powrie (Con)	5,105	13.2	18.8	Ian Hail
Dr Elizabeth Dick (LD)	2,972	7.7	7.5	Dr Elizabeth Dick
Majority	11,859	30.6	23.1	

Electorate: 57,346 Turnout: 38,807 (67.7%)

DUNFERMLINE EAST, E Scotland. Gordon Brown's safe seat, cuts at Rosyth naval base an issue

Candidates 97	97 votes	97%	92%	Candidates
Gordon Brown (Lab)	24,441	66.8	62.9	Gordon Brown
John Ramage (SNP)	5,690	15.6	14.7	John Mellon
Iain Mitchell (Con)	3,656	10	16.3	Stuart Randall
Jim Tolson (LD)	2,164	5.9	6.1	John Mainland
Majority	18,751	51.2	46.6	

Electorate: 52,072 Turnout: 36,583 (70.3%)

DUNFERMLINE WEST, E Scotland. Lab seat, urban, English-born Lab MP

Candidates 97	97 votes	97%	92%	Candidates
Rachel Squire (Lab)	19,338	53.1	41.5	Rachel Squire
John Lloyd (SNP)	6,984	19.2	19.8	Brian Goodall
Elizabeth Harris (LD)	4,963	13.6	15.6	Russell McPhate
Kevin Newton (Con)	4,606	12.6	23	James Mackie
Majority	12,354	33.9	18.5	

Electorate: 52,467 Turnout: 36,434 (69.4%)

DURHAM, CITY OF, Durham. Beautiful historic city, very safe Lab seat

Candidates 97	97 votes	97%	92%	Candidates
Gerry Steinberg (Lab)	31,102	63.3	53.3	Gerry Steinberg
Richard Clark (Con)	8,598	17.5	23.7	Nick Cartmell
Dr Nigel Martin (LD)	7,499	15.3	21.5	Carol Woods
Majority	22,504	45.8	29.6	

Electorate: 69,340 Turnout: 49,135 (70.9%)

DURHAM NORTH, Durham. Strong Lab seat, mainly urban, working class

Candidates 97	97 votes	97%	92%	Candidates
Giles Radice (Lab)	33,142	70.3	59.9	
Mark Hardy (Con)	6,843	14.5	24.9	Matthew Palmer
Brian Moore (LD)	5,225	11.1	15.3	Carole Field
Majority	26,299	55.8	35	

Electorate: 67,890 Turnout: 47,168 (69.5%)

DURHAM NORTH WEST, Durham. Hilly, ex-industrial small towns, totally safe for Lab

Candidates 97	97 votes	97%	92%	Candidates
Hilary Armstrong (Lab)	31,855	68.8	58.0	Hilary Armstrong
L St John Howe (Con)	7,101	15.3	27.3	William Clouston
Anthony Gillings (LD)	4,991	10.8	14.6	Alan Ord
Majority	24,754	53.5	30.7	
Electorate: 67,156 Turnout: 46,319 (69%)				

EALING ACTON & SHEPHERD'S BUSH, W London. Thought to be marginal in 97 but now seems safe Lab, urban, large non-white population

Candidates 97	97 votes	97%	92%	Candidates
Clive Soley (Lab)	28,052	58.4	46.4	Clive Soley
Barbara Yerolemou (Con)	12,405	25.8	39.4	Justine Greening
Andrew Mitchell (LD)	5,163	10.7	12.1	Martin Tod
Majority	15,647	32.6	7	
Electorate: 72,078 Turnout: 48,064 (66.7%)				

EALING NORTH, W London. Heathrow dominated, Lab secure, large non-white population

Candidates 97	97 votes	97%	92%	Candidates
Stephen Pound (Lab)	29,904	53.7	35.8	Stephen Pound
Harry Greenway (Con)	20,744	37.2	51.4	Charles Walker
Anjan Gupta (LD)	3,887	7	10.8	Francesco Fruzza
Majority	9,160	16.5	15.6	
Electorate: 78,144 Turnout: 55,726 (71.3%)				

EALING SOUTHALL, W London. Strongly Asian, safe Lab

Candidates 97	97 votes	97%	92%	Candidates
Piara Khabra (Lab)	32,791	60	45.3	Piara Khabra
John Penrose (Con)	11,368	20.8	36.3	Daniel Kawczynski
Nikki Thomson (LD)	5,687	10.4	8.2	Baldev Sharma
Majority	21,423	49.6	9	
Electorate: 81,704 Turnout: 54,642 (66.9%)				

EASINGTON, Durham. 2nd safest Lab seat, ex-mining, skilled manual

Candidates 97	97 votes	97%	92%	Candidates
John Cummings (Lab)	33,600	80.2	72.7	John Cummings
Jason Hollands (Con)	3,588	8.6	16.7	Philip Lovel
Jim Heppell (LD)	3,025	7.2	10.6	
Majority	30,012	71.6	56	
Electorate: 62,518 Turnout: 41,895(67%)				

EASTBOURNE, E Sussex. Con seat, LD longshot, seaside, many pensioners

Candidates 97	97 votes	97%	92%	Candidates
Nigel Waterson (Con)	22,183	42.1	53	
Chris Berry (LD)	20,189	38.3	41.2	Chris Berry
David Lines (Lab)	6,576	12.5	4.7	Gillian Roles
Majority	1,994	3.8	11.8	
Electorate: 72,347 Turnout: 52,667 (72.8%)				

EAST HAM, E London. Very Lab seat, urban, strongly Asian

Candidates 97	97 votes	97%	92%	Candidates
Stephen Timms (Lab)	25,779	64.6	54	Stephen Timms
Miss Angela Bray (Con)	6,421	16.1	32	Peter Campbell
I Khan (SLP)	2,697	6.8		
Majority	19,358	48.5	22	
Electorate: 65,591 Turnout: 39,889 (60.8%)				

EAST KILBRIDE, W Scotland. Strong Lab seat, part new town, some SNP votes

Candidates 97	97 votes	97%	92%	Candidates
Adam Ingram (Lab)	27,584	56.5	47.4	Adam Ingram
George Gebbie (SNP)	10,200	20.9	23.6	Archie Buchanan
Clifford Herbertson (Con)	5,863	12	18.6	Margaret McCulloch
K Philbrick (LD)	3,527	7.2	10.4	Ewan Hawthorn
Majority	17,384	35.6	23.8	

Electorate: 65,229 Turnout: 48,796 (74.8%)

EASTLEIGH, Hampshire. Suburbs outside Southampton, LD held 97 but Con, Lab target

Candidates 97	97 votes	97%	92%	Candidates
David Chidgey (LD)	19,453	35.1	29.7	David Chidgey
Stephen Reid (Con)	18,699	33.7	50.9	Conor Burns
Alan Lloyd (Lab)	14,883	26.8	19.5	Sam Jaffa
Majority	754	1.4	21.2	

Electorate: 72,154 Turnout: 55,494 (76.9%)

EAST LOTHIAN, E Scotland. Lab seat, some ex-mining, also smart coastal towns with Con voters

Candidates 97	97 votes	97%	92%	Candidates
John Home Robertson (Lab)	22,881	52.7	45.5	Anne Picking
Murdo Fraser (Con)	8,660	19.9	30.2	Hamish Mair
David McCarthy (SNP)	6,825	15.7	13.3	Ms Hilary Brown
Alison MacAskill (LD)	4,575	10.5	11.1	Judy Hayman
Majority	14,221	32.8	15.3	

Electorate: 57,441 Turnout: 43,432 (75.6%)

EASTWOOD, W Scotland. Glasgow stockbroker belt, shock Lab win 97, likely Con gain

Candidates 97	97 votes	97%	92%	Candidates
Jim Murphy (Lab)	20,766	39.7	24.1	Jim Murphy
Paul Cullen (Con)	17,530	33.5	46.6	Raymond Robertson
Douglas Yates (SNP)	6,826	13.1	12.5	Stewart Maxwell
Dr Christopher Mason (LD)	6,110	11.7	16.4	Allan Steele
Majority	3,236	6.2	22.5	

Electorate: 66,697 Turnout: 52,235 (78.3%)

ECCLES, Greater Manchester. Central Salford, strong Lab seat, inner city, working class

Candidates 97	97 votes	97%	92%	Candidates
Ian Stewart (Lab)	30,468	66.7	57.6	Ian Stewart
Gregory Barker (Con)	8,552	18.7	31.1	Peter Caillard
Robert Boyd (LD)	4,905	10.7	9.6	Bob Boyd
Majority	21,916	48	26.5	

Electorate: 69,645 Turnout: 45,690 (65.6%)

EDDISBURY, Cheshire. Prosperous rural Cheshire, always Con but Lab did well in 97 and byelection

Candidates 97	97 votes	97%	92%	Candidates
Alastair Goodlad (Con)	21,027	42.5	52.7	Stephen O'Brien
Margaret Hanson (Lab)	19,842	40.1	31.1	Bill Eyres
David Reaper (LD)	6,540	13.2	14.9	Paul Roberts
Majority	1,185	2.4	21.6	

Electorate: 65,256 Turnout: 49,450 (75.8%)

EDINBURGH CENTRAL, E Scotland. Fairly safe for Lab, elegant city centre

Candidates 97	97 votes	97%	92%	Candidates
Alistair Darling (Lab)	20,125	47.1	38.5	Alistair Darling
Michael Scott-Hayward (Con)	9,055	21.2	29.4	Alastair Orr
Fiona Hyslop (SNP)	6,750	15.8	15.2	Dr Ian McKee
F Utting (LD)	5,605	13.1	14.8	Kevin Lang
Majority	11,070	25.9	9.1	

Electorate: 63,695 Turnout: 42,735 (67.1%)

EDINBURGH EAST & MUSSELBURGH, E Scotland. Strong Lab seat, urban

Candidates 97	97 votes	97%	92%	Candidates
Gavin Strang (Lab)	22,564	53.6	44.7	Gavin Strang
Derrick White (SNP)	8,034	19.1	17.9	Rob Munn
Ken Ward (Con)	6,483	15.4	24	
Callum MacKellar (LD)	4,511	10.7	11.5	Gary Peacock
Majority	14,530	34.5	20.7	

Electorate: 59,647 Turnout: 42,118 (70.6%)

EDINBURGH NORTH & LEITH, E Scotland. Pairing of smart New Town and developing port district

Candidates 97	97 votes	97%	92%	Candidates
Malcolm Chisholm (Lab)	19,209	46.9	34.9	Mark Lazarowicz
Anne Dana (SNP)	8,231	20.1	20.3	Kaukab Stewart
Ewen Stewart (Con)	7,312	17.9	24.8	Iain Mitchell
Hillary Campbell (LD)	5,335	13	11.7	Sebastian Tombs
Majority	10,978	26.8	10.1	

Electorate: 61,617 Turnout: 40,945 (66.5%)

EDINBURGH PENTLANDS, E Scotland. Council estates and smart suburbs, Malcolm Rifkind seeks to regain for Con

Candidates 97	97 votes	97%	92%	Candidates
Dr Lynda Clark (Lab)	19,675	43	31.2	Dr Lynda Clark
Malcolm Rifkind (Con)	14,813	32.4	40.2	Malcolm Rifkind
Stewart Gibb (SNP)	5,952	13	15.7	Dr Stuart Crawford
Jenniger Dawe (LD)	4,575	10	12.7	David Walker
Majority	4,862	10.6	9	

Electorate: 59,635 Turnout: 45,742 (76.7%)

EDINBURGH SOUTH, E Scotland. Elegant Lab ex-marginal, Con win seems far prospect

Candidates 97	97 votes	97%	92%	Candidates
Nigel Griffiths (Lab)	20,993	46.8	41.5	Nigel Griffiths
E Smith (Con)	9,541	21.3	32.2	Gordon Buchan
Michael Pringle (LD)	7,911	17.6	13.2	Marilyne MacLaren
John Hargreaves (SNP)	5,791	12.9	12.9	Heather Williams
Majority	11,452	25.5	9.3	

Electorate: 62,467 Turnout: 44,838 (71.8%)

EDINBURGH WEST, E Scotland. LDs finally won in 97, held in 99 Scottish elections, look secure now

Candidates 97	97 votes	97%	92%	Candidates
Donald Gorrie (LD)	20,578	43.2	29.9	John Barrett
Lord James Douglas-Hamilton (Con)	13,325	28	38.2	Iain Whyte
Lesley Hinds (Lab)	8,948	18.8	17.4	Elspeth Alexandra
Graham Sutherland (SNP)	4,210	8.8	12.5	Alyn Smith
Majority	7,253	15.2	8.3	

Electorate: 61,132 Turnout: 47,631 (77.9%)

EDMONTON, N London. Massive Lab gain in 97, large black population

Candidates 97	97 votes	97%	92%	Candidates
Andrew Love (Lab)	27,029	60.3	45	Andrew Love
Dr Ian Twinn (Con)	13,557	30.2	46.3	David Burrowes
Andrew Wiseman (LD)	2,847	6.3	8.3	Douglas Taylor
Majority	13,472	30.1	1.3	

Electorate: 63,718 Turnout: 44,838 (70.4%)

ELLESMERE PORT & NESTON, Cheshire. Industrial (oil and cars) commuting, working class

Candidates 97	97 votes	97%	92%	Candidates
Andrew Miller (Lab)	31,310	59.6	47.8	Andrew Miller
Lynn Turnbull (Con)	15,275	29.1	42.1	Gareth Williams
Joanna Pemberton (LD)	4,673	8.9	8.9	Stuart Kelly
Majority	16,035	30.5	5.7	

Electorate: 67,573 Turnout: 52,562 (77.8%)

ELMET, W Yorkshire. Con marginal, Lab gain 97, Leeds outer suburbs, Con need to form government

Candidates 97	97 votes	97%	92%	Candidates
Colin Burgon (Lab)	28,348	52.4	41.9	Colin Burgon
Spencer Batiste (Con)	19,569	36.2	47.5	Michael Hayman
Brian Jennings (LD)	4,691	8.7	10.5	Madeleine Kirk
Majority	8,779	16.2	5.6	

Electorate: 70,423 Turnout: 54,095 (76.8%)

ELTHAM, S London. New Lab heartland gained in 97, suburban, white collar, no sign Con revival

Candidates 97	97 votes	97%	92%	Candidates
Clive Efford (Lab)	23,710	54.6	40.1	Clive Efford
Clive Blackwood (Con)	13,528	31.2	40.1	Sharon Massey
Amanda Taylor (LD)	3,701	8.5	15.5	Martin Morris
Majority	10,182	23.4	0.1 (Con)	

Electorate: 57,358 Turnout: 43,428 (75.7%)

ENFIELD NORTH, N London. Lab took in 97, Con longshot, outer suburbs

Candidates 97	97 votes	97%	92%	Candidates
Joan Ryan (Lab)	24,148	50.7	34.9	Joan Ryan
Mark Field (Con)	17,326	36.3	52.9	Nick De Bois
Mike Hopkins (LD)	4,264	8.9	11.1	Hilary Leighter
Majority	6,822	14.4	18	

Electorate: 67,680 Turnout: 47,669 (70.4%)

ENFIELD SOUTHGATE, N London. Hit the news in 97 ejecting Michael Portillo, likely revert to Con

Candidates 97	97 votes	97%	92%	Candidates
Stephen Twigg (Lab)	20,570	44.2	26.2	Stephen Twigg
Michael Portillo (Con)	19,137	41.1	57.9	John Flack
Jeremy Browne (LD)	4,966	10.7	14.4	Wayne Hoban
Majority	1,433	3.1	31.7	

Electorate: 65,796 Turnout: 46,533 (70.7%)

EPPING FOREST, Essex. Rich outer suburbs, safe for Con even in 97

Candidates 97	97 votes	97%	92%	Candidates
Eleanor Laing (Con)	24,117	45.5	59.8	Eleanor Laing
Stephen Murray (Lab)	18,865	35.6	22.6	Christopher Naylor
Stephen Robinson (LD)	7,074	13.3	16.7	Michael Heavens
Majority	5,252	9.9	37.2	

Electorate: 72,795 Turnout: 53,007 (72.8%)

EPSOM & EWELL, Surrey. Strong Con seat, stockbroker belt, managerial

Candidates 97	97 votes	97%	92%	Candidates
Sir Archie Hamilton (Con)	24,717	45.6	61.1	Chris Grayling
Philip Woodford (Lab)	13,192	24.3	15.1	Charles Mansell
John Vincent (LD)	12,380	22.8	23.2	John Vincent
Majority	11,525	21.3	37.9	

Electorate: 73,221 Turnout: 54,181 (74%)

EREWASH, Derbyshire. Lab took in 97, mainly urban, skilled manual, still big Con vote

Candidates 97	97 votes	97%	92%	Candidates
Elizabeth Blackman (Lab)	31,196	51.7	38.2	Elizabeth Blackman
Angela Knight (Con)	22,061	36.6	47.2	Gregor MacGregor
Dr Martin Garnett (LD)	5,181	8.6	13.6	Martin Garnett
Majority	9,135	15.1	9	

Electorate: 77,402 Turnout: 60,338 (78%)

ERITH & THAMESMEAD, S London. Lab seat, contains struggling riverside new town, white collar

Candidates 97	97 votes	97%	92%	Candidates
John Austin (Lab)	25,812	62.1	43	John Austin
Nadim Zahawi (Con)	8,388	20.2	31.6	Mark Brooks
Alex Grigg (LD)	5,001	12	25.4	James Kempton
Majority	17,424	41.9	11.4	

Electorate: 62,887 Turnout: 41,587 (66.1%)

ESHER & WALTON, Surrey. Strong Con seat, stockbroker belt, managerial, Con reselection battle

Candidates 97	97 votes	97%	92%	Candidates
Ian Taylor (Con)	26,747	49.8	60.7	Ian Taylor
Julie Reay (Lab)	12,219	22.8	17.4	Joe McGowan
Gary Miles (LD)	10,937	20.4	21.9	Mark Marsh
Majority	14,528	27	38.8	

Electorate: 72,382 Turnout: 53,667 74.1

ESSEX NORTH, Essex. Secure Con seat, mainly rural, managerial

Candidates 97	97 votes	97%	92%	Candidates
Bernard Jenkin (Con)	22,480	43.9	57.7	Bernard Jenkin
Timothy Young (Lab)	17,004	33.2	19.1	Philip Hawkins
Andrew Phillips (LD)	10,028	19.6	22.2	
Majority	5,476	10.7	35.5	

Electorate: 68,008 Turnout: 51,209 (75.3%)

EXETER, Devon. Big win for Blairite Ben Bradshaw in 97, should hold with ease

Candidates 97	97 votes	97%	92%	Candidates
Ben Bradshaw (Lab)	29,398	47.5	36.2	Ben Bradshaw
Adrian Rogers (Con)	17,693	28.6	41.1	Anne Jobson
Dennis Brewer (LD)	11,148	18	19.4	Richard Copus
Majority	11,705	18.9	4.9	

Electorate: 79,154 Turnout: 61,864 (78.2%)

FALKIRK EAST, C Scotland. Mixed Central belt seat, SNP longshot

Candidates 97	97 votes	97%	92%	Candidates
Michael Connarty (Lab)	23,344	56.1	44.2	Michael Connarty
Keith Brown (SNP)	9,959	23.9	28.4	Isobel Hutton
Malcolm Nicol (Con)	5,813	14	20.2	
Rodger Spillane (LD)	2,153	5.2	7.3	Karen Utting
Majority	13,385	32.2	15.8	

Electorate: 56,791 Turnout: 41,595 (73.2%)

FALKIRK WEST, C Scotland. Strong Lab seat, urban

Candidates 97	97 votes	97%	92%	Candidates
Dennis Canavan (Lab)	22,772	59.3	51.5	Eric Joyce
David Alexander (SNP)	8,989	23.4	23.5	David Kerr
Carol Buchanan (Con)	4,639	12.1	18.9	
D Houston (LD)	1,970	5.1	6.2	Hugh O'Donnell
Majority	13,783	35.9	28	

Electorate: 52,850 Turnout: 38,370 (72.6%)

FALMOUTH & CAMBORNE, Cornwall. Con in 92, Lab 97, could go LD next but Lab favourites

Candidates 97	97 votes	97%	92%	Candidates
Candy Atherton (Lab)	18,151	33.8	29.2	Candy Atherton
Sebastian Coe (Con)	15,463	28.8	36.9	Nick Serpell
Terrye Jones (LD)	13,512	25.2	31.2	Julian Brazil
Majority	2,688	5	5.7	

Electorate: 71,383 Turnout: 53,632 (75.1%)

FAREHAM, Hampshire. Strong Con seat, seaside, professional

Candidates 97	97 votes	97%	92%	Candidates
Sir Peter Lloyd (Con)	24,436	46.8	60.6	Mark Hoban
Michael Prior (Lab)	14,078	27	14.9	James Carr
Grace Hill (LD)	10,234	19.6	23.2	Hugh Pritchard
Majority	10,358	19.8	37.4	

Electorate: 68,786 Turnout: 52,177 (75.9%)

FAVERSHAM & KENT MID, Kent. Con seat, mainly rural, middle class, strong Lab second place 97

Candidates 97	97 votes	97%	92%	Candidates
Andrew Rowe (Con)	22,016	44.4	59.2	Hugh Robertson
Alan Stewart (Lab)	17,843	36	23	Grahame Birchall
Bruce Parmenter (LD)	6,138	12.4	17	Mike Sole
Majority	4,173	8.4	36.2	

Electorate: 67,490 Turnout: 49,606 (73.5%)

FELTHAM & HESTON, W London. Lab since 92, outer suburbs, white collar

Candidates 97	97 votes	97%	92%	Candidates
Alan Keen (Lab)	27,836	59.7	45.5	Alan Keen
Patrick Ground (Con)	12,563	26.9	42.9	Liz Mammatt
Colin Penning (LD)	4,264	9.1	11.6	Andy Darley
Majority	15,273	32.8	2.6	

Electorate: 71,093 Turnout: 46,621 (65.6%)

FERMANAGH & SOUTH TYRONE, Northern Ireland. Unionist, split nationalist vote, MP leaving, rural

Candidates 97	97 votes	97%	92%	Candidates
Ken Maginnis (UUP)	24,862	51.5	52.4	James Cooper
Gerry McHugh (SF)	11,174	23.1	19.1	Michelle Gildernew
Tommy Gallagher (SDLP)	11,060	22.9	22.9	Tommy Gallagher
S Farry (Alliance)	977	2	1.7	
Majority	13,688	28.4	29.4	

Electorate: 64,600 Turnout: 48,290 (74.8%)

FIFE CENTRAL, E Scotland. Strong Lab seat, industrial

Candidates 97	97 votes	97%	92%	Candidates
Henry McLeish (Lab)	23,912	58.7	50.7	
Tricia Marwick (SNP)	10,199	25	24.9	David Alexander
Jacob Rees-Mogg (Con)	3,669	9	17.4	Jeremy Balfour
Ross Laird (LD)	2,610	6.4	6.9	Elizabeth Riches
Majority	13,713	33.7	25.8	

Electorate: 58,315 Turnout: 40,765 (69.9%)

FIFE NORTH EAST, E Scotland. Smart, rural E Scotland, LD since 87, now secure

Candidates 97	97 votes	97%	92%	Candidates
Menzies Campbell (LD)	21,432	51.2	5.6	Menzies Campbell
The Hon Adam Bruce (Con)	11,076	26.5	38.5	Mike Scott-Hayward
Colin Welsh (SNP)	4,545	10.9	8.6	Kris Murray-Brown
Charles Milne (Lab)	4,301	10.3	46.4	Clare Brennan
Majority	10,356	24.7	7.9	

Electorate: 58,793 Turnout: 41,839 (71.2%)

FINCHLEY & GOLDERS GREEN, N London. Once Margaret Thatcher's seat, shock Lab win 97

Candidates 97	97 votes	97%	92%	Candidates
Rudi Vis (Lab)	23,180	46.1	30.9	Rudi Vis
John Marshall (Con)	19,991	39.7	54.7	John Marshall
Jonathan Davies (LD)	5,670	11.3	12.8	Sarah Teather
Majority	3,189	6.4	23.8	

Electorate: 72,225 Turnout: 50,306 (69.7%)

FOLKESTONE & HYTHE, Kent. Easier than expected Con win 97, Michael Howard secure against split opposition

Candidates 97	97 votes	97%	92%	Candidates
Michael Howard (Con)	20,313	39	52.3	Michael Howard
David Laws (LD)	13,981	26.9	35.3	Peter Carroll
Peter Doherty (Lab)	12,939	24.9	12.1	Albert Catterall
Majority	6,332	12.1	17	

Electorate: 71,152 Turnout: 52,050 (73.2%)

FOREST OF DEAN, Gloucestershire. Lab marginal, Cons must win places like this to take power

Candidates 97	97 votes	97%	92%	Candidates
Diana Organ (Lab)	24,203	48.2	42.4	Diana Organ
Paul Marland (Con)	17,860	35.6	41	Mark Harper
A Lynch (LD)	6,165	12.3	16.1	David Gayler
Majority	6,343	12.6	1.4	
Electorate: 63,465 Turnout: 50,184 (79.1%)				

FOYLE, Northern Ireland. Strong SDLP seat,urban, based on Derry

Candidates 97	97 votes	97%	92%	Candidates
John Hume (SDLP)	25,109	52.5	54	John Hume
Mitchel McLaughlin (SF)	11,445	23.9	17.3	Mitchel McLaughlin
William Hay (DUP)	10,290	21.5	25	William Hay
H Boll (Alliance)	817	1.7	2	Colm Cavanagh
Majority	13,664	28.6	28.9	
Electorate: 67,620 Turnout: 47,815 (70.7%)				

FYLDE, Lancashire. Strong Con seat, seaside, middle class

Candidates 97	97 votes	97%	92%	Candidates
Michael Jack (Con)	25,443	48.9	60.2	Michael Jack
John Garrett (Lab)	16,480	31.7	18.6	
Bill Greene (LD)	7,609	14.6	20.7	John Begg
Majority	8,963	17.2	39.5	
Electorate: 71,385 Turnout: 52,067 (72.9%)				

GAINSBOROUGH, Lincolnshire. Now strong Con seat, mainly rural, rightwing Con MP

Candidates 97	97 votes	97%	92%	Candidates
Edward Leigh (Con)	20,593	43.1	53.4	Edward Leigh
Paul Taylor (Lab)	13,767	28.8	20.9	Alan Rhodes
Neil Taylor (LD)	13,436	28.1	25.8	Steve Taylor
Majority	6,826	14.3	27.6	
Electorate: 64,105 Turnout: 47,796 (74.6%)				

GALLOWAY & UPPER NITHSDALE, SW Scotland. Isolated, scenic south Scotland, SNP gain from Con 97

Candidates 97	97 votes	97%	92%	Candidates
Alasdair Morgan (SNP)	18,449	43.9	36.4	Malcolm Fleming
Ian Lang (Con)	12,825	30.5	42	Peter Duncan
Katy Clark (Lab)	6,861	16.3	13	
John McKerchar (LD)	2,700	6.4	8.6	Neil Wallace
Majority	5,624	13.4	5.6	
Electorate: 52,751 Turnout: 42018 (79.7%)				

GATESHEAD EAST & WASHINGTON WEST, Tyne & Wear. Strong Lab seat, urban

Candidates 97	97 votes	97%	92%	Candidates
Joyce Quin (Lab)	31,047	72.1	58	Joyce Quin
Jacqui Burns (Con)	6,097	14.2	27.7	Elizabeth Campbell
Alan Ord (LD)	4,622	10.7	14.3	Ron Beadle
Majority	24,950	57.9	30.3	
Electorate: 64,114 Turnout: 43,081 (67.2%)				

GEDLING, Nottinghamshire. Nottingham commuters, Lab gain 97 but Con target now

Candidates 97	97 votes	97%	92%	Candidates
Vernon Coaker (Lab)	24,390	46.8	34.4	Vernon Coaker
Andrew Mitchell (Con)	20,588	39.5	53.2	Jonathan Bullock
Ray Poynter (LD)	5,180	9.9	12.1	
Majority	3,802	7.3	18.8	
Electorate: 68,820 Turnout: 52,164 (75.8%)				

GILLINGHAM, Kent. Lab surge in 97 saw them take this urban seat, amazing if party holds it next time

Candidates 97	97 votes	97%	92%	Candidates
Paul Clark (Lab)	20,187	39.8	23.8	Paul Clark
James Couchman (Con)	18,207	35.9	52	Tim Butcher
Robert Sayer (LD)	9,649	19	23.5	Jonathan Hunt
Majority	1,980	3.9	28.2	

Electorate: 70,389 Turnout: 50,683 (72%)

GLASGOW ANNIESLAND, W Scotland. Outer suburbs, held by Lab in by-election after Donald Dewar's death

Candidates 97	97 votes	97%	92%	Candidates
Donald Dewar (Lab)	20,951	61.8	53.1	John Robertson
Dr William Wilson (SNP)	5,797	17.1	17	Grant Thoms
Andrew Brocklehurst (Con)	3,881	11.5	15.6	Stewart Connell
Christopher McGinty (LD)	2,453	7.2	13.7	Christopher McGinty
Majority	15,154	44.7	36.1	

Electorate: 52,955 Turnout: 33,879 (64%)

GLASGOW BAILLIESTON, W Scotland. Strong Lab seat, outer suburbs, much council housing

Candidates 97	97 votes	97%	92%	Candidates
James Wray (Lab)	20,925	65.7	63.2	James Wray
Patsy Thomson (SNP)	6,085	19.1	22.6	Lachlan McNeill
M Kelly (Con)	2,468	7.7	9.9	David Comrie
S Rainger (LD)	1,217	3.8	4.3	Charles Dundas
Majority	14,840	46.6	40.6	

Electorate: 51,151 Turnout: 31,853 (62.3%)

GLASGOW CATHCART, W Scotland. Hard to imagine this seat was ever Con, mixed suburbs

Candidates 97	97 votes	97%	92%	Candidates
John Maxton (Lab)	19,158	57.4	49.3	Tom Harris
Maire Whitehead (SNP)	6,193	18.5	19.1	Josephine Docherty
Alistair Muir (Con)	4,248	12.7	21.5	Richard Cook
Callan Dick (LD)	2,302	6.9	7.2	Tom Henery
Majority	12,965	38.9	27.8	

Electorate: 49,312 Turnout: 33,390 (67.7%)

GLASGOW GOVAN, W Scotland. Poor, ex-shipbuilding, Lab even in Scottish elections, SNP challenge

Candidates 97	97 votes	97%	92%	Candidates
Mohammed Sarwar (Lab)	14,216	44.1	43	Mohammed Sarwar
Nicola Sturgeon (SNP)	11,302	35.1	27.6	Karen Neary
William Thomas (Con)	2,839	8.8	19.7	Mark Menzies
Robert Stewart (LD)	1,918	5.9	5.6	Bob Stewart
Majority	2,914	9	15.4	

Electorate: 49,836 Turnout: 32,242 (64.7%)

GLASGOW KELVIN, W Scotland. Grand inner city, includes Hillhead, now safe Lab

Candidates 97	97 votes	97%	92%	Candidates
George Galloway (Lab)	16,643	51	46.9	George Galloway
Sandra White (SNP)	6,978	21.4	19.3	Frank Rankin
Elspeth Buchanan (LD)	4,629	14.2	18.9	Tamsin Mayberry
Duncan McPhie (Con)	3,539	10.8	13.2	Davina Rankin
Majority	9,665	29.6	27.6	

Electorate: 57,438 Turnout: 32,654 (56.9%)

GLASGOW MARYHILL, W Scotland. Strong Lab seat, council estates

Candidates 97	97 votes	97%	92%	Candidates
Maria Fyfe (Lab)	19,301	64.9	62.6	
John Wailes (SNP)	5,037	16.9	19.3	Alex Dingwall
Elspeth Attwooll (LD)	2,119	7.1	6.7	Stuart Callison
S Baldwin (Con)	1,747	5.9	9.6	Gawain Towler
Majority	14,264	48	43.3	

Electorate: 52,522 Turnout: 29,721 (56.6%)

GLASGOW POLLOK, W Scotland. Lab dominance challenged by local socialist Tommy Sheridan

Candidates 97	97 votes	97%	92%	Candidates
Ian Davidson (Lab)	19,653	59.9	49.9	Ian Davidson
David Logan (SNP)	5,862	17.9	25	David Ritchie
Tommy Sheridan (SS)	3,639	11.1	–	Keith Baldassara
E Hamilton (Con)	1,979	6	8.2	Roy O'Brien
Majority	13,791	42	24.9	
Electorate: 49,284 Turnout: 32,802 (66.6%)				

GLASGOW RUTHERGLEN, W Scotland. Strong Lab seat, outer suburbs, SNP remote second

Candidates 97	97 votes	97%	92%	Candidates
Thomas McAvoy (Lab)	20,430	57.5	53.4	Thomas McAvoy
Iain Gray (SNP)	5,423	15.3	16	Anne McLaughlin
Robert Brown (LD)	5,167	14.5	11.7	David Jackson
David Campbell Bannerman (Con)	3,288	9.3	19.2	Malcolm Macaskill
Majority	15,007	42.2	34.2	
Electorate: 50,645 Turnout: 35,521 (70.1%)				

GLASGOW SHETTLESTON, W Scotland. Strong Lab seat, inner city, includes Gorbals

Candidates 97	97 votes	97%	92%	Candidates
David Marshall (Lab)	19,616	73.2	65.5	David Marshall
Humayun Hanif (SNP)	3,748	14	16	Jim Byrne
Colin Simpson (Con)	1,484	5.5	12.2	Campbell Murdoch
K Hiles (LD)	1,061	4	6.1	
Majority	15,868	59.2	49.5	
Electorate: 47,990 Turnout: 26,813 (55.9%)				

GLASGOW SPRINGBURN, W Scotland. Strong Lab seat, inner city, ex-railway works

Candidates 97	97 votes	97%	92%	Candidates
Michael Martin (Speaker)	22,534	71.4	64.9	Michael Martin
John Brady (SNP)	5,208	16.5	20	Sandy Bain
Mark Holdsworth (Con)	1,893	6	10.9	Charlie Garton-Jones
Jim Alexander (LD)	1,349	4.3	4.3	
Majority	17,326	54.9	44.9	
Electorate: 53,473 Turnout: 31,577 (59.1%)				

GLOUCESTER, Gloucestershire. The seat that gave Lab a majority in 97, Con longshot

Candidates 97	97 votes	97%	92%	Candidates
Tess Kingham (Lab)	28,943	50	36.8	Parmjit Dhanda
Douglas French (Con)	20,684	35.7	45.5	Paul James
Peter Munisamy (LD)	6,069	10.5	17.6	Tim Bullamore
Majority	8,259	14.3	8.7	
Electorate: 78,682 Turnout: 57,914 (73.6%)				

GORDON, NE Scotland. LD triumph 97 against Con challenge, big, rural, rising SNP support

Candidates 97	97 votes	97%	92%	Candidates
Malcolm Bruce (LD)	17,999	42.6	27.2	Malcolm Bruce
John Porter (Con)	11,002	26	48	Nanette Milne
Richard Lochhead (SNP)	8,435	20	19	Rhona Kemp
Lindsay Kirkhill (Lab)	4,350	10.3	6.3	Ellis Thorpe
Majority	6,997	16.6	20.8	
Electorate: 58,767 Turnout: 42,245 (71.9%)				

GOSPORT, Hampshire. Seaside, working class, remarkable safe Con seat thanks to Royal Navy base

Candidates 97	97 votes	97%	92%	Candidates
Peter Viggers (Con)	21,085	43.6	58.1	Peter Viggers
Ivan Gray (Lab)	14,827	30.7	13.6	Richard Williams
Steve Hogg (LD)	9,479	19.6	28	Roger Roberts
Majority	6,258	12.9	30.1	
Electorate: 68,829 Turnout: 48,355 (70.3%)				

GOWER, S Wales. Lab seat, Welsh-speaking

Candidates 97	97 votes	97%	92%	Candidates
Martin Caton (Lab)	23,313	53.8	50	Martin Caton
Alun Cairns (Con)	10,306	23.8	35	John Bushell
Howard Evans (LD)	5,624	13	10	Sheila Waye
Elwyn Williams (PC)	2,226	5.1	4	
Majority	13,007	30	25	

Electorate: 57,691 Turnout: 43,336 (75.1%)

GRANTHAM & STAMFORD, Lincolnshire. Con seat, mainly rural plus small towns, Lab close in 97

Candidates 97	97 votes	97%	92%	Candidates
Quentin Davies (Con)	22,672	42.8	58	Quentin Davies
Peter Denning (Lab)	19,980	37.7	26	John Robinson
John Sellick (LD)	6,612	12.5	16	Jane Carr
Majority	2,692	5.1	32	

Electorate: 72,310 Turnout: 52,970 (73.3%)

GRAVESHAM, Kent. Bellwether seat, small Lab majority makes it a distant Con target

Candidates 97	97 votes	97%	92%	Candidates
Chris Pond (Lab)	26,460	49.7	40	Chris Pond
Jacques Arnold (Con)	20,681	38.8	49.6	Jacques Arnold
Dr M Canet (LD)	4,128	7.8	8.9	Bruce Parmenter
Majority	5,779	10.9	9.6	

Electorate: 69,234 Turnout: 53,253 (76.9%)

GREAT GRIMSBY, Humberside. Lab seat, fishing, working class

Candidates 97	97 votes	97%	92%	Candidates
Austin Mitchell (Lab)	25,765	59.8	51	Austin Mitchell
Dean Godson (Con)	9,521	22.1	36.2	James Cousins
Andrew De Freitas (LD)	7,810	18.1	12.8	Andrew de Freitas
Majority	16,244	37.7	14.8	

Electorate: 65,043 Turnout: 43,096 (66.3%)

GREAT YARMOUTH, Norfolk. Lab gain 97, urban, port and holiday makers, Con longshot

Candidates 97	97 votes	97%	92%	Candidates
Anthony David Wright (Lab)	26,084	53.4	38	Anthony Wright
Michael Carttiss (Con)	17,416	35.6	47.9	Charles Reynolds
Derek Wood (LD)	5,381	11	13.6	
Majority	8,668	17.8	9.9	

Electorate: 68,625 Turnout: 48,881 (71.2%)

GREENOCK & INVERCLYDE, W Scotland. Strong Lab seat, industrial (especially electronics), some hills

Candidates 97	97 votes	97%	92%	Candidates
Dr Norman Godman (Lab)	19,480	56.2	47.8	David Cairns
Brian Goodall (SNP)	6,440	18.6	17	Andrew Murie
Rod Ackland (LD)	4,791	13.8	13.9	Chic Brodie
Hugo Swire (Con)	3,976	11.5	21.1	Alister Haw
Majority	13,040	37.6	26.7	

Electorate: 48,818 Turnout: 34,687 (71.1%)

GREENWICH & WOOLWICH, S London. Lab safe now SDP era over, urban, large black population

Candidates 97	97 votes	97%	92%	Candidates
Nick Raynsford (Lab)	25,630	63.4	44.6	Nick Raynsford
Michael Mitchell (Con)	7,502	18.6	18.2	Richard Forsdyke
Cherry Luxton (LD)	5,049	12.5	35.1	Russell Pyne
Majority	18,128	44.8	9.5	

Electorate: 61,352 Turnout: 40,403 (65.9%)

GUILDFORD, Surrey. Strong Con seat, mainly urban, professional

Candidates 97	97 votes	97%	92%	Candidates
Nicholas St Aubyn (Con)	24,230	42.5	55.4	Nicholas St Aubyn
Margaret Sharp (LD)	19,439	34.1	32.9	Sue Doughty
Joseph Burns (Lab)	9,945	17.5	11.4	Joyce Still
Majority	4,791	8.4	22.5	

Electorate: 75,540 Turnout: 56,958 (75.4%)

HACKNEY NORTH & STOKE NEWINGTON, N London. Strong Lab seat, inner city, high unemployment

Candidates 97	97 votes	97%	92%	Candidates
Diane Abbott (Lab)	21,110	65.2	57.8	Diane Abbott
Michael Lavender (Con)	5,483	16.9	26.9	
Douglas Taylor (LD)	3,306	10.2	11.5	Meral Ece
Majority	15,627	48.3	30.9	

Electorate: 62,045 Turnout: 32,382 (52.2%)

HACKNEY SOUTH & SHOREDITCH, N London. Intemperate local politics, council cuts, Con, LD, Green activity

Candidates 97	97 votes	97%	92%	Candidates
Brian Sedgemore (Lab)	20,048	59.4	53.4	Brian Sedgemore
Martin Pantling (LD)	5,068	15	15	Tony Vickers
Christopher O'Leary (Con)	4,494	13.3	29	Paul White
Majority	14,980	44.4	24.4	

Electorate: 61,728 Turnout: 33,746 (54.7%)

HALESOWEN & ROWLEY REGIS, W Midlands. Safe Lab, mainly urban, working class

Candidates 97	97 votes	97%	92%	Candidates
Sylvia Heal (Lab)	26,366	54.1	44.5	Sylvia Heal
John Kennedy (Con)	16,029	32.9	44.7	Les Jones
Elaine Todd (LD)	4,169	8.5	9.9	Patrick Harley
Majority	10,337	21.2	0.2	

Electorate: 66,245 Turnout: 48,761 (73.6%)

HALIFAX, W Yorkshire. Lab recovered ground 97, now safe, urban, skilled manual, Pennine hills

Candidates 97	97 votes	97%	92%	Candidates
Alice Mahon (Lab)	27,465	54.3	43.5	Alice Mahon
Robert Light (Con)	16,253	32.1	42.7	James Walsh
Ed Waller (LD)	6,059	12	12.7	John Durkin
Majority	11,212	22.2	0.8	

Electorate: 71,701 Turnout: 50,556 (70.5%)

HALTEMPRICE & HOWDEN, E Yorkshire. Strong Con seat, rural, middle class, based on Beverley

Candidates 97	97 votes	97%	92%	Candidates
David Davis (Con)	21,809	44	59.3	David Davis
Diana Wallis (LD)	14,295	28.8	25.2	Jon Neal
George McManus (Lab)	11,701	23.6	15.3	Leslie Howell
Majority	7,514	15.2	34.1	

Electorate: 65,602 Turnout: 49,550 (75.5%)

HALTON, Cheshire. Chemical plants, includes Runcorn, Widnes, very safe for Lab

Candidates 97	97 votes	97%	92%	Candidates
Derek Twigg (Lab)	31,497	70.9	59.6	Derek Twigg
Philip Balmer (Con)	7,847	17.7	30.3	Chris Davenport
Janet Jones (LD)	3,263	7.3	8.8	Peter Walker
Majority	23,650	53.2	29.3	

Electorate: 64,987 Turnout: 44,439 (68.4%)

HAMILTON NORTH & BELLSHILL, W Scotland. Strong Lab seat, industrial

Candidates 97	97 votes	97%	92%	Candidates
Dr John Reid (Lab)	24,322	64	58.3	John Reid
Michael Matheson (SNP)	7,255	19.1	20	
Gordon McIntosh (Con)	3,944	10.4	15.2	
Keith Legg (LD)	1,924	5.1	6.8	
Majority	17,067	44.9	38.3	

Electorate: 53,607 Turnout: 37,999 (70.9%)

HAMILTON SOUTH, W Scotland. Lab seat, just held in 99 by-election, industrial, SNP longshot

Candidates 97	97 votes	97%	92%	Candidates
George Robertson (Lab)	21,709	65.6	57	Bill Tynan
Ian Black (SNP)	5,831	17.6	19.7	John Wilson
Robert Kilgour (Con)	2,858	8.6	16.1	Neil Richardson
Richard Pitts (LD)	1,693	5.1	6.6	John Oswald
Majority	15,878	48	3.6	

Electorate: 46,562 Turnout: 33,091 (71.1%)

HAMMERSMITH & FULHAM, W London. Lab marginal, middle class, Con outside bet

Candidates 97	97 votes	97%	92%	Candidates
Iain Coleman (Lab)	25,262	46.8	38.6	Iain Coleman
Matthew Carrington (Con)	21,420	39.6	51.6	Matthew Carrington
Alexi Sugden (LD)	4,728	8.8	8.3	Jon Burden
Majority	3,842	7.2	13	

Electorate: 78,637 Turnout: 54,026 (68.7%)

HAMPSHIRE EAST, Hampshire. Utterly safe for Con

Candidates 97	97 votes	97%	92%	Candidates
Michael Mates (Con)	27,927	48	60.6	Michael Mates
Bob Booker (LD)	16,337	28.1	27.5	Robert Booker
Bob Hoyle (Lab)	9,945	17.1	9.4	
Majority	11,590	19.9	33.1	

Electorate: 76,604 Turnout: 58128 (75.9%)

HAMPSHIRE NORTH EAST, Hampshire. Fast growing suburbs and villages, strong Con seat

Candidates 97	97 votes	97%	92%	Candidates
James Arbuthnot (Con)	26,017	50.9	64	James Arbuthnot
Ian Mann (LD)	11,619	22.7	25.1	Mike Plummer
Peter Dare (Lab)	8,203	16	9.2	
Majority	14,398	28.2	38.9	

Electorate: 69,110 Turnout: 51,111 (74%)

HAMPSHIRE NORTH WEST, Hampshire. Strong Con seat, mainly rural plus Andover, middle class

Candidates 97	97 votes	97%	92%	Candidates
Sir George Young (Con)	24,730	45.2	58.1	Sir George Young
Charles Fleming (LD)	13,179	24.1	28	Alex Bentley
Michael Mumford (Lab)	12,900	23.6	12.6	
Majority	11,551	21.1	30.1	

Electorate: 73,221 Turnout: 54,667 (74.7%)

HAMPSTEAD & HIGHGATE, N London. Ultra-middle class, once Con, now safe for Lab Glenda Jackson

Candidates 97	97 votes	97%	92%	Candidates
Glenda Jackson (Lab)	25,275	57.4	46.2	Glenda Jackson
Elizabeth Gibson (Con)	11,991	27.2	40.8	Andrew Mennear
Bridget Fox (LD)	5,481	12.4	11	Jonathan Simpson
Majority	13,284	30.2	5.4	

Electorate: 64,889 Turnout: 44,031 (67.9%)

HARBOROUGH, Leicestershire. Easy Con win 97 thanks to decline in LD vote, rural, middle class

Candidates 97	97 votes	97%	92%	Candidates
Edward Garnier (Con)	22,170	41.8	52.7	Edward Garnier
Mark Cox (LD)	15,646	29.5	34.4	Jill Hope
Nick Holden (Lab)	13,332	25.2	12.3	Raj Jethwa
Majority	6,524	12.3	18.3	

Electorate: 70,424 Turnout: 53,007 (75.3%)

HARLOW, Essex. Lab easy win 97, new town, skilled manual

Candidates 97	97 votes	97%	92%	Candidates
Bill Rammell (Lab)	25,861	54.1	42.8	Bill Rammell
Jerry Hayes (Con)	15,347	32.1	46	Robert Halfon
Lorna Spenceley (LD)	4,523	9.5	11.2	Lorna Spenceley
Majority	10,514	22	3.2	

Electorate: 64,072 Turnout: 47,812 (74.6%)

HARROGATE & KNARESBOROUGH, N Yorkshire. Elegant twin towns, LD gain 97, Con return looks unlikely

Candidates 97	97 votes	97%	92%	Candidates
Phil Willis (LD)	24,558	51.5	33.4	Phil Willis
Norman Lamont (Con)	18,322	38.5	51.8	Andrew Jones
Barbara Boyce (Lab)	4,151	8.7	13.5	Alastair MacDonald
Majority	6,236	13	18.4	

Electorate: 65,155 Turnout: 47,653 (73.1%)

HARROW EAST, N London. Massive Lab win 97, large Asian community

Candidates 97	97 votes	97%	92%	Candidates
Tony McNulty (Lab)	29,923	52.5	33.8	Tony McNulty
Hugh Dykes (Con)	20,189	35.4	52.9	Peter Wilding
Baldev Sharma (LD)	4,697	8.2	10.8	George Kershaw
Majority	9,734	17.1	19.1	

Electorate: 79,846 Turnout: 56,985 (71.4%)

HARROW WEST, N London. Plush ex-Con seat, Lab gain 97, now top Con target

Candidates 97	97 votes	97%	92%	Candidates
Gareth Thomas (Lab)	21,811	41.5	22.5	Gareth Thomas
Robert Hughes (Con)	20,571	39.2	55.2	Danny Finkelstein
Pash Nandhra (LD)	8,127	15.5	20.2	Christopher Noyce
Majority	1,240	2.3	32.7	

Electorate: 72,004 Turnout: 52,506 (72.9%)

HARTLEPOOL, NE England. MP is serial resigner Peter Mandelson, talk of ousting him but unlikely

Candidates 97	97 votes	97%	92%	Candidates
Peter Mandelson (Lab)	26,997	60.7	51.9	Peter Mandelson
Michael Horsley (Con)	9,489	21.3	34.9	Gus Robinson
Reginald Clark (LD)	6,248	14.1	13.3	Nigel Boddy
Majority	17,508	39.4	17	

Electorate: 67,712 Turnout: 44,452 (65.6%)

HARWICH, Essex. Outstanding Lab result 97, Con must want to take it back, port and retirement towns

Candidates 97	97 votes	97%	92%	Candidates
Ivan Henderson (Lab)	20,740	38.8	24.7	Ivan Henderson
Iain Sproat (Con)	19,524	36.5	51.7	Ian Sproat
Ann Elvin (LD)	7,037	13.1	23.2	Peter Wilcock
Majority	1,216	2.3	27	

Electorate: 75,775 Turnout: 53,514 (70.6%)

HASTINGS & RYE, E Sussex. LDs wanted this 97 but Lab won from third, declining seaside town

Candidates 97	97 votes	97%	92%	Candidates
Michael Jabez Foster (Lab)	16,867	34.4	15.7	Michael Foster
Jacqui Lait (Con)	14,307	29.2	47.6	Mark Coote
Monroe Palmer (LD)	13,717	28	35.2	Graem Peters
Majority	2,560	5.2	12.4	

Electorate: 70,388 Turnout: 49,069 (69.7%)

HAVANT, Hampshire. Con base of thinker David Willetts, mainly urban, not posh

Candidates 97	97 votes	97%	92%	Candidates
David Willetts (Con)	19,204	39.7	52.9	David Willetts
Lynne Armstrong (Lab)	15,475	32	19.8	Peter Guthrie
M Kooner (LD)	10,806	22.4	26.1	Helena Cole
Majority	3,729	7.7	26.8	

Electorate: 68,420 Turnout: 48,322 (70.6%)

HAYES & HARLINGTON, W London. Once marginal, now Lab, airport, large Asian community

Candidates 97	97 vote	97%	92%	Candidates
John McDonnell (Lab)	25,458	62	44.8	John McDonnell
Andrew Retter (Con)	11,167	27.2	44.9	Robert McLean
Anthony Little (LD)	3,049	7.4	10.3	Nahid Boethe
Majority	14,291	34.8	0.1	

Electorate: 56,828 Turnout: 41,091 (72.3%)

HAZEL GROVE, Greater Manchester. Huge LD win 97, commuting, middle class, looks almost safe

Candidates 97	97 votes	97%	92%	Candidates
Andrew Stunell (LD)	26,883	54.5	43.1	Andrew Stunell
Brendan Murphy (Con)	15,069	30.5	44.8	Nadine Bargery
Jeffrey Lewis (Lab)	5,882	11.9	11.7	Martin Miller
Majority	11,814	24	1.7	

Electorate: 63,693 Turnout: 49,340 (77.5%)

HEMEL HEMPSTEAD, Hertfordshire. Prosperous new town, white collar, Lab could lose on Con surge

Candidates 97	97 votes	97%	92%	Candidates
Tony McWalter (Lab)	25,175	45.7	32.5	Tony McWalter
Robert Jones (Con)	21,539	39.1	49.9	Paul Ivey
Patricia Lindsley (LD)	6,789	12.3	15.4	Neil Stuart
Majority	3,636	6.6	17.4	

Electorate: 71,467 Turnout: 55,092 (77.1%)

HEMSWORTH, W Yorkshire. Famous as place they were said to weigh Lab votes not count, poor

Candidates 97	97 votes	97%	92%	Candidates
Jon Trickett (Lab)	32,088	70.6	63.8	Jon Trickett
Norman Hazel (Con)	8,096	17.8	25.8	Elizabeth Truss
Jaki Kirby (LD)	4,033	8.9	10.4	Ed Waller
Majority	23,992	52.8	38	

Electorate: 66,964 Turnout: 45,477 (67.9%)

HENDON, N London. Easy gain for Lab in 97, mixed suburbs, Con longshot

Candidates 97	97 votes	97%	92%	Candidates
Andrew Dismore (Lab)	24,683	49.3	33.5	Andrew Dismore
John Gorst (Con)	18,528	37	53.6	Richard Evans
Wayne Casey (LD)	5,427	10.8	11.7	Wayne Casey
Majority	6,155	12.3	20.1	

Electorate: 76,194 Turnout: 50,036 (65.7%)

HENLEY, Oxfordshire. Floppy-haired Boris Johnson replaces Michael Heseltine as local Con MP

Candidates 97	97 votes	97%	92%	Candidates
Michael Heseltine (Con)	23,908	46.4	60	Boris Johnson
Tim Horton (LD)	12,741	24.7	23.9	Catherine Bearder
Duncan Enright (Lab)	11,700	22.7	14.8	Janet Matthews
Majority	11,167	21.7	36.1	

Electorate: 66,423 Turnout: 51,543 (77.6%)

HEREFORD, Herefordshire. LDs finally took 97, 99 Euro elections calamity for them, Con target

Candidates 97	97 votes	97%	92%	Candidates
Paul Keetch (LD)	25,198	47.9	41.3	Paul Keetch
Colin Shephard (Con)	18,550	35.3	47	Virginia Taylor
Chris Chappell (Lab)	6,596	12.6	10.6	David Hallam
Majority	6,648	12.6	5.7	

Electorate: 69,864 Turnout: 52,553 (75.2%)

HERTFORD & STORTFORD, Hertfordshire. Mixed rural and prosperous towns, managerial

Candidates 97	97 votes	97%	92%	Candidates
Bowen Wells (Con)	24,027	44	56.5	Mark Prisk
Simon Speller (Lab)	17,142	31.4	16.9	Simon Speller
Michael Wood (LD)	9,679	17.7	25.5	Madeleine Goldspink
Majority	6,885	12.6	31	

Electorate: 71,759 Turnout: 54,561 (76%)

HERTFORDSHIRE NORTH EAST, Hertfordshire. Strong Con seat, part new town, managerial

Candidates 97	97 votes	97%	92%	Candidates
Oliver Heald (Con)	21,712	41.8	51.7	
Ivan Gibbons (Lab)	18,624	35.8	21.3	
Steve Jarvis (LD)	9,493	18.3	26.4	Alison Kingman
Majority	3,088	6	25.3	

Electorate: 67,161 Turnout: 51,995 (77.4%)

HERTFORDSHIRE SOUTH WEST, Hertfordshire. Strong Con seat, stockbroker belt near London

Candidates 97	97 votes	97%	92%	Candidates
Richard Page (Con)	25,462	46	59.2	
M Wilson (Lab)	15,441	27.9	17.4	
Ann Shaw (LD)	12,381	22.3	22.6	Ed Featherstone
Majority	10,021	18.1	36.6	

Electorate: 71,671 Turnout: 55,411 (77.3%)

HERTSMERE, Hertfordshire. Just outside London, Thameslink commuters, will stay Con

Candidates 97	97 votes	97%	92%	Candidates
James Clappison (Con)	22,305	44.3	57.8	
Beth Kelly (Lab)	19,230	38.2	21.8	Hilary Broderick
Ann Gray (LD)	6,466	12.8	19.7	Paul Thompson
Majority	3,075	6.1	36	

Electorate: 68,011 Turnout: 50,348 (74%)

HEXHAM, Northumberland. Rural, huge, Borders, Lab surge 97 but Con hung on by 222 votes

Candidates 97	97 votes	97%	92%	Candidates
Peter Atkinson (Con)	17,701	38.8	52.4	
Ian McMann (Lab)	17,479	38.3	24.2	Paul Brannen
Dr Philip Carr (LD)	7,959	17.4	21.7	Philip Latham
Majority	222	0.5	28.2	

Electorate: 58,914 Turnout: 45,671 (77.5%)

HEYWOOD & MIDDLETON, Greater Manchester. Outer Rochdale, some Con voters, safe Lab

Candidates 97	97 votes	97%	92%	Candidates
Jim Dobbin (Lab)	29,179	57.7	46.5	Jim Dobbin
Sebastian Grigg (Con)	11,637	23	31.6	Marilyn Hopkins
David Clayton (LD)	7,908	15.6	20	
Majority	17,542	34.7	14.9	

Electorate: 73,897 Turnout: 50,550 (68.4%)

HIGH PEAK, Derbyshire. Kinder Scout and Dark Peak hills, small towns, swings between Con, Lab

Candidates 97	97 votes	97%	92%	Candidates
Tom Levitt (Lab)	29,052	50.8	37.9	Tom Levitt
Charles Hendry (Con)	20,261	35.5	46	Simon Chapman
Sue Barber (LD)	6,420	11.2	14.8	Peter Ashenden
Majority	8,791	15.3	8.1	

Electorate: 72,315 Turnout: 57,153 (79%)

HITCHIN & HARPENDEN, Hertfordshire. Prosperous London commuters, safe for Con Peter Lilley

Candidates 97	97 votes	97%	92%	Candidates
Peter Lilley (Con)	24,038	45.9	61.4	
Rosemary Sanderson (Lab)	17,367	33.1	17.9	Alan Amos
Chris White (LD)	10,515	20.1	19.8	John Murphy
Majority	6,671	12.8	41.6	

Electorate: 67,218 Turnout: 52,427 (78%)

HOLBORN & ST PANCRAS, C London. Typical inner city plus West End fringe

Candidates 97	97 votes	97%	92%	Candidates
Frank Dobson (Lab)	24,707	65	54.3	Frank Dobson
Julian Smith (Con)	6,804	17.9	28.2	Roseanne Serelli
Justine McGuiness (LD)	4,750	12.5	13.9	Nathaniel Green
Majority	17,903	47.1	26.1	

Electorate: 63,037 Turnout: 37,997 (60.3%)

HORNCHURCH, E London. Outer London, was Con, Essex traditions, ex MP runs again

Candidates 97	97 votes	97%	92%	Candidates
John Cryer (Lab)	22,066	50.2	34.5	John Cryer
Robin Squire (Con)	16,386	37.3	53.5	Robin Squire
Rabi Martin (LD)	3,446	7.8	11.1	
Majority	5,680	12.9	19	

Electorate: 60,775 Turnout: 43,941 (72.3%)

HORNSEY & WOOD GREEN, N London. Plush N London heights plus Cypriots, once marginal

Candidates 97	97 votes	97%	92%	Candidates
Barbara Roche (Lab)	31,792	61.7	48.5	Barbara Roche
Helena Hart (Con)	11,293	21.9	39.2	Jason Hollands
Lynne Featherstone (LD)	5,794	11.3	10	Lynne Featherstone
Majority	20,499	39.8	9.3	

Electorate: 74,537 Turnout: 51,487 (69.1%)

HORSHAM, W Sussex. Very prosperous, very safe Con, elects Francis Maude

Candidates 97	97 votes	97%	92%	Candidates
Francis Maude (Con)	29,015	50.8	62.3	Francis Maude
Maureen Millson (LD)	14,153	24.8	22.8	Hubert Carr
M Walsh (Lab)	10,691	18.7	11.9	
Majority	14,862	26	39.5	

Electorate: 75,431 Turnout: 57,165 (75.8%)

HOUGHTON & WASHINGTON EAST, Tyne & Wear. New town plus older ex-mining centres, very Lab

Candidates 97	97 votes	97%	92%	Candidates
Fraser Kemp (Lab)	31,946	76.4	67	Fraser Kemp
Philip Booth (Con)	5,391	12.9	21.7	Tony Devenish
Keith Miller (LD)	3,209	7.7	11.3	Richard Ormerod
Majority	26,555	63.5	45.3	

Electorate: 67,343 Turnout: 41,823 (62.1%)

HOVE, E Sussex. Grand, next to Brighton, lost to Lab in 97, if Con can't regain Hague will despair

Candidates 97	97 votes	97%	92%	Candidates
Ivor Caplin (Lab)	21,458	44.6	24.5	Ivor Caplin
Robert Guy (Con)	17,499	36.4	49	Jenny Langston
Tom Pearce (LD)	4,645	9.7	19.4	Harold de Souza
Majority	3,959	8.2	24.5	

Electorate: 69,016 Turnout: 48,121 (69.7%)

HUDDERSFIELD, W Yorkshire. Lab seat, urban, some poverty

Candidates 97	97 votes	97%	92%	Candidates
Barry Sheerman (Lab)	25,171	56.5	48.7	Barry Sheerman
Bill Forrow (Con)	9,323	20.9	33.9	Paul Baverstock
Gordon Beever (LD)	7,642	17.2	15.9	
Majority	15,848	35.6	14.8	

Electorate: 65,824 Turnout: 44,554 (67.7%)

HUNTINGDON, Cambridgeshire. Thriving, ex-John Major, safest Con seat in the land

Candidates 97	97 votes	97%	92%	Candidates
John Major (Con)	31,501	55.3	60	Jonathan Djanogly
Jason Reece (Lab)	13,361	23.5	14.5	Takki Sulaiman
Matthew Owen (LD)	8,390	14.7	21.4	Michael Pope
Majority	18,140	31.8	38.6	

Electorate: 76,094 Turnout: 56,963 (74.9%)

HYNDBURN, Lancashire. Once Lab-Con marginal, mainly urban, skilled manual

Candidates 97	97 votes	97%	92%	Candidates
Greg Pope (Lab)	26,831	55.6	46.8	Greg Pope
Peter Britcliffe (Con)	15,383	31.9	43.2	Peter Britcliffe
Les Jones (LD)	4,141	8.6	9.6	
Majority	11,448	23.7	3.6	
Electorate: 66,806 Turnout: 48,272 (72.3%)				

ILFORD NORTH, E London. Once strong Con seat, suburban, impressive if Lab holds on

Candidates 97	97 votes	97%	92%	Candidates
Linda Perham (Lab)	23,135	47.4	29.9	Linda Perham
Vivian Bendall (Con)	19,911	40.8	57.8	Vivian Bendall
Alan Dean (LD)	5,049	10.3	12.3	Gavin Stollar
Majority	3,224	6.6	27.9	
Electorate: 68,218 Turnout: 48,845 (71.6%)				

ILFORD SOUTH, E London. Less prosperous part of borough, Lab now look extremely safe here

Candidates 97	97 votes	97%	92%	Candidates
Mike Gapes (Lab)	29,273	58.5	42.1	Mike Gapes
Neil Thorne (Con)	15,073	30.1	46.9	Suresh Kumar
Aina Khan (LD)	3,152	6.3	10.4	Ralph Scott
Majority	14,200	28.4	4.8	
Electorate: 72,104 Turnout: 50,019 (69.4%)				

INVERNESS EAST, NAIRN & LOCHABER, N Scotland. LD lost 92, now Lab, SNP target, beautiful, big

Candidates 97	97 votes	97%	92%	Candidates
David Stewart (Lab)	16,187	33.9	23.2	David Stewart
Fergus Ewing (SNP)	13,848	29	25.1	Angus MacNeil
Stephen Gallagher (LD)	8,364	17.5	26.7	Patsy Kenton
Mary Scanlon (Con)	8,355	17.5	23.5	Richard Jenkins
Majority	2,339	4.9	1.6	
Electorate: 65,701 Turnout: 47,768 (72.7%)				

IPSWICH, Suffolk. Ex-marginal, now looks safer for Lab, mixed socially

Candidates 97	97 votes	97%	92%	Candidates
Jamie Cann (Lab)	25,484	52.7	43.9	Jamie Cann
Stephen Castle (Con)	15,048	31.1	43.3	Edward Wild
Nigel Roberts (LD)	5,881	12.2	11.4	
Majority	10,436	21.6	0.6	
Electorate: 66,947 Turnout: 48,362 (72.2%)				

ISLE OF WIGHT. Britain's biggest electorate, LD won in 70s and regained 97, could be tight fight

Candidates 97	97 votes	97%	92%	Candidates
Dr Peter Brand (LD)	31,274	42.7	11.4	
Andrew Turner (Con)	24,868	34	43.3	Andrew Turner
Deborah Gardiner (Lab)	9,646	13.2	43.9	Deborah Gardiner
Majority	6,406	8.7	0.6	
Electorate: 101,680 Turnout: 73,159 (72%)				

ISLINGTON NORTH, N London. Not the Blair's end of the borough, poor, radical Lab MP Jeremy Corbyn

Candidates 97	97 votes	97%	92%	Candidates
Jeremy Corbyn (Lab)	24,834	69.3	57.4	Jeremy Corbyn
James Kempton (LD)	4,879	13.6	15.1	Laura Willoughby
Simon Fawthrop (Con)	4,631	12.9	23.7	Neil Rands
Majority	19,955	55.7	33.7	
Electorate: 57,385 Turnout: 35,860 (62.5%)				

ISLINGTON SOUTH & FINSBURY, N London. Part grand, part poor, LDs win council, Lab general elections

Candidates 97	97 votes	97%	92%	Candidates
Chris Smith (Lab)	22,079	62.5	51.2	Chris Smith
Sarah Ludford (LD)	7,516	21.3	23.2	Keith Sharp
David Berens (Con)	4,587	13	24.7	Nicky Morgan
Majority	14,563	41.2	26.5	
Electorate: 55,468 Turnout: 35,316 (63.7%)				

ISLWYN, S Wales. Thought Lab stronghold until PC won at Welsh elections, anyone's guess now

Candidates 97	97 votes	97%	92%	Candidates
Don Touhig (Lab)	26,995	74.2	74.3	Don Touhig
Chris Worker (LD)	3,064	8.4	5.7	
Russell Walters (Con)	2,864	7.9	14.9	Philip Howells
Darren Jones (PC)	2,272	6.2	3.9	
Majority	23,931	65.8	68.6	
Electorate: 50,540 Turnout: 36,404 (72%)				

JARROW, Tyne & Wear. South Tyne, ex-shipbuilding, always Lab

Candidates 97	97 votes	97%	92%	Candidates
Stephen Hepburn (Lab)	28,497	64.9	62.5	Stephen Hepburn
Mark Allatt (Con)	6,564	14.9	23.4	Donald Wood
Tim Stone (LD)	4,865	11.1	14.1	James Selby
Majority	21,933	50	39.1	
Electorate: 63,827 Turnout: 43,942 (68.8%)				

KEIGHLEY, W Yorkshire. Includes Brontes' parsonage, was Con–Lab marginal until 97

Candidates 97	97 votes	97%	92%	Candidates
Ann Cryer (Lab)	26,039	50.6	40.8	Ann Cryer
Gary Waller (Con)	18,907	36.7	47.4	Simon Cooke
Mike Doyle (LD)	5,064	9.8	10.6	Mike Doyle
Majority	7,132	13.9	6.6	
Electorate: 67,231 Turnout: 51,480 (76.6%)				

KENSINGTON & CHELSEA, W London. No risk for MP Michael Portillo, Con even at by-election

Candidates 97	97 votes	97%	92%	Candidates
Alan Clark (Con)	19,887	53.6	16.7	
Robert Atkinson (Lab)	10,368	28	68.2	Simon Stanley
Robert Woodthorpe Browne (LD)	5,668	15.3	13.2	
Majority	9,519	25.6	51.5	
Electorate: 67,786 Turnout: 37,088 (54.7%)				

KETTERING, Northamptonshire. Amazing Lab win 97, will surely go Con next time

Candidates 97	97 votes	97%	92%	Candidates
Philip Sawford (Lab)	24,650	43.3	31.9	Philip Sawford
Roger Freeman (Con)	24,461	42.9	52.7	Philip Hollobone
Roger Aron (LD)	6,098	10.7	15.4	
Majority	189	0.4	20.8	
Electorate: 75,153 Turnout: 56,957 (75.8%)				

KILMARNOCK & LOUDOUN, W Scotland. Industrial, independent area SW of Glasgow, SNP target

Candidates 97	97 votes	97%	92%	Candidates
Desmond Browne (Lab)	23,621	49.8	44.8	Desmond Browne
Alex Neil (SNP)	16,365	34.5	30.7	John Brady
Douglas Taylor (Con)	5,125	10.8	19	Donald Reece
John Stewart (LD)	1,891	4	5.5	John Stewart
Majority	7,256	15.3	14.1	
Electorate: 61,376 Turnout: 47,409 (77.2%)				

KINGSTON & SURBITON, S London. LD Ed Davey just took from Con in 97, he'll need Lab tactical votes to hold

Candidates 97	97 votes	97%	92%	Candidates
Edward Davey (LD)	20,411	36.7	25.9	
Richard Tracey (Con)	20,355	36.6	53	David Shaw
Sheila Griffin (Lab)	12,811	23	19.6	Phil Woodford
Majority	56	0.1	27.1	

Electorate: 73,878 Turnout: 55,665 (75.3%)

KINGSTON UPON HULL EAST, E Yorkshire. Stamping ground of MP John Prescott, very safe, docks

Candidates 97	97 votes	97%	92%	Candidates
John Prescott (Lab)	28,870	71.3	63	John Prescott
Angus West (Con)	5,552	13.7	23.8	Sandip Verma
Jim Wastling (LD)	3,965	9.8	12.6	Jo Swinson
Majority	23,318	57.6	39.2	

Electorate: 68,733 Turnout: 40,486 (58.9%)

KINGSTON UPON HULL NORTH, E Yorkshire. Safe Lab but university, a few LD voters

Candidates 97	97 votes	97%	92%	Candidates
Kevin McNamara (Lab)	25,542	65.8	55.9	Kevin McNamara
David Lee (Con)	5,837	15	23.6	Paul Charlson
David Nolan (LD)	5,667	14.6	20	
Majority	19,705	50.8	32.3	

Electorate: 68,105 Turnout: 38,794 (57%)

KINGSTON UPON HULL WEST & HESSLE, E Yorkshire. City centre plus north end of Humber Bridge, safe

Candidates 97	97 votes	97%	92%	Candidates
Alan Johnson (Lab)	22,520	58.7	51.6	Alan Johnson
Bob Tress (LD)	6,995	18.2	17.4	
Cormach Moore (Con)	6,933	18.1	30.3	John Sharp
Majority	15,525	40.5	21.3	

Electorate: 65,840 Turnout: 38,354 (58.3%)

KINGSWOOD, Bristol. Once Con, now looks safe Lab, east of Bristol

Candidates 97	97 votes	97%	92%	Candidates
Dr Roger Berry (Lab)	32,181	53.7	40.6	Dr Roger Berry
Jon Howard (Con)	17,928	29.9	45.8	Robert Marven
Jeanne Pinkerton (LD)	7,672	12.8	13.6	Christopher Greenfield
Majority	14,253	23.8	5.2	

Electorate: 77,026 Turnout: 59,887 (77.7%)

KIRKCALDY, E Scotland. Forth coastline plus ex-industrial towns, secure Lab, some SNP votes

Candidates 97	97 votes	97%	92%	Candidates
Lewis Moonie (Lab)	18,730	53.6	45.6	Lewis Moonie
Stewart Hosie (SNP)	8,020	22.9	22.6	Shirley-Anne Somerville
Charlotte Black (Con)	4,779	13.7	22.1	
John Mainland (LD)	3,031	8.7	9.7	
Majority	10,710	30.7	23	

Electorate: 52,186 Turnout: 34,973 (67%)

KNOWSLEY NORTH & SEFTON EAST, Merseyside. Strong Lab seat, outer suburbs, high unemployment

Candidates 97	97 votes	97%	92%	Candidates
George Howarth (Lab)	34,747	69.9	54.4	George Howarth
Carl Doran (Con)	8,600	17.3	26.8	Keith Chapman
David Bamber (LD)	5,499	11.1	15.6	Richard Roberts
Majority	26,147	52.6	27.6	

Electorate: 70,918 Turnout: 49,703 (70.1%)

KNOWSLEY SOUTH, Merseyside. Biggest majority in Britain in terms of votes, Ford's Jaguar factory

Candidates 97	97 votes	97%	92%	Candidates
Edward O'Hara (Lab)	36,695	77.1	69.5	Eddie O'Hara
Gary Robertson (Con)	5,987	12.6	20.5	Paul Jemetta
Cliff Mainey (LD)	3,954	8.3	9	David Smithson
Majority	30,708	64.5	49	

Electorate: 70,532 Turnout: 47,590 (67.5%)

LAGAN VALLEY, Northern Ireland. Strong Unionist seat, mainly urban, fast growing

Candidates 97	97 votes	97%	92%	Candidates
Jeffrey Donaldson (UUP)	24,560	55.4	66.9	Jeffrey Donaldson
Seamus Close (Alliance)	7,635	17.2	11.8	
Edwin Poots (DUP)	6,005	13.6		
Delores Kelly (SDLP)	3,436	7.8	9.1	
Majority	16,925	38.2	55.1	

Electorate: 71,225 Turnout: 44,310 (62.2%)

LANCASHIRE WEST, Lancashire. Once marginal, now safe Lab, inc. struggling Skelmersdale new town

Candidates 97	97 votes	97%	92%	Candidates
Colin Pickthall (Lab)	33,022	60.3	49.4	Colin Pickthall
Christopher Varley (Con)	15,903	29.1	42.3	Jeremy Myers
Arthur Wood (LD)	3,938	7.2	7	
Majority	17,119	31.2	7.1	

Electorate: 73,175 Turnout: 54,729 (74.8%)

LANCASTER & WYRE, Lancashire. Knife-edge Lab gain 97, Lab Lancaster plus Con rural surrounds

Candidates 97	97 votes	97%	92%	Candidates
Hilton Dawson (Lab)	25,173	42.8	33	Hilton Dawson
Keith Mans (Con)	23,878	40.6	52.1	Steve Barclay
John Humberstone (LD)	6,802	11.6	14	Liz Scott
Majority	1,295	2.2	19.1	

Electorate: 78,168 Turnout: 58,862 (75.3%)

LEEDS CENTRAL, W Yorkshire. Usually safe Lab, lowest post-war turnout (19.5%) in 99 by-election almost gave seat to LDs

Candidates 97	97 votes	97%	92%	Candidates
Derek Fatchett (Lab)	25,766	69.6	63.7	Hilary Benn
Edward Wild (Con)	5,077	13.7	22.4	Victoria Richmond
David Freeman (LD)	4,164	11.3	14	
Majority	20,689	55.9	41.3	

Electorate: 67,664 Turnout: 37,009 (54.7%)

LEEDS EAST, W Yorkshire. Strong Lab seat, inner city, much council housing, some Asian voters

Candidates 97	97 votes	97%	92%	Candidates
George Mudie (Lab)	24,151	67.5	57.7	George Mudie
John Emsley (Con)	6,685	18.7	28.3	Barry Anderson
Madeleine Kirk (LD)	3,689	10.3	14	
Majority	17,466	48.8	29.4	

Electorate: 56,963 Turnout: 35,792 (62.8%)

LEEDS NORTH EAST, W Yorkshire. Once safe Con, Lab gain 97, probably Lab in future

Candidates 97	97 votes	97%	92%	Candidates
Fabian Hamilton (Lab)	22,368	49.2	36.8	Fabian Hamilton
Timothy Kirkhope (Con)	15,409	33.9	45.4	Owain Rhys
Dr Bill Winlow (LD)	6,318	13.9	16.7	Jonathan Brown
Majority	6,959	15.3	8.6	

Electorate: 63,185 Turnout: 45,509 (72%)

LEEDS NORTH WEST, W Yorkshire. Outer suburbs, professional, Lab gain from 3rd in 97

Candidates 97	97 votes	97%	92%	Candidates
Harold Best (Lab)	19,694	39.9	27.3	Harold Best
Dr Keith Hampson (Con)	15,850	32.1	43	Adam Pritchard
Barbara Pearce (LD)	11,689	23.7	27.8	David Hall-Matthews
Majority	3,844	7.8	15.2	
Electorate: 69,971 Turnout: 49,376 (70.6%)				

LEEDS WEST, W Yorkshire. Once Lib, now safe Lab again, Aire valley

Candidates 97	97 votes	97%	92%	Candidates
John Battle (Lab)	26,819	66.7	55.1	John Battle
John Whelan (Con)	7,048	17.5	26.2	John Robertshaw
Nigel Amor (LD)	3,622	9	8.9	
Majority	19,771	49.2	28.9	
Electorate: 63,965 Turnout: 40,220 (62.9%)				

LEICESTER EAST, Leicestershire. Inner city, strongly Asian, controversial MP Keith Vaz

Candidates 97	97 votes	97%	92%	Candidates
Keith Vaz (Lab)	29,083	65.5	56.3	Keith Vaz
Simon Wilton (Con)	10,661	24	33.7	John Mugglestone
Jay Matabudul (LD)	3,105	7	8.1	Jim Marshall
Majority	18,422	41.5	22.6	
Electorate: 64,012 Turnout: 44,402 (69.4%)				

LEICESTER SOUTH, Leicestershire. Lab seat, mixed residential, strongly Asian, Lab secure

Candidates 97	97 votes	97%	92%	Candidates
James Marshall (Lab)	27,914	58	52.3	
Christopher Heaton-Harris (Con)	11,421	23.7	34.6	Richard Hoile
B Coles (LD)	6,654	13.8	11.7	Parmjit Singh Gill
Majority	16,493	34.3	17.7	
Electorate: 71,750 Turnout: 48,114 (67.1%)				

LEICESTER WEST, Leicestershire. Lab now secure, most white in city

Candidates 97	97 votes	97%	92%	Candidates
Patricia Hewitt (Lab)	22,580	55.2	46.8	Patricia Hewitt
Richard Thomas (Con)	9,716	23.7	38.5	Chris Shaw
Mark Jones (LD)	5,795	14.2	13.3	Andrew Vincent
Majority	12,864	31.5	8.3	
Electorate: 64,570 Turnout: 40,914 (63.4%)				

LEICESTERSHIRE NORTH WEST, Leicestershire. Big Lab gain 97, should hold, ex-mining, residential

Candidates 97	97 votes	97%	92%	Candidates
David Taylor (Lab)	29,332	56.4	43.8	David Taylor
Robert Goodwill (Con)	16,113	31	45.4	Nick Weston
Stan Heptinstall (LD)	4,492	8.6	10.4	
Majority	13,219	25.4	1.6	
Electorate: 65,068 Turnout: 52,025 (80%)				

LEIGH, Greater Manchester. Old-fashioned heartland Lab seat, ex-mining, working class

Candidates 97	97 votes	97%	92%	Candidates
Lawrence Cunliffe (Lab)	31,652	68.9	59.3	
Edward Young (Con)	7,156	15.6	27.3	Andrew Oxley
Peter Hough (LD)	5,163	11.2	12.4	
Majority	24,496	53.3	32	
Electorate: 69,908 Turnout: 45,920 (65.7%)				

LEOMINSTER, Herefordshire. Lib hope in 70s, now fairly safe Con but MP joined Lab 98

Candidates 97	97 votes	97%	92%	Candidates
Peter Temple-Morris (Con)	22,888	45.3	56.3	Bill Wiggin
Terry James (LD)	14,053	27.8	27.8	Celia Downie
Richard Westward (Lab)	8,831	17.5	12.3	Stephen Hart
Majority	8,835	17.5	28.5	
Electorate: 65,993 Turnout: 50,553 (76.6%)				

LEWES, E Sussex. Gained by busy LD campaigner Norman Baker 97, could hold on

Candidates 97	97 votes	97%	92%	Candidates
Norman Baker (LD)	21,250	43.2	39.1	
Tim Rathbone (Con)	19,950	40.6	51.3	Simon Sinnatt
Dr Mark Patton (Lab)	5,232	10.6	8.2	Paul Richards
Majority	1,300	2.6	12.2	

Electorate: 64,340 Turnout: 49,169 (76.4%)

LEWISHAM DEPTFORD, S London. Strong Lab seat, inner city, large black population

Candidates 97	97 votes	97%	92%	Candidates
Joan Ruddock (Lab)	23,827	70.8	60.6	Joan Ruddock
Irene Kimm (Con)	4,949	14.7	27.6	Cordelia McCartney
Kofi Appiah (LD)	3,004	8.9	11.8	Andrew Wiseman
Majority	18,878	56.1	33	

Electorate: 58,141 Turnout: 33,644 (57.9%)

LEWISHAM EAST, S London. Suburban, large black population, once marginal

Candidates 97	97 votes	97%	92%	Candidates
Bridget Prentice (Lab)	21,821	58.3	45.4	Bridget Prentice
Philip Hollobone (Con)	9,694	25.9	42.8	David McInnes
David Buxton (LD)	4,178	11.2	11.4	David Buxton
Majority	12,127	32.4	2.6	

Electorate: 56,332 Turnout: 37,408 (66.4%)

LEWISHAM WEST, S London. Suburban, large black population, once marginal

Candidates 97	97 votes	97%	92%	Candidates
Jim Dowd (Lab)	23,273	62	47	Jim Dowd
Clare Whelan (Con)	8,956	23.8	42.8	Gary Johnson
Kathy McGrath (LD)	3,672	9.8	9.9	Richard Thomas
Majority	14,317	38.2	4.2	

Electorate: 58,659 Turnout: 37,544 (64%)

LEYTON & WANSTEAD, N London. Safe Lab seat, urban, large non-white population

Candidates 97	97 votes	97%	92%	Candidates
Harry Cohen (Lab)	23,922	60.8	45.8	Harry Cohen
Robert Vaudry (Con)	8,736	22.2	30.9	Edward Heckels
Charles Anglin (LD)	5,920	15.1	20.5	Alex Wilcock
Majority	15,186	38.6	14.9	

Electorate: 62,175 Turnout: 39,322 (63.2%)

LICHFIELD, Staffordshire. Colourful Con MP just held on in 97, should do better next time

Candidates 97	97 votes	97%	92%	Candidates
Michael Fabricant (Con)	20,853	42.9	57	
Susan Woodward (Lab)	20,615	42.4	20.5	Martin Machray
Phillip Bennion (LD)	5,473	11.3	5.7	Phillip Bennion
Majority	238	0.5	36.5	

Electorate: 62,720 Turnout: 48,593 (77.5%)

LINCOLN, Lincolnshire. Lab heritage restored after Con spell in 80s, hard-to-reach small city

Candidates 97	97 votes	97%	92%	Candidates
Gillian Merron (Lab)	25,563	54.9	46	Gillian Merron
Tony Brown (Con)	14,433	31	44.2	Christine Talbot
Lisa Gabriel (LD)	5,048	10.8	8.8	Lisa Gabriel
Majority	11,130	23.9	1.8	

Electorate: 65,484 Turnout: 46,548 (71.1%)

LINLITHGOW, E Scotland. Edinburgh airport plus small town, ex-shale mines, SNP target

Candidates 97	97 votes	97%	92%	Candidates
Tam Dalyell (Lab)	21,469	54.1	49.2	Tam Dalyell
Kenneth MacAskill (SNP)	10,631	26.8	30.1	Jim Sibbald
Tom Kerr (Con)	4,964	12.5	13.7	
Andrew Duncan (LD)	2,331	5.9	6.9	Martin Oliver
Majority	10,838	27.3	19.1	

Electorate: 53,706 Turnout: 39,654 (73.8%)

LIVERPOOL GARSTON, Merseyside. Strong Lab seat though LDs run council, suburban

Candidates 97	97 votes	97%	92%	Candidates
Maria Eagle (Lab)	26,667	61.3	51.1	Maria Eagle
Flo Clucas (LD)	8,250	19	21.6	Paula Keaveney
Nigel Gordon-Johnson (Con)	6,819	15.7	25	Helen Sutton
Majority	18,417	42.3	26.1	

Electorate: 66,755 Turnout: 43,482 (65.1%)

LIVERPOOL RIVERSIDE, Merseyside. City centre, high unemployment, some LD councilors

Candidates 97	97 votes	97%	92%	Candidates
Louise Ellman (Lab)	26,858	70.4	68.4	Louise Ellman
B Fraenkel (LD)	5,059	13.3	18.4	Richard Marbrow
D Sparrow (Con)	3,635	9.5	10.9	Judith Edwards
Majority	21,799	57.1	50	

Electorate: 73,429 Turnout: 38,135 (51.9%)

LIVERPOOL WALTON, Merseyside. Strong Lab seat, inner city, high unemployment

Candidates 97	97 votes	97%	92%	Candidates
Peter Kilfoyle (Lab)	31,516	78.4	72.4	Peter Kilfoyle
Richard Roberts (LD)	4,478	11.1	12	Kiron Reid
Mark Kotecha (Con)	2,551	6.3	12.5	Stephen Horgan
Majority	27,038	67.3	59.9	

Electorate: 67,527 Turnout: 40,207 (59.5%)

LIVERPOOL WAVERTREE, Merseyside. Now Lab, onetime LD marginal, suburban, working class

Candidates 97	97 votes	97%	92%	Candidates
Jane Kennedy (Lab)	29,592	64.4	41.3	Jane Kennedy
Richard Kemp (LD)	9,891	21.5	34.7	Christopher Newby
Christopher Malthouse (Con)	4,944	10.8	12.5	Geoffrey Allen
Majority	19,701	42.9	6.6	

Electorate: 73,063 Turnout: 45,918 (62.8%)

LIVERPOOL WEST DERBY, Merseyside. Outer suburbs, council estates, Libs (not LD) 2nd in 97

Candidates 97	97 votes	97%	92%	Candidates
Robert Wareing (Lab)	30,002	71.2	64.6	Robert Wareing
Stephen Radford (Lib)	4,037	9.6		
Ann Hines (LD)	3,805	9	15.3	
Majority	25,965	61.6	49	

Electorate: 68,682 Turnout: 42,157 (61.4%)

LIVINGSTON, E Scotland. Lab seat,SNP longshot, new town

Candidates 97	97 votes	97%	92%	Candidates
Robin Cook (Lab)	23,510	54.9	45.8	Robin Cook
Peter Johnston (SNP)	11,763	27.5	9.1	Graham Sutherland
Hugh Craigie Halkett (Con)	4,028	9.4	18.1	
E Hawthorn (LD)	2,876	6.7	25.9	Gordon Mackenzie
Majority	11,747	27.4	19.9	

Electorate: 60,296 Turnout: 42,834 (71%)

LLANELLI, W Wales. Rugby playing south-west Wales, PC pulled of a shock win in 99 Welsh elections

Candidates 97	97 votes	97%	92%	Candidates
Denzil Davies (Lab)	23,851	57.9	54.5	Denzil Davies
Marc Phillips (PC)	7,812	19	15.7	Dyfan Jones
Andrew Hayes (Con)	5,003	12.1	17	
Majority	16,039	38.9	37.5	
Electorate: 58,322 Turnout: 41,211 (70.7%)				

LONDONDERRY EAST, Northern Ireland. Strong Unionist seat, rural, scenic north coast

Candidates 97	97 votes	97%	92%	Candidates
William Ross (UUP)	13,558	35.6	64.9	
Gregory Campbell (DUP)	9,764	25.6	–	
Arthur Doherty (SDLP)	8,273	21.7	19.9	
Malachy O'Kane (SF)	3,463	9.1	3.5	
Majority	3,794	10	45	
Electorate: 58,831 Turnout: 38,102 (64.8%)				

LOUGHBOROUGH, Leicestershire. Lab marginal,Con target seat, suburban

Candidates 97	97 votes	97%	92%	Candidates
Andrew Reed (Lab)	25,448	48.6	39.8	Andy Reed
Kenneth Andrew (Con)	19,736	37.7	46.8	Neil Lyon
Diana Brass (LD)	6,190	11.8	11.3	
Majority	5,712	10.9	7	
Electorate: 68,945 Turnout: 52,365 (76%)				

LOUTH & HORNCASTLE, Lincolnshire. Coast and north Lincs towns, rural

Candidates 97	97 votes	97%	92%	Candidates
Sir Peter Tapsell (Con)	21,699	43.4	52.7	
John Hough (Lab)	14,799	29.6	13.7	David Bolland
Fiona Martin (LD)	12,207	24.4	31.7	Fiona Martin
Majority	6,900	13.8	21	
Electorate: 68,824 Turnout: 49,953 (72.6%)				

LUDLOW, Shropshire. Big, rural, hills and small towns, LDs have longterm hopes

Candidates 97	97 votes	97%	92%	Candidates
Christopher Gill (Con)	19,633	42.4	51.6	Martin Taylor-Smith
Ian Huffer (LD)	13,724	29.7	25.6	Matthew Green
Nuala O'Kane (Lab)	11,745	25.4	21.4	Nigel Knowles
Majority	5,909	12.7	26	
Electorate: 61,267 Turnout: 46,285 (75.5%)				

LUTON NORTH, Bedfordshire. Urban, Lab gain 97, some Tory voters make it Con longshot

Candidates 97	97 votes	97%	92%	Candidates
Kelvin Hopkins (Lab)	25,860	54.6	37.2	Kelvin Hopkins
David Senior (Con)	16,234	34.3	51.2	Amanda Sater
Kathryn Newbound (LD)	4,299	9.1	10.1	Bob Hoyle
Majority	9,626	20.3	14	
Electorate: 64,617 Turnout: 47,332 (73.2%)				

LUTON SOUTH, Bedfordshire. Airport, closing car plant, Lab gain 97, now looks safe

Candidates 97	97 votes	97%	92%	Candidates
Margaret Moran (Lab)	26,428	54.8	43.2	Margaret Moran
Graham Bright (Con)	15,109	31.4	44.3	Gordon Henderson
K Fitchett (LD)	4,610	9.6	11.2	Rabi Martins
Majority	11,319	23.4	1.1	
Electorate: 68,395 Turnout: 48,184 (70.4%)				

MACCLESFIELD, Cheshire. Prosperous town at foot of Peak hills, Con but many LD voters

Candidates 97	97 votes	97%	92%	Candidates
Nicholas Winterton (Con)	26,888	49.6	56	
Janet Jackson (Lab)	18,234	33.6	22.9	Stephen Carter
Mike Flynn (LD)	9,075	16.7	20.7	Mike Flynn
Majority	8,654	16	33.1	

Electorate: 72,049 Turnout: 54,197 (75.2%)

MAIDENHEAD, Berkshire. Strong Con seat, managerial, secure even in 97

Candidates 97	97 votes	97%	92%	Candidates
Theresa May (Con)	25,344	49.8	61.6	
Andrew Ketteringham (LD)	13,363	26.3	29.8	Kathryn Newbound
Denise Robson (Lab)	9,205	18.1	8.6	John O'Farrell
Majority	11,981	23.5	31.8	

Electorate: 67,302 Turnout: 50,889 (75.6%)

MAIDSTONE & THE WEALD, Kent. Safe mixed seat of famous Con MP Ann Widdecombe

Candidates 97	97 votes	97%	92%	Candidates
Ann Widdecombe (Con)	23,657	44.1	56.1	Ann Widdecombe
John Morgan (Lab)	14,054	26.2	12.5	Mark Davis
Jane Nelson (LD)	11,986	22.4	30.3	Kathryn Newbound
Majority	9,603	17.9	25.8	

Electorate: 72,466 Turnout: 53,608 (74%)

MAKERFIELD, Greater Manchester. Massively strong Lab seat, mainly urban, skilled manual

Candidates 97	97 votes	97%	92%	Candidates
Ian McCartney (Lab)	33,119	73.6	63.3	Ian McCartney
Michael Winstanley (Con)	6,942	15.4	24.4	
Bruce Hubbard (LD)	3,743	8.3	9.2	
Majority	26,177	58.2	38.9	

Electorate: 45,014 Turnout: 67,358 (66.8%)

MALDON & CHELMSFORD EAST, Essex. Strong Con seat, Essex coast, mainly rural, managerial

Candidates 97	97 votes	97%	92%	Candidates
John Whittingdale (Con)	24,524	48.7	63.9	
Kevin Freeman (Lab)	14,485	28.7	12.8	Russell Kennedy
Graham Pooley (LD)	9,758	19.4	22	Jane Jackson
Majority	10,039	20	51.1	

Electorate: 66,184 Turnout: 50,387 (76.1%)

MANCHESTER BLACKLEY, Greater Manchester. Strong Lab seat, inner city, high unemployment

Candidates 97	97 votes	97%	92%	Candidates
Graham Stringer (Lab)	25,042	70	62.2	Graham Stringer
Steve Barclay (Con)	5,454	15.3	26	Lance Stanbury
Simon Wheale (LD)	3,937	11	11	
Majority	19,588	54.7	36.2	

Electorate: 62,227 Turnout: 35,756 (57.5%)

MANCHESTER CENTRAL, Greater Manchester. Now trendy city centre plus poor surrounds, safe Lab

Candidates 97	97 votes	97%	92%	Candidates
Tony Lloyd (Lab)	23,803	71	69.1	Tony Lloyd
Alison Firth (LD)	4,121	12.3	10.5	
Simon McIlwaine (Con)	3,964	11.8	19.4	Aaron Powell
Majority	19,682	58.7	49.7	

Electorate: 63,815 Turnout: 33,537 (52.6%)

MANCHESTER GORTON, Greater Manchester. Inner city, high unemployment, LD vote creeping up

Candidates 97	97 votes	97%	92%	Candidates
Gerald Kaufman (Lab)	23,704	65.3	62.3	Gerald Kaufman
Dr Jackie Pearcey (LD)	6,362	17.5	14	Dr Jackie Pearcey
Guy Senior (Con)	4,249	11.7	19.5	
Majority	17,342	47.8	42.8	

Electorate: 64,348 Turnout: 36,311 (56.4%)

MANCHESTER WITHINGTON, Greater Manchester. Strong Lab seat, gentrifying suburbs, some LD activity

Candidates 97	97 votes	97%	92%	Candidates
Keith Bradley (Lab)	27,103	61.6	52.7	Keith Bradley
Jonathan Smith (Con)	8,522	19.4	31.3	Julian Samways
Yasmen Zalzala (LD)	6,000	13.6	14.2	Yasmin Zalzala
Majority	18,581	42.2	21.4	

Electorate: 66,116 Turnout: 44,027 (66.6%)

MANSFIELD, Nottinghamshire. Recovering from closure of coal mines, utterly safe for Lab

Candidates 97	97 votes	97%	92%	Candidates
Alan Meale (Lab)	30,556	64.4	54.4	Alan Meale
Tim Frost (Con)	10,038	21.2	33.1	William Wellesley
Phil Smith (LD)	5,244	11.1	12.6	
Majority	20,518	43.2	21.3	

Electorate: 67,056 Turnout: 47,426 (70.7%)

MEDWAY, Kent. Urban, white collar, Lab gained 97, Con must take to form government

Candidates 97	97 votes	97%	92%	Candidates
Robert Marshall-Andrews (Lab)	21,858	48.9	34.6	Robert Marshall-Andrews
Dame Peggy Fenner (Con)	16,504	36.9	52.3	Mark Reckless
Roger Roberts (LD)	4,555	10.2	9.6	
Majority	5,354	12	17.7	

Electorate: 61,736 Turnout: 44,742 (72.5%)

MEIRIONNYDD NANT CONWY, NW Wales. Very small electorate, hilly, very safe for PC

Candidates 97	97 votes	97%	92%	Candidates
Elfyn Llwyd (PC)	12,465	50.7	44	Elfyn Llwyd
Hefin Rees (Lab)	5,660	23	18.8	Denise Jones
Jeremy Quin (Con) ·	3,922	16	26.5	Lisa Francis
Bobby Feeley (LD)	1,719	7	8.9	
Majority	6,805	27.7	25.2	

Electorate: 32,345 Turnout: 24,575 (76%)

MERIDEN, W Midlands. Once Lab but Con held even in 97, suburbs east of Birmingham

Candidates 97	97 votes	97%	92%	Candidates
Caroline Spelman (Con)	22,997	42	55.1	
Brian Seymour-Smith (Lab)	22,415	41	30.9	Christine Shawcroft
Tony Dupont (LD)	7,098	13	14	
Majority	582	1	24.2	

Electorate: 76,286 Turnout: 54,718 (71.7%)

MERTHYR TYDFIL & RHYMNEY, S Wales. Most votes go to Lab, valleys, unemployment

Candidates 97	97 votes	97%	92%	Candidates
Edward Rowlands (Lab)	30,012	76.7	71.6	Dai Havard
Duncan Anstey (LD)	2,926	7.5	11.3	
Jonathan Morgan (Con)	2,508	6.4	11.1	Richard Cuming
Alun Cox (PC)	2,344	6	6.1	Robert Hughes
Majority	27,086	69.2	60.3	

Electorate: 56,507 Turnout: 39,141 (69.3%)

MIDDLESBROUGH, NE England. Strong Lab seat, urban, high unemployment

Candidates 97	97 votes	97%	92%	Candidates
Stuart Bell (Lab)	32,925	71.4	61.1	Stuart Bell
Liam Bentham (Con)	7,907	17.2	29.9	Alex Finn
Miss Alison Charlesworth (LD)	3,934	8.5	9	
Majority	25,018	54.2	31.2	

Electorate: 70,930 Turnout: 46,097 (65%)

MIDDLESBROUGH SOUTH & CLEVELAND EAST, NE England. Ought to be marginal but huge Lab win in 97

Candidates 97	97 votes	97%	92%	Candidates
Dr Ashok Kumar (Lab)	29,319	54.7	43.3	Dr Ashok Kumar
Michael Bates (Con)	18,712	34.9	45.8	Barbara Harpham
Hamish Garrett (LD)	4,004	7.5	10.9	
Majority	10,607	19.8	2.5	
Electorate: 70,480 Turnout: 53,587 (76%)				

MIDLOTHIAN, E Scotland. Gladstone made it famous but Lab win with ease, south of Edinburgh, SNP longshot

Candidates 97	97 votes	97%	92%	Candidates
Eric Clarke (Lab)	18,861	53.5	48.2	David Hamilton
Laurence Millar (SNP)	8,991	25.5	23.2	Ian Goldie
Anne Harper (Con)	3,842	10.9	17.6	
Richard Pinnock (LD)	3,235	9.2	10	Jacqueline Bell
Majority	9,870	28	25	
Electorate: 47,552 Turnout: 35,249 (74.1%)				

MILTON KEYNES NORTH EAST, Buckinghamshire. Lab just won in 97, Con banker for gain next time

Candidates 97	97 votes	97%	92%	Candidates
Brian White (Lab)	20,201	39.4	23.7	
Peter Butler (Con)	19,961	39	51.6	Marion Rix
Graham Mabbutt (LD)	8,907	17.4	23	David Yeoward
Majority	240	0.4	27.9	
Electorate: 70,394 Turnout: 51,236 (72.8%)				

MILTON KEYNES SOUTH WEST, Buckinghamshire. New town plus Bletchley of Enigma fame, Lab safe now

Candidates 97	97 votes	97%	92%	Candidates
Dr Phyllis Starkey (Lab)	27,298	53.8	37.4	Dr Phyllis Starkey
Barry Legg (Con)	17,006	33.5	46.6	Iain Stewart
Peter Jones (LD)	6,065	11.9	14.5	Nazar Mohammed
Majority	10,292	20.3	-9.2	
Electorate: 71,070 Turnout: 50,758 (71.4%)				

MITCHAM & MORDEN, S London. Once Con marginal, now Lab, outer suburbs, white collar

Candidates 97	97 votes	97%	92%	Candidates
Siobhain McDonagh (Lab)	27,984	58.4	43.1	Siobhain McDonagh
Angela Rumbold (Con)	14,243	29.7	46.5	Harry Stokes
Nick Harris (LD)	3,632	7.6	9.2	
Majority	13,741	28.7	3.4	
Electorate: 65,385 Turnout: 47,946 (73.3%)				

MOLE VALLEY, Surrey. Strong Con seat, mainly rural, middle class

Candidates 97	97 votes	97%	92%	Candidates
Sir Paul Beresford (Con)	26,178	48	61.4	
Stephen Cooksey (LD)	15,957	29.3	28.6	Celia Savage
Christopher Payne (Lab)	8,057	14.8	9.4	Dan Redford
Majority	10,221	18.7	32.8	
Electorate: 69,139 Turnout: 54,524 (78.9%)				

MONMOUTH, S Wales. Marginal, Lab gain 97, Con won 99 Welsh elections, English borders

Candidates 97	97 votes	97%	92%	Candidates
Huw Edwards (Lab)	23,404	47.7	41	Huw Edwards
Roger Evans (Con)	19,226	39.2	47.3	Roger Evans
Mark Williams (LD)	4,689	9.6	10.9	Neil Parker
N Warry (Ref)	1,190	2.4	0.8	
Majority	4,178	8.5	6.3	
Electorate: 60,703 Turnout: 49,025 (80.8%)				

MONTGOMERYSHIRE, Mid Wales. Very rural, almost always LD, safe for unusual MP Lembit Öpik, hit by foot and mouth

Candidates 97	97 votes	97%	92%	Candidates
Lembit Öpik (LD)	14,647	45.9	48.5	Lembit Öpik
Glyn Davies (Con)	8,344	26.1	32.7	David Jones
Angharad Davies (Lab)	6,109	19.1	12.4	Paul Davies
H Jones (PC)	1,608	5	4.8	David Senior
Majority	6,303	19.8	15.8	

Electorate: 42,618 Turnout: 31,925 (74.9%)

MORAY, NE Scotland. SNP now safe, rural NE Scotland including Elgin, some Con votes

Candidates 97	97 votes	97%	92%	Candidates
Margaret Ewing (SNP)	16,529	41.6	44.6	Angus Robertson
Andrew Findlay (Con)	10,963	27.6	37.5	
Lewis Macdonald (Lab)	7,886	19.8	11.9	
Debra Storr (LD)	3,548	8.9	6	Linda Gorn
Majority	5,566	14	7.1	

Electorate: 58,302 Turnout: 39,766 (68.2%)

MORECAMBE & LUNESDALE, Lancashire. Big Lab win 97, declining seaside town, Con longshot now

Candidates 97	97 votes	97%	92%	Candidates
Geraldine Smith (Lab)	24,061	48.9	29.4	Geraldine Smith
Mark Lennox-Boyd (Con)	18,096	36.7	49.2	David Nuttall
June Greenwell (LD)	5,614	11.4	19.1	
Majority	5,965	12.2	19.8	

Electorate: 68,013 Turnout: 49,249 (72.4%)

MORLEY & ROTHWELL, W Yorkshire. Lab seat, urban, skilled manual, Con remote 2nd

Candidates 97	97 votes	97%	92%	Candidates
John Gunnell (Lab)	26,836	58.5	49.5	Colin Challen
Alan Barraclough (Con)	12,086	26.3	36.9	David Schofield
Mitchell Galdas (LD)	5,087	11.1	13	Stewart Golton
Majority	14,750	32.2	12.6	

Electorate: 68,385 Turnout: 45,897 (67.1%)

MOTHERWELL & WISHAW, W Scotland. Strong Lab seat, steel industry jobs gone

Candidates 97	97 votes	97%	92%	Candidates
Frank Roy (Lab)	21,020	57.4	56.5	Frank Roy
James McGuigan (SNP)	8,229	22.5	21.4	James McGuigan
Scott Dickson (Con)	4,024	11	15.6	
Alex Mackie (LD)	2,331	6.4	6.1	
Majority	12,791	34.9	35.1	

Electorate: 52,252 Turnout: 36,619 (70.1%)

NEATH, S Wales. Totally safe Lab seat, valleys, Lab minister Peter Hain is MP

Candidates 97	97 votes	97%	92%	Candidates
Peter Hain (Lab)	30,324	73.5	68	Peter Hain
Dr Dewi Evans (Con)	3,583	8.7	15.2	David Devine
T Jones (PC)	3,344	8.1	11.3	
Frank Little (LD)	2,597	6.3	5.4	
Majority	26,741	64.8	52.8	

Electorate: 55,524 Turnout: 41,243 (74.3%)

NEWARK, Nottinghamshire. Lab gain 97, major Con target, MP restored after court ruling

Candidates 97	97 votes	97%	92%	Candidates
Fiona Jones (Lab)	23,496	45.2	35.8	Fiona Jones
Richard Alexander (Con)	20,480	39.4	50.4	Patrick Mercer
Peter Harris (LD)	5,960	11.5	13	David Harding-Price
Majority	3,016	5.8	14.6	

Electorate: 69,763 Turnout: 51,971 (74.5%)

NEWBURY, Berkshire. LD held easily 97, hope to do so again, bypass was issue, also new Vodafone HQ

Candidates 97	97 votes	97%	92%	Candidates
David Rendel (LD)	29,887	52.9	37.1	
Richard Benyon (Con)	21,370	37.8	55.9	Richard Benyon
Paul Hannon (Lab)	3,107	5.5	6.1	Steve Billcliffe
Majority	8,517	15.1	18.8	

Electorate: 73,680 Turnout: 56,476 (76.7%)

NEWCASTLE-UNDER-LYME, Staffordshire. Lab in no danger here, ex-mining and potteries

Candidates 97	97 votes	97%	92%	Candidates
Llin Golding (Lab)	27,743	56.5	47.9	Paul Farrelly
Marcus Hayes (Con)	10,537	21.4	29.6	Mike Flynn
Dr Robin Studd (LD)	6,858	14	21.9	Jerry Roodhouse
Majority	17,206	35.1	18.3	

Electorate: 66,686 Turnout: 49,129 (73.7%)

NEWCASTLE UPON TYNE CENTRAL, Tyne & Wear. Bigger Con vote than might expect, professional

Candidates 97	97 votes	97%	92%	Candidates
Jim Cousins (Lab)	27,272	59.2	47.9	Jim Cousins
Brooks Newmark (Con)	10,792	23.4	29.6	Aidan Ruff
Ruth Berry (LD)	6,911	15	21.9	Stephen Psallidas
Majority	16,480	35.8	18.3	

Electorate: 69,781 Turnout: 46,088 (66%)

NEWCASTLE UPON TYNE EAST & WALLSEND, Tyne & Wear. Strong Lab seat, inner city, inc. Byker and river

Candidates 97	97 votes	97%	92%	Candidates
Nick Brown (Lab)	29,607	71.2	57.2	Nick Brown
Jeremy Middleton (Con)	5,796	13.9	22.5	Tim Troman
Graham Morgan (LD)	4,415	10.6	18.7	David Ord
Majority	23,811	57.3	34.7	

Electorate: 63,271 Turnout: 41,589 (65.7%)

NEWCASTLE UPON TYNE NORTH, Tyne & Wear. Lab seat, now safe, once 3-way, suburban

Candidates 97	97 votes	97%	92%	Candidates
Doug Henderson (Lab)	28,125	62.2	49.4	Doug Henderson
Greg White (Con)	8,793	19.4	31.8	Phillip Smith
Peter Allen (LD)	6,578	14.5	18.8	Graham Soult
Majority	19,332	42.8	17.6	

Electorate: 65,357 Turnout: 45,229 (69.2%)

NEW FOREST EAST, Hampshire. Woods plus growing shoreline suburbs, safe Con despite LD activity

Candidates 97	97 votes	97%	92%	Candidates
Dr Julian Lewis (Con)	21,053	42.9	53.1	
George Dawson (LD)	15,838	32.3	33.4	
Alan Goodfellow (Lab)	12,161	24.8	12.7	Alan Goodfellow
Majority	5,215	10.6	19.7	

Electorate: 65,717 Turnout: 49,052 (74.6%)

NEW FOREST WEST, Hampshire. Very safe Con, Bournemouth borders plus forest

Candidates 97	97 votes	97%	92%	Candidates
Desmond Swayne (Con)	25,149	50.6	60.7	
Bob Hale (LD)	13,817	27.8	30.5	
David Griffiths (Lab)	7,092	14.3	8.2	
Majority	11,332	22.8	30.2	

Electorate: 66,522 Turnout: 49,750 (74.8%)

NEWPORT EAST, S Wales. Urban terraces, safe for ex-Con, now Lab minister Alan Howarth, hit by steel closure

Candidates 97	97 votes	97%	92%	Candidates
Alan Howarth (Lab)	21,481	57.7	55	Alan Howarth
David Evans (Con)	7,958	21.4	31.4	Ian Oakley
Alistair Cameron (LD)	3,880	10.4	11.9	Alistair Cameron
Majority	13,523	36.3	23.6	

Electorate: 50,997 Turnout: 37,258 (73.1%)

NEWPORT WEST, S Wales. Safe base for Lab campaign Paul Flynn, amazing was Con in 83

Candidates 97	97 votes	97%	92%	Candidates
Paul Flynn (Lab)	24,331	60.5	53.1	Paul Flynn
Peter Clarke (Con)	9,794	24.4	36	Dr William Morgan
Stanley Wilson (LD)	3,907	9.7	9.5	Veronica Watkins
Majority	14,537	36.1	17.1	

Electorate: 53,914 Turnout: 40,202 (74.6%)

NEWRY & ARMAGH, Northern Ireland. Rural, Catholic south of province

Candidates 97	97 votes	97%	92%	Candidates
Seamus Mallon (SDLP)	22,904	43	49.3	
Danny Kennedy (UUP)	18,015	33.8	36.3	
Pat McNamee (SF)	11,218	21.1	12.5	
P Whitcroft (Alliance)	1,015	1.9	1.9	
Majority	4,889	9.2	13.1	

Electorate: 70,652 Turnout: 53,275 (75.4%)

NORFOLK MID, Norfolk. Strong Con seat, rural plus broads, Lab surge 97 saw Con almost lose

Candidates 97	97 votes	97%	92%	Candidates
Keith Simpson (Con)	22,739	39.6	54.6	
Daniel Zeichner (Lab)	21,403	37.3	26.1	Daniel Zeichner
Sue Frary (LD)	8,617	15	19	
Majority	1,336	2.3	28.5	

Electorate: 75,311 Turnout: 57,457 (76.3%)

NORFOLK NORTH, Norfolk. Interesting LD target, almost took 97, Lab vote key to result

Candidates 97	97 votes	97%	92%	Candidates
David Prior (Con)	21456	36.5	54.6	
Norman Lamb (LD)	20163	34.3	19	Norman Lamb
Michael Cullingham (Lab)	14736	25.1	26.1	Michael Gates
Majority	1,293	2.2	28.5	

Electorate: 77,112 Turnout: 58,813 (76.3%)

NORFOLK NORTH WEST, Norfolk. Mainly rural, part working class, inc. King's Lynn, Con target

Candidates 97	97 votes	97%	92%	Candidates
Dr George Turner (Lab)	25,250	43.8	33.6	Dr George Turner
Henry Bellingham (Con)	23,911	41.5	52.1	Henry Bellingham
E Knowles (LD)	5,513	9.6	13.8	
Majority	1,339	2.3	18.5	

Electorate: 77,083 Turnout: 57,597 (74.7%)

NORFOLK SOUTH, Norfolk. Still safe Con seat, rural, middle class, long distance commuters

Candidates 97	97 votes	97%	92%	Candidates
John MacGregor (Con)	24,935	40.2	52.4	Richard Bacon
Barbara Hacker (LD)	17,557	28.3	26.9	Anne Lee
J Ross (Lab)	16,188	26.1	18.4	Mark Wells
Majority	7,378	11.9	25.5	

Electorate: 79,239 Turnout: 62,097 (78.4%)

NORFOLK SOUTH WEST, Norfolk. Narrow Con win in 97, small towns, rural

Candidates 97	97 votes	97%	92%	Candidates
Gillian Shephard (Con)	24,694	42	54.7	
Adrian Hefferman (Lab)	22,230	37.8	27	Anne Hanson
David Bucton (LD)	8,178	13.9	18.2	
Majority	2,464	4.2	27.7	

Electorate: 80,236 Turnout: 58,796 (73.3%)

NORMANTON, W Yorkshire. Outside Wakefield, safe for Lab but some Con votes

Candidates 97	97 votes	97%	92%	Candidates
William O'Brien (Lab)	26,046	60.6	51.1	William O'Brien
Fiona Bulmer (Con)	10,153	23.6	35.6	Graham Smith
David Ridgway (LD)	5,347	12.4	13.3	
Majority	15,893	37	15.5	

Electorate: 62,979 Turnout: 43,004 (68.3%)

NORTHAMPTON NORTH, Northamptonshire. Lab gained 97 with majority of exactly 10,000, probably safe now

Candidates 97	97 votes	97%	92%	Candidates
Sally Keeble (Lab)	27,247	52.7	38.6	Sally Keeble
Tony Marlow (Con)	17,247	33.4	45.8	John Whelan
Lesley Dunbar (LD)	6,579	12.7	15.2	Richard Church
Majority	10,000	19.3	7.2	

Electorate: 73,664 Turnout: 51,698 (70.2%)

NORTHAMPTON SOUTH, Northamptonshire. Unexpected, tight, Lab win in 97, partly rural

Candidates 97	97 votes	97%	92%	Candidates
Tony Clarke (Lab)	24,214	42.4	30.2	Tony Clarke
Michael Morris (Con)	23,470	41.1	55.7	Shailesh Vara
Tony Worgan (LD)	6,316	11.1	14.1	Andrew Simpson
Majority	744	1.3	25.5	

Electorate: 79,384 Turnout: 57,105 (71.9%)

NORTHAVON, Bristol. Commuter land north of Bristol, remarkable LD gain in 97, battle to hold

Candidates 97	97 votes	97%	92%	Candidates
Prof Steve Webb (LD)	26,500	42.4	34.5	
Sir John Cope (Con)	24,363	39	51.8	Carrie Ruxton
Ronald Stone (Lab)	9,767	15.6	12.1	Robert Hall
Majority	2,137	3.4	17.3	

Electorate: 78,943 Turnout: 62,530 (79.2%)

NORWICH NORTH, Norfolk. City's less grand suburbs, ought to be safe for Lab

Candidates 97	97 votes	97%	92%	Candidates
Dr Ian Gibson (Lab)	27,346	49.7	40.3	Dr Ian Gibson
Dr Roger Kinghorn (Con)	17,876	32.5	44.2	Kay Mason
Paul Young (LD)	6,951	12.6	14.6	
Majority	9,470	17.2	3.9	

Electorate: 55,057 Turnout: 72521 (75.9%)

NORWICH SOUTH, Norfolk. City centre and university, big Lab win in 97 but some Con votes still

Candidates 97	97 votes	97%	92%	Candidates
Charles Clarke (Lab)	26,267	51.7	46	Charles Clarke
Bashir Khanbhai (Con)	12,028	23.7	38.1	Andrew French
Andrew Aalders-Dunthorne (LD)	9,457	18.6	14.1	Andrew Aalders-Dunthorne
Majority	14,239	28	7.9	

Electorate: 70,009 Turnout: 50,801 (72.6%)

NOTTINGHAM EAST, Nottinghamshire. Edge of city, Lab gain 92 but now looks utterly safe

Candidates 97	97 votes	97%	92%	Candidates
John Heppell (Lab)	24,755	62.3	52.6	John Heppell
Andrew Raca (Con)	9,336	23.5	36.4	Richard Allan
Kevin Mulloy (LD)	4,008	10.1	7.8	Tim Ball
Majority	15,419	38.8	16.2	

Electorate: 65,581 Turnout: 39,744 (60.6%)

NOTTINGHAM NORTH, Nottinghamshire. Once Con, now safe Lab city suburbs

Candidates 97	97 votes	97%	92%	Candidates
Graham Allen (Lab)	27,203	65.7	55.7	Graham Allen
Gillian Shaw (Con)	8,402	20.3	35.1	Martin Wright
Rachel Oliver (LD)	3,301	8	8.6	
Majority	18,801	45.4	20.6	

Electorate: 65,698 Turnout: 41,401 (63%)

NOTTINGHAM SOUTH, Nottinghamshire. Developing city centre plus university, mixed suburbs, leftwing MP

Candidates 97	97 votes	97%	92%	Candidates
Alan Simpson (Lab)	26,825	55.3	47.7	Alan Simpson
Brian Kirsch (Con)	13,461	27.7	41.8	Wendy Manning
Gary Long (LD)	6,265	12.9	10	Kevin Mulloy
Majority	13,364	27.6	5.9	

Electorate: 72,418 Turnout: 48,520 (67%)

NUNEATON, Warwickshire. Once marginal, now safe Lab Midlands town

Candidates 97	97 votes	97%	92%	Candidates
Bill Olner (Lab)	30,080	56.2	45.8	Bill Olner
Richard Blunt (Con)	16,540	30.9	43	Mark Lancaster
Ron Cockings (LD)	4,732	8.8	11.2	
Majority	13,540	25.3	2.8	

Electorate: 72,032 Turnout: 53,513 (74.3%)

OCHIL, C Scotland. SNP target, low hills between Forth and Tay rivers, mostly urban

Candidates 97	97 votes	97%	92%	Candidates
Martin O'Neill (Lab)	19,707	45	43.1	Martin O'Neill
George Reid (SNP)	15,055	34.4	26.1	Keith Brown
Allan Hogarth (Con)	6,383	14.6	24	
Ann Watters (LD)	2,262	5.2	6.9	
Majority	4,652	10.6	17	

Electorate: 56,571 Turnout: 43,786 (77.4%)

OGMORE, S Wales. Safe Lab ex-mining valleys west of Cardiff

Candidates 97	97 votes	97%	92%	Candidates
Sir Raymond Powell (Lab)	28,163	74	71.7	Sir Raymond Powell
David Unwin (Con)	3,716	9.8	15.1	Richard Hill
Kirsty Williams (LD)	3,510	9.2	6.8	
J Rogers (PC)	2,679	7	6.3	
Majority	24,447	64.2	56.6	

Electorate: 52,078 Turnout: 38,068 (73.1%)

OLD BEXLEY & SIDCUP, S London. Has sent Ted Heath to parliament for 50 years, very suburban

Candidates 97	97 votes	97%	92%	Candidates
Sir Edward Heath (Con)	21,608	42	56.3	Derek Conway
Richard Justham (Lab)	18,039	35.1	21.1	Jim Dickson
Iain King (LD)	8,284	16.1	20.9	Belinda Ford
Majority	3,569	6.9	35.2	

Electorate: 68,043 Turnout: 51,391 (75.5%)

OLDHAM EAST & SADDLEWORTH, Greater Manchester. Mix of Oldham terraces and ex-Yorkshire hills, LD high hopes

Candidates 97	97 votes	97%	92%	Candidates
Philip Woolas (Lab)	22,546	41.7	30.2	Philip Woolas
Chris Davies (LD)	19,157	35.4	34.4	Howard Sykes
John Hudson (Con)	10,666	19.7	35.4	Craig Heeley
Majority	3,389	6.3	1	

Electorate: 73,188 Turnout: 54,101 (73.9%)

OLDHAM WEST & ROYTON, Greater Manchester. New Lab seat, urban, large Asian community

Candidates 97	97 votes	97%	92%	Candidates
Michael Meacher (Lab)	26,894	58.8	49.1	Michael Meacher
Jonathan Lord (Con)	10,693	23.4	38.1	Duncan Reed
Howard Cohen (LD)	5,434	11.9	11.4	Marc Ramsbottom
Majority	16,201	35.4	11	

Electorate: 69,202 Turnout: 45,738 (66.1%)

ORKNEY & SHETLAND, N Scotland. Probably safe for LDs despite new candidate, most remote in UK

Candidates 97	97 votes	97%	92%	Candidates
Jim Wallace (LD)	10,743	52	46.4	Alistair Carmichael
James Paton (Lab)	3,775	18.3	19.8	
Willie Ross (SNP)	2,624	12.7	11.2	John Mowat
Hope Vere Anderson (Con)	2,527	12.2	22	
Majority	6,968	33.7	26.6	
Electorate: 32,291 Turnout: 20,665 (64%)				

ORPINGTON, S London. Con for 30 years but LDs want to repeat past glory

Candidates 97	97 votes	97%	92%	Candidates
John Horam (Con)	24,417	40.6	55.3	
Chris Maines (LD)	21,465	35.7	28.3	Chris Maines
Sue Polydorou (Lab)	10,753	17.9	14.8	
Majority	2,952	4.9	27	
Electorate: 78,749 Turnout: 60,162 (76.4%)				

OXFORD EAST, Oxfordshire. Failing car industry, gentrifying terraces, safe Lab but LDs winning council seats

Candidates 97	97 votes	97%	92%	Candidates
Andrew Smith (Lab)	27,205	56.8	50.2	Andrew Smith
Jonathan Djanogly (Con)	10,540	22	33.5	Cheryl Potter
George Kershaw (LD)	7,038	14.7	14	Steve Goddard
Majority	16,665	34.8	16.7	
Electorate: 69,339 Turnout: 47,877 (69%)				

OXFORD WEST & ABINGDON, Oxfordshire. Inspector Morse territory, LD big gain 97, should hold

Candidates 97	97 votes	97%	92%	Candidates
Evan Harris (LD)	26,268	42.9	35.8	
Laurence Harris (Con)	19,983	32.7	46.2	Ed Matts
Susan Brown (Lab)	12,361	20.2	16.1	Gillian Kirk
Majority	6,285	10.2	10.4	
Electorate: 79,329 Turnout: 61,196 (77.1%)				

PAISLEY NORTH, W Scotland. Strong Lab seat, mainly urban, parts very deprived

Candidates 97	97 votes	97%	92%	Candidates
Irene Adams (Lab)	20,295	59.5	51.9	Irene Adams
Ian Mackay (SNP)	7,481	21.9	23.5	George Adam
Kenneth Brookes (Con)	3,267	9.6	15.7	
Alan Jelfs (LD)	2,365	6.9	7.7	
Majority	12,814	37.6	28.4	
Electorate: 49,725 Turnout: 34,135 (68.6%)				

PAISLEY SOUTH, W Scotland. Strong Lab seat, MP killed himself in 97, some SNP support

Candidates 97	97 votes	97%	92%	Candidates
Gordon McMaster (Lab)	21,482	57.5	50.8	Douglas Alexander
William Martin (SNP)	8,732	23.4	24.6	Brian Lawson
Eileen McCartin (LD)	3,500	9.4	8.9	
R Reid (Con)	3,237	8.7	15.4	
Majority	12,750	34.1	26.2	
Electorate: 54,040 Turnout: 37,351 (69.1%)				

PENDLE, Lancashire. Small Lancashire towns which have voted Lab recently, remains of Con support

Candidates 97	97 votes	97%	92%	Candidates
Gordon Prentice (Lab)	25,059	53.3	44.2	Gordon Prentice
John Midgley (Con)	14,235	30.3	40.3	Rasjid Skinner
Tony Greaves (LD)	5,460	11.6	15	
Majority	10,824	23	3.9	
Electorate: 63,048 Turnout: 47,035 (74.6%)				

PENRITH & THE BORDER, Cumbria. England's largest seat in area, splendid countryside, hit by foot and mouth

Candidates 97	97 votes	97%	92%	Candidates
David Maclean (Con)	23,300	47.6	58.7	
Geyve Walker (LD)	13,067	26.7	29	Geyve Walker
Margaret Meling (Lab)	10,576	21.6	11	Michael Boaden
Majority	10,233	20.9	29.7	

Electorate: 66,496 Turnout: 48,961 (73.6%)

PERTH, NE Scotland. SNP look secure in big, once-Con seat

Candidates 97	97 votes	97%	92%	Candidates
Roseanna Cunningham (SNP)	16,209	36.4	34.4	Annabelle Ewing
John Godfrey (Con)	13,068	29.3	40.5	
Douglas Alexander (Lab)	11,036	24.8	13.2	Marion Dingwall
Chic Brodie (LD)	3,583	8	12	
Majority	3,141	7.1	6.1	

Electorate: 60,313 Turnout: 44,551 (73.9%)

PETERBOROUGH, Cambridgeshire. Sizeable Lab gain 97, Blairite MP has seemed to struggle

Candidates 97	97 votes	97%	92%	Candidates
Helen Brinton (Lab)	24,365	50.3	37.8	Helen Brinton
Jacqueline Foster (Con)	17,042	35.2	49.5	Stewart Jackson
David Howarth (LD)	5,170	10.7	9.3	
Majority	7,323	15.1	11.7	

Electorate: 65,926 Turnout: 48,427 (73.5%)

PLYMOUTH DEVONPORT, Devon. Once SDP, now very secure for Lab

Candidates 97	97 votes	97%	92%	Candidates
David Jamieson (Lab)	31,629	60.9	47	David Jamieson
Anthony Johnson (Con)	12,562	24.2	35.6	John Glen
Richard Copus (LD)	5,570	10.7	13.2	Keith Baldry
Majority	19,067	36.7	11.4	

Electorate: 74,482 Turnout: 51,963 (69.8%)

PLYMOUTH SUTTON, Devon. Mixed city suburbs, Lab gain 97, Con longshot

Candidates 97	97 votes	97%	92%	Candidates
Linda Gilroy (Lab)	23,881	50.1	39.8	Linda Gilroy
A Crisp (Con)	14,441	30.3	41.8	Oliver Colvile
Steve Melia (LD)	6,613	13.9	16.4	Alan Connett
Majority	9,440	19.8	2	

Electorate: 70,666 Turnout: 47,652 (67.4%)

PONTEFRACT & CASTLEFORD, W Yorkshire. Strong Lab seat, ex-mining, working class

Candidates 97	97 votes	97%	92%	Candidates
Yvette Cooper (Lab)	31,339	75.7	69.9	Yvette Cooper
Adrian Flook (Con)	5,614	13.6	20.9	Pamela Singleton
Wesley Paxton (LD)	3,042	7.3	9.2	Wesley Paxton
Majority	25,725	62.1	49	

Electorate: 62,350 Turnout: 41,396 (66.4%)

PONTYPRIDD, S Wales. Strong Lab seat, ex-mining

Candidates 97	97 votes	97%	92%	Candidates
Dr Kim Howells (Lab)	29,290	63.9	60.8	Dr Kim Howells
Nigel Howells (LD)	6,161	13.4	8.5	Ed Townsend
Jonathan Cowen (Con)	5,910	12.9	20.3	Prudence Dailey
Owain Llewelyn (PC)	2,977	6.5	9.1	Bleddyn Hancock
Majority	23,129	50.5	52.3	

Electorate: 64,184 Turnout: 45,855 (71.4%)

POOLE, Dorset. Con even in 97, some LDs, urban, retirement

Candidates 97	97 votes	97%	92%	Candidates
Robert Syms (Con)	19,726	42.1	55.1	
Alan Tetlow (LD)	14,428	30.8	29.3	Nick Westbrook
Haydn White (Lab)	10,100	21.6	11.7	David Watt
Majority	5,298	11.3	25.8	

Electorate: 66,078 Turnout: 46,810 (70.8%)

POPLAR & CANNING TOWN, E London. Changing Docklands, some costly houses, much poverty too

Candidates 97	97 votes	97%	92%	Candidates
Jim Fitzpatrick (Lab)	24,807	63.2	51.2	Jim Fitzpatrick
Bene't Steinberg (Con)	5,892	15	25.7	Robert Marr
Janet Ludlow (LD)	4,072	10.4	19.5	
Majority	18,915	48.2	25.5	

Electorate: 67,172 Turnout: 39,268 (58.5%)

PORTSMOUTH NORTH, Hampshire. Naval centre, partly working class, Con target

Candidates 97	97 votes	97%	92%	Candidates
Syd Rapson (Lab)	21,339	47.1	33.2	Syd Rapson
Peter Griffiths (Con)	17,016	37.6	50.7	Chris Day
Steve Sollitt (LD)	4,788	10.6	15.1	Darren Sanders
Majority	4,323	9.5	17.5	

Electorate: 64,538 Turnout: 45,270 (70.1%)

PORTSMOUTH SOUTH, Hampshire. LDs regained in 97 on reduced share of vote, tight fight next time

Candidates 97	97 votes	97%	92%	Candidates
Mike Hancock (LD)	20,421	39.5	42	
David Martin (Con)	16,094	31.1	42.5	Philip Warr
Alan Burnett (Lab)	13,086	25.3	14.6	Graham Heaney
Majority	4,327	8.4	0.5	

Electorate: 80,514 Turnout: 51,695 (64.2%)

PRESELI PEMBROKESHIRE, W Wales. Oil, docks and St David's, strong Con vote but Lab probably secure

Candidates 97	97 votes	97%	92%	Candidates
Jackie Lawrence (Lab)	20,477	48.3	38.1	Jackie Lawrence
Robert Buckland (Con)	11,741	27.7	39.5	Stephen Crabb
Jeffrey Clarke (LD)	5,527	13	12.3	Alexander Dauncey
Alun Lloyd Jones (PC)	2,683	6.3	8.6	Rhys Sinnet
Majority	8,736	20.6	1.4	

Electorate: 54,088 Turnout: 42,403 (78.4%)

PRESTON, Lancashire. Strong Lab seat, once had cotton industry, working class

Candidates 97	97 votes	97%	92%	Candidates
Audrey Wise (Lab)	29,220	60.8	53.1	Mark Hendrick
Paul Gray (Con)	10,540	21.9	39.5	Graham O'Hare
Bill Chadwick (LD)	7,045	14.7	12.3	Bill Chadwick
Majority	18,680	38.9	13.6	

Electorate: 72,933 Turnout: 48,074 (65.9%)

PUDSEY, W Yorkshire. Housing outside Leeds, Lab gain 97, ought to hold

Candidates 97	97 votes	97%	92%	Candidates
Paul Truswell (Lab)	25,370	48.1	29.1	Paul Truswell
Peter Bone (Con)	19,163	36.3	43.7	John Procter
Dr Jonathan Brown (LD)	7,375	14	26.4	Stephen Boddy
Majority	6,207	11.8	14.6	

Electorate: 70,922 Turnout: 52,731 (74.4%)

PUTNEY, S London. Lab ousted David Mellor in 97, Con target now

Candidates 97	97 votes	97%	92%	Candidates
Tony Colman (Lab)	20,084	45.7	36.6	Tony Colman
David Mellor (Con)	17,108	38.9	52.2	Michael Simpson
Russell Pyne (LD)	4,739	10.8	9.6	Anthony Burrett
Majority	2,976	6.8	15.6	

Electorate: 60,175 Turnout: 43,995 (73.1%)

RAYLEIGH, Essex. Suburbs outside Southend, very safe for Con

Candidates 97	97 votes	97%	92%	Candidates
Dr Michael Clark (Con)	25,516	49.7	61.1	Mark Francois
Raymond Ellis (Lab)	14,832	28.9	14.8	Paul Clark
Sid Cumberland (LD)	10,137	19.8	21.9	Geoff Williams
Majority	10,684	20.8	39.2	

Electorate: 68,736 Turnout: 51,314 (74.7%)

READING EAST, Berkshire. Once a Con certainty, now Lab, close next time, dense suburbs

Candidates 97	97 votes	97%	92%	Candidates
Jane Griffiths (Lab)	21,461	42.7	28.9	
John Watts (Con)	17,666	35.2	49.1	Barry Tanswell
Sam Samuel (LD)	9,307	18.5	20.4	Tom Dobrashian
Majority	3,795	7.5	20.2	

Electorate: 71,586 Turnout: 50,220 (70.2%)

READING WEST, Berkshire. Marginal seat gained in 97 by sharp, clever Lab backbencher Martin Salter

Candidates 97	97 votes	97%	92%	Candidates
Martin Salter (Lab)	21,841	45.1	28.7	Martin Salter
Nicholas Bennett (Con)	18,844	38.9	52.4	Stephen Reid
Dee Tomlin (LD)	6,153	12.7	17.8	Polly Martin
Majority	2,997	6.2	23.7	

Electorate: 69,072 Turnout: 48,389 (70.1%)

REDCAR, NE England. Lab seat, chemical industry, Mo Mowlam standing down

Candidates 97	97 votes	97%	92%	Candidates
Dr Marjorie Mowlam (Lab)	32,975	67.3	53.6	Vera Baird
Andrew Isaacs (Con)	11,308	23.1	34	Chris Main
Joyce Benbow (LD)	4,679	9.6	12.4	Stan Wilson
Majority	21,667	44.2	19.6	

Electorate: 68,965 Turnout: 48,959 (71%)

REDDITCH, Worcestershire. Lab gain in 97, new town, Lab should hold while it keeps a parliamentary majority

Candidates 97	97 votes	97%	92%	Candidates
Jacqui Smith (Lab)	22,280	49.8	40.4	Jacqui Smith
Miss Anthea McIntyre (Con)	16,155	36.1	47.1	Karen Lumley
Malcolm Hall (LD)	4,935	11	11.7	Michael Ashall
Majority	6,125	13.7	6.7	

Electorate: 60,841 Turnout: 44,748 (73.5%)

REGENT'S PARK & KENSINGTON NORTH, N London. Mixed socially, some poverty, secure Lab seat

Candidates 97	97 votes	97%	92%	Candidates
Karen Buck (Lab)	28,367	59.9	48.3	Karen Buck
Paul McGuinness (Con)	13,710	29	41.1	Peter Wilson
Emily Gasson (LD)	4,041	8.5	7.9	
Majority	14,657	30.9	7.2	

Electorate: 73,752 Turnout: 47,344 (64.2%)

REIGATE, Surrey. Strongly Con but some Lab, LD votes too, prosperous Surrey town

Candidates 97	97 votes	97%	92%	Candidates
Crispin Blunt (Con)	21,123	43.8	57.5	Peter Hobbins
Andrew Howard (Lab)	13,382	27.8	17.5	Simon Charleton
Peter Samuel (LD)	9,615	20	24.1	
Majority	7,741	16	33.4	
Electorate: 64,750 Turnout: 48,174 (74.4%)				

RENFREWSHIRE WEST, W Scotland. MP suspended from Lab in 97, SNP longshot

Candidates 97	97 votes	97%	92%	Candidates
Tommy Graham (Lab)	18,525	46.6		
Colin Campbell (SNP)	10,546	26.5	20.6	Carol Puthucheary
Charles Cormack (Con)	7,387	18.6	27.8	
P MacPherson (LD)	3,045	7.7	8.4	Alex Mackie
Majority	7,979	20.1	7.2	
Electorate: 52,348 Turnout: 39,786 (76%)				

RHONDDA, S Wales. Usually safe Lab, PC won in 99 Welsh elections, amazing if Lab lose now

Candidates 97	97 votes	97%	92%	Candidates
Allan Rogers (Lab)	30,381	74.5	74.5	Chris Bryant
Leanne Wood (PC)	5,450	13.4	11.8	Leanne Wood
Dr Rodney Berman (LD)	2,307	5.7	5.3	
Steven Whiting (Con)	1,551	3.8	7.8	
Majority	24,931	61.1	62.7	
Electorate: 57,104 Turnout: 40,807 (71.5%)				

RIBBLE SOUTH, Lancashire. Key marginal, Lab gain 97, inc. Leyland trucks

Candidates 97	97 votes	97%	92%	Candidates
David Borrow (Lab)	25,856	46.8	34.8	
R Atkins (Con)	20,772	37.6	49.8	
T Farron (LD)	5,879	10.6	14.8	Mark Alcock
Majority	5,084	9.2	15	
Electorate: 71,670 Turnout: 55,231 (77.1%)				

RIBBLE VALLEY, Lancashire. Reverting to safe Con type after LD byelection win in 90

Candidates 97	97 votes	97%	92%	Candidates
Nigel Evans (Con)	26,702	46.7	52.6	
Michael Carr (LD)	20,062	35.1	38.2	Michael Carr
Marcus Johnstone (Lab)	9,013	15.8	8.7	Marcus Johnstone
Majority	6,640	11.6	14.4	
Electorate: 72,663 Turnout: 57,221 (78.7%)				

RICHMOND, N Yorkshire. William Hague's safe seat, dales, fells and farmland

Candidates 97	97 votes	97%	92%	Candidates
William Hague (Con)	23,326	48.9	60.4	
Steve Merritt (Lab)	13,275	27.8	11.5	Fay Tinnion
Jane Harvey (LD)	8,773	18.4	27.1	Edward Forth
Majority	10,051	21.1	33.3	
Electorate: 65,058 Turnout: 47,741 (73.4%)				

RICHMOND PARK, S London. LDs will be eager to hold this 97 gain after years of near misses

Candidates 97	97 votes	97%	92%	Candidates
Dr Jennifer Tonge (LD)	25,393	44.7	37.6	
Jeremy Hanley (Con)	22,442	39.5	51.8	Tom Harris
Sue Jenkins (Lab)	7,172	12.6	8.8	Barry Langford
Majority	2,951	5.2	14.2	
Electorate: 71,571 Turnout: 56,853 (79.4%)				

ROCHDALE, Greater Manchester. Looks safe for Lab now after LD spell finally broken in 97

Candidates 97	97 votes	97%	92%	Candidates
Lorna Fitzsimons (Lab)	23,758	49.4	37.7	Lorna Fitzsimons
Elizabeth Lynne (LD)	19,213	40	37.9	
Mervyn Turnberg (Con)	4,237	8.8	23.2	Elaina Cohen
Majority	4,545	9.4	0.2	

Electorate: 68,529 Turnout: 48,082 (70.2%)

ROCHFORD & SOUTHEND EAST, Essex. Strong Con seat, suburban, white collar

Candidates 97	97 votes	97%	92%	Candidates
Sir Teddy Taylor (Con)	22,683	48.7	59	
Nigel Smith (Lab)	18,458	39.7	27.5	Chris Dandridge
Paula Smith (LD)	4,387	9.4	11.8	
Majority	4,225	9	31.5	

Electorate: 72,847 Turnout: 46,535 (63.9%)

ROMFORD, N London. Outer suburbs, almost Essex, prosperous, Lab shock gain 97

Candidates 97	97 votes	97%	92%	Candidates
Eileen Gordon (Lab)	18,187	43.2	28.3	Eileen Gordon
Sir Michael Neubert (Con)	17,538	41.6	58.1	Andrew Rosindell
Nigel Meyer (LD)	3,341	7.9	12.4	Nigel Meyer
Majority	649	1.6	29.8	

Electorate: 5,9611 Turnout: 42,119 (70.7%)

ROMSEY, Hampshire. Seemed safe for Con until heavy defeat by LDs in 00 byelection, tight now

Candidates 97	97 votes	97%	92%	Candidates
Michael Colvin (Con)	23,834	46	63.2	Paul Raynes
Mark Cooper (LD)	15,249	29.4	23.1	
Joanne Ford (Lab)	9,623	18.6	12.9	Stephen Roberts
Majority	8,585	16.6	40.1	

Electorate: 67,305 Turnout: 51,821 (77%)

ROSSENDALE & DARWEN, Lancashire. Lab gained in 92 and have settled in since, small towns and moors

Candidates 97	97 votes	97%	92%	Candidates
Janet Anderson (Lab)	27,470	53.6	43.6	Janet Anderson
Trisha Buzzard (Con)	16,521	32.3	43.5	George Lee
Brian Dunning (LD)	5,435	10.6	11.8	Brian Dunning
Majority	10,949	21.3	0.1	

Electorate: 69,749 Turnout: 51,208 (73.4%)

ROSS, SKYE & INVERNESS WEST, N Scotland. If Charles Kennedy loses this huge seat LDs will despair

Candidates 97	97 votes	97%	92%	Candidates
Charles Kennedy (LD)	15,472	38.7	38.7	Charles Kennedy
Donnie Munro (Lab)	11,453	28.7	18.9	Donald Crichton
Margaret Paterson (SNP)	7,821	19.6	18.8	Jean Urquhart
Mary MacLeod (Con)	4,368	10.9	21.9	
Majority	4,019	10	19.8	

Electorate: 55,639 Turnout: 39,955 (71.8%)

ROTHER VALLEY, S Yorkshire. William Hague's birthplace but utterly safe for Lab

Candidates 97	97 votes	97%	92%	Candidates
Kevin Barron (Lab)	31,184	67.6	60.5	Kevin Barron
Steven Stanbury (Con)	7,699	16.7	26.9	James Duddridge
Stan Burgess (LD)	5,342	11.6	12.7	
Majority	23,485	50.9	33.6	

Electorate: 68,622 Turnout: 46,157 (67.3%)

ROTHERHAM, S Yorkshire. Struggling town after pit closures, safe Lab

Candidates 97	97 votes	97%	92%	Candidates
Dr Denis MacShane (Lab)	26,852	71.3	63.9	Dr Denis MacShane
Simon Gordon (Con)	5,383	14.3	23.7	Richard Powell
David Wildgoose (LD)	3,919	10.4	12.3	
Majority	21,469	57	40.2	

Electorate: 59,895 Turnout: 37,650 (62.9%)

ROXBURGH & BERWICKSHIRE, SE Scotland. Seems safe for quiet LD Archie Kirkwood

Candidates 97	97 votes	97%	92%	Candidates
Archy Kirkwood (LD)	16,243	46.5	46.5	
Douglas Younger (Con)	8,337	23.9	34.2	
Helen Eadie (Lab)	5,226	15	8.8	Catherine Maxwell-Stuart
Malcolm Balfour (SNP)	3,959	11.3	10.6	Roderick Campbell
Majority	7,906	22.6	12.3	

Electorate: 47,259 Turnout: 34,931 (73.9%)

RUGBY & KENILWORTH, Warwickshire. Shock win for Lab in 97, terrible news for Con if they don't take it next time

Candidates 97	97 votes	97%	92%	Candidates
Andy King (Lab)	26,356	43.1	32	Andy King
James Pawsey (Con)	25,861	42.3	52.4	David Martin
Jerry Roodhouse (LD)	8,737	14.3	15.3	
Majority	495	0.8	20.4	

Electorate: 79,384 Turnout: 61,205 (77.1%)

RUISLIP-NORTHWOOD, N London. Strong Con seat, outer suburbs

Candidates 97	97 votes	97%	92%	Candidates
John Wilkinson (Con)	22,526	50.2	62.9	
Paul Barker (Lab)	14,732	32.9	19.9	
Chris Edwards (LD)	7,279	16.2	16.7	Mike Cox
Majority	7,794	17.3	43	

Electorate: 60,392 Turnout: 44,833 (74.2%)

RUNNYMEDE & WEYBRIDGE, Surrey. New strong Con seat, stockbroker belt, managerial

Candidates 97	97 votes	97%	92%	Candidates
Philip Hammond (Con)	25,051	48.6	61.4	
Ian Peacock (Lab)	15,176	29.4	16	Jane Briginshaw
Geoffrey Taylor (LD)	8,397	16.3	21.1	Chris Bushill
Majority	9,875	19.2	40.3	

Electorate: 72,176 Turnout: 51,561 (71.4%)

RUSHCLIFFE, Nottinghamshire. Elects Ken Clarke, commuting, middle class

Candidates 97	97 votes	97%	92%	Candidates
Kenneth Clarke (Con)	27,558	44.4	54.4	
Jocelyn Pettitt (Lab)	22,503	36.2	23.2	Hanif Adeel
Sam Boote (LD)	8,851	14.3	20	Jeremy Hargreaves
Majority	5,055	8.2	31.2	

Electorate: 78,735 Turnout: 62,112 (78.9%)

RUTLAND & MELTON, Rutland, Leicestershire. Revived, independent minded small county, always Con

Candidates 97	97 votes	97%	92%	Candidates
Alan Duncan (Con)	24,107	45.8	61.4	
John Meads (Lab)	15,271	29	15.7	Matthew O'Callaghan
Kim Lee (LD)	10,112	19.2	20.8	Kim Lee
Majority	8,836	16.8	40.6	

Electorate: 70,150 Turnout: 52,630 (75%)

RYEDALE, N Yorkshire. Once LD but since Con held in 97 will keep, Yorkshire Moors

Candidates 97	97 votes	97%	92%	Candidates
John Greenway (Con)	21,351	43.8	55.4	
Keith Orrell (LD)	16,293	33.4	30	Keith Orrell
Alison Hiles (Lab)	8,762	18	14.6	David Ellis
Majority	5,058	10.4	25.4	

Electorate: 65,215 Turnout: 48,783 (74.8%)

SAFFRON WALDEN, Essex. Strong Con seat, managerial, rural

Candidates 97	97 votes	97%	92%	Candidates
Sir Alan Haselhurst (Con)	25,871	45.3	56.6	
Melvin Caton (LD)	15,298	26.8	28.6	Elfreda Tealby-Watson
Malcolm Fincken (Lab)	12,275	21.5	14.4	Tania Rogers
Majority	10,573	18.5	28	

Electorate: 7,4097 Turnout: 57,050 (77%)

SALFORD, Greater Manchester. Strong Lab seat, inner city, high unemployment

Candidates 97	97 votes	97%	92%	Candidates
Hazel Blears (Lab)	22,848	69	59.1	Hazel Blears
Elliot Bishop (Con)	5,779	17.4	26.5	Chris King
Norman Owen (LD)	3,407	10.3	12.6	Norman Owen
Majority	17,069	51.6	32.6	

Electorate: 58,610 Turnout: 33,122 (56.5%)

SALISBURY, Wiltshire. Smart county town and surrounds, LD threat has faded

Candidates 97	97 votes	97%	92%	Candidates
Robert Key (Con)	25,012	42.9	52	
Jane Emmerson-Peirce (LD)	18,736	32.2	37.2	Yvonne Emmerson-Peirce
R Rogers (Lab)	10,242	17.6	9	Sue Mallory
Majority	6,276	10.7	14.8	

Electorate: 78,973 Turnout: 58,239 (73.7%)

SCARBOROUGH & WHITBY, N Yorkshire. Between moors and sea, notable Lab win 97

Candidates 97	97 votes	97%	92%	Candidates
Lawrie Quinn (Lab)	24,791	45.6	29.9	Lawrie Quinn
John Sykes (Con)	19,667	36.2	49.8	John Sykes
Martin Allinson (LD)	7,672	14.1	18.9	
Majority	5,124	9.4	19.9	

Electorate: 75,861 Turnout: 54,321 (71.6%)

SCUNTHORPE, Humberside. Lab seat, industrial, skilled manual

Candidates 97	97 votes	97%	92%	Candidates
Elliot Morley (Lab)	25,107	60.4	54.3	Elliot Morley
Martyn Fisher (Con)	10,934	26.3	35.9	Bernard Theobald
G Smith (LD)	3,497	8.4	7.7	Bob Tress
Majority	14,173	34.1	18.4	

Electorate: 41,574 Turnout: 60,392 (68.8%)

SEDGEFIELD, Durham. Tony Blair's seat, small towns, borders Hague's Richmond

Candidates 97	97 votes	97%	92%	Candidates
Tony Blair (Lab)	33,526	71.2	62.2	Tony Blair
Elizabeth Pitman (Con)	8,383	17.8	28.1	Douglas Carswell
Ronald Beadle (LD)	3,050	6.5	9.7	
Majority	25,143	53.4	34.1	

Electorate: 64,923 Turnout: 47,116 (72.6%)

SELBY, N Yorkshire. Some mining still but could revert to Tories, flat

Candidates 97	97 votes	97%	92%	Candidates
John Grogan (Lab)	25,838	45.9	35.7	John Grogan
Kenneth Hind (Con)	22,002	39.1	51.2	Michael Mitchell
Ted Batty (LD)	6,778	12	13.1	
Majority	3,836	6.8	15.5	

Electorate: 75,141 Turnout: 56,316 (74.9%)

SEVENOAKS, Kent. A safe Con seat just south of London

Candidates 97	97 votes	97%	92%	Candidates
Michael Fallon (Con)	22,776	45.4	57.6	
John Hayes (Lab)	12,315	24.6	16.1	Caroline Humphreys
Roger Walshe (LD)	12,086	24.1	24.6	Clive Gray
Majority	10,461	20.8	33	
Electorate: 66,473 Turnout: 50,149 (75.4%)				

SHEFFIELD ATTERCLIFFE, S Yorkshire. Strong Lab seat, ex-steel, skilled manual

Candidates 97	97 votes	97%	92%	Candidates
Clive Betts (Lab)	28,937	65.3	57.5	Clive Betts
Brendan Doyle (Con)	7,119	16.1	26.3	John Perry
Gail Smith (LD)	6,973	15.7	14.7	Gail Smith
Majority	21,818	49.2	31.2	
Electorate: 68,548 Turnout: 44,318 (64.7%)				

SHEFFIELD BRIGHTSIDE, S Yorkshire. Strong Lab seat, elects David Blunkett, outer suburbs

Candidates 97	97 votes	97%	92%	Candidates
David Blunkett (Lab)	24,901	73.5	70.4	David Blunkett
Francis Butler (LD)	4,947	14.6	12.5	Alison Firth
Christopher Buckwell (Con)	2,850	8.4	16.8	Matthew Wilson
Majority	19,954	58.9	53.6	
Electorate: 58,930 Turnout: 33,865 (57.5%)				

SHEFFIELD CENTRAL, S Yorkshire. Strong Lab seat, inner city, high unemployment, rising LD vote

Candidates 97	97 votes	97%	92%	Candidates
Richard Caborn (Lab)	23,179	63.6	59.6	Richard Caborn
Ali Qadar (LD)	6,273	17.2	18.9	Ali Qadar
Martin Hess (Con)	4,341	11.9	18.7	Noelle Brelsford
Majority	16,906	46.4	40.7	
Electorate: 68,667 Turnout: 36,419 (53%)				

SHEFFIELD HALLAM, S Yorkshire. Cons wiped out by LDs 97, should keep, grand, hilly, green

Candidates 97	97 votes	97%	92%	Candidates
Richard Allan (LD)	23,345	51.3	30.7	
Sir Irvine Patnick (Con)	15,074	33.1	49.6	John Harthman
Stephen Conquest (Lab)	6,147	13.5	18.4	
Majority	8,271	18.2	18.9	
Electorate: 62,834 Turnout: 45,479 (72.4%)				

SHEFFIELD HEELEY, S Yorkshire. Strong Lab seat, outer suburbs

Candidates 97	97 votes	97%	92%	Candidates
Bill Michie (Lab)	26,274	60.7	55.7	Meg Munn
Roger Davison (LD)	9,196	21.3	18.4	David Willis
John Harthman (Con)	6,767	15.6	25.9	Carolyn Abbott
Majority	17,078	39.4	37.3	
Electorate: 66,599 Turnout: 43,266 (65%)				

SHEFFIELD HILLSBOROUGH, S Yorkshire. Suburban, skilled manual, LDs faded, could still surprise

Candidates 97	97 votes	97%	92%	Candidates
Helen Jackson (Lab)	30,150	56.9	46.2	Helen Jackson
Arthur Dunworth (LD)	13,699	25.8	34.3	John Commons
David Nuttall (Con)	7,707	14.5	19.5	Graham King
Majority	16,451	31.1	11.9	
Electorate: 74,641 Turnout: 53,024 (71%)				

SHERWOOD, Nottinghamshire. Once mining, also once Con, now secure Lab

Candidates 97	97 votes	97%	92%	Candidates
Paddy Tipping (Lab)	33,071	58.5	47.5	Paddy Tipping
Roland Spencer (Con)	16,259	28.8	42.9	Brandon Lewis
Bruce Moult (LD)	4,889	8.6	9.6	Peter Harris
Majority	16,812	29.7	4.6	
Electorate: 74,788 Turnout: 56,533 (75.6%)				

SHIPLEY, W Yorkshire. Shock Lab win for young candidate 97, Con target

Candidates 97	97 votes	97%	92%	Candidates
Christopher Leslie (Lab)	22,962	43.4	28.5	Christopher Leslie
Sir Marcus Fox (Con)	19,966	37.8	50.4	David Senior
John Cole (LD)	7,984	15.1	20	
Majority	2,996	5.6	21.9	

Electorate: 69,281 Turnout: 52,872 (76.3%)

SHREWSBURY & ATCHAM, Shropshire. Lab won from 3rd 97, likely Con gain now

Candidates 97	97 votes	97%	92%	Candidates
Paul Marsden (Lab)	20,484	37	26	
Derek Conway (Con)	18,814	34	45.8	Anthea McIntyre
A Wooland (LD)	13,838	25	27	Jonathan Rule
Majority	1,670	3	18.8	

Electorate: 73,542 Turnout: 55,344 (75.3%)

SHROPSHIRE NORTH, Shropshire. Just stayed Con 97, Welsh borders and flat farmland

Candidates 97	97 votes	97%	92%	Candidates
Owen Paterson (Con)	20,730	40.2	50.8	
Ian Lucas (Lab)	18,535	36	26.2	
John Stevans (LD)	10,489	20.4	23	
Majority	2,195	4.2	24.6	

Electorate: 70,852 Turnout: 51,518 (72.7%)

SITTINGBOURNE & SHEPPEY, Kent. Unexpected Lab gain 97, Tories plan to retake

Candidates 97	97 votes	97%	92%	Candidates
Derek Wyatt (Lab)	18,723	40.6	23.9	Derek Wyatt
Roger Moate (Con)	16,794	36.4	48.8	Adrian Lee
Roger Truelove (LD)	8,447	18.3	26.8	
Majority	1,929	4.2	22	

Electorate: 63,849 Turnout: 46,162 (72.3%)

SKIPTON & RIPON, N Yorkshire. Hilly base of Con Europhile David Curry, safe

Candidates 97	97 votes	97%	92%	Candidates
David Curry (Con)	25,294	46.5	57.9	
Thomas Mould (LD)	13,674	25.2	27.3	Bernard Bateman
Robert Marchant (Lab)	12,171	22.4	14.8	Michael Dugher
Majority	11,620	21.3	30.6	

Electorate: 72,042 Turnout: 54,351 (75.4%)

SLEAFORD & NORTH HYKEHAM, Lincolnshire. Strong Con seat, rural, based on Grantham

Candidates 97	97 votes	97%	92%	Candidates
Douglas Hogg (Con)	23,358	43.9	58.4	
Sean Hariss (Lab)	18,235	34.3	21.9	Elizabeth Donnelly
John Marriot (LD)	8,063	15.2	16.6	
Majority	5,123	9.6	36.5	

Electorate: 71,486 Turnout: 53,176 (74.4%)

SLOUGH, Berkshire. Lab gain 97, dense suburbs and big Asian community

Candidates 97	97 votes	97%	92%	Candidates
Fiona Mactaggart (Lab)	27,029	56.6	44.1	Fiona Mactaggart
Peta Bushcombe (Con)	13,958	29.2	44	Diana Coad
Chris Bushell (LD)	3,509	7.4	7.2	Keith Kerr
Majority	13,071	27.4	0.1	

Electorate: 70,282 Turnout: 47,732 (67.9%)

SOLIHULL, W Midlands. Safe, leafy Con suburb outside Birmingham

Candidates 97	97 votes	97%	92%	Candidates
John M Taylor (Con)	26,299	44.6	60.8	
Mike Southcombe (LD)	14,902	25.3	21	Jo Byron
Rachel Harris (Lab)	14,334	24.3	16.7	Brendan O'Brien
Majority	11,397	19.3	39.8	

Electorate: 78,897 Turnout: 58,906 (74.7%)

SOMERTON & FROME, Somerset. Narrowly won by LD David Heath in 97, he needs to cut Lab vote to stay

Candidates 97	97 votes	97%	92%	Candidates
David Heath (LD)	22,684	39.5	40.3	
Mark Robinson (Con)	22,554	39.3	47.4	Jonathan Marland
Bob Ashford (Lab)	9,385	16.3	10.4	Andrew Perkins
Majority	130	0.2	7.1	

Electorate: 73,987 Turnout: 57,403 (77.6%)

SOUTHAMPTON ITCHEN, Hampshire. East of port city, urban, Lab took 92

Candidates 97	97 votes	97%	92%	Candidates
John Denham (Lab)	29,498	54.8	44	John Denham
Peter Fleet (Con)	15,289	28.4	42.1	Caroline Nokes
David Harrison (LD)	6,289	11.7	13.9	Mark Cooper
Majority	14,209	26.4	1.9	

Electorate: 76,868 Turnout: 53,858 (70.1%)

SOUTHAMPTON TEST, Hampshire. Once marginal, now safe Lab, west part of city

Candidates 97	97 votes	97%	92%	Candidates
Dr Alan Whitehead (Lab)	28,396	54.1	45.5	Alan Whitehead
James Hill (Con)	14,712	28.1	40.4	Richard Gueterbock
Alan Dowden (LD)	7,171	13.7	13.1	John Shaw
P Day (Ref)	1,397	2.7	5.1	

Electorate: 72,983 Turnout: 52,441 (71.9%)

SOUTHEND WEST, Essex. Probably secure for Con but has LD undercurrents, seaside

Candidates 97	97 votes	97%	92%	Candidates
David Amess (Con)	18,029	38.8	54.7	
Nina Stimson (LD)	15,414	33.1	30.9	Richard de Ste Croix
Alan Harley (Lab)	10,600	22.8	12.3	Paul Fisher
Majority	2,615	5.7	23.8	

Electorate: 66,493 Turnout: 46,514 (70%)

SOUTH HOLLAND & THE DEEPINGS, Lincolnshire. Strong Con seat, rural

Candidates 97	97 votes	97%	92%	Candidates
John Hayes (Con)	24,691	49.3	57	
John Lewis (Lab)	16,700	33.3	24.1	Graham Walker
Peter Millen (LD)	7,836	15.6	18.9	
Majority	7,991	16	32.9	

Electorate: 69,641 Turnout: 50,129 (72%)

SOUTHPORT, Merseyside. LD regained 97, new candidate has tight fight with Con, north of Liverpool

Candidates 97	97 votes	97%	92%	Candidates
Ronnie Fearn (LD)	24,346	48.1	41.5	John Pugh
Matthew Banks (Con)	18,186	35.9	47	Laurence Jones
Sarah Norman (Lab)	6,129	12.1	10.2	Paul Brant
Majority	6,160	12.2	–	

Electorate: 70,194 Turnout: 50,596 (72.1%)

SOUTH SHIELDS, Tyne & Wear. Strong Lab seat, ex-shipbuilding, skilled manual

Candidates 97	97 votes	97%	92%	Candidates
David Clark (Lab)	27,834	71.4	61.1	David Clark
Mark Hoban (Con)	5,681	14.6	26.6	
David Ord (LD)	3,429	8.8	12.3	Marshall Grainger
Majority	22,153	56.8	34.5	

Electorate: 62,261 Turnout: 38,978 (62.6%)

SOUTHWARK NORTH & BERMONDSEY, S London. Lab snap at LD heels here, Tate Modern and Thames shore

Candidates 97	97 votes	97%	92%	Candidates
Simon Hughes (LD)	19,831	48.6	51.4	
Jeremy Fraser (Lab)	16,444	40.3	34.5	Kingsley Abrams
Grant Shapps (Con)	2,835	6.9	12	
Majority	3,387	8.3	16.9	

Electorate: 65,598 Turnout: 40,795 (62.2%)

SPELTHORNE, Surrey. Strong Con seat, mainly urban, white collar

Candidates 97	97 votes	97%	92%	Candidates
David Wilshire (Con)	23,306	44.9	58.5	
Keith Dibble (Lab)	19,833	38.2	22.9	Andrew Shaw
Edward Glynn (LD)	6,821	13.1	16.5	
Majority	3,473	6.7	35.6	

Electorate: 70,561 Turnout: 51,917 (73.6%)

ST ALBANS, Hertfordshire. Remarkable Lab gain from 3rd, Con prospect

Candidates 97	97 votes	97%	92%	Candidates
Kerry Pollard (Lab)	21,338	42	25	Kerry Pollard
David Rutley (Con)	16,879	33.2	45.7	Charles Elphicke
Anthony Rowlands (LD)	10,692	21	28	Nick Rijke
Majority	4,459	8.8	17.7	

Electorate: 65,560 Turnout: 50,805 (77.5%)

ST HELENS NORTH, Merseyside. Strong Lab seat, industrial, skilled manual

Candidates 97	97 votes	97%	92%	Candidates
David Watts (Lab)	31,953	64.9	57.9	David Watts
Pelham Walker (Con)	8,536	17.3	28.5	Simon Pearce
John Beirne (LD)	6,270	12.7	13.1	John Beirne
Majority	23,417	47.6	29.4	

Electorate: 71,380 Turnout: 49,230 (69%)

ST HELENS SOUTH, Merseyside. Strong Lab seat, glass industry, skilled manual

Candidates 97	97 votes	97%	92%	Candidates
Gerry Bermingham (Lab)	30,367	68.6	61	Gerry Bermingham
Mary Russell (Con)	6,628	15	24.5	Lee Rotherham
Brian Spencer (LD)	5,919	13.4	13.9	Brian Spencer
Majority	23,739	53.6	36.5	

Electorate: 66,526 Turnout: 44,258 (66.5%)

ST IVES, Cornwall. Land's End and Scilly Isles, LD gain 97, likely hold

Candidates 97	97 votes	97%	92%	Candidates
Andrew George (LD)	23,966	44.5	40.1	
Williams Rogers (Con)	16,796	31.2	42.9	Joanna Richardson
Christopher Fagen (Lab)	8,184	15.2	16	William Morris
Majority	7,170	13.3	2.8	

Electorate: 71,680 Turnout: 53,901 (75.2%)

STAFFORD, Staffordshire. Midlands town plus surrounds, Lab gain 97, likely to hold

Candidates 97	97 votes	97%	92%	Candidates
David Kidney (Lab)	24,606	47.5	34.9	David Kidney
David Cameron (Con)	20,292	39.2	48.1	Philip Cochrane
Pam Hornby (LD)	5,480	10.6	16.5	
Majority	4,314	8.3	13.2	

Electorate: 58,610 Turnout: 33,122 (56.5%)

STAFFORDSHIRE MOORLANDS, Staffordshire. Rough hill country near Derbyshire, plus Lab towns

Candidates 97	97 votes	97%	92%	Candidates
Charlotte Atkins (Lab)	26,686	52.2	40.9	Charlotte Atkins
Dr Andrew Ashworth (Con)	16,637	32.5	38.7	Marcus Hayes
Christina Jebb (LD)	6,191	12.1	17.4	John Redfern
Majority	10,049	19.7	2.2	

Electorate: 66,095 Turnout: 51,117 (77.3%)

STAFFORDSHIRE SOUTH, Staffordshire. Strong Con seat, mainly rural

Candidates 97	97 votes	97%	92%	Candidates
Sir Patrick Cormack (Con)	25,568	50	59.2	
Judith LeMaistre (Lab)	17,747	34.7	25.8	Paul Kalinauckas
Jamie Calder (LD)	5,797	11.3	15.1	
Majority	7,821	15.3	33.4	

Electorate: 68,895 Turnout: 51,114 (74.2%)

STALYBRIDGE & HYDE, Greater Manchester. Lab seat, outer suburbs, working class

Candidates 97	97 votes	97%	92%	Candidates
Tom Pendry (Lab)	25,363	58.9	51.6	James Purnell
Nick de Bois (Con)	10,557	24.5	35.9	
Martin Cross (LD)	5,169	12	9	
Majority	14,806	34.4	15.7	

Electorate: 65,468 Turnout: 43,081 (65.8%)

STEVENAGE, Hertfordshire. Barbara Follett took from Con in 97 and expects to keep it

Candidates 97	97 votes	97%	92%	Candidates
Barbara Follett (Lab)	28,440	55.3	38.6	Barbara Follett
Timothy Wood (Con)	16,858	32.8	43.9	Graeme Quar
Alex Wilcock (LD)	4,588	8.9	17.1	Harry Davies
Majority	11,582	22.5	5.3	

Electorate: 66,889 Turnout: 51,386 (76.8%)

STIRLING, C Scotland. Key Lab gain from Con 1997, SNP now look challengers

Candidates 97	97 votes	97%	92%	Candidates
Anne McGuire (Lab)	20,382	47.4	38.6	Anne McGuire
Michael Forsyth (Con)	13,971	32.5	39.2	
Ewan Dow (SNP)	5,752	13.4	14.5	Fiona Macaulay
Alastair Tough (LD)	2,675	6.2	6.7	
Majority	6,411	14.9	0.6	

Electorate: 52,490 Turnout: 42,958 (81.8%)

STOCKPORT, Greater Manchester. Lab seat, urban, safer than ever before

Candidates 97	97 votes	97%	92%	Candidates
Ann Coffey (Lab)	29,338	62.9	48	Ann Coffey
Stephen Fitzsimmons (Con)	10,426	22.3	37.9	John Allen
S Roberts (LD)	4,951	10.6	12.8	Mark Hunter
Majority	18,912	40.6	10.1	

Electorate: 65,232 Turnout: 46,669 (71.5%)

STOCKTON NORTH, Cleveland. Strong Lab seat, chemical industry

Candidates 97	97 votes	97%	92%	Candidates
Frank Cook (Lab)	29,726	66.8	54	Frank Cook
Bryan Johnston (Con)	8,369	18.8	32.9	Amanda Vigar
Suzanne Fletcher (LD)	4,816	10.8	12	David Freeman
Majority	21,357	48	21.1	

Electorate: 64,380 Turnout: 44,474 (69.1%)

STOCKTON SOUTH, Cleveland. Lab gained at last in 97, Cons finished here for time being

Candidates 97	97 votes	97%	92%	Candidates
Dari Taylor (Lab)	28,790	55.2	35.6	Dari Taylor
Tim Delvin (Con)	17,205	33	45	Tim Devlin
Peter Monck (LD)	4,721	9.1	19.4	Suzanne Fletcher
Majority	11,585	22.2	9.4	

Electorate: 68,470 Turnout: 52,116 (76.1%)

STOKE-ON-TRENT CENTRAL, Staffordshire. Strong Lab seat, pottery industry, skilled manual

Candidates 97	97 votes	97%	92%	Candidates
Mark Fisher (Lab)	26,662	66.2	58	Mark Fisher
Neil Jones (Con)	6,738	16.7	27.9	Jill Clark
Edward Fordham (LD)	4,809	11.9	13.6	Gavin Webb
Majority	19,924	49.5	30.1	

Electorate: 64,113 Turnout: 40,245 (62.8%)

STOKE-ON-TRENT NORTH, Staffordshire. Strong Lab seat, mainly urban, skilled manual

Candidates 97	97 votes	97%	92%	Candidates
Joan Walley (Lab)	25,190	65.1	54.8	Joan Walley
Christopher Day (Con)	7,798	20.2	33.7	Benjamin Browning
H Jebb (LD)	4,141	10.7	10.5	Henry Jebb
Majority	17,392	44.9	21.1	

Electorate: 59,030 Turnout: 38,666 (65.5%)

STOKE-ON-TRENT SOUTH, Staffordshire. Lab seat, suburban, skilled manual

Candidates 97	97 votes	97%	92%	Candidates
George Stevenson (Lab)	28,645	62	49.8	George Stevenson
Sheila Scott (Con)	10,342	22.4	36.7	Philip Bastiman
Peter Barnett (LD)	4,710	10.2	13	
Majority	18,303	39.6	13.1	

Electorate: 69,968 Turnout: 46,236 (66.1%)

STONE, Staffordshire. Base for Con Eurosceptic William Cash, inc. Alton Towers

Candidates 97	97 votes	97%	92%	Candidates
William Cash (Con)	24,859	46.8	56	William Cash
John Wakefield (Lab)	21,041	39.6	28.9	
Barry Stamp (LD)	6,392	12	13.6	
Majority	3,818	7.2	27.1	

Electorate: 68,241 Turnout: 53,074 (77.8%)

STOURBRIDGE, W Midlands. Lab took in 97, Con longshot, mainly urban

Candidates 97	97 votes	97%	92%	Candidates
Debra Shipley (Lab)	23,452	47.2	38.3	Debra Shipley
Warren Hawksley (Con)	17,807	35.8	48.8	Stephen Eyre
Chris Bramhall (LD)	7,123	14.3	11.8	Chris Bramall
Majority	5,645	11.4	10.5	

Electorate: 64,966 Turnout: 49,701 (76.5%)

STRANGFORD, Northern Ireland. Strong Unionist seat, commuting

Candidates 97	97 votes	97%	92%	Candidates
John D Taylor (UUP)	18,431	44.3	49	
Iris Robinson (DUP)	12,579	30.2	19.9	
Kieran McCarthy (Alliance)	5,467	13.1	16.1	
Peter O'Reilly (SDLP)	2,775	6.7		
Majority	5,852	14.1	29.2	

Electorate: 69,980 Turnout: 41,619 (59.5%)

STRATFORD-ON-AVON, Warwickshire. Secure for Cons, especially as tied opposition

Candidates 97	97 votes	97%	92%	Candidates
John Maples (Con)	29,967	48.3	58.8	
Dr S Juned (LD)	15,861	25.5	25.6	Susan Juned
Stewart Stacey (Lab)	12,754	20.5	13.4	Mushtaq Hussain
Majority	14,106	22.8	33.2	

Electorate: 81,433 Turnout: 62,099 (76.3%)

STRATHKELVIN & BEARSDEN, W Scotland. Middle class outer Glasgow which seems safe for Lab

Candidates 97	97 votes	97%	92%	Candidates
Sam Galbraith (Lab)	26,278	52.9	46.1	
David Sharpe (Con)	9,986	20.1	32.6	
Graeme McCormick (SNP)	8,111	16.3	12.9	Calum Smith
John Morrison (LD)	4,252	8		Gordon Macdonald
Majority	16,292	32.8	13.5	

Electorate: 62,974 Turnout: 49,712 (78.9%)

STREATHAM, S London. Brixton to suburbs, once Con now safe Lab

Candidates 97	97 votes	97%	92%	Candidates
Keith Hill (Lab)	28,181	62.8	49.4	Keith Hill
Ernest Noad (Con)	9,758	21.7	38.4	Stephen Hocking
Roger O'Brien (LD)	6,082	13.6	10	Roger O'Brien
Majority	18,423	41.1	11	

Electorate: 74,509 Turnout: 44,885 (60.2%)

STRETFORD & URMSTON, Greater Manchester. Safe Lab, suburban, white collar

Candidates 97	97 votes	97%	92%	Candidates
Beverley Hughes (Lab)	28,480	58.5	48.9	Beverley Hughes
John Gregory (Con)	14,840	30.5	40.8	Jonathan Mackie
John Bridges (LD)	3,978	8.2	9.2	
Majority	13,640	28	8.1	

Electorate: 69,913 Turnout: 48,695 (69.7%)

STROUD, Gloucestershire. Notable Lab win in 97 which is unlikely to be repeated

Candidates 97	97 votes	97%	92%	Candidates
David Drew (Lab)	26,170	42.7	29.4	David Drew
Roger Knapman (Con)	23,260	37.9	46.2	Neil Carmichael
Paul Hodgkinson (LD)	9,502	15.5	21.6	Janice Beasley
Majority	2,910	4.8	16.8	

Electorate: 77,493 Turnout: 61,347 (79.2%)

SUFFOLK CENTRAL & IPSWICH NORTH, Suffolk. Strong Con seat, mainly urban, middle class

Candidates 97	97 votes	97%	92%	Candidates
Michael Lord (Con)	22,493	42.6	55.8	
Carole Jones (Lab)	18,955	35.9	20.7	
Mione Goldspink (LD)	10,886	20.6	21.9	
Majority	3,538	6.7	35.1	

Electorate: 70,221 Turnout: 52,823 (75.2%)

SUFFOLK COASTAL, Suffolk. Inc. Felixstowe, Woodbridge and Sizewell nuclear plant

Candidates 97	97 votes	97%	92%	Candidates
John Gummer (Con)	21,696	38.6	52.4	
Mark Campbell (Lab)	18,442	32.8	23.3	Nigel Gardner
Alexandra Jones (LD)	12,036	21.4	22.7	Janice Beasley
Majority	3,254	5.8	29.1	

Electorate: 74,218 Turnout: 56,256 (75.8%)

SUFFOLK SOUTH, Suffolk. Strong Con seat, rural, middle class

Candidates 97	97 votes	97%	92%	Candidates
Tim Yeo (Con)	19,402	37.3	51.3	
Paul Bishop (Lab)	15,227	29.3	21.8	
Kathy Pollard (LD)	14,395	27.7	26.2	
Majority	4,175	8	25.1	

Electorate: 67,322 Turnout: 51,975 (77.2%)

SUFFOLK WEST, Suffolk. Just remained Con 97, mostly rural, inc Newmarket

Candidates 97	97 votes	97%	92%	Candidates
Richard Spring (Con)	20,081	40.9	53.8	
Michael Jefferys (Lab)	18,214	37.1	24	
Adrian Graves (LD)	6,892	14	21.3	
Majority	1,867	3.8	29.8	

Electorate: 68,637 Turnout: 49,082 (71.5%)

SUNDERLAND NORTH, Tyne & Wear. Strong Lab seat, inner city, skilled manual

Candidates 97	97 votes	97%	92%	Candidates
William Etherington (Lab)	26,067	68.2	59.6	William Etherington
Andrew Selous (Con)	6,370	16.7	27.8	Michael Harris
Geoffrey Pryke (LD)	3,973	10.4	10.9	
Majority	19,697	51.5	31.8	

Electorate: 64,711 Turnout: 38,213 (59.1%)

SUNDERLAND SOUTH, Tyne & Wear. First to declare in 97, now very safe Lab

Candidates 97	97 votes	97%	92%	Candidates
Chris Mullin (Lab)	27,174	68.1	57.5	Chris Mullin
Tim Schofield (Con)	7,536	18.9	29.3	Jim Boyd
John Lennox (LD)	4,606	11.5	11.8	
Majority	19,638	49.2	28.2	
Electorate: 67,937 Turnout: 39,925 (58.8%)				

SURREY EAST, Surrey. Strong Con seat, commuting, managerial

Candidates 97	97 votes	97%	92%	Candidates
Peter Ainsworth (Con)	27,389	50.1	61.1	
B Ford (LD)	12,296	22.5	26.9	Jeremy Pursehouse
David Ross (Lab)	11,573	21.2	10.5	
Majority	15,093	27.6	34.2	
Electorate: 72,851 Turnout: 54,656 (75%)				

SURREY HEATH, Surrey. Strong Con seat, stockbroker belt, middle class

Candidates 97	97 votes	97%	92%	Candidates
Nick Hawkins (Con)	28,231	51.6	63.7	
D Newman (LD)	11,944	21.8	23.1	Mark Lelliott
S Jones (Lab)	11,511	21	11.3	James Norman
Majority	16,287	29.8	40.6	
Electorate: 73,813 Turnout: 54,724 (74.1%)				

SURREY SOUTH WEST, Surrey. Con base for Virginia Bottomley, LDs active but missed in 97

Candidates 97	97 votes	97%	92%	Candidates
Virginia Bottomley (Con)	25,165	44.6	58.5	
Neil Sherlock (LD)	22,471	39.8	33.5	Simon Cordon
Margaret Leicester (Lab)	5,333	9.4	6.4	
Majority	2,694	4.8	25	
Electorate: 72,349 Turnout: 56,458 (78%)				

SUSSEX MID, Sussex. Strong Con seat, rural, managerial, commuters

Candidates 97	97 votes	97%	92%	Candidates
Nicholas Soames (Con)	23,231	43.5	58.9	
Margaret Collins (LD)	16,377	30.6	28.2	Lesley Wilkins
M Hamilton (Lab)	9,969	18.6	10.6	
Majority	6,854	12.9	30.7	
Electorate: 68,783 Turnout: 53,463 (77.7%)				

SUTTON & CHEAM, S London. Great LD-Con fight, LD took 97, both candidates run again

Candidates 97	97 votes	97%	92%	Candidates
Paul Burstow (LD)	19,919	42.3	33.8	Paul Burstow
Lady Olga Maitland (Con)	17,822	37.8	55.2	Lady Olga Maitland
Mark Allison (Lab)	7,280	15.5	9.9	Lisa Homan
Majority	2,097	4.5	21.4	
Electorate: 62,785 Turnout: 47,092 (75%)				

SUTTON COLDFIELD, W Midlands. Very safe Con outer Birmingham, new Con candidate

Candidates 97	97 votes	97%	92%	Candidates
Sir Norman Fowler (Con)	27,373	52.2	65.2	Andrew Mitchell
Alan York (Lab)	12,488	23.8	15	Robert Pocock
Jim Whorwood (LD)	10,139	19.3	19.3	Martin Turner
Majority	14,885	28.4	45.9	
Electorate: 71,863 Turnout: 52,401 (72.9%)				

SWANSEA EAST, S Wales. Lab will lose no sleep over this ultra-safe seat

Candidates 97	97 votes	97%	92%	Candidates
Donald Anderson (Lab)	29,151	75.4	69.7	Donald Anderson
Catherine Dibble (Con)	3,582	9.3	17.2	Paul Morris
Elwyn Jones (LD)	3,440	8.9	9.5	Robert Speht
M Pooley (PC)	1,308	3.4	3.6	
Majority	25,569	66.1	52.5	

Electorate: 57,373 Turnout: 38,674 (67.4%)

SWANSEA WEST, S Wales. Very Lab, though suburban with shrunken Con vote

Candidates 97	97 votes	97%	92%	Candidates
Alan Williams (Lab)	22,748	56.2	53	Alan Williams
Andrew Baker (Con)	8,289	20.5	31.4	Margaret Harper
John Newbury (LD)	5,872	14.5	10.5	Mike Day
D Lloyd (PC)	2,675	6.6	3.8	Ian Titherington
Majority	14,459	35.7	21.6	

Electorate: 58,703 Turnout: 40,469 (68.9%)

SWINDON NORTH, Wiltshire. Lab gain in 97, should hold, boom town plus local area

Candidates 97	97 votes	97%	92%	Candidates
Michael Wills (Lab)	24,029	49.8	42.7	Michael Wills
Guy Opperman (Con)	16,341	33.9	40.9	
Mike Evemy (LD)	6,237	12.9	14.6	
Majority	7,688	15.9	1.8	

Electorate: 65,535 Turnout: 48,270 (73.7%)

SWINDON SOUTH, Wiltshire. Lab gain 97 but now just about marginal

Candidates 97	97 votes	97%	92%	Candidates
Julia Drown (Lab)	23,943	46.8	30.8	Julia Drown
Simon Coombs (Con)	18,298	35.8	48.9	
Stanley Pajak (LD)	7,371	14.4	18.7	
Majority	5,645	11	18.1	

Electorate: 70,206 Turnout: 51,162 (72.9%)

TAMWORTH, Staffordshire. Probably secure for Lab, Midlands, Con longshot

Candidates 97	97 votes	97%	92%	Candidates
Brian Jenkins (Lab)	25,808	51.8	39.2	Brian Jenkins
Lady Lightbown (Con)	18,312	36.7	49.3	Louise Gunter
J Pinkett (LD)	4,025	8.1	9.9	Jennifer Pinkett
Majority	7,496	15.1	10.1	

Electorate: 67,204 Turnout: 49,854 (74.2%)

TATTON, Cheshire. Famous for electing Ind Martin Bell in 97, this time it will go Con

Candidates 97	97 votes	97%	92%	Candidates
Martin Bell (Ind)	29,354	60.2		
Neil Hamilton (Con)	18,277	37.5	62.2	George Osborne
S Hill (Ind C)	295	0.6		
Majority	11,077	22.7	43.2	

Electorate: 63,822 Turnout: 48,792 (76.5%)

TAUNTON, Somerset. LDs gained 97, plan to hold on, Con outside bet

Candidates 97	97 votes	97%	92%	Candidates
Jackie Ballard (LD)	26,064	42.7	40.8	Jackie Ballard
David Nicholson (Con)	23,621	38.7	46	Adrian Flook
Elizabeth Lisgo (Lab)	8,248	13.5	12.7	Andrew Govier
Majority	2,443	4	5.2	

Electorate: 79,783 Turnout: 61,011 (76.5%)

TAYSIDE NORTH, NE Scotland. SNP took from Con in 97, should consolidate now

Candidates 97	97 votes	97%	92%	Candidates
John Swinney (SNP)	20,447	44.8	38.8	Peter Wishart
Bill Walker (Con)	16,287	35.7	46.4	
Ian McFartridge (Lab)	5,141	11.3	7	
Peter Regent (LD)	3,716	8.2	7.9	Julia Robertson
Majority	4,160	9.1	7.6	
Electorate: 61,397 Turnout: 45,591 (74.3%)				

TEIGNBRIDGE, Devon. Con seat, LD longshot, rural

Candidates 97	97 votes	97%	92%	Candidates
Patrick Nicholls (Con)	24,679	39.2	50.3	
Richard Younger-Ross (LD)	24,398	38.8	35.1	Richard Younger-Ross
Sue Dann (Lab)	11,311	18	13	Christopher Bain
Majority	281	0.4	15.2	
Electorate: 81,667 Turnout: 62,945 (77.1%)				

TELFORD, Shropshire. Lab seat, new town, many social problems

Candidates 97	97 votes	97%	92%	Candidates
Bruce Grocott (Lab)	21,456	57.8	52.8	Bruce Grocott
Bernard Gentry (Con)	10,166	27.4	33.3	Andrew Henderson
Nathaniel Green (LD)	4,371	11.8	12.4	Sally Wiggin
Majority	11,290	30.4	19.5	
Electorate: 56,558 Turnout: 37,112 (65.6%)				

TEWKESBURY, Gloucestershire. Easy Con win in 97, mainly urban, M5 corridor

Candidates 97	97 votes	97%	92%	Candidates
Laurence Robertson (Con)	23,859	45.8	53.8	
John Sewell (LD)	14,625	28	35.2	Stephen Martin
Sarah Tustin (Lab)	13,665	26.2	10.1	Keir Dhillon
Majority	9,234	17.8	18.6	
Electorate: 68,207 Turnout: 52,149 (76.5%)				

THANET NORTH, Kent. Since Cons won here in 97 they are bound to do so again

Candidates 97	97 votes	97%	92%	Candidates
Roger Gale (Con)	21,586	44.1	57.2	
Iris Johnston (Lab)	18,820	38.4	23.5	
Paul Kendrick (LD)	5,576	11.4	17.7	
Majority	2,766	5.7	33.7	
Electorate: 71,112 Turnout: 48,955 (68.8%)				

THANET SOUTH, Kent. inc Ramsgate, Broadstairs, Aitken lost to Lab in 97, Con target

Candidates 97	97 votes	97%	92%	Candidates
Dr Stephen Ladyman (Lab)	20,777	46.2	28.1	
Jonathan Aitken (Con)	17,899	39.8	51.7	Mark Macgregor
Barbara Hewitt-Silk (LD)	5,263	11.7	18.3	
Majority	2,878	6.4	23.6	
Electorate: 62,791 Turnout: 44,988 (71.6%)				

THURROCK, Essex. Contains Lakeside shops, Thames shore, Lab voters

Candidates 97	97 votes	97%	92%	Candidates
Andrew MacKinlay (Lab)	29,896	63.3	45.9	Andrew MacKinlay
Andrew Rosindell (Con)	12,640	26.8	43.7	Mike Penning
J White (LD)	3,843	8.1	9.5	
Majority	17,256	36.5	2.2	
Electorate: 71,600 Turnout: 47,212 (65.9%)				

TIVERTON & HONITON, Devon. LDs hoped to win here in 97 but just missed, likely Con hold

Candidates 97	97 votes	97%	92%	Candidates
Angela Browning (Con)	24,438	41.3	51.3	
Dr J Barnard (LD)	22,785	38.5	31.7	Jim Barnard
John King (Lab)	7,598	12.8	11	Isabel Owen
Majority	1,653	2.8	19.6	

Electorate: 75,744 Turnout: 59,129 (78.1%)

TONBRIDGE & MALLING, Kent. Strong Con seat, commuting, managerial

Candidates 97	97 votes	97%	92%	Candidates
Sir John Stanley (Con)	23,640	48	60.8	
Barbara Withstandley (Lab)	13,410	27.2	17.1	Victoria Hayman
Keith Brown (LD)	9,467	19.2	20.7	Merilyn Canet
Majority	10,230	20.8	40.1	

Electorate: 64,798 Turnout: 49,229 (76%)

TOOTING, S London. Southern part of Tory borough of Wandsworth, but seat safe for Lab

Candidates 97	97 votes	97%	92%	Candidates
Tom Cox (Lab)	27,516	59.7	48.2	Tom Cox
James Hutchings (Con)	12,505	27.1	40.1	Alexander Nicoll
Simon James (LD)	4,320	9.4	7.4	Simon James
Majority	15,011	32.6	8.1	

Electorate: 66,652 Turnout: 46,105 (69.2%)

TORBAY, Devon. LDs squeaked in 97, Con stormed back since on council, Con target

Candidates 97	97 votes	97%	92%	Candidates
Adrian Sanders (LD)	21,094	39.6	39.8	
Rupert Allason (Con)	21,082	39.5	49.9	Christian Sweeting
Michael Morey (Lab)	7,923	14.9	9.6	John McKay
Majority	12	0.1	10.1	

Electorate: 72,258 Turnout: 53,322 (73.8%)

TORFAEN, S Wales. Strong Lab seat, part new town, working class, based on Pontypool

Candidates 97	97 votes	97%	92%	Candidates
Paul Murphy (Lab)	29,863	69.1	64.1	Paul Murphy
N Parish (Con)	5,327	12.3	20.3	Jason Evans
J Gray (LD)	5,249	12.1	13.1	
Majority	24,536	56.8	43.8	

Electorate: 60,343 Turnout: 43,245 (71.7%)

TORRIDGE & WEST DEVON, Devon. LDs just won 97, will be tight this time, big, inc. Dartmoor, hit by foot and mouth

Candidates 97	97 votes	97%	92%	Candidates
John Burnett (LD)	24,744	41.8	41.7	
Ian Liddle-Grainger (Con)	22,787	38.5	47.1	Geoffrey Cox
David Brenton (Lab)	7,319	12.4	9.5	David Brenton
Majority	1,957	3.3	5.4	

Electorate: Turnout: (%)

TOTNES, Devon. Tight Con win in 97 against LDs, south Devon coast

Candidates 97	97 votes	97%	92%	Candidates
Anthony Steen (Con)	19,637	36.5	50.8	
Rob Chave (LD)	18,760	34.9	35.6	Rachel Oliver
Victor Ellery (Lab)	8,796	16.4	12.1	Thomas Wildy
Majority	877	1.6	15.2	

Electorate: 70,473 Turnout: 53,769 (76.3%)

TOTTENHAM, N London. Strong Lab seat, inner city, Lab held in 00 byelection

Candidates 97	97 votes	97%	92%	Candidates
Sir Anthony Grant (Lab)	26,121	69.3	56.5	David Lammy
Andrew Scantlebury (Con)	5,921	15.7	29.8	Uma Fernandes
Neil Hughes (LD)	4,064	10.8	11.4	Meher Khan
Majority	20,200	53.6	26.7	

Electorate: 66,173 Turnout: 37,704 (57%)

TRURO & ST AUSTELL, Cornwall. LD seat since 74, mainly urban, retirement

Candidates 97	97 votes	97%	92%	Candidates
Matthew Taylor (LD)	27,502	48.5	50.5	Matthew Taylor
Neil Badcock (Con)	15,001	26.4	38.3	Tim Bonner
Michael Dooley (Lab)	8,697	15.3	9.8	David Phillips
Majority	12,501	22.1	12.2	

Electorate: 76,824 Turnout: 56,747 (73.9%)

TUNBRIDGE WELLS, Kent. Strong Con seat, commuting, managerial, Archie Norman MP failed on frontbench

Candidates 97	97 votes	97%	92%	Candidates
Archie Norman (Con)	21,853	45.2	55	
Tony Clayton (LD)	14,347	29.7	29.5	Keith Brown
Peter Warner (Lab)	9,879	20.4	14.7	Ian Carvell
Majority	7,506	15.5	25.5	

Electorate: 65,259 Turnout: 48,354 (74.1%)

TWEEDDALE, ETTRICK & LAUDERDALE, SE Scotland. LDs survived Lab challenge in 97, should be more secure next time

Candidates 97	97 votes	97%	92%	Candidates
Michael Moore (LD)	12,178	31.2	35	
Keith Geddes (Lab)	10,689	27.4	16.4	George McGregor
Alister Jack (Con)	8,623	22.1	30.7	
Ianin Goldie (SNP)	6,671	17.1	17.2	Richard Thomson
Majority	1,489	3.8	18.6	

Electorate: 50,891 Turnout: 39,001 (76.6%)

TWICKENHAM, S London. LDs took in 97, leafy outer London

Candidates 97	97 votes	97%	92%	Candidates
Dr Vincent Cable (LD)	26,237	45.1	39.3	
Toby Jessel (Con)	21,956	37.8	49.6	Nick Longworth
E Tutchell (Lab)	9,065	15.6	10.4	Dean Rogers
Majority	4,281	7.3	10.3	

Electorate: 73,281 Turnout: 58,144 (79.3%)

TYNE BRIDGE, Tyne & Wear. Strong Lab seat, inner city, high unemployment

Candidates 97	97 votes	97%	92%	Candidates
David Clelland (Lab)	26,767	76.8	66.8	David Clelland
Adrian Lee (Con)	3,861	11.1	22.1	James Cook
M Wallace (LD)	2,785	8	11.1	Jonathan Wallace
Majority	22,906	65.7	44.7	

Electorate: 61,058 Turnout: 34,850 (57.1%)

TYNEMOUTH, Tyne & Wear. Con lost to Lab in 97, some smart seaside towns, Lab should hold

Candidates 97	97 votes	97%	92%	Candidates
Alan Campbell (Lab)	28,318	55.4	42.3	Alan Campbell
Martin Callanan (Con)	17,045	33.3	48.6	Karl Poulsen
Andrew Duffield (LD)	4,509	8.8	8.1	Penny Reid
Majority	11,273	22.1	6.3	

Electorate: 66,341 Turnout: 51,153 (77.1%)

TYNESIDE NORTH, Tyne & Wear. Strong Lab seat, inner city, working class

Candidates 97	97 votes	97%	92%	Candidates
Stephen Byers (Lab)	32,810	72.7	61	Stephen Byers
Michael MacIntrye (Con)	6,167	13.7	26	
Tommy Mulvenna (LD)	4,762	10.6	13	Simon Reed
Majority	26,643	59	35	

Electorate: 66,449 Turnout: 45,121 (67.9%)

TYRONE WEST, Northern Ireland. Catholic majority, but split SDLP-SF vote let UUP in last time, up for grabs

Candidates 97	97 votes	97%	92%	Candidates
William Thompson (UUP)	16,003	34.6	–	
Joe Byrne (SDLP)	14,842	32.1	31	
Pat Doherty (SF)	14,280	30.9	19.9	
Ann Gormley (Alliance)	829	1.8	4.7	
Majority	1,161	2.5	11.1	

Electorate: 58,168 Turnout: 46,275 (79.6%)

ULSTER MID, Northern Ireland. SF won on highest UK turnout in 97, expect to hold

Candidates 97	97 votes	97%	92%	Candidates
Martin McGuinness (SF)	20,294	40.1	24.1	
Rev William McCrea (DUP)	18,411	36.3	41	
Denis Haughey (SDLP)	11,205	22.1	30.6	
E Bogues (Alliance)	460	0.9	2.6	
Majority	1,883	3.8	10.5	

Electorate: 58,836 Turnout: 50,669 (86.1%)

UPMINSTER, E London. Remarkable Lab gain 97, end of District line, London borders

Candidates 97	97 votes	97%	92%	Candidates
Keith Darvill (Lab)	19,085	46.2	30.1	Keith Darvill
Sir Nicholas Bonsor (Con)	16,315	39.5	54.2	Angela Watkinson
Pamela Peskett (LD)	3,919	9.5	15.7	
Majority	2,770	6.7	24.1	

Electorate: 57,148 Turnout: 41,319 (72.3%)

UPPER BANN, Northern Ireland. David Trimble's seat, rural, some Catholic voters

Candidates 97	97 votes	97%	92%	Candidates
David Trimble (UUP)	20,836	43.6	59	David Trimble
Brid Rodgers (SDLP)	11,584	24.2	23.4	
Bernadette O'Hagan (SF)	5,773	12.1	6.1	
M Carrick (DUP)	5,482	11.5	–	
Majority	9,252	19.4	35.5	

Electorate: 70,398 Turnout: 47,787 (67.9%)

UXBRIDGE, N London. Cons just held in 97 and by-election though Lab won in 66

Candidates 97	97 votes	97%	92%	Candidates
Michael Shersby (Con)	18,095	43.6	56.4	
D Williams (Lab)	17,371	41.8	29	Dave Salisbury-Jones
Dr Andrew Malyan (LD)	4,528	10.9	12.5	Catherine Royce
Majority	724	1.8	27.4	

Electorate: 57,497 Turnout: 41,545 (72.3%)

VALE OF CLWYD, NE Wales. Lab won in 97, Con will try to take these north Wales towns

Candidates 97	97 votes	97%	92%	Candidates
Chris Ruane (Lab)	20,617	52.7	38.8	Chris Ruane
David Edwards (Con)	11,662	29.8	43.7	Brendan Murphy
Daniel Munford (LD)	3,425	8.8	12.4	
G Kensler (PC)	2,301	5.9	4.8	John Penri Williams
Majority	8,955	22.9	4.9	

Electorate: 52,418 Turnout: 39,132 (74.7%)

VALE OF GLAMORGAN, South Glamorgan. Perpetual Con marginal which went heavily Lab in 97

Candidates 97	97 votes	97%	92%	Candidates
John Smith (Lab)	29,054	53.9	44.3	John Smith
Walter Sweeney (Con)	18,522	34.4	44.3	Lady Susan Inkin
Suzanne Campbell (LD)	4,945	9.2	9.2	Dewi Smith
M Corp (PC)	1,393	2.6	–	
Majority	10,532	19.5	–	

Electorate: 67,213 Turnout: 53,914 (80.2%)

VALE OF YORK, N Yorkshire. Flatlands between Yorkshire Moors and the Dales, safe for Con even in 97

Candidates 97	97 votes	97%	92%	Candidates
Anne McIntosh (Con)	23,815	44.7	60.6	
Matthew Carter (Lab)	14,094	26.5	11.1	Christopher Jukes
Charles Hall (LD)	12,656	23.8	27.8	Greg Stone
Majority	9,721	18.2	32.8	

Electorate:70,077 Turnout: 53,265 (76%)

VAUXHALL, S London. Strong Lab seat, inner city

Candidates 97	97 votes	97%	92%	Candidates
Kate Hoey (Lab)	24,920	63.8	56.1	Kate Hoey
Keith Kerr (LD)	6,260	16	14.4	Greg Stone
Richard Bacon (Con)	5,942	15.2	26.6	Gareth Compton
Majority	18,660	47.8	29.5	

Electorate: 70,402 Turnout: 39,066 (55.5%)

WAKEFIELD, W Yorkshire. Suburban, working class and now very safe for Lab

Candidates 97	97 votes	97%	92%	Candidates
David Hinchliffe (Lab)	28,977	57.4	48.2	David Hinchliffe
Jonathan Peacock (Con)	14,373	28.5	40.5	Thelma Karran
Douglas Dale (LD)	5,656	11.2	11.3	Douglas Dale
Majority	14,604	28.9	7.7	

Electorate: 73,210 Turnout: 50,486 (69%)

WALLASEY, Merseyside. Outer Liverpool suburbs, Con until 92, now secure Lab

Candidates 97	97 votes	97%	92%	Candidates
Angela Eagle (Lab)	30,264	64.6	48.9	Angela Eagle
Patricia Wilcock (Con)	11,190	23.9	41.9	Lesley Rennie
Peter Reisdorf (LD)	3,899	8.3	7.7	Peter Reisdorf
Majority	19,074	40.7	7	

Electorate: 63,714 Turnout: 46,843 (73.5%)

WALSALL NORTH, W Midlands. Lab, urban, working class, some Cons

Candidates 97	97 votes	97%	92%	Candidates
David Winnick (Lab)	24,517	56.6	46.7	David Winnick
Michael Bird (Con)	11,929	27.5	39.4	
T O'Brien (LD)	4,050	9.4	12.7	
Majority	12,588	29.1	7.3	

Electorate: 67,586 Turnout: 43,302 (64.1%)

WALSALL SOUTH, W Midlands. Residential, large Asian community, north of Birmingham

Candidates 97	97 votes	97%	92%	Candidates
Bruce George (Lab)	25,024	57.9	48.2	Bruce George
Leslie Leek (Con)	13,712	31.7	41.9	Mike Bird
Harry Harris (LD)	2,698	6.2	8.3	
Majority	11,312	26.2	6.3	

Electorate: 64,221 Turnout: 43,240 (67.3%)

WALTHAMSTOW, N London. Good Lab performance in 97 puts this out of Con reach

Candidates 97	97 votes	97%	92%	Candidates
Neil Gerrard (Lab)	25,287	63.1	44.3	Neil Gerrard
J Andrew (Con)	8,138	20.3	37.2	Nick Boys Smith
J Jackson (LD)	5,491	13.7	15.8	Peter Dunphy
Majority	17,149	42.8	7.1	

Electorate: 63,817 Turnout: 40,055 (62.8%)

WANSBECK, Northumberland. Strong Lab seat, ex-mining, working class, LD distant second

Candidates 97	97 votes	97%	92%	Candidates
Denis Murphy (Lab)	29,569	65.5	59.7	Denis Murphy
Alan Thompson (LD)	7,202	15.9	15.3	Alan Thompson
Paul Green (Con)	6,299	13.9	23.6	Rachel Lake
Majority	22,367	49.6	36.1	
Electorate: 62,998 Turnout: 45,172 (71.7%)				

WANSDYKE, Somerset. South of Bristol, small towns, once Con, now Con target

Candidates 97	97 votes	97%	92%	Candidates
Dan Norris (Lab)	24,117	44.1	27.3	Dan Norris
Mark Prisk (Con)	19,318	35.3	47.2	Chris Watt
Jeff Manning (LD)	9,205	16.8	23.6	Gail Coleshill
Majority	4,799	8.8	19.9	
Electorate: 69,032 Turnout: 54,722 (79.3%)				

WANTAGE, Oxfordshire. Strong Con seat, rural, professional

Candidates 97	97 votes	97%	92%	Candidates
Robert Jackson (Con)	22,311	39.8	54.1	
Celia Wilson (Lab)	16,222	28.9	19.4	Stephen Beer
J G A Riley (LD)	14,862	26.5	25	Neil Fawcett
Majority	6,089	10.9	34.7	
Electorate: 71,657 Turnout: 56,059 (78.2%)				

WARLEY, W Midlands. Lab seat, urban, large Asian community

Candidates 97	97 votes	97%	92%	Candidates
John Spellar (Lab)	24,813	63.8	53.1	John Spellar
Christopher Pincher (Con)	9,362	24.1	34.3	Mark Pritchard
Jeremy Pursehouse (LD)	3,777	9.7	11.4	
Majority	15,451	39.7	18.8	
Electorate: 59,757 Turnout: 38,893 (65.1%)				

WARRINGTON NORTH, Cheshire. Lab seat, inner city

Candidates 97	97 votes	97%	92%	Candidates
Helen Jones (Lab)	31,827	62.1	53.2	Helen Jones
Ray Lacey (Con)	12,300	24	34.9	James Usher
Ian Greenhalgh (LD)	5,308	10.4	11.3	Roy Smith
Majority	19,527	38.1	18.3	
Electorate: 72,693 Turnout: 51,251 (70.5%)				

WARRINGTON SOUTH, Cheshire. Safe in 97, could be marginal in less good year for Lab

Candidates 97	97 votes	97%	92%	Candidates
Helen Southworth (Lab)	28,721	52.1	40.8	Helen Southworth
Christopher Grayling (Con)	17,914	32.5	45.7	Caroline Mosley
Peter Walker (LD)	7,199	13.1	13	Roger Barlow
Majority	10,807	19.6	4.9	
Electorate: 72,261 Turnout: 55,082 (76.2%)				

WARWICK & LEAMINGTON, Warwickshire. Impressive Lab gain in 97, twin towns, Con target

Candidates 97	97 votes	97%	92%	Candidates
James Plaskitt (Lab)	26,747	44.5	31.2	James Plaskitt
Sir Dudley Smith (Con)	23,349	38.9	49.5	David Campbell Bannerman
Nigel Hicks (LD)	7,133	11.9	17.1	
Majority	3,398	5.6	18.3	
Electorate: 79,373 Turnout: 60,091 (75.7%)				

WARWICKSHIRE NORTH, Warwickshire. Lab seem to have made this safe, ex-mining, working class

Candidates 97	97 votes	97%	92%	Candidates
Mike O'Brien (Lab)	31,669	58.4	46.1	Mike O'Brien
Stephen Hammond (Con)	16,902	31.2	43.6	Geoff Parsons
Bill Powell (LD)	4,040	7.4	10.3	
Majority	14,767	27.2	2.5	
Electorate: 72,601 Turnout: 54,239 (74.7%)				

WATFORD, Hertfordshire. Remarkable Lab gain in 97, close to London, will be tight battle

Candidates 97	97 votes	97%	92%	Candidates
Claire Ward (Lab)	25,019	45.3	34	Claire Ward
R Gordon (Con)	19,227	34.8	48.1	Michael McManus
Andrew Canning (LD)	9,272	16.8	16.8	Duncan Hames
Majority	5,792	10.5	14.1	

Electorate: 74,015 Turnout: 55,236 (74.6%)

WAVENEY, Suffolk. Eastern, coastal seat, Lab took with ease in 97

Candidates 97	97 votes	97%	92%	Candidates
Bob Blizzard (Lab)	31,486	56	39.7	Bob Blizzard
David Porter (Con)	19,393	34.5	47	Lee Scott
Christopher Thomas (LD)	5,054	9	12.8	David Young
Majority	12,093	21.5	7.3	

Electorate: 75,266 Turnout: 56,251 (74.7%)

WEALDEN, E Sussex. Strong Con seat, rural, wooded, managerial

Candidates 97	97 votes	97%	92%	Candidates
Sir Geoffrey Johnson Smith (Con)	29,417	49.8	61.7	Charles Hendry
Michael Skinner (LD)	15,213	25.7	27.1	Steve Murphy
Nicholas Levine (Lab)	10,185	17.2	9.2	Kathy Fordham
Majority	14,204	24.1	34.6	

Electorate: 79,519 Turnout: 59,099 (74.3%)

WEAVER VALE, Cheshire. Lab seat, salt mining, inc. Northwich

Candidates 97	97 votes	97%	92%	Candidates
Mike Hall (Lab)	27,244	56.4	48.8	Mike Hall
James Byrne (Con)	13,796	28.6	35.7	Carl Cross
Nigel Griffiths (LD)	5,949	12.3	14.5	Nigel Griffiths
Majority	13,448	27.8	13.1	

Electorate: 66,011 Turnout: 48,301 (73.2%)

WELLINGBOROUGH, Northamptonshire. Noted Lab win in 97, likely to revert to Con mainly urban, skilled manual

Candidates 97	97 votes	97%	92%	Candidates
Paul Stinchcombe (Lab)	24,854	44.2	33.9	Paul Stinchcombe
Peter Fry (Con)	24,667	43.8	53.4	Peter Bone
Peter Smith (LD)	5,279	9.4	12.7	Peter Gaskell
Majority	187	0.4	19.5	

Electorate: 74,954 Turnout: 56,289 (75.1%)

WELLS, Somerset. LDs just missed in 97 thanks to Lab surge, Glastonbury and Mendip hills

Candidates 97	97 votes	97%	92%	Candidates
David Heathcoat-Amory (Con)	22,208	39.4	49.6	
H Gold (LD)	21,680	38.5	38	Graham Oakes
Michael Eavis (Lab)	10,204	18.1	10.6	Andy Merryfield
Majority	528	0.9	11.6	

Electorate: 72,178 Turnout: 56,380 (78.1%)

WELWYN HATFIELD, Hertfordshire. Lab took in 97, new town, professional

Candidates 97	97 votes	97%	92%	Candidates
Melanie Johnson (Lab)	24,936	47.1	36	Melanie Johnson
David Evans (Con)	19,341	36.5	47.5	Grant Shapps
Rodney Schwartz (LD)	7,161	13.5	16	Daniel Cooke
Majority	5,595	10.6	11.5	

Electorate: 67,395 Turnout: 52,968 (78.6%)

WENTWORTH, S Yorkshire. Named after stately home but mostly ex-mining land, safe Lab

Candidates 97	97 votes	97%	92%	Candidates
John Healey (Lab)	30,225	72.3	68.5	John Healey
Karl Hamer (Con)	6,266	15	21.8	Mike Roberts
James Charters (LD)	3,867	9.3	9.6	David Wildgoose
Majority	23,959	57.3	46.7	

Electorate: 63,951 Turnout: 41,781 (65.3%)

WEST BROMWICH EAST, W Midlands. Lab seat, mainly urban, working class

Candidates 97	97 votes	97%	92%	Candidates
Peter Snape (Lab)	23,710	57.2	47.9	
Brian Matsell (Con)	10,126	24.4	37.9	David MacFarlane
Martyn Smith (LD)	6,179	14.9	13.3	Ian Garrett
Majority	13,584	32.8	10	
Electorate: 63,401 Turnout: 41,487 (65.4%)				

WEST BROMWICH WEST, W Midlands. Now Lab since Speaker retired, by-election 2000

Candidates 97	97 votes	97%	92%	Candidates
Betty Boothroyd (Speaker)	23,969	65.3	50.6	
R Silvester (Lab)	8,546	23.3	37.6	Adrian Bailey
S Edwards (Nat Dem)	4,181	11.4	11.8	
Majority	15,423	42	13	
Electorate: 67,496 Turnout: 36,696 (54.4%)				

WEST HAM, E London. Strong Lab seat, inner city

Candidates 97	97 votes	97%	92%	Candidates
Tony Banks (Lab)	24,531	72.9	57.9	Tony Banks
Mark MacGregor (Con)	5,037	15	30	Syed Kamall
S McDonough (LD)	2,479	7.4	9.6	
Majority	19,494	57.9	27.9	
Electorate: 57,058 Turnout: 33,661 (59%)				

WESTBURY, Wiltshire. Con seat, LDs faded in 97, mainly urban

Candidates 97	97 votes	97%	92%	Candidates
David Faber (Con)	23,037	40.6	52.2	Andrew Murrison
John Miller (LD)	16,969	29.9	33.9	David Vigar
Kevin Small (Lab)	11,969	21.1	10.6	Sarah Cardy
Majority	6,068	10.7	18.3	
Electorate: 74,301 Turnout: 56,751 (76.4%)				

WESTERN ISLES, NW Scotland. Lab seat, SNP longshot, Gaelic speaking

Candidates 97	97 votes	97%	92%	Candidates
Calum MacDonald (Lab)	8,955	55.6	47.8	Calum MacDonald
Anne Lorne Gillies (SNP)	5,379	33.4	37.2	Alasdair Nicholson
James McGrigor (Con)	1,071	6.6	8.5	
Neil Mitchison (LD)	495	3.1	3.4	
Majority	3,576	22.2	10.6	
Electorate: 22,983 Turnout: 16,106 (70.1%)				

WESTMORLAND & LONSDALE, Cumbria. Fells and Lancs coast, traditionally Con but LDs rising, hit by foot and mouth

Candidates 97	97 votes	97%	92%	Candidates
Tim Collins (Con)	21,463	42.3	56.9	
Stanley Collins (LD)	16,942	33.4	27.5	Tim Farron
John Harding (Lab)	10,452	20.6	15.1	John Bateson
Majority	4,521	8.9	29.4	
Electorate: 68,389 Turnout: 50,809 (74.3%)				

WESTON-SUPER-MARE, Somerset. Seaside, retirement, LDs took in 97 but Cons revived locally, target

Candidates 97	97 votes	97%	92%	Candidates
Brian Cotter (LD)	21,407	40.1	38.5	
M E Daly (Con)	20,133	37.7	48.1	John Penrose
D Kraft (Lab)	9,557	17.9	11.4	Derek Kraft
Majority	1,274	2.4	9.6	
Electorate: 72,445 Turnout: 53,377 (73.7%)				

WIGAN, Greater Manchester. Strong Lab seat, mainly urban, working class

Candidates 97	97 votes	97%	92%	Candidates
Roger Stott (Lab)	30,043	68.6	60.6	Neil Turner
Mark Loveday (Con)	7,400	16.9	25.3	Mark Page
Trevor Beswick (LD)	4,390	10	11.7	Trevor Beswick
Majority	22,643	51.7	35.3	

Electorate: 64,689 Turnout: 43,819 (67.7%)

WILTSHIRE NORTH, Wiltshire. Con seat even in 97, mainly rural, managerial

Candidates 97	97 votes	97%	92%	Candidates
James Gray (Con)	25,390	43.8	56.2	
Simon Cordon (LD)	21,915	37.8	31.5	Hugh Pym
Nigel Knowles (Lab)	8,261	14.2	10.2	
Majority	3,475	6	24.7	

Electorate: 77,236 Turnout: 58,013 (75.1%)

WIMBLEDON, S London. Shock Lab gain in 97, if this is held Tories will weep

Candidates 97	97 votes	97%	92%	Candidates
Roger Casale (Lab)	20,674	42.8	23.3	Roger Casale
Dr Charles Goodson-Wickes (Con)	17,684	36.6	53	Stephen Hammond
A Willott (LD)	8,014	16.6	21.3	
Majority	2,990	6.2	29.7	

Electorate: 64,070 Turnout: 48,354 (75.5%)

WINCHESTER, Hampshire. Dramatic history, LD gain by 2 in 97, held by 21,000 in by-election

Candidates 97	97 votes	97%	92%	Candidates
Mark Oaten (LD)	26,100	42.1	36.9	
Gerald Malone (Con)	26,098	42.1	51.7	Andrew Hayes
Patrick Davies (Lab)	6,528	10.5	7.5	Stephen Wyeth
Majority	2	0	14.8	

Electorate: 78,883 Turnout: 62,054 (78.7%)

WINDSOR, Berkshire. New strong Con seat, stockbroker belt, managerial

Candidates 97	97 votes	97%	92%	Candidates
Michael Trend (Con)	24,476	48.2	56.3	Nick Pinfield
Chris Fox (LD)	14,559	28.7	29.1	
Amanda Williams (Lab)	9,287	18.3	12.4	Mark Muller
Majority	9,917	19.5	27.2	

Electorate: 69,132 Turnout: 50,781 (73.5%)

WIRRAL SOUTH, Merseyside. Lab gain in 97 after byelection, mainly rural, middle class

Candidates 97	97 votes	97%	92%	Candidates
Ben Chapman (Lab)	24,499	50.9	34.6	Ben Chapman
Leslie Byrom (Con)	17,495	36.4	50.8	Tony Millard
Phillip Gilchrist (LD)	5,018	10.4	13.1	Phillip Gilchrist
Majority	7,004	14.5	16.2	

Electorate: 59,372 Turnout: 48,095 (81%)

WIRRAL WEST, Merseyside, Middle class, suburban, Lab just took 97, Con target

Candidates 97	97 votes	97%	92%	Candidates
Stephen Hesford (Lab)	21,035	44.9	31	Stephen Hesford
David Hunt (Con)	18,297	39	52.7	Chris Lynch
John Thornton (LD)	5,945	12.7	14.6	Simon Holbrook
Majority	2,738	5.9	21.7	

Electorate: 60,907 Turnout: 46,890 (77%)

WITNEY, Oxfordshire. Mainly rural, managerial, MP joined Lab after election, certain Con gain

Candidates 97	97 votes	97%	92%	Candidates
Shaun Woodward (Con)	24,282	43.1	57.8	David Cameron
Alexander Hollingsworth (Lab)	17,254	30.6	18.1	
Angela Lawrence (LD)	11,202	19.9	22.5	Gareth Epps
Majority	7,028	12.5	35.3	

Electorate: 73,519 Turnout: 56,401 (76.7%)

WOKING, Surrey. Strong Con seat, stockbroker belt, professional

Candidates 97	97 votes	97%	92%	Candidates
Humfrey Malins (Con)	19,553	38.4	59.1	
P Goldenberg (LD)	13,875	27.3	27.1	Alan Hilliar
C Hanson (Lab)	10,695	21	13.4	Sabir Hussain
Majority	5,678	11.1	32	

Electorate: 70,053 Turnout: 50,914 (72.7%)

WOKINGHAM, Berkshire. Strong Con seat, stockbroker belt, managerial, votes for John Redwood

Candidates 97	97 votes	97%	92%	Candidates
John Redwood (Con)	25,086	50.1	61.7	
Royce Longton (LD)	15,721	31.4	25.6	Royce Longton
Patricia Colling (Lab)	8,424	16.8	11.3	Matthew Syed
Majority	9,365	18.7	36.1	

Electorate: 66,161 Turnout: 50,108 (75.7%)

WOLVERHAMPTON NORTH EAST, W Midlands. White, working class, Lab gain in 92, now safe

Candidates 97	97 votes	97%	92%	Candidates
Ken Purchase (Lab)	24,534	59.3	49	Ken Purchase
David Harvey (Con)	11,547	27.9	41.4	Maria Miller
Brian Niblett (LD)	2,214	5.3	7.4	
Majority	12,987	31.4	7.6	

Electorate: 61,642 Turnout: 41,403 (67.2%)

WOLVERHAMPTON SOUTH EAST, W Midlands. Strong Lab seat, industrial, working class

Candidates 97	97 votes	97%	92%	Candidates
Dennis Turner (Lab)	22,202	63.7	56.7	Dennis Turner
William Hanbury (Con)	7,020	20.2	31.7	Adrian Pepper
Richard Whitehouse (LD)	3,292	9.5	9.5	Peter Wild
Majority	15,182	43.5	25	

Electorate: 54,291 Turnout: 34,830 (64.2%)

WOLVERHAMPTON SOUTH WEST, W Midlands. Lab gain 97, suburban, large Asian community

Candidates 97	97 votes	97%	92%	Candidates
Jenny Jones (Lab)	24,657	50.4	39.9	
Nicholas Budgen (Con)	19,539	39.9	49.3	David Chambers
M Green (LD)	4,012	8.2	8.5	Mike Dixon
Majority	5,118	10.5	9.4	

Electorate: 67,482 Turnout: 48,921 (72.5%)

WOODSPRING, Somerset. Strong Con seat, partly by sea, commuting, managerial

Candidates 97	97 votes	97%	92%	Candidates
Dr Liam Fox (Con)	24,425	44.4	53.3	
Nan Kirsen (LD)	16,691	30.4	31.7	Colin Eldridge
D Sander (Lab)	11,377	20.7	12.4	Chanel Stevens
Majority	7,734	14	21.6	

Electorate: 69,971 Turnout: 54,927 (78.5%)

WORCESTER, Worcestershire. Lab took in 97, will 'Worcester woman' switch back?

Candidates 97	97 votes	97%	92%	Candidates
Michael Foster (Lab)	25,848	50.1	39.9	Michael Foster
Nicholas Bourne (Con)	18,423	35.7	45.5	Richard Adams
Paul Chandler (LD)	6,462	12.5	13.1	Paul Chandler
Majority	7,425	14.4	5.6	

Electorate: 69,234 Turnout: 51,619 (74.6%)

WORCESTERSHIRE MID, Worcestershire. Strong Con seat, mainly rural, managerial

Candidates 97	97 votes	97%	92%	Candidates
Peter Luff (Con)	24,092	47.4	54.9	
Diane Smith (Lab)	14,680	28.9	17.6	
David Barwick (LD)	9,458	18.6	26.1	Robert Woodthorpe-Browne
Majority	9,412	18.5	28.8	

Electorate: 68,381 Turnout: 50,819 (74.3%)

WORCESTERSHIRE WEST, Worcestershire. Strong Con seat, rural, pleasant edge of Cotswolds

Candidates 97	97 votes	97%	92%	Candidates
Sir Michael Spicer (Con)	22,223	45	54.7	
Michael Hadley (LD)	18,377	37.2	29.3	Mike Hadley
Neil Stone (Lab)	7,738	15.7	13.8	
Majority	3,846	7.8	25.4	

Electorate: 64,712 Turnout: 49,344 (76.3%)

WORKINGTON, Cumbria. Remote ex-mining industrial coast, very working class

Candidates 97	97 votes	97%	92%	Candidates
Dale Campbell-Savours (Lab)	31,717	64.2	54.2	Tony Cunningham
Robert Blunden (Con)	12,061	24.4	36.4	Tim Stoddart
Phillip Roberts (LD)	3,967	8	7.5	
Majority	19,656	39.8	17.8	

Electorate: 65,766 Turnout: 49,374 (75.1%)

WORSLEY, Greater Manchester. Strong Lab seat, mainly urban

Candidates 97	97 votes	97%	92%	Candidates
Terry Lewis (Lab)	29,083	62.2	53.8	Terry Lewis
Damian Garrido (Con)	11,342	24.2	32.1	Tobias Ellwood
Robert Bleakley (LD)	6,356	13.6	12.7	Robert Bleakley
Majority	17,741	38	21.7	

Electorate: 68,978 Turnout: 46,781 (67.8%)

WORTHING EAST & SHOREHAM, W Sussex. Con held 97, LD longshot, seaside, pensioners

Candidates 97	97 votes	97%	92%	Candidates
Tim Loughton (Con)	20,864	40.5	51.4	
Martin King (LD)	15,766	30.6	33.7	Paul Elgood
Mark Williams (Lab)	12,335	23.9	13.3	
Majority	5,098	9.9	17.7	

Electorate: 70,770 Turnout: 51,569 (72.9%)

WORTHING WEST, W Sussex. Strong Con seat, seaside, white collar

Candidates 97	97 votes	97%	92%	Candidates
Peter Bottomley (Con)	23,733	46.1	61.7	
Christopher Hare (LD)	16,020	31.1	27.5	James Walsh
John Adams (Lab)	8,347	16.2	8.7	Alan Butcher
Majority	7,713	15	34.2	

Electorate: 71,329 Turnout: 51,442 (72.1%)

WREKIN, THE, Shropshire. Surrounds Telford, part rural, Con target

Candidates 97	97 votes	97%	92%	Candidates
Peter Bradley (Lab)	21,243	46.9	31.9	Peter Bradley
Peter Bruinvels (Con)	18,218	40.2	47.8	Jacob Rees-Mogg
Ian Jenkins (LD)	5,807	12.8	19.3	Ian Jenkins
Majority	3,025	6.7	15.9	

Electorate: 59,126 Turnout: 45,268 (76.6%)

WREXHAM, NE Wales. Lab seat, mainly urban, working class

Candidates 97	97 votes	97%	92%	Candidates
Dr John Marek (Lab)	20,450	56.1	50	Ian Lucas
Stuart Andrew (Con)	8,688	23.9	32.4	Felicity Elphick
Andrew Thomas (LD)	4,833	13.3	15	Ron Davies
Majority	11,762	32.2	17.6	

Electorate: 50,741 Turnout: 36,422 (71.8%)

WYCOMBE, Buckinghamshire. Strong Con seat, mainly urban, middle class

Candidates 97	97 votes	97%	92%	Candidates
Sir Raymond Whitney (Con)	20,890	39.9	53.3	Paul Goodman
Chris Bryant (Lab)	18,520	35.4	21.4	Chauhdry Shafique
Paul Bensilum (LD)	9,678	18.5	23	Dee Tomlin
Majority	2,370	4.5	30.3	

Electorate: 73,589 Turnout: 52,319 (71.1%)

WYRE FOREST, Worcestershire. Kidderminster, Bewdley, woodland, Lab in 97

Candidates 97	97 votes	97%	92%	Candidates
David Lock (Lab)	26,843	48.8	31.2	David Lock
Anthony Coombs (Con)	19,897	36.1	47.5	Mark Simpson
David Cropp (LD)	4,377	8	21.3	
Majority	6,946	12.7	16.3	

Electorate: 73,062 Turnout: 55,055 (75.4%)

WYTHENSHAWE & SALE EAST, Greater Manchester. Outer suburbs, working class, some Con votes

Candidates 97	97 votes	97%	92%	Candidates
Paul Goggins (Lab)	26,448	58.1	49.5	Paul Goggins
A Fleming (Con)	11,429	25.1	34.9	Susan Fildes
Vanessa Tucker (LD)	5,639	12.4	14.5	Vanessa Tucker
Majority	15,019	33	14.6	

Electorate: 71,986 Turnout: 45,533 (63.3%)

YEOVIL, Somerset. New LD candidate gives Con chance, more urban than some expect

Candidates 97	97 votes	97%	92%	Candidates
Sir Paddy Ashdown (LD)	26,349	48.7	51.7	David Laws
Nicholas Cambrook (Con)	14,946	27.7	36.9	Marco Forgione
Joe Conway (Lab)	8,053	14.9	9.6	Joe Conway
Majority	11,403	21	14.8	

Electorate: 74,165 Turnout: 54,053 (72.9%)

YNYS MÖN, NW Wales. Really Anglesey, PC, Welsh speaking, island, ferry port

Candidates 97	97 votes	97%	92%	Candidates
Ieuan Wyn Jones (PC)	15,756	39.5	37.1	
Owen Edwards (Lab)	13,275	33.2	23.5	Albert Owen
Gwilym Owen (Con)	8,569	21.5	34.6	Albie Fox
D Burnham (LD)	1,537	3.8	4.4	
Majority	2,481	6.3	13.6	

Electorate: 52,951 Turnout: 39,930 (75.4%)

YORK, CITY OF, N Yorkshire. Now safe Lab, mixed town, industrial, university, tourism

Candidates 97	97 votes	97%	92%	Candidates
Hugh Bayley (Lab)	34,956	59.9	49.1	
Simon Mallett (Con)	14,433	24.7	39.2	
Andrew Waller (LD)	6,537	11.2	10.6	Andrew Waller
Majority	20,523	35.2	9.9	

Electorate: 79,383 Turnout: 58,345 (73.5%)

YORKSHIRE EAST, E Yorkshire. Rural, safe Con seat, runs along coast

Candidates 97	97 votes	97%	92%	Candidates
John Townend (Con)	20,904	42.7	50.6	
Ian Male (Lab)	17,567	35.9	26.5	
David Leadley (LD)	9,070	18.5	22.9	Mary-Rose Hardy
Majority	3,337	6.8	24.1	

Electorate: 69,408 Turnout: 48,971 (70.6%)

Table 36 By-elections in the 1997 parliament

UXBRIDGE July 31 1997
Elected: John Randall

Con	John Randall	16,288	51.1%
Lab	Andrew Slaughter	12,522	39.3%
Lib Dem	Keith Kerr	1,792	5.6%
Majority	3,766	Con hold	
Swing	5% Lab to Con		

Cause: death of Sir Michael Shersby, May 8 1997

PAISLEY SOUTH November 6 1997
Elected: Douglas Alexander

Lab	Douglas Alexander	10,346	44.1%
SNP	I Blackford	7,615	32.5%
Lib Dem	E McCartin	2,582	11%
Majority	2,731	Lab hold	
Swing	11.2% Lab to SNP		

Cause: death of Gordon McMaster, July 28 1997

BECKENHAM November 20 1997
Elected: Jacqui Lait

Con	Jacqui Lait	13,162	41.2%
Lab	Bob Hughes	11,935	37.4%
Lib Dem	Rosemary Vetterlein	5,864	18.4%
Majority	1,227	Con hold	
Swing	2.6% Con to Lab		

Cause: resignation of Piers Merchant, October 21 1997

WINCHESTER November 20 1997
Elected: Mark Oaten

Lib Dem	Mark Oaten	37,006	68%
Con	Gerry Malone	15,450	28.4%
Lab	Patrick Davies	944	1.7%
Majority	21,556	Lib Dem hold	
Swing	19.8% Con to Lib Dem		

Cause: general election result overturned by High Court

LEEDS CENTRAL June 10 1999
Elected: Hilary Benn

Lab	Hilary Benn	6,361	47.3%
Lib Dem	Peter Wild	4,068	30.2%
Con	William Edward Wild	1,618	12%
Majority	2,293	Lab hold	
Swing	20.5% Lab to Lib Dem		

Cause: death of Derek Fatchett, May 9 1999

EDDISBURY July 22 1999
Elected: Stephen O'Brien

Con	Stephen O'Brien	15,465	44.8%
Lab	Margaret Hanson	13,859	40.2%
Lib Dem	Paul Roberts	4,757	13.8%
Majority	1,606	Con hold	
Swing	1.1% Lab to Con		

Cause: resignation of Sir Alistair Goodlad, June 28 1999

WIGAN September 23 1999
Elected: Neil Turner
Lab	Neil Turner	9,641	59.6%
Con	Thomas Peet	2,912	18%
Lib Dem	Jonathan Rule	2,148	13.3%
Majority	6,729	Lab-hold	
Swing	5.1% Lab to Con		

Cause: death of Roger Stott, August 8 1999

HAMILTON SOUTH September 23 1999
Elected: Bill Tynan
Lab	Bill Tynan	7,172	36.8 %
SNP	Annabelle Ewing	6,616	34%
SSP	Shareen Blackall	1,847	9.5 %
Con	Charles Ferguson	1,406	7.2 %
Majority	556	Lab hold	
Swing	22.6% Lab to SNP		

Cause: George Robertson elevated to House of Lords, August 24 1999

KENSINGTON & CHELSEA November 25 1999
Elected: Michael Portillo
Con	Michael Portillo	11,004	56.4%
Lab	John Atkinson	4,298	22%
Lib Dem	Robert Browne	1,831	9.4%
Majority	6,706	Con hold	
Swing	4.4% Lab to Con		

Cause: death of Alan Clark, September 5 1999

CEREDIGION February 3 2000
Elected: Simon Thomas
PC	Simon Thomas	10,716	42.8%
Lib Dem	Mark Williams	5,768	23%
Con	Paul Davies	4,138	16.5%
Lab	Maria Battle	3,612	14.4%
Majority	4,948	PC hold	
Swing	5.5% Lab to PC		

Cause: resignation of Cynog Dafis, January 10 2000

ROMSEY May 4 2000
Elected: Sandra Gidley
Lib Dem	Sandra Gidley	19,571	50.6%
Con	Timothy Palmer	16,260	42%
Lab	Andrew Howard	1,451	3.7%
Majority	3,311	Lib Dem gain	
Swing	12.6% Con to Lib Dem		

Cause: death of Michael Colvin, February 24 2000

TOTTENHAM June 22 2000
Elected: David Lammy
Lab	David Lammy	8,785	53.5%
Lib Dem	Duncan Hames	3,139	19.1%
Con	Jane Ellison	2,634	16%
Majority	5,646	Lab hold	
Swing	12% Lab to Lib Dem		

Cause: death of Bernie Grant, April 8 2000

SOUTH ANTRIM September 21 2000
Elected: William McCrea

DUP	William McCrea	11,601	38%
UUP	David Burnside	10,779	35.3%
SDLP	Donovan McClelland	3,495	11.4%
Sinn Fein	Martin Meehan	2,611	8.5%
Alliance	David Ford	2,031	6.5%
Majority	822	DUP gain	

Swing unavailable, no DUP candidate 1997
Cause: death of Clifford Forsythe, April 27 2000

GLASGOW ANNIESLAND November 23 2000
Elected: John Robertson

Lab	John Robertson	10,539	52.1%
SNP	Grant Thoms	4,202	20.8%
Con	Dorothy Luckhurst	2,188	10.8%
Lib Dem	Christopher McGinty	1,630	8.1%
Majority	6,337	Lab hold	
Swing	6.7% Lab to SNP		

Cause: death of Donald Dewar, October 11 2000

PRESTON November 23 2000
Elected: Mark Hendrick

Lab	Mark Hendrick	9,765	45.7%
Con	Graham O'Hare	5,339	25%
Lib Dem	Bill Chadwick	3,454	16.2%
Majority	4,426	Lab hold	
Swing	9.1% Lab to Con		

Cause: death of Audrey Wise, September 2 2000

WEST BROMWICH November 23 2000
Elected: Adrian Bailey

Lab	Adrian Bailey	9,640	51.1%
Con	Karen Bissell	6,408	33.9%
Lib Dem	Sadie Smith	1,791	9.5%
Majority	3,232	Lab hold	

Swing unavailable, seat uncontested 1997
Cause: resignation of Speaker, Betty Boothroyd, October 23 2000

FALKIRK WEST December 21 2000
Elected: Eric Joyce

Lab	Eric Joyce	8,492	43.5%
SNP	David Kerr	7,787	39.9%
Con	Craig Stevenson	1,621	8.3%
SSP	Iain Hunter	989	5.1%
Lib Dem	Hugh O'Donnell	615	3.2%
Majority	705	Lab gain*	
Swing	16.5% Lab to SNP		

Cause: resignation of Dennis Canavan, November 21 2000

* Labour MP Dennis Canavan was expelled, 25 March 1999

Table 37 Twenty seats with the lowest turnout 1997

		% of registered electorate
1	Liverpool Riverside	51.9
2	Hackney North & Stoke Newington	52.2
3	Manchester, Central	52.6
4	Sheffield Central	53.0
5	Birmingham Ladywood	54.2
6	West Bromwich West	54.4
7	Hackney South & Shoreditch	54.7
8	Leeds Central	54.7
9	Kensington & Chelsea	54.7
10	Vauxhall	55.5
11	Glasgow, Shettleston	55.9
12	Manchester Gorton	56.4
13	Camberwell & Peckham	56.5
14	Salford	56.5
15	Glasgow Maryhill	56.6
16	Glasgow Kelvin	56.9
17	Kingston upon Hull North	57.0
18	Tottenham	57.0
19	Tyne Bridge	57.1
20	Birmingham Sparkbrook & Small Heath	57.1

Table 38 Twenty seats with highest turnout 1997

		% of registered electorate
1	Mid Ulster	86.1
2	Brecon & Radnorshire	82.2
3	Stirling	81.8
4	Wirral South	81.0
5	Monmouth	80.8
6	Cardiff North	80.2
7	Vale of Glamorgan	80.2
8	Ayr	80.2
9	North West Leicestershire	80.0
10	Galloway & Upper Nithsdale	79.7
11	West Tyrone	79.6
12	Richmond Park	79.4
13	Twickenham	79.3
14	Wansdyke	79.3
15	Northavon	79.2
16	Stroud	79.2
17	Forest of Dean	79.1
18	High Peak	79.0
19	Strathkelvin & Bearsden	78.9
20	Dover	78.9

Table 39 Twenty constituencies with largest registered electorates, 1997

1	Isle of Wight	101,680
2	Bristol West	84,870
3	Ealing Southall	81,704
4	Teignbridge	81,667
5	Stratford-on-Avon	81,433
6	Portsmouth South	80,514
7	Devizes	80,383
8	South West Norfolk	80,236
9	Croydon Central	80,152
10	Daventry	80,151
11	North Cornwall	80,076
12	Harrow East	79,846
13	Taunton	79,783
14	Wealden	79,519
15	Northampton South	79,384
16	Rugby & Kenilworth	79,384
17	City of York	79,383
18	Warwick & Leamington	79,373
19	Oxford West & Abingdon	79,329
20	Bracknell	79,292

Table 40 Twenty constituencies with the smallest registered electorates, 1997

1	Western Isles	22,983
2	Orkney & Shetland	32,291
3	Meirionnydd Nant Conwy	32,345
4	Caithness, Sutherl& & Easter Ross	41,566
5	Montgomeryshire	42,618
6	Hamilton South	46,562
7	Caernarfon	46,815
8	Roxburgh & Berwickshire	47,259
9	Midlothian	47,552
10	Glasgow Shettleston	47,990
11	Cumbernauld & Kilsyth	48,031
12	Cynon Valley	48,286
13	Greenock & Inverclyde	48,818
14	Glasgow Pollok	49,284
15	Glasgow Cathcart	49,312
16	Argyll & Bute	49,450
17	Cunninghame South	49,543
18	Paisley North	49,725
19	Glasgow Govan	49,836
20	Aberavon	50,025

Table 41 Turnout at general elections 1945–97

	Total votes	% of electorate
1945	25,085,978	72.7
1950	28,772,671	84.0
1951	28,595,668	82.5
1955	26,760,498	76.7
1959	27,859,241	78.8
1964	27,655,374	77.1
1966	27,263,606	75.8
1970	28,344,798	72.0
1974 Feb	31,333,226	78.7
1974 Oct	29,189,178	72.8
1979	31,220,010	76.0
1983	30,671,136	72.7
1987	32,529,568	75.3
1992	33,612,693	77.7
1997	31,287,702	71.5

Table 42 Local elections 2001

On May 3 local elections take place in the following English counties and unitary authorities. In the county councils and the Isle of Wight unitary authority, every seat is up for election. In all the other unitary authorities, one-third of seats will be contested. There are no elections in Scotland, Wales, London or English metropolitan districts.

COUNTIES

Authority	Party with control
Bedfordshire	Con
Buckinghamshire	Con
Cambridgeshire	Con
Cheshire	NoC
Cornwall and Isles of Scilly	NoC
Cumbria	Lab
Derbyshire	Lab
Devon	Lib Dem
Dorset	NoC
Durham	Lab
East Sussex	NoC
Essex	NoC
Gloucestershire	NoC
Hampshire	Con
Hertfordshire	Con
Kent	Con
Lancashire	Lab
Leicestershire	NoC
Lincolnshire	Con
Norfolk	NoC
Northamptonshire	Lab
Northumberland	Lab
North Yorkshire	Con
Nottinghamshire	Lab
Oxfordshire	NoC
Shropshire	NoC
Somerset	Lib Dem
Staffordshire	Lab
Suffolk	NoC
Surrey	Con
Warwickshire	NoC
West Sussex	Con
Wiltshire	Con
Worcestershire	NoC

ENGLISH UNITARY AUTHORITIES

Authority	Party with control
Bristol	Lab
Halton	Lab
Isle of Wight	NoC
Peterborough	NoC
Reading	Lab
Slough	Lab
Southend-on-Sea	Con
Thurrock	Lab
Warrington	Lab
Wokingham	NoC

NoC – No overall control

Source: Labour party, Guardian Research and Information department. The political affiliation figures were taken from each local authority in May 2000.

Table 43 Scottish parliamentary elections, May 6 1999

Party	Constituency MSPs	Regional MSPs	Total MSPs	Share of seats %	Constituency vote	Share of constituency votes %	Regional list votes	Share of regional list votes, %
Lab	52*	3	56*	43.4	908,346	38.8	786,818	33.6
SNP	7	28	35	27.1	672,768	28.7	638,644	27.3
Con	0**	18	18**	14.0	364,425	15.6	359,109	15.4
Lib Dem	12	5	17	13.2	333,269	14.2	290,760	12.4
Green	0	1	1	0.8	0	0.0	84,024	3.6
Falkirk West	1	0	1	0.8	18,511	0.8	27,700	1.2
Scottish Socialist	0	1	1	0.8**	23,654	1.0	46,635	2.0
Others	0	0	0	0	21,605	0.9	105,221	4.4
Total	73	56	129		2,342,578		2,338,911	

Turnout: 58%

*Now 1 fewer, Ayr lost to Conservatives at by-election, Dec 1999.
**Gained Ayr at by-election, Dec 1999.

Table 44 Welsh assembly elections, May 6 1999

	Top-up vote %	Direct vote %	Top-up seats	Direct seats	Total seats
Conservative	16.5	15.8	8	1	9
Labour	35.5	37.6	1	27	28
Lib Dem	12.5	13.5	3	3	6
Plaid Cymru	30.6	28.4	8	9	17
Others	4.9	4.7	0	0	0

Table 45 Northern Ireland assembly elections, June 25 1998

Party	Number of seats	Total votes 000s	Share of the vote %
Ulster Unionists	28	172,225	22.0
Social Democratic Labour party	24	177,963	21.3
Democratic Unionist party	20	145,917	18.0
Sinn Fein	18	142,858	17.7
Alliance party	6	52,636	6.5
Women's Coalition	3	13,019	1.6
Progressive Unionists	2	20,634	2.6
UK Unionists*	5	36,541	4.5
Independent unionists**	3	24,339	3.0
Others	0	18,199	2.3

*UK Unionist party split on 15 January 1999. Four members formed the Northern Ireland Unionist party, one of whom has since been expelled and currently sits as an independent. There is now only one UKUP Assembly member.
** Three elected independent members joined forces to form the United Unionist Assembly party on 21 September 1998.

Table 46 London mayoral election, May 4 2000

		First preference	%	Second preference	%	Final
Ken Livingstone	Independent	667,877	0.4	178,809	0.1	776,427
Steve Norris	Con	464,434	0.3	188,041	0.1	564,137
Frank Dobson	Lab	223,884	0.1	228,095	0.2	–
Susan Kramer	Lib Dem	203,452	0.1	404,815	0.3	–
Ram Gidoomal	Christian Peoples Alliance	42,060	0	56,489	0	–
Darren Johnson	Green	38,121	0	192,764	13.6	–
Michael Newland	BNP	33,568	0	45,337	0	–
Damian Hockney	Ukip	16,234	0	43,672	0	–
Geoffrey Ben-Nathan	Pro-motorist Small Shop	9,956	0	23,021	0	–
Ashwin Kumarn Tanna	Independent	9,015	0	41,766	0	–
Geoffrey Clements	Natural Law	5,470	0	18,185	0	–

Source: DETR

Table 47 European parliamentary elections, June 10 1999

GREAT BRITAIN

Party	Votes	%	Seats
Con	3,578,217	35.8	36
Lab	2,803,821	28	29
Lib Dem	1,266,549	12.7	10
SNP	268,528	2.7	2
PC	185,235	1.9	2
Green	625,378	6.3	2
Ukip	696,057	7	3
Pro-Euro Con	138,097	1.4	
BNP	102,644	1	
Liberal	93,051	0.9	
Scottish Lab	86,749	0.9	
Scottish Socialist	39,720	0.4	
Natural Law	20,329	0.2	
Socialist Alliance	7,203	0.1	
Humanist	2,586	0	
Weekly Worker	1,724	0	
Socialist	1,510	0	
Other	84,872	0.8	
Total	**10,002,270**	**100**	**84**

NORTHERN IRELAND (1st preferences)

DUP	192,762	28.4	1
SDLP	190,731	28.1	1
UUP	119,507	17.6	1
SF	117,643	17.3	
PUP	22,494	3.3	
UKUP	20,283	3	
Alliance	14,391	2.1	
Natural Law	998	0.1	
Total	**678,809**	**100**	**3**

Source: House of Commons Library

Table 48 General election, May 1 1997

	Total votes	% of total vote	Candidates	MPs elected	Lost deposits
Labour	13,518,167	43.2	639	418	0
Con	9,600,943	30.7	648	165	8
Lib Dem	5,242,947	16.8	639	46	13
Ref	811,849	2.6	547	0	505
SNP	621,550	2	72	6	0
UU	258,349	0.8	16	10	1
SDLP	190,814	0.6	18	3	3
PC	161,030	0.5	40	4	15
SF	126,921	0.4	17	2	4
DUP	107,348	0.3	9	2	0
Ukip	105,722	0.3	193	0	192
Green	63,991	0.2	95	0	95
Alliance	62,972	0.2	17	0	6
Socialist Labour	52,109	0.2	64	0	61
Liberal	45,166	0.1	55	0	53
BNP	35,832	0.1	57	0	54
Natural Law	30,604	0.1	197	0	197
Speaker	23,969	0.1	1	1	0
ProLife Alliance	19,332	0.1	56	0	56
UKUP	12,817	0	1	1	0
PUP	10,928	0	3	0	0
National Democrat	10,829	0	21	0	20
Scottish Socialist Alliance	9,740	0	16	0	15
National Front	2,716	0	6	0	6
Others	159,639	0.5	297	1	289
Total	31,286,284	100	3,724	659	1,593